GRAY HORSE TROOP
FOREVER SOLDIERS

5/7 Cav History —
Vietnam 1967 - 68
Iraq 2005
GARRYOWEN / WAR PAINT

[signature] Dec 2015

CHARLES BAKER

POWDER RIVER PUBLICATIONS

GOOD MORNING VIETNAAAAMM
TV LAND 8000 Mi.
MIDDIES
SANDS OF MALFUNCTION
RUE SANS JOIE
VERY MUDDY
HEAVEN
LZ JACK
LZ LONG
17
HELL
CITADEL
POOH BAH
1
UNCLE BEN'S
PLATOON HQS 300 Mi.
ABLE DECKER JUNGLE
CHANEL NO. 5
A SHAU VALLEY
548
547
CB

GRAY HORSE TROOP/Forever Soldiers
By Charles Baker

Published by Charles Baker & Associates, Inc., dba Powder River Publications
October 2013
ISBN: 978-0-9888111-0-2

Cover and Layout by Gamel Design.

Maps, diagrams and illustrations by Charles Baker.

Photographs mostly from Charles Baker, some with permission of fellow veterans, and some from the public domain.

Printing: CREATESPACE

Second Revision September 2014.

This book was printed in the United States of America.

TABLE OF CONTENTS

ADDENDA

Forward

This is a personal account about the Vietnam War, not a scholarly work by a "military historian." Even so, it is accurate in terms of the big picture — the missions, plans and operations for the day. The sources for these matters are the Daily Journals and summaries, the writings of others, conversations with many of our veterans, as well as my personal records and vivid memories of memorable days. One thing I discovered along the way — talking to five guys about a battle results in at least three different battles. Therefore this book is told from the perspective of a battalion operations officer who was down with the rifle companies on difficult days, and otherwise not far away.

This accounting also relies on the citations on individual awards for valor to help piece together the battles and skirmishes — Bronze Star (V) and above. In the northern sector of South Vietnam, the war escalated dramatically in the fall of 1967, and stayed that way for two years. There were many award recommendations. There needed to be. Recommendations went back to the rear on pages torn out of our little green notebooks, often wet, poorly written, very sketchy. Finalized paperwork did not flow immediately back to the field for review and approval during the Battle of Hue — Tet 68, Khe Sanh and the A Shau Valley. Initiators were not always there. Officers rode out on medevac birds, or rotated out to new jobs. The clerks in the S-1 shop did the best they could writing these citations. Many veterans with whom I have spoken regarding their award start off with "well, that's not exactly what I did."

Nevertheless, the main battles always involved several medal recipients, and the write ups collectively capture what happened that day. The recipients more than earned these awards. There could have been a lot more. People got missed.

Thirty-seven years later, this author traveled for several weeks with the same unit in Iraq. A lot has changed. A lot remains the same. Comparisons are sprinkled throughout this work.

Charles R. "Charlie" Baker

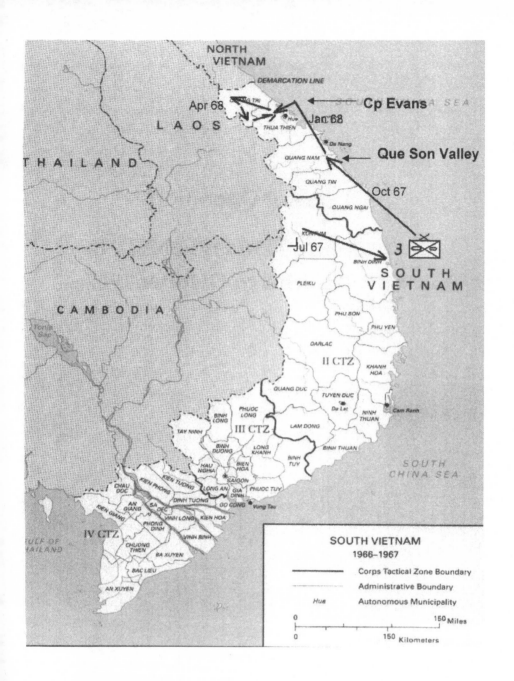

SOUTH VIETNAM
1966–1967

Corps Tactical Zone Boundary

Administrative Boundary

Hue Autonomous Municipality

0 — 150 Miles

0 — 150 Kilometers

CHAPTER 1

WELCOME TO 5/7 CAV, BROTHER

It was 21 July 2004. *(That's how we write dates in the Army.)* A large number of dignitaries sat beneath the canopy of the reviewing stand, including several retired generals, the 3rd Infantry Division Commander, and many retired veterans of the Vietnam War. Ft. Stewart, Georgia, was a hot and dusty place that day, just the kind of dusty old Army Post that dusty old soldiers love.

Facing the reviewing stand on the far side of the parade ground stood a line of company formations — the five companies of the 1st Battalion, 3rd Air Defense Artillery — along with the 3rd Infantry Division Band. Centered on these six units was the color guard. The four color bearers held the United States Flag, The US Army flag, The 3rd Air Defense Artillery flag, and one uncased flag in a canvas cover.

The men of the 1st Battalion, 3rd Air Defense Artillery, looked sharp in their dress greens and black berets. *(We say 1/3 ADA, for short.)* Many of them had seen action with the battalion on the dusty road to Baghdad in March of 2003. No enemy aircraft showed up when the 3rd Infantry Division went through the berm into Iraq on March 20th, and it was not long before 1/3 ADA received an alternate mission to operate as an armored reconnaissance unit. Up around the Euphrates River, they took their turn at the point of the spear for the 3rd Infantry Division.

The legendary 3rd ID, "Rock of the Marne." Audie Murphy and all that. 1/3 ADA was one of the battalions that reached the center of Baghdad on 9 April 2003 when the statue of Saddam came down. Several of the men standing on the field this day had experienced real combat action during the brief but intense movement to contact operations into Baghdad. This was a proud unit indeed, about to have its colors replaced by another flag.

The battalion commander and his staff came to attention, marched across the field to a position in front of the color guard, and faced about. He was a cavalry officer, not an air defense officer, and had taken command of the battalion only three months earlier. He proudly wore his tanker boots, and the silver spurs he had earned as a young lieutenant in the cavalry. This parade on Cottrell Field was being conducted in the traditions of the cavalry, with the commands being given by signals from the bugler.

The 5th Battalion 7th Cavalry Vietnam Veterans Association, with more than a thousand members, had been contacted in March of 2004 by the new commander, Lt. Col. Petery. Word about the Reactivation Parade had spread throughout the association. Many of the most active members flew in from across the country. It had been thirty years in mothballs for their unit.

Following the battalion adjutant's preparatory command "Colors Front and Center", the bugler sounded the command of execution with one sharp note, prompting the band to play, and the Commander, his staff and the six-man color guard to step off. They looked sharp as they marched across the field toward us and halted in front of the reviewing stand. The 1st Brigade Commander and Colonel (Retired) John Long, President of our battalion Vietnam Veterans Association moved forward and took their positions to pass the flags. The red artillery flag was furled and put into an olive drab canvas case. The yellow cavalry colors, topped by many campaign ribbons, came out of its canvas case, was unfurled and handed to John Long. He passed it to the Brigade Commander, who passed it to the battalion commander. At that moment, all the men standing formation on Cottrell Field would be cavalry troopers in 5th Squadron, 7th U.S. Cavalry, whether they liked it or not. *(5/7 Cav for short.)* The 5/7 Cav would be a cavalry squadron, rather than an infantry battalion this time around. The troopers would have the option of retaining their air defense specialty, but make no mistake — they would be trained and fight as cavalry troopers in Iraq in 2005, whether they liked it or not. The Volunteer Army. You volunteer at the enlistment office. Everything is mandatory after that.

During the ceremony, a listing of all the campaigns of 5/7 Cav was read. The great majority of the men on Cottrell Field on 21 July 2004 knew no additional details of the battalion's history beyond this list. They knew little if anything about their new unit during the Indian Wars leading up to that fateful day at Little Bighorn. They knew nothing about their new battalion in WW II, Korea, or the Vietnam War. The 5/7 Cav had been among the first to Manila in the Big War, and was the first into several places in Vietnam. We had a lot of history.

The Color Guard turned about, marched back across the field. Lt. General (Ret.) James B. Vaught was seated in the first row of the bleachers. Just before the Commanding General of the 3rd ID began to speak, he moved forward and commandeered the microphone. Three stars can do things like that, and the two-star promptly moved aside. Vaught talked with great force and authority — not unlike when he took command of the battalion on 27 January 1968. His little talks in Vietnam were always focused on the soldiers, leaving the details of the operation to guys like me. He was no different on this memorable day, telling the young soldiers in plain language some of what they needed to know about being a young cavalry scout in combat, to include doing their job, taking the initiative, but being back to fight again tomorrow.

The last step before the troops passed in review was to sing the songs. The newly reactivated 5th Squadron, Seventh U.S. Cavalry first sang their new song, "Sgt. Flynn." Then they sang the 3rd Infantry Division song "I'm a Dog Faced Soldier". And finally, the Army song "The Caissons Go Rolling Along." Back when I was young, the Army had adopted the Artillery Song to become the official "Army Song," frosting off those Infantrymen who cared about such things.

For the veterans, it was a grand day, as the colors of 5/7 Cav passed in review thirty-three years after they had come home from Vietnam. I sat in the bleachers during the final march by, with my wife telling me to get pictures. But my mind was halfway around the world to the west, thinking about my first day with 5/7 Cav.

12 January 1968
LZ Colt – Que Son Valley

I had already been in Vietnam since early July 1967 with the 3rd Brigade, 1st Cavalry Division. I was a young infantry officer on my first tour in Vietnam. As the Headquarters Commandant, I had moved the Brigade Headquarters in July from Dak To on the Laotian border to Binh Dinh on the coast, and northward to LZ Baldy in the Que Son Valley on 1 October 1967. The 1st Cavalry Division had moved north to I Corps to join the Marines.

It was around 1530 hours on 12 January 1968 when I stepped off the struts of the UH1B "Huey" helicopter, lowered my head, and ran out from under the whirling rotor blades. *(3:30 pm in civilian speak.)* As soon as I was clear, the bird lifted off and sent a fine layer of dust and grit down the back of my shirt. Two soldiers stood by the helipad, hands on hips, dressed in fatigue pants, boots, and nothing else. They had long since given up shaking the dirt out of their longer-than-regulation hair. Two sorry-looking soldiers, but they had really great tans. I was used to the slovenly appearance of 1st Cavalry Division soldiers by this time. The troopers in the Infantry battalions took great pains to not be mistaken for any of us back on the coast. *(Some still do, even in their fifties and sixties.)*

When the gravel and dust stopped falling, I was looking at a barren and sun-baked place. Not a cloud in the sky. No trees. No shade. It was hot and it was dry. Maybe 95 Fahrenheit. Heat shimmered off the barrels of the six-gun battery of 105mm howitzers spread across the top of the hill. Down the slope I could see some of the sandbag-covered perimeter bunkers. Behind or on top of each bunker was a pup tent made of two ponchos joined together by the snaps: sleeping quarters for two soldiers. In the Infantry in Vietnam, we used the buddy system. Every man had a buddy, even if you hated his guts. The two-man fighting positions on this hill were spread farther apart than I was used to seeing back at LZ Baldy, home of the Brigade Headquarters. Much farther apart. Too far apart, perhaps.

I had been dropped off at Landing Zone Colt. The 1st Cavalry Division had more than four hundred of its own helicopters, and carried its infantrymen into battle by heliborne assault. So we called all of our bases Landing Zones. LZ for short. *(In Iraq they are FOBs — forward operating bases. In Iraq you can't find the rear. Only forward. In Vietnam, there was lots of rear — practically the whole coast.)*

LZ Colt was the location of the 5/7 Cav forward command post, located in the middle of the infamous Que Son Valley. Infamous for all the good Marines killed or wounded there, dating back to 1963. A big boulder rose about ten feet up at the very top of the hill. A sandbag-covered structure was built against the long side of this boulder, and sprouted numerous antennae from the roof. It was clearly the Battalion Tactical Operations Center — the TOC — my new place of business.

Picking up my gear, I headed that way, needing no directions from the ragamuffins at the pad. *(Nor would the enemy looking on from the surrounding villages and hills.)*

I was temporarily blinded when I walked into the dark, musty bunker. Radios hummed away on two small tables against the far wall. Two soldiers sat talking in front of the radios. A large acetate-covered map was mounted on the wall between them. A standard military 1:50,000 contour map, it covered the Que Son Valley area, about 30 kilometers south of Da Nang. A few other men were shooting the breeze around a large table at the back of the room. Finally someone noticed that an officer had entered, and they all stood up and came forward. One of the sergeants gathered them around and introduced each man individually.

I said "I am your new boss," and someone in the back said "we know." I had very little more to say, and they all went back to work or play.

I was probably not what they expected in an infantry major. I had been a major all of two days, and could pass for nineteen. Reed-thin, Buddy Holly glasses, but Senior Jump Wings and a Ranger Tab helped some. Everyone was very friendly and polite, and made me feel welcome. I had worked directly for their battalion commander when he was back at Brigade in the fall, and he had requested me for this position. I also knew before I got there that I was replacing an unpopular senior major. Even so, I had to be just one more career officer fighting the Cold War to these men. Another Lifer to run their lives, and hopefully not lose it for them.

Not more than fifteen minutes went by before Lt. Col. Jack Long came into the TOC. His real name was Herlihy, but someone with good sense nicknamed him Jack. He greeted me with his ever-present wintry smile and kind words. He and his Artillery Fire Support Officer *("FSO")*, a captain named John, had just returned from flying around the valley, where they had been observing the company operations. John excused himself and went about his business. He had his own table, radio, map board, and RTO. John's job was to bring us the artillery. He was very important.

Jack spent about fifteen minutes bringing me up to speed on the situation, before departing to get some chow. Not more than two minutes after he left, an intense voice came crackling in over the battalion command radio net. "FAST FLANKER 65, this is HARD HITTER 6, over."

HARD HITTER 6 was the company commander of Charlie Company, except we could not use "Charlie" in that war. The bad guys were Charlie. The Viet Cong. VC, for short. Victor Charlie in the Army phonetic alphabet. Charlie was the bad guy. The good guys were in C Company, along with their friends in Alpha, Bravo and Delta Companies.

FAST FLANKER was the battalion call sign. FAST FLANKER 6 was the battalion commander's call sign, and 65 was for the radio operators in his forward command post. The young soldier sitting at the right side radio immediately answered with "HARD HITTER 6, this is FAST FLANKER 65, over."

The heavy-breathing HARD HITTER 6 was obviously moving at the double time as he reported having "a platoon in heavy contact with an NVA force of unknown size. I am moving in their direction." He added "I have some men down."

The Que Son Valley crawled with NVA units of the 2d NVA Division. They had chewed on the 5th Marines until we got there in October of '67. And now they were chewing on us. The RTO in front of me immediately pushed to talk and called FAST FLANKER 4 – our Supply Officer back at LZ Baldy — telling him to crank up ammo re-supply. At the same time, the RTO on the left radio picked up his handset and called the Brigade TOC on the Brigade Command Net. He paraphrased the Hard Hitter report and asked them to crank up Dustoff. *(Dustoff was our lingo for the medical evacuation helicopter. Medevac. Dustoff. We have multiple names for practically everything in the Army. Now it's Air Evac in Iraq and Afghanistan.)*

My Assistant Operations Officer, a captain I had just met, stood there silently taking it all in. The specialists and sergeants seemed to be running the show. I began to wonder what we officers were for, so of course I grabbed the mike. "HARD HITTER 6, this is FAST FLANKER 3, over." 3 stands for Operations Officer. Also called the S-3. That was me.

When HARD HITTER 6 answered, I asked him about artillery right before a round left one of the howitzers just outside the TOC. I then asked him for their location, prompting the RTO on the right to impatiently tap his grease pencil at a spot on the map. (Coordinates BT014365). I then asked if he needed scout birds and gunships, and finally got an answer. "Roger that, over." I was finally getting to contribute, when in walked the boss.

I briefed the CO — clear, concise, and complete — skills gained from seven years as an infantry and cavalry officer. I already had six months as a battalion S-3 in Berlin Brigade before coming to Vietnam. I knew stuff. "Crank up the bird," said the CO. I reached for my gear and the CO quickly said, "you'd better stay behind for this one." He and John the FSO turned and went out the door. I was quite disappointed. Crushed, actually.

As the CO was lifting off, I got back on the horn to higher headquarters, the 3d Brigade of the First Cavalry Division. I gave them a more detailed situation report, and requested scout birds and gunships.

Earlier in the day, the 1st Platoon of C Company had moved cautiously across an open area toward a wooded area at the bottom of the mountain below C Company's operating base. They were in the hills north of LZ Ross. It was very quiet one second and thunderous the next. The forward men of the forward squads had not seen the covered spider holes and other skillfully camouflaged machinegun positions dug into the thick bamboo hedgerows. The NVA soldiers were the masters of camouflage. To be honest, we were the opposite. A company-sized NVA force, maybe 100 men, was deployed in what turned out to be a large U-shape ambush site. The entire platoon had entered the open end of the "U", and were caught in the kill zone. They were taking intense small arms fire from the front and both flanks.

SSG McCrary's point squad had men go down immediately. McCrary quickly spotted an automatic weapon emplacement that seemed to be doing most of the damage, and assaulted the position without hesitation. He quickly destroyed the enemy machinegun, and just as quickly was killed in action against a hostile force. Douglas MacArthur McCrary's family received a Silver Star Medal in a little black box. 1st Lt. Benjamin Franklin McClary had been killed eleven months earlier serving in the very same company in 5/7 Cav. Two Sons from patriotic families.

The four-man fire team at the back of McCrary's squad immediately assaulted forward to covered positions, led by Specialist Fourth Class Bill Port. *(The ten-man rifle squad in the Infantry is organized around two fire teams and a squad leader.)* Two other men behind this squad crawled forward to administer first aid. Eventually all the wounded men were pulled into an area offering some cover.

The platoon leader, a lieutenant named Tom Golden, was severely wounded, but was able to crawl around organizing his platoon into a defensive perimeter. It wasn't long before the NVA assaulted with on-rushing infantrymen. Though also wounded, Sgt Wooleyham took over McCrary's squad and led them in repelling several enemy rushes. At one point the NVA and our troopers were trading grenades and rifle fire from only a few yards apart.

NVA soldiers were also maneuvering around behind the platoon in an effort to encircle and cut them off from reinforcements. By that same time, another platoon, the 3rd Platoon, had gotten down to the base of the hill, and the Platoon Leader gave Sgt Roden's squad the mission to go across the paddy first. They were covered by fire from Sgt. Lee Danielson's squad.

NVA in the tree line across the paddy took the 3rd Platoon under fire as Roden's point man, Baldwin, stepped out of cover. As it turned out, Roden and Baldwin were the only two to make it across. They ran across the open ground and quickly found themselves close to an NVA machinegun position. They were taken under fire and had a grenade go off right next to them without serious effect. These two gallant troopers destroyed the enemy gun position, before realizing that they were alone out there. They were fortunate to fight their way out, running for dear life back across the paddy to rejoin their platoon. When they got there, they learned that the very popular and respected Lee Danielson had been killed by the enemy fire.

In the meantime, in the pinned-down 1st Platoon, Sp4 Coleman had seen the NVA circling around to cut them off completely, and he unhesitatingly attacked them. Coleman eliminated several enemy positions, and kept the door open for his platoon's eventual withdrawal.

The 2d Platoon under Lt. Kibbon arrived in the area and became engaged further over on the other flank. Kibbon had moved out across the paddy in front of his platoon, and was hit by enemy fire halfway across. His platoon came under intense enemy fire and went to ground in the furrows of the rice paddy. Lt. Kibbon, although painfully wounded, put out intense covering fire from his position in the paddy while his platoon sergeant got the rest of platoon back to the cover of the paddy dike. Platoon Sergeant Birmingham organized and prepared the platoon to assault forward, this time using a good base of supporting fire by one of his squads. Under Birmingham's firm leadership, along with Kibbon's continuing fire support, the platoon successfully assaulted across the paddy and rolled up some of the enemy positions on one flank of Golden's platoon.

At about 1700 hours, as dark was approaching, LTC. Long air-assaulted two platoons from Alpha Company very visibly onto a nearby hill (Coordinates BT002366) to reinforce C Company. These factors along with the gallant actions of the 2d and 3d Platoons enabled the men of 1st Platoon to begin to fight their way backward out of this predicament.

It was dark when the word spread throughout the platoon to begin moving back. Bill Port and his fire team were behind an embankment, with the mission of covering the withdrawal. Port had been badly wounded in the hand. He was missing three fingers. A man in a position next to them attempted to move back and was cut down in open area. Seeing this, Bill Port unhesitatingly rushed out through intense fire, picked the man up and carried him back to safety. Port returned through heavy fire and rejoined his fire team in their forward fighting position. On the next assault by the NVA, a grenade came over the embankment and landed at their feet. Port shouted "grenade" and hurled himself toward it to shield the others. He didn't move again after the blast. Port's actions saved the three other men from being hit, and further inspired them to continue covering the withdrawal until everyone was out. As the men of 1st Platoon moved backward in the dark, firing at the NVA muzzle blasts, they could no longer find and bring out their three KIAs. In the heat of the battle, Port, Spangler and McClary were left on the field.

C Company attacked back into the contact area at first light the next morning to recover their three bodies. The NVA were gone. There were lots of blood trails. Many an NVA soldier had gone to meet Buddha the previous day, but the NVA had taken their bodies with them. They apparently took Port too, because we could not find him anywhere. Spangler and McClary were found right where they had fallen.

When I received the report that they could not find Port, I immediately told them to scour the entire wooded area, leave no stone unturned, and report back when they had done so. An hour later, the answer was the same. There had been little doubt in anyone's mind that Port was killed by the grenade, but now no one would quite swear to it on paper. We had no choice but to report Bill Port as missing in action. MIA.

Among fighter pilots, MIAs are inevitable. They become heroes. In the Infantry, you are not supposed to get captured. Infantry MIAs do not automatically become heroes. In the Infantry, everything about MIAs is bad news. Real bad news. My first day as Fast Flanker 3 resulted in an MIA. It also resulted in the award of the Medal of Honor to Bill Port. Many Medals of Honor are the direct result of a screwed up situation, and 12 January 1968 was no exception.

I fired off a note to my wife the next day.

Dear Nancy,

Vietnam is a truly awful place now that I am back. Everything is filth, discomfort and utterly repulsive. We (3rd Brigade) lost about 45 guys while you and I were on the beach... 2 men are missing which is the most tragic thing in the war. Many medals have been won.

Charlie seems to be lasting longer than our Brigade S-2 seems to think he could. We have underestimated him this time. Instead of running back into the mountains he has stayed in the valley and our helicopters are full of holes.

Arrived at LZ Colt last evening to become the S-3 of the 5th Battalion 7th Cavalry. When I arrived one of our companies was in a heavy contact but today is quiet. We are writing up one of our soldiers for the Medal of Honor. He dived on a grenade and saved his guys.

The battalion commander is an old pro named Jack Long. He was the Deputy Brigade Commander who used to drive me nuts back at LZ Gail and LZ Sandra. Underneath his rough exterior he has a heart of gold.

Everyone here is first class and polite and it is so nice to be among good people again.

*   *   *   *   *

It was so long ago. The next morning, as I drove home from the Reactivation Parade, I was amazed at how the memories were so vivid. Like it was just last week.

CHAPTER 2

OPERATING INDEPENDENTLY

I don't totally believe in fate, but it was somewhat ironic that I came to be the Operations Officer of a battalion in the 7th Cavalry. As a child, I lived deep in the heart of Powder River. The site of the Little Big Horn Battle was only 90 miles north, where Custer and his 7th Cavalry had been soundly defeated by the Sioux and Cheyenne. When I was in the first grade in Buffalo, Wyoming, old Jim Gatchell ran the drugstore and fed us ice cream cones on Saturday mornings for singing "God Bless America." Gatchell personally knew many of the Cheyenne who had fought at the Little Big Horn. Billy Hughes and I would play Indians and Cavalry on a little hill west of town. One of us would be the mighty Cheyenne warriors, and the other would be the 7th Cavalry. On top of the hill where we played was the falling-down remains of a wooden burial platform. Scattered around in the grass were lots of arrowheads. Maybe the ghost of the old Cheyenne Indian Chief buried on that little hill got me sent to the 7th Cavalry in 1968, hoping I would get my ass shot full of holes.

As the new FAST FLANKER 3, I knew I was following in the footsteps of a lot of interesting characters. Deju vu is for historians — every new experience is a new experience — but I was not new to being an operations officer. Actually, I had started with the Cuban Missile Crisis. Another vivid memory.

29 October 1962
Ft. Campbell, Kentucky

Everything that could be done had been done. Nothing left to do but wait for the order to chute up and get on the plane. My eighteen months of recon platoon command were over, I was now a 1st Lieutenant, and the operations officer of the 101st Airborne Division's reconnaissance company, Troop B, 17th Cavalry.

I sat on my parachute, chin in my hands, thinking about nothing in particular. Just watching troopers coming and going, milling about, chewing the fat. The place was Polk Army Airfield at Ft. Campbell. The Russians had ships loaded with ICBMs coming across the Atlantic toward Cuba. They also had bombers stationed in Cuba, presumably with nuclear weapons on board.

A few days earlier we had watched John F Kennedy address the nation on television. Early on he said: "*... missiles in Cuba add to an already clear and present danger...*" Somewhere in the middle he described Cuba in terms of: "*... an area well known to have a special and historical relationship to the United States...* " (*which seems to have been forgotten since then.*) Among other actions and initiatives, he said: "**Should these offensive military preparations continue, thus increasing the threat to the hemisphere, further action will be justified. I** *have directed the Armed Forces to prepare for any eventualities."* And he closed with: *"It shall be the policy of this Nation to regard any nuclear missile launched from Cuba against any nation in the Western Hemisphere as an attack by the Soviet Union on the United States, requiring a full retaliatory response upon the Soviet Union."*

Right after JFK's speech, we went to DEFCON 3 at Ft. Campbell. All leaves and passes were cancelled, and we began preparing all our equipment for a possible invasion of Cuba. Three days later, as Russians ships continued to plow forward, we were ordered to DEFCON 2. The 101st Airborne Division immediately went on full alert. Goodbye families. We were quarantined in the barracks. I was called into the CO's office, filled out a top secret security clearance form, and was whisked away to a group of tents inside a barbed wire area. It was the division plans area. A bunch of tents put up in a vacant lot, surrounded by barbed wire, and guarded by MPs in full battle gear. There were buildings all over post, but they put up tents to plan the operation. The only bugs in these tents were actual living insects. The 101st Airborne Division had put on its war face.

It was inside this little tent city where I read the division's top secret war plans, operations orders, intelligence estimates, and aerial photos that seemed to come in every few hours. By the end of the second day, I had put together the operations orders for the Troop, gotten the approval of my troop commander, and briefed it to a horde of senior officers at Division Headquarters. I was twenty-four at the time.

Early on the morning of 29 October 1962, the officers and senior NCOs of B/17 Cav stood in our troop dayroom listening to John F Kennedy again on television. I believe it was closed circuit — directed at the Armed Forces. I cannot find a transcript anywhere. It was short and sweet. Immediately after his speech, we mounted up on trucks and went to Polk Army Airfield. The wee small hours of 30 October, fewer than twenty-fours away, were going to be a traumatic experience for Cubans, Russians and Americans alike.

There had been very little sleep during the last three days. Now, waiting for the word to mount the C-130s, I should have been lying against my parachute like half the soldiers were, getting caught up on rest. But I was too excited on the inside as I sat there looking bored stiff on the outside. The day was wearing on, getting close to the magic hour beyond which we would not meet the planned arrival time over the sugarcane fields. I just sat there, checking my watch from time to time, and started thinking about my wife and baby boy. They were at our modest little officer's quarters less than a mile away, or maybe out for a wagon ride in the neighborhood. I didn't even get to kiss them goodbye.

In fewer than twelve hours, the five platoons of the division's reconnaissance company, Troop B, 17th US Cavalry, would be jumping out of C-130s in the middle of the night. Jump altitude was set at five hundred feet. A few of the old sergeants of Troop B had done that one. Jumping in the dark at five hundred feet is another issue. The drop zones were in the vast cane fields between the ocean and the escarpment, which quickly rises some five hundred feet above sea level. The selected drop area was one mile in from the beach, and three miles long.

Our mission was to locate enemy gun positions along a three mile stretch of the high ground overlooking the drop zone on the coast. Our C-130 Hercules aircraft would fly down the cane fields parallel to the beach, and just below the top of the escarpment, hopefully below the radars of the anti-aircraft missiles known to be up there. I had seen the photos with my brand new Top Secret Clearance just that morning. Soviet-built missile sites were not that far inland. The five C-130s would drop the platoons about one quarter mile apart down the cane field area. The platoons would gather up their men, get off the drop zone, and move out toward the high ground in their assigned zones. Our captain commanding the troop would operate from his rear command post in the trees down at the edge of the drop zone. I was going with the center platoon.

We had maybe three hours before the Screaming Eagles of the legendary 101st Airborne Division would have eight thousand parachutists coming out of a continuous line of planes. It would just be getting light, and any Cuban or Russian soldiers located on the escarpment would be completely terrorized *(or maybe not.)*

Every available aircraft was involved. The nearly worn-out C-119s. The C-123s. The big C-124s. And the brand new C-130 Hercules for the lucky ones like the division's elite Troop B, 17th Cavalry. You knew you were going to clear the trees at the end of the Polk Army Airfield runway when you took off in a C-130. The Screaming Eagles and the All-Americans of the 82nd Airborne Division would lead the way into Cuba, just as they had led the way into France eighteen years earlier.

The enemy soldiers on the escarpment, assuming they were still there after the gigantic parachute drop that morning, would also get to see a vast armada of ships rise up on the horizon, bringing another one hundred and forty thousand soldiers and marines. The Cuban Invasion would be big. Real Big.

Each of our platoons would spread out into two or three patrols to advance in their assigned zone. They would have only three hours of darkness to get to the top and find any enemy positions that could bring fire on the cane fields below. We were definitely planning to go up the hill that night, until the word came down at about 1600 hours. Jack and Nikita had worked things out. We never got on the planes.

Some old generals say that the President's deal with Mr. Kruschev got reported to the Commanding General of the of the huge invasion force only forty-five minutes before the point of no return. The President was a great hero for staring down the Russians. We of the 101st Airborne Division didn't get the little bronze star on our jump wings. Like any good Airborne Infantry Ranger lieutenant with absolutely no combat experience, I pouted all the way back to the barracks. The sergeants who had seen combat in Korea were delirious with joy, and very thankful that John Kennedy had saved their lives.

We had spent many tense eighteen-hour days almost invading Cuba, but got home to our families in no time flat after the word came down. It was almost like nothing had happened. And for the vast majority of Americans, nothing had happened.

From the perspective of the media, and consequently the historians, the Cuban Missile Crisis ended on 29 October, 1962. But not really. The bombers were still in Cuba. It was just not headline news anymore.

Throughout the first three weeks of November we sat on the edge of our seats at Ft. Campbell, expecting to go to back to DEFCON 2, return to Polk Army airfield and draw parachutes. In a time-line news summary of key events about the Cuban Missile Crisis, there was only one more item after 29 October.

"November 21, 1962: Just over a month after the crisis began, JFK terminates the quarantine when Khrushchev agrees after several weeks of tense negotiations at the UN to withdraw Soviet IL-28 nuclear bombers from Cuba."

Three decades later a Soviet military official would reveal that mobile tactical nuclear weapons *(e.g., the bombers)* and more than 40,000 Soviet troops were in place in Cuba throughout this time for use in the event of an American invasion.

I had the great fortune of being assigned to Troop B, 17th Cavalry. An infantry officer getting to be a cavalry officer. We trained and operated with very little supervision from our captain, and were normally on independent missions for the division, or attached to one of the Infantry Brigades. Our captain mainly held the fort somewhere. Life was great in the cavalry for a lieutenant, compared to being a closely supervised 2d lieutenant in a rifle company commanded by a captain, who might be over-supervised by a colonel concerned altogether too much about sergeant's work. And it got me started as an operations officer early in my service.

CHAPTER 3

BACK IN THE ARMY

Motivation to go to Iraq began to percolate after the Reactivation Parade in July 2004. Many of us Vietnam Vets had attended the battalion party in Savannah that evening. I met the battalion commander, all the troop commanders and many of the junior officers. The whole scene was surreal. Sitting with the young lieutenants and their wives took me back to the life of a young officer in a combat unit. Nothing had changed in forty years. Some things live on in the Infantry and Cavalry. The people come and go, but the unit lives on. A battalion takes on a life of its own.

At the party I mentioned to LTC. Petery that I was writing about 5/7 Cav from my experiences back in 1968. He was quick to invite me to come to Iraq and ride with them as an embedded writer. I couldn't imagine doing anything like that at the time. I half-seriously commented that maybe I should.

The next day I dashed off an e-mail to my favorite West Point classmates:

> *The incoming commander was brief, as he should be, but gave very promising remarks. The troops on the field were sharp as knives. The company and field grade officers were very gracious and articulate. The NCOs were ominous-looking warriors. As the separate companies passed by, I remembered the instances where I had gone with each of them many years earlier on one action or another. At the end we sang "I'm a Dog Faced Soldier" — then we sang The Army Song. Nothing has changed since our days down in the battalion. The wives are still beautiful. The young officers still carry that naive but essential look of indestructibility. The NCOs show lots of personal power. The rail-thin PFC with severe acne still lurks over by the wall, waiting for the day that he'll have to be the one to bail us all out and get the Distinguished Service Cross. It was another great day to be in the Army.*

I was a retired Colonel living in Atlanta, but I had been treading water ever since 1968. I may have reached the rank of Colonel, but I was stuck on Major. FAST FLANKER 3. That's me. I retired in 1983, disenchanted by the whole thing, and never looked back for a minute. But that changed on 9/11.

We apparently won the Cold War by 1989, but it has been endless war ever since. Endless little wars all around the globe. Eating up the world's precious resources. Israel and the Arabs. Panama. Granada. Lebanon. Afghanistan for the Ruskies, and now us. Wars raging all the time in various far-off places we don't want to know about, such as in Africa. I had tuned it all out in favor of golf and distance races. Well, until September 11, 2001. It was Reveille for me. Back in the Army.

Everyone remembers that dreadful morning. I had come downstairs half-awake, turned on the TV and then my computer. I caught a glimpse from the latest action movie — in this case, an airliner flying into the top of a skyscraper in Manhattan

— as I was going into the kitchen to turn on the coffee. Returning to the den, I was jolted awake by the second plane moving from right to left across the screen. I started hearing the program.

(Holy shit. This ain't no freakin movie. It is World War III.)

I stood frozen in the middle of the room, mesmerized by the second plane, as it disappeared into the upper floors of the World Trade Center building. And not much later the buildings started to drop. *(It's only been twelve fucking years since we won the Cold War, and we spent 58,000 guys in Nam for this? I knew from profanity, after a career in the Infantry. And maybe "spent" is awfully callous… but that's what we did.)*

The memory of seventy men sent to the Black Marble during my six months as Battalion S-3 in 1968 came back in full force. And three times that many were wounded bad enough to be medevaced. God only knows what happened to many of them.

And then the Pentagon got hit. I immediately called one of my closest classmates to check on his wife who worked for the Department of Army. She was fine. Her office was demolished, but she had been a hundred feet up the hall at the time.

For the next weeks and months, I thought of little else but the life I had led up until then, and how meaningless it all seemed in the face of the 9/11 tragedy, and how depressing it was to see the paranoia landing on America like a big cloud of smog.

After the Berlin Wall came down in 1989 and the Vietnam Wall went up, I was beginning to think we had achieved something. Communism lost, and the world was saved. Okay, so no one talked intelligently about what to do now that the Red Menace was gone. But, life was good. The only problem seemed to be something about Wahabi… or Al Quaida somebody.

In addition to the hostages in Iran, the crazy Arabs killed 200 plus US Marines in Lebanon in 1983, hijacked a TWA plane full of people in 1985, hijacked a cruise ship the same year, fired a missile into one of our ships, one of their biggest players violated the sovereignty of Kuwait, and on and on and on. But I had just walked away in disgust when I retired, maybe even earlier. By 2001 I didn't know much anymore, and wasn't much interested. The terrorists were just more of the same old hapless Arabs firing their rifles in the air. They were still the most incredibly incompetent soldiers that warfare has ever known. Wasn't it just about their hating the Israelis? Had they really affected us here in TV Land, other than in Boca Raton and NYC?

But now it's WW III. Thirty short years after my outfit came home from Vietnam, the Arabs attacked New York City. NEW YORK CITY! And in the unfolding weeks, our response was heroic. Isn't it always?

It took us no time at all after 11 September 2011 to announce the culprits, Sheikh Osama Bin Laden and his wife-beating al Quaida followers in Afghanistan. Within a few months the Air Force kicked the stuffing out of them in nothing flat. Some of our smart bombs were not so smart around Tora Bora, but, hey, war is hell. And we didn't exactly take the high ground at yet another place we won't mention in Afghanistan. And, not uninterestingly, we dropped a chemical bomb on the Talibans every bit as powerful as those pesky small nuclear bombs we were railing about.

But at least The Sheikh was on the run — hiding in a cave somewhere. We were doing something about the radical fundamentalist's use of terrorism as a political strategy. Don and his generals were all smiles in their all-too-frequent press conferences. They were no different than the Gulf War guys when it came to thirst for exposure, reminding me of the nervous new lieutenant on his first training exercise. He would call in hourly all night with "commo check, how do you hear this station, over?" Finally the captain answers with, "We hear you too loud and too often, out." Over the course of my life I had watched the news media transition from news reporters to entertainers. Now the generals too? My ingrained cynicism, conceived in the 9th grade and delivered in Vietnam, was growing beyond control.

Back in 1991 we had knocked Iraq from a conventional war capability back to no better than guerilla warfare. We could have sent the Iraq military force all the way back to zero capability had we only finished the job. For a couple years after 9/11, I felt personally lost. Hundreds of thousands of good people had died fighting the Cold War, and for what. We were going down the drain. No one seemed to be doing anything right. It seemed like every generation coming up was too egotistical to learn anything from the past. We even have Whahabis living all over the place in America, and all we can do is guarantee them freedom of religion under the Constitution — even if they are not citizens yet — even if they are a built-in haven for terrorists. And no profiling allowed. No sir. Even the weather was against us. El Nino, that little sumbitch. And what about the young people this time around? They seemed awfully quiet, for a change.

AMERICA TOWN

I know I should be happy in your land
It's not all that wild to me
Not that I want to be any other where
I know its hell out there

Here in the borders of America Town
All of the dollies are spinning round and round
Hail to the chief
Let's just drag them all down
There's got to be a hero somewhere

Used to get annoyed at the fire and the flag

Now it just seems old to me
(Everyone is old to me)
And I know we'd kick your ass
But first I'll take a nap tonight
And know someone's looking over me

John Ondrasik — Five For Fighting

In 2002 I was no longer treading water. I was starting to dog-paddle a bit. Gone since 1975, I had a lot of swimming to do. No news is good news had been my mantra. Just get up, two cups of coffee, run on the beach, and go from there. I didn't know anything about politics anyway, and still don't, so why worry about it. Not gonna teach this old dog new tricks. *(Thinking of more clichés. Give me a minute.)* But at least I was interested in what was happening to the Army. I had some notion of what the Army used to be about, and definite opinions about what it should be about. By 2002 I was becoming active with my battalion's association for veterans, and following the operations in Afghanistan with interest.

On 11 November 2002, I went to D.C. for Veterans Day. It was cool and drizzly for the Vietnam Veterans Parade from the Washington Monument down to The Wall. The rain was light but steady. The temperature was in the 50s. Nevertheless, several thousand Nam Vets showed up for the parade. They had marched in a lot of rain in Vietnam. Some have been marching in the rain during much of their remaining lives. The forty-man platoon of Veterans from my battalion of the 7th U. S. Cavalry had the honor of being the lead unit.

We marched right behind the band and the 1st Cavalry Division Color Guard. Our own Color Guard from our battalion veteran's association led us down the Avenue. We were sometimes in step, and sometimes not. We ran the spectrum from private first class to general. A very tall and distinguished-looking gentleman stood out a few rows back in the formation, looking sharp in his blue blazer with two shiny silver stars on the front of his Stetson. Near the back was a little guy in a raggedy fatigue shirt over shorts and sandals, with the deep tan of a fishing boat captain. In between were all the various types of Nam Vets, and included corporate executives and PTSD patients. Some of the executives were PTSD patients. Most of the men were showing their age, but they had a spring in their step. There was a lot of banter going on. We were a happy group. Happy survivors.

Some of the 5/7 Cav men wore striking black satin jackets and black Stetson hats emblematic of the cavalry, but sprinkled throughout the group were a few guys still wearing their old fatigue jackets. One such man was me, Fast Flanker 3. I was halfway back, marching along, proud to be in the same row with Bold Eagle 6, the Sergeant Major, and a couple other legendary heroes of the battalion. I suspect I was different, though, with my very erect posture, like a young soldier on parade in spite of my advanced age. My fatigue jacket was not plain and scruffy, like you saw everywhere after the war. I had my 1st Cavalry Division patch on my right sleeve, signifying service in combat with the division. On my left sleeve I wore my Ranger Tab above the Vietnamese Ranger patch that I earned on my second tour in Vietnam. I had my senior jump wings, my Vietnamese Ranger Badge, and my prized Combat Infantryman's Badge. I was the only guy in the formation wearing a fatigue jacket on the one hand, but with all the bells and whistles on the other. It was like I was trying to be the war protester, but couldn't quite let go of the Army.

The platoon came to the end of the march, halted, broke ranks and headed for The Wall. As I came along, I just had to step in front of the Color Guard still standing at attention with the flags, and quietly say, "Y'all are a fine looking color guard. Great job." It seemed to me that a couple chests went noticeably higher. That's Fast Flanker 3, ever the officer. In 1968 the troops called me Major, or Sir. At least when I was around. No one called me by my first name, that's for sure. I sometimes referred to myself as Fast Flanker 3, like some of the athletes who talk about themselves in third person. And I still do. Nowadays to the '68 vintage veterans in the association who remembered me, I am still the Major. They can't quite break that mold of slight discomfort around the officers. The association is all about the old days.

Everyone trooped over to the sidewalk leading down to the massive v-shaped wall dug into the earth — the Vietnam War Memorial in Washington, D.C. When you win, the generals sit on their bronze horses in the various circles around town, or stand on pedestals around the Plain at West Point. But Vietnam was a different kind of war. The men who got honored were primarily the thousands of 19 to 22 year-olds. Their names are carved into the shiny black marble. Row upon row. More than 58,000 men. Somewhere between one and eight women — I'm not sure. Other groups have sprinkled the nearby area with their own statues and monuments since The Wall became such a hit, but you can't get away from The Wall. The cost of these particular young people will not be forgotten anytime soon. They aren't lumped together under some symbolic sculpture. They aren't numbers. They are exact names right in your face.

Before long, I found myself standing in front of Panel 37 E. Jim Thomas stood next to me. Jim was looking for his friend Joe Begotka, who had been a fellow radio-telephone operator in the battalion headquarters back in '68. *(RTOs, they were called.)*

While Jim looked for Begotka, I searched the panel for William Port. The loss of Bill Port turned out to be an amazing story. He didn't die on the night of 12 January 1968. Instead, he turned up in a North Vietnamese POW camp, where for the next ten months he was an inspirational leader of his fellow prisoners. He eventually died from his terrible wounds and treatment at the hands of his captors. He was so inspirational, in fact, that his fellow prisoners recommended him for the Medal of Honor for his period of captivity. Bill Port's remains were recovered from the North Vietnamese in 1985. Bill Port may have earned two MOHs, but regardless of this story, he is carried on The Wall as killed in action on the 12th of January, 1968, and was posthumously awarded the Medal of Honor for his actions on that day.

Looking for Bill Port, I found Wally Crum, a classmate at West Point. We had served together in Berlin Brigade in '63. Wally was an advisor down in the Mekong Delta when he was killed. There were so many names crowded into such a short period, twenty to thirty names per day, about five to six names per line. I ended up going two panels further until familiar names started jumping out at me.

"Hey, I found Port!"

I looked around, and Jim had moved further down the wall. I felt foolish for my outburst. The front of the wall is quiet, even with a crowd. A Cemetery. A very quiet place. There are so many names on panel 34E. Looking upward, it was hard for an old guy like me to keep my eye on someone after I had found him. I lost Port twice but found him again. There was Max Spangler in the same row — Row 39. Spangler was eighteen years old, and was killed early in the battle. And, there was Doug McClary in the next row above Port and Spangler. And Castaldi was there too. Danielson too. The battalion lost too many men from C Company that day. Too many.

My thoughts were interrupted by a teenager standing next to me. She asked, "When were you over there?"

"1968", I responded.

"Marines?"

"No, Army."

"How long were you in the Army?" she added.

"Forever, I think."

"Oh. My grandfather was in the Army too", she said.

"How long?"

"Well — I guess you could say forever," she said, with tears brimming in her eyes.

CHAPTER 4

INDIAN COUNTRY

A few months after the Reactivation Parade in July 2004, a scholarly classmate of mine posed some serious questions in the San Francisco Chronicle, and my interest picked up. The catalyst for his article was the outbreak of "Support Our Troops" ribbons, the "latest vehicular sign du jour," he called it. He asked, "What, exactly, would they like the rest of us to do?" - implying that there are no such ribbons on the backs of his family cars. He raised many issues, such as the similarities of the government's justifying the two wars, and of course the troubling questions of the losses of 58,000 men in Vietnam, and now 1200 in Iraq. He closed with "I wish I knew the answers to these questions because then I could decide what 'Support Our Troops' really means."

I just had to give him a piece of my mind - that the troops know little of politics, that when the country calls, they haul. Most everyone must have been thinking the same thing, because the outpouring of patriotism has become dangerously strong. I told him that "support our troops simply means support our troops." The fact that he had bailed after his first tour in Vietnam and joined the flower people was certainly a factor in my response.

I went to Ft. Stewart a couple times to see some training and get to know the current troopers better. I got myself appointed as the association's Liaison Officer to the battalion. The 5/7 Cav began deploying to Iraq right after the holidays. The equipment had gone by sea beginning after Thanksgiving 2004, and the troops started flying on 9 January 2005.

Three short weeks before the battalion was scheduled to deploy, I went up for a final visit in December. At the urging of Captain Ralph Elder, B Troop Commander, I arranged my trip so that I could attend Reveille and run with the 500-man battalion. At the end of the run, I seized the opportunity to take the stand, and complimented the entire battalion on the fact that every man finished, also commenting that the straggler group was only one minute back with a handful of guys.

I told them about the infamous ten-mile physical training run of the 2d Battalion 6th Infantry in Berlin in 1966, in which I, as the Battalion S-3, had commanded the straggler group. Those not carted off to the hospital outnumbered the largest of the five companies by a significant amount by the end of the run. And we came in at least fifteen minutes behind. It was a bloodbath. Almost ended the fine career of the battalion commander, it did.

My battalion commander in Berlin was a PT nut. As a new 2d lieutenant, he had been a mortar platoon leader in the first days of the Korean War in 1951, and half his men were shot in the back retreating to the next ridgeline. They were too fat and too out of shape to outrun the North Koreans. He was ahead of his time in 1966. By the early eighties, all soldiers had gym shorts, t-shirts and running shoes; and the soldiers of all branches were running their asses off most every morning. Some run on flexible steel legs nowadays.

In the fall of 2004, I would have liked to tell all the lieutenants and captains everything that I knew about the history of 5/7 Cav. But I also knew they would be far too busy dealing with the present, and getting ready to go to Iraq within a few months. They had their own war to fight. Just like we did before them. I could only guess about what the volunteer soldiers of today would want to know about the history of their unit. 5/7 Cav has some history.

The 7th U.S. Cavalry was created to fight the Indians in the western territories in 1866, right after the Civil War. Under the command of Lt. Colonel George Custer, the 7th Cavalry was horse-mounted cavalry. They were more accurately described as horse-mounted infantry – because they went out to fight, not just to scout out the enemy. For WW II and Korea, they were organized as infantry, with half-track troop carriers for mobility. In Vietnam, the 7th Cavalry grew from nine companies to three separate airmobile infantry battalions assigned to the 1st Cavalry Division — airmobile because the rifle companies were maneuvered about the battle area in formations of UH1B Helicopters. One thing is constant in the US Army, we reorganize for the moment.

Most of the experienced troopers in 1866 had come from the storied Fighting 69th Infantry, a volunteer regiment from New York City that became legendary during the Civil War. The "Fighting 69th" allegedly got their name from General Robert E. Lee, who had personally seen them coming more than once. The 7th Cavalry's mission was to quell the Indians terrorizing the westward-advancing settlers. They fought the Sioux and Cheyenne right past my hometown of Buffalo, Wyoming — deep in Powder River. Powder River — a mystical place. *The last hunting ground.*

E Company of the original 7th Cavalry Regiment, being the fifth company alpha-betically, is the forerunner of the 5th Battalion. *Now 5th Squadron.* Each company had specific colored horses, enabling Lt. Col. Custer to identify his units on the battlefield. E Company rode dapple grays. On 27 June 1876, E Company and four other companies went with Custer up the grassy ridge north of the vast village of teepees along the Little Bighorn River. According to historians, George Custer sent E and F down the Medicine Tail Coulee to the ford, where they ran straight into hundreds of Cheyenne warriors. The Cheyenne attacked straight at and around E and F Company, killing the retreating cavalrymen as they continued to the high ground in pursuit of Custer and the other three companies. As stated in Welch's great book, *Killing Custer,* on page 165: "Com-panies E and F, under Captain Yates, did make it to the ford. Many Indian accounts describe a well-organized detachment of soldiers on gray horses actually getting into the water. This was Company E, led by Lieutenant Algeron Smith. Company E was the most noticeable of the companies on their light-colored mounts. At the Battle of Little Bighorn, the Indians described the movements of this company as being all over the battlefield until the end." The Indians called them the Gray Horse Troop.

Algeron "A.E." Smith was killed in the battle. Historians are very unclear about how many men rode with the Gray Horse Troop that day, and if all of them were killed or not. As many as twenty-eight are alleged to have fallen in the coulee, and that may have been everyone in field that day. In any event, George Custer became a household name, while the troopers of his command faded into the obscurity of the Montana hills.

The original Irish veterans of the Fighting 69th brought their songs with them to the 7th Cavalry in 1866. During the Indian Wars, they would sit around the fire at night singing Irish ballads such as "Sgt. Flynn."

SGT. FLYNN

Ten thousand Braves are riding, Sgt. Flynn.
In the Black Hills they are hiding, Sgt. Flynn.
Crazy Horse and Sitting Bull,
They will get their bellies full of lead and steel, from the men of Garryowen!

We'll dismount and fight the heathens Sgt. Flynn.
While there's still a trooper breathin Sgt. Flynn.
In the face of sheer disaster,
Keep those carbines firing faster.
Let those volleys ring for dear old Garryowen!

GARRYOWEN, GARRYOWEN, GARRYOWEN.
In this valley of Montana all alone.
There are better days to be,
For the Seventh Cavalry,
When we charge again for dear old GARRYOWEN!

There are many old stanzas, but these lyrics of "Sgt. Flynn" were obviousy added after these Irishmen and their commander, George Custer, met Tatanka Yotanka's braves on the Little Big Horn River. Sitting Bull to us. And his tactical commander, Tasunka Witko. Crazy Horse.

The 7th Cavalry regimental crest includes the word Garryowen on the bottom scroll. Garry and Owen are split by the saber, looking like a person's name rather than the one word that it is. The term garryowen actually was a beer garden in Ireland frequented by the town rowdies. Garryowen started with the 69th and was brought to the 7th.

All ancient history. The history of 5/7 Cavalry started for me in October of 1967 while hanging around the Brigade TOC at LZ Baldy.

October 1967
Que Son Valley
South Vietnam

The 3d Brigade had moved north to the Hiep Duc District of Quang Nam Province on 1 October 1967, freeing the 5th Marine Regiment to move up to Danang. In this regard, the Brigade was attached to the American Division for command and control. The 7th Cavalry went deep into Indian Country when they moved into the Que Son Valley. Almost as deep as Powder River. The Que Son Valley is about 30 kilometers ("clicks") long and maybe 15 to 20 clicks wide, surrounded on three sides by jungle-covered mountains. Two rivers run from west to east out of the valley and hit the ocean about 50 clicks south of Da Nang. The wide valley floor of the Que Son was an extremely fertile rice bowl. Dating back to 1965, this valley was dominated by numerous VC battalions and separate companies. Starting in 1967 it became a haven for the 2nd NVA Division coming into South Vietnam after the long trek down the Ho Chi Minh Trail through Laos. Its three regiments were assembled in the mountains surrounding the valley that summer. By the fall of 1967, they were itching for a fight. It was a brutal place for the foot-mobile 5th Marines before we replaced them in October. Find a veteran who was in the 5th Marines in summer of 1967, and ask him about the Que Son Valley.

The 3d Brigade Headquarters, with two battalions, started arriving at LZ Baldy on 1 October, and one battalion (2/12 Cav) was immediately sent out to the west end of the valley to take over an existing Marine base. They called it LZ Ross. The 2/12 Cav commander was LTC. Ross. 1/7 Cav operated out of LZ Baldy and was assigned an area of operations ("AO") along the coast, east of Route One.

5/7 Cav came into LZ Baldy a few days later, to be deployed into the center of the valley about halfway to LZ Ross. On 7 October they air-assaulted onto a piece of slightly higher ground in the middle of the valley, where they established a firebase for one battery of 105mm howitzers, along with their battalion command post. LZ Colt was the name. Getting off to a very rough start is its fame.

LZ Colt was not "good ground," as we in the Infantry would say. The hill was really just a dome-shaped rise above the surrounding terrain. It was within view from a nearby hill of equal elevation, affording the enemy excellent observation. The floor of the valley was predominately flat terrain, only 10 meters above sea level. LZ Colt was only 23 meters, and not even a hill on the west and north side. In order to operate throughout the valley floor, however, an artillery battery had to be somewhere in this general area. The location of the artillery overruled the infantry tactical considerations. Col. McKenna, the Brigade Commander, had weighed these risks relative to the need for an artillery battery in the center of the valley.

Unfortunately, the 3d Brigade also pushed the 5/7 Cav out to LZ Colt before they could deliver the required defense materials. Through the first two days they received only enough barbed wire for a single strand obstacle. Several factors combined to create this problem. The Third Brigade had just arrived on 1 October, and much of the

30

helicopter assets were still getting set up out on the coast. Additionally, the 5th Marines were unhelpful when it came to the handoff of property and materials. Of much greater impact, though, was the onset of the monsoon season. It started raining on the 7th, and got serious on the night of 8-9 October with high winds and 13 inches of downpour in the space of a few hours. It blew most of our tents down on top of us at the Brigade HQs, and caused the loss of one day for moving anything anywhere. Within 48 hours the rice paddies went from dry to full of water.

LZ Colt was a mess of mud and water-filled bunkers on the 9th of October. In addition to barbed wire, they were also missing lots of other defense materials such as additional claymore mines and trip flares. B Company defended this poor piece of ground.

The Brigade Commander may have weighed the risks, but he didn't have nearly enough information about the risks he was taking. Being there only a week, the Brigade S-2 Intelligence officer had little appreciation of the magnitude of enemy strength in the Que Son. And he did not know there were five NVA battalions within easy reach of LZ Colt on 9 October. Three of them, the battalions of the 3d NVA Regiment of the 2d NVA Division, were in the final stages of preparation for an attack against LZ Colt that very night.

Making matters worse that day, the Brigade Commander directed that two of the battalion's three available rifle companies be air-assaulted into the mountains 10 clicks to the south of LZ Colt in response to intelligence reports about a large NVA force located there. 3rd Brigade was still in separate company operations mode, e.g., spreading their companies out searching for the elusive enemy. The war in Vietnam was a company operations war up to that point. Aggressive brigade commanders, with little to do, could easily fall to the temptation of dictating the maneuver of companies. Micro-management was definitely in vogue, starting with the Secretary of Defense. 3d Brigade had a very aggressive brigade commander at the time.

In the wee small hours of the night of 9-10 October, the NVA commenced a 61mm mortar attack. The very first round landed in the commander's tent, killing the S-3 instantly and grievously wounding the commander. At the same time, 2 to 3 squads of NVA sappers penetrated the flimsy barbed wire barriers and ran to the top of the highground, throwing grenades and satchel charges into tents and the TOC.

Sappers are not unlike our Rangers. They preceded major assaults. They conducted raids. They were the elites. Each sapper carried a satchel charge to throw into a tent or a bunker door. Explosives were among their main weapons — *(not unlike today's terrorists. Sappers were not terrorists, though. They were soldiers. They attacked US and South Vietnamese military units and installations. They generally did not blow up women and children on their way into church or at the town market.)*

The NVA had totally surprised the 3rd Brigade with their ability to mount a significant operation against LZ Colt in such a short period. By the time their preliminary work was finished, although it was at the cost of all their sappers, they had succeeded in killing or wounding all the officers in the 5/7 Cav HQS.

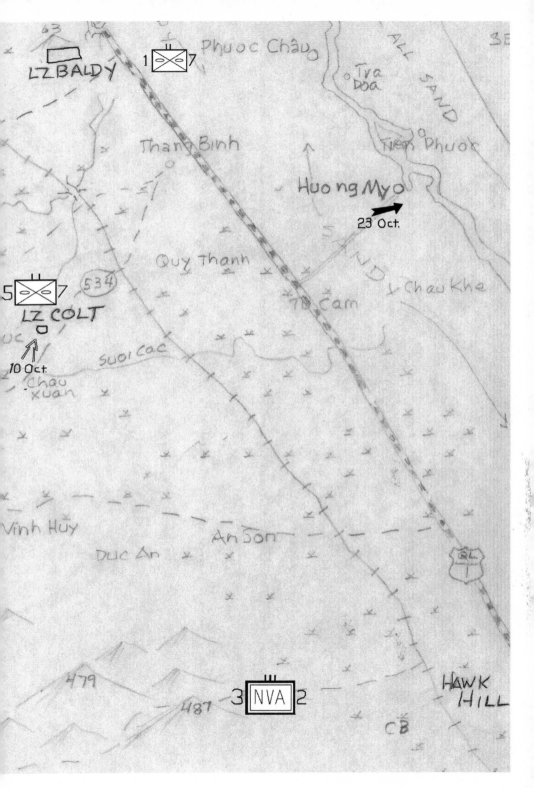

LZ BALDY

1 ☒ 7

Phuoc Châu

Tra Doa

All Sand

Se

Thang Binh

Tien Phuoc

Huong My

23 Oct.

Quy Thanh

Chau Khe

5 ☒ 7

LZ COLT

534

Tu Cam

Sand

10 Oct.

Suoi Cac

Chau Xuan

Vinh Huy

An Son

Duc An

QL 1

479

487

3 NVA 2

Hawk Hill

CB

33

The NVA mortar men had known right where to land their opening mortar rounds. In addition to severely wounding the Battalion Commander, four 5/7 Cav men were killed — Major Moore, the S-3; Capt. Aubert, the Headquarters Company commander; 2Lt. Pinchot, and Sp4. Davis. Additional KIAs were Capt. Denis O' Connor, who was the FSO, and two other men from 1/21 Arty — Pfc Miley and Sp4. Ertel. All the other officers in the battalion command group were wounded in varying degrees, to include Capt. Howard Prince, the assistant S-3.

But the 2d Division of the NVA was also surprised, maybe more so, by our ability to respond. The commander of the NVA battalion preparing to attack Colt from the north had been discovered by a 1/9 Air Cav scout bird making his reconnaissance from a nearby hill. He and his group were killed by 1/9 gun birds, and his part of the attack never got started. At about 0340 hours the next morning, within minutes after the sappers struck, C Battery, 1/21 Arty had three of its 105mm tubes lowered and putting direct fire into the woods to the south of the LZ. Helicopter gunships and ARA birds showed up in increasing numbers, like bees to honey. Artillery rounds from the batteries at other firebases showed up. A Specter gun bird showed up. The attack of the other two battalions never made it to the wire. One of the two battalions was decimated.

A sketch of the sapper's assault plan was found on the body of one of the dead sappers after the battle was over. One of the survivors in the battalion operations sections secured this diagram, and saw to it that it got to Captain Howard Prince, who was the assistant S-3 that night. Howard had been shot in the foot and hit by mortar fragments, and was one of at least thirty men evacuated that morning. He returned to duty later, and assumed command of B Company shortly before my arrival on 12 January.

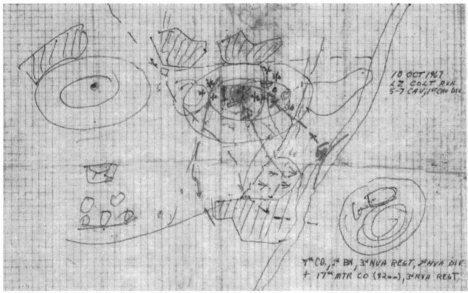

Captured Diagram of NVA Attack of LZ Colt, 10 Oct

34

Bret Coulson, the nephew of 2Lt Craig Pinchot, who was killed that night, wrote a very detailed article entitled *The Battle at LZ Colt, Republic of South VIETNAM, 10 October 1967.* He describes in detail the build up toward this battle, all the enemy elements involved, and credits many of the heroic actions that took place.

3rd Brigade was definitely winning its little corner of the war. At least until 9-10 October. LTC Jack Long, who was my boss at Brigade headquarters, took off for LZ Colt the morning after the attack to assume command of 5/7 Cav. He had been one of two deputy brigade commanders, anxious to get a battalion. He had the challenge of rebuilding the operational part of his battalion staff from scratch, in addition to operating in the middle of three NVA regiments and another five battalions of VC.

The battalions changed COs every six months, giving more lieutenant colonels a chance to punch their career ticket, get a medal or two, and stay in the race for general. Many of these guys had been squirreled away in desk jobs for years. But LTC Long was not your typical pencil pusher. He was about to earn his third Combat Infantryman's Badge — WWII, Korea, and now Vietnam. He didn't need another Silver Star either.

Up to that point in the valley, 5/7 Cav had received little if any good intel from Brigade, even though Troop B was killing NVA all over the place. To me, it sounded no different from my previous seven years in training. Information constantly flowed upward from the units, but seldom came back in the form of timely intelligence. *(During recent debates about the inadequacies of our intelligence system for Iraq and Afghanistan, a retired general actually said on Fox TV that our intelligence capability is so bad, that tactical commanders on the ground have to generate their own tactical intelligence. I was stunned. I had not known it any other way. What US Army had he been in for his 30 years, I wondered?)*

The loss of most of the 5/7 Cav command group at LZ Colt certainly made the headlines around the division, but to the troops on the ground, it had not been much of a battle. The battalion had a much bigger fight a couple weeks later in a place named Huong My, not that long after Jack took command.

23 October 1967
Huong My

1/7 Cav was assigned the area east of the highway out to the ocean. The Truong Giang River was in fact an inland waterway between the mainland and what came to be known as Cigar Island. Sorties by 1/9 Air Cav birds down this waterway were resulting in 5 to 10 enemy killed every day, and the Brigade S-2 was obtaining reports indicating that numerous NVA and VC units were located out in this area.

The land east of the river to the ocean was almost all sand, and there were extensive sandy areas between the highway and the inland waterway as well. Starting on 13 Oct, the 1/9 Air Cav began a campaign starting at the north end of the 3rd Brigade AO, working southward to search the areas astride the inland waterway. They searched with a continuous stream of two bird teams. A red and a white. The pilot and a scout in a little H-13 "bubble" helicopter were flying right on the deck along the dikes and bamboo hedgerows, peeking into the bushes, looking for camouflaged enemy soldiers. Up above, the red bird was ready to pounce. Right away on the 13th, the white birds began finding black uniformed VC individuals, armed with AK-47s, trying not to be seen or trying to evade. They were engaging these VC at very close range.

On 17 October, in response to incoming intelligence, the Americal Division moved their 1st Squadron, of the 1st Armored Cavalry Regiment up to Hill 29 just north of Tam Ky. *(That would be 1/1 ACR)* They named their base Hawk Hill. It was just west of the highway about 15 kilometers south of Baldy. 1/1 ACR was mounted in M48 tanks and M113 armored personnel carriers (APCs). They had an air cav component as well. The 1/1 ACR was new to Vietnam starting in August, and had not seen much action yet.

On 19 Oct the 1/9 scout birds started finding numerous enemy in khaki uniforms in the Phu 'O' Chau area. Khaki meant North Vietnam Army. NVA. The 3rd Brigade began an operation on 20 Oct, with 2 companies of 1/7 air-assaulting into LZs just outside of Phu 'O' Chau to sweep southward. Alpha Troop of the 1/1 ACR swept northward.

1/9 Air Cav teams searched between the two units advancing toward each other. They started finding squad-sized groups of NVA soldiers trying to evade, and as the day wore on the NVA started holding their ground and returning fire. At some point, the troop from 1/1 ACR got ambushed, and suffered numerous casualties. This was their first experience losing men against a well-armed NVA unit. A day-long battle ensued, in which many NVA were killed, but the main force escaped across the river toward the ocean.

Tom Solenberger was the CO of our Delta Company. Highly respected by his troops, as well as by Col McKenna, the Brigade Commander, from the earlier days down in the An Loa Valley. Tom recalled being alerted to airlift from LZ Colt at 1130 on the 20th, and they finally got picked up at 1530 hours. They air assaulted into a location 8 clicks in from the ocean to a green LZ and set up a perimeter.

The 1/7 Cav and 1/1 ACR operation continued the next day, with 1/7 air-assaulting onto Cigar Island, and A Troop, 1/1 ACR swimming their APCs over. The two units went southward down Cigar Island side by side. Alpha Company, 1/7 Cav, was ambushed on the right flank close to the river, and suffered many wounded. On their left, Alpha Troop 1/1 ACR got into contact as well, and this battle raged well into the day.

In the meantime, Delta 5/7 Cav sent out platoon patrols in all directions with no contact. They must have come into the Phu O Chao area behind 1/7 going across the river. *(There are no map coordinates for these actions in October, only guesses about locations. When I went to the National Archives in College Park, Maryland back in 2003, the folder with the battalion journals for October 67 was missing. All the other*

36

months were present. This pertained to all of the 1st Cav battalion journals. My contact at the Archives indicates that the files they have today are as they came from DA in 1987. Interesting.)

Tom Solenberger moved his company on foot 6 clicks to the south on 22 October. The route took them through a highly cultivated area, comprised of small rectangular plots surrounded by earthen banks 1 to 2 meter-high. The constant dikes were hard to climb over and slowed their movement. At suppertime, LTC Long flew in and took Tom on an aerial recon to select an LZ where Delta Company would CA into the next morning, 23 October. *("CA" means combat air-assault.)*

Bert Chloe of 1/9 Air Cav wrote a great book called *Flashing Sabers*. He includes chapters about Phu Chau on 20-21 Oct and Huong My on 23 Oct. In his presentation of facts about 23 Oct, the operation involved having the 5/7 Cav sweep toward Huong My from the south, and if they made contact, elements of 1/7 Cav would CA closer to the river, and the enemy would be caught in the middle

1/9 Cav started operating at first light. Quoting from Chloe's book:

"At O645 FLASHING SABER 14 *(Warrant Officer Brown)* and FLASHING SABER 25 *(Warrant Officer Feig)* checked in with the 5/7 Cav Bn S-3 for guidance. S-3 said to concentrate mostly in front of center company" *(Implying 2 other companies)* "FS14 came up on D/5/7 command net to tell them he would be screening to their front, and said they would remain on Delta net."

"At 0710 FS14 found 2 NVA in bunker, neutralized them."

"At 0800 FS14 observed 2 VC in black PJs with AKs, who ran into a bunker. Destroyed bunker, confirmed 1 KIA."

Delta lifted off at 0800 hours and landed thereafter on a green LZ south of road, moved northward across the road to an open area, set up perimeter, and issued further orders from there. *(Green signified no enemy presence.)* It could not have been very far from the pick up location down to the LZ, and the air-assault could have hit the ground as early as 0815. The LZ was an open sandy area, and the rotors kicked a big cloud of fine sand dust.

Lt. Jim Bass was the Platoon Leader of 2d Platoon, and said the air-assault was uneventful. "We had done a hundred of these since I joined the company in late June. The first thing we did was clean weapons." Greg Trujillo, the Platoon Sergeant, recalls that they had moved out quickly from the LZ to perform their mission, and did not have time to field strip their weapons and do a thorough cleaning.

Solenberger's diagram of his plan shows the 2d Platoon moving out at 0830, and he recalls the 3rd Platoon moving out at the same time. "We set up our CP, and dropped our packs. I then sent the 2nd Plt. back across the road to the east, with orders to sweep toward and into the town from the south. The 3rd Platoon went east to sweep the area and move into the town from the north." The 1st Platoon remained with Solenberger.

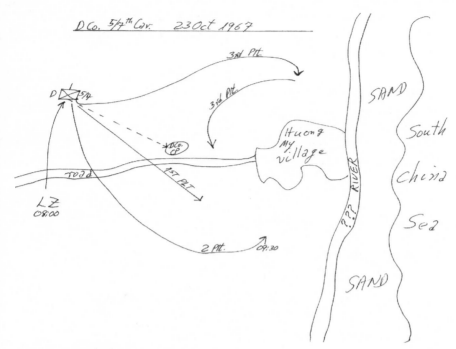

Solenberger's Diagram

The 2d Platoon moved out toward the village, and advanced over at least 5 or 6 paddy dikes that surrounded rectangular agriculture plots maybe 30 to 50 meters square. They could see the village in the distance.

On the north axis, Ric Wetherbee, 1st Sqad Ldr in 3rd Platoon, recalls that they started off single file atop the dikes, heading generally toward the area they were assigned. The rest of the company disappeared, and the platoon was traveling alone. After an hour of this they came into a small oasis of shade trees and took a break.

According to Bert Chloe in *Flashing Saber*, D/5/7 Cav called the scout team at 0915 to request assistance in locating a sniper firing at their left flank platoon. WO Rice and his supporting Red Bird searched the terrain for well over an hour, finally found a sniper, and killed him, before leaving station, replaced by the team of Thomas and Brown. That would suggest sometime after 10:45

Shortly after Thomas and Brown came on station, they began spotting numerous NVA evading into bunkers located inside hooches in a small village. Brown attacked the hooches and received heavy fire. Thomas informed the S-3 of 5/7 Cav, recommending the battalion maneuver in their direction. Solenberger has no recollection of receiving this information that 1/9 Cav reported to the S-3 of 5/7 Cav. He also had received no specific intelligence from anyone about the possibility of an NVA battalion or more being in the search area.

LT Bass was right behind his point man when they came upon a hooch some distance out from the village and ran into a woman and a NVA soldier, who had lots of gear like maybe he was a medic. "We surprised them, and grabbed the NVA as a prisoner." Bass led his platoon along the dike that teed into a final and much higher dike along the edge of the village. "As we reached the top of the dike, I looked down into an area that was much larger, and appeared to be a village common area. I found myself looking at NVA soldiers. Rifles were stacked. One guy was in a hammock. It was surreal. They stared at us. We stared back. Finally someone reached for a gun. All hell broke loose."

2d Platoon maneuvered sideways initially before assaulting over the dike. One squad began to maneuver to flank the enemy positions, led by Dean Messersmith who quickly moved past Lt. Bass and ran along the dike that bordered the common area. After about 30 or 40 yards that dike teed into another dike that bordered what appeared to be a shallow irrigation ditch. At this point Dean Messersmith was shot by an enemy dug into a large plant just beyond the dike. Bass says, "Frenchy Bossout was in front of me, got up to the same spot and was shot in the neck. I sprayed the area with my CAR-15, with Frenchy yelling at me for a grenade. He put the grenade in the plant." Sp4 Jack Stevens remembered "Dean Messersmith throwing smoke, and after that, total confusion. People were going forward, backward, right, left. Frenchy, Angus and Mitch were down."

Bert Chloe went on to say that sometime after their report of the strong enemy position, "D/5/7 reached the area, began maneuvering into the area, and came under intense fire. The 2d platoon became pinned down. The Red bird co-pilot was wounded, and Thomas & Brown departed station."

Squad leader, Kirk Adams, was following Lt. Bass, and says "It started when Frenchy was shot. James Mitchell was blinded. Neubill and Hunter went down. I made it back to the dike, there was a media camera guy there, and I almost shot him. There was too much activity. Chaotic. The snipers were well hidden. We threw smoke."

Platoon Sergeant Trujillo crawled out to get Messersmith, and had one of those miracle hits — a bullet thru the helmet but not thru Greg. He suffered a bloody flesh wound on the side of his head, but was otherwise ok, and made it back to the dike. LT Bass made Trujillo go back on a medevac, in case he had a concussion or was hurt worse than he thought.

There was a news team following Bass's platoon, and they produced a 6 minute news clip *(now viewable on YouTube)* that shows Lt. Bass on the radio debating with Capt. Solenberger about going out after Messersmith. Against Solenberger's opinion, Lt. Bass organized a base of covering fire, and his Medic, Doc McBride and two others, ran out and pulled him back. Unfortunately, Messersmith did not survive. A few others lay wounded out in front of their position, to include James Mitchell shot in the head and blinded. He lay out there all afternoon.

Far over to the north, 3rd Platoon was taking their breather when they "suddenly heard all hell open up from the direction of the other platoons. We were too far away to see anything, so we stayed put and listened to the radio."

Solenberger requested and received air support which was coordinated by Lt. Bass since Solenberger could not see the action in the flat terrain criss-crossed by high dikes.

It was late morning when all this action exploded on Delta company. Since the 3rd Platoon was moving around the left without contact, Solenberger decided to commit his 1st Platoon to move southeast to assist the 2nd Platoon. He also moved his CP down to the north side of the road, but still could not see much due to the high dikes.

LT Ballo, the Artillery FO, went with 1st Platoon. The platoon was led by SFC Ford, whose plan was to send three squads toward the village on three parallel dikes. Ballo says, "I tried to tell him to recon by fire first, but he was going to do it his way. When they walked right into the ambush, everyone went down." George Lawson was in one of the flank squads, and reports that "Me and Harvey and George Vineyard were in the rear of the squad bringing up the rear.. is the reason we made it back alive.. my rifle blew up in my face from the sand and I think Harvey and George were just jammed...George Vineyard was shot by a sniper.. it's strange to me to this day thinking about Ford across from us and him motioning...to us to come on with him, and right off they were all mowed down.. and there was nothing we could do but watch..."

Soon after the 1st Plt. crossed the road and were ambushed in the rice paddies, Solenberger lost commo with the Platoon. Based on the times involved in the platoon maneuvers, I believe 1st Platoon came into the edge of the village well to the left of 2d Platoon, and the two platoons were engaged in separate actions.

Solenberger, hearing the volume of fire and losing all communications with 1st Platoon, called for his 3rd Platoon to move south without going into the town, in an effort to relieve the pressure on the 1st and 2nd. It took the 3rd Platoon, under Lt. Hayes, 15 to 20 minutes double-timing along the dikes, to get to the contact area. They went to the sound of the firing, and ended coming up to the same dike from which the 1st Platoon had launched their failed assault. They found themselves looking across an open square at a much higher than normal dike fronted by bamboo and trees. It looked like a fortress. 3rd Platoon got no radio response from the other platoons, and had no information to go on.

They saw movement in the trees masking the big dike wall to their front, and fired a grenade round into the trees above the movement. "Immediately about twelve of our guys came into the open waving, and yelling at us. It was the 1st Platoon men not killed or severely wounded by the ambush. When they went across to them, they learned of the devastating ambush that had trapped most of the 1st Platoon. The NVA had let the platoon fully enter the paddies before opening up at close range. Some were killed where they stood. Some tried to return fire. None of the M-16s worked for more than a few rounds before jamming in the sand. Some managed to jump over a dike thinking they were escaping, only to be mowed down from further spider holes on the next adjacent dikes. The NVA positions were invisible. It was a perfect trap."

1st Platoon had eight KIAs spread among this and two other squares. Almost everyone else in the platoon was wounded to some degree. The survivors of 1st Platoon had no operable M-16s at this point, and went back to the company CP across the road. Wetherbee climbed up the dike and observed the situation. "There were men dead and dying, weapons, and personal gear strewn about. I saw no sign of the enemy. It was apparent that roughly half the platoon was still out there dead or wounded."

It wasn't long before the 3d Platoon made their own fatal error. After a heated discussion about assaulting straight ahead to retrieve the casualties, or trying first to flank the enemy positions, Wetherbee took his squad far around to the right to flank the NVA positions on the far dike. Just as they were approaching the likely enemy spider hole locations, Wetherbee looked across to see his Platoon Leader leading a squad across the paddy and routing the enemy out of their positions. The assaulting squad disappeared through a wall of foliage in hot pursuit of the evading enemy soldiers, and within seconds were met by a heavy volume of fire. The six men in the squad were killed, and the lieutenant staggered back severely wounded. Another skillful ambush by the NVA. Another rush to save people, only to lose more.

In the space of an hour, the Company Commander had his entire company pinned down through the piecemeal deployment of his three platoons against a strong NVA defensive network of hidden spider holes spread throughout a maze of dikes and agriculture plots. Things were out of control for D Company before anyone could do anything about it.

LTC Long arrived at the company CP with his command and control helicopter taking numerous hits. Long said "he would order A Co, to come down from the north and B Co would come up from the south. He then flew away." At some point after LTC Long had come in, Col McKenna came in to Tom's CP, and his C&C bird took so many hits they had to strand him there. Solenberger was struck by McKenna's calm demeanor, as he sat back against a tree and calmly said he was sure that Tom was going to get him out of there.

Not unlike D Company being all spread out, it was also business as usual in the battalion. According to Lt. Bob Trimble, XO of B Company, the "three companies of 5/7 Cav went into three totally separate areas that day. That's the way we operated at that time." I trust Trimble's word implicitly and, based on subsequent experience, I know in my heart that 5/7 Cav received little if anything of the intelligence being reported to Brigade S-2 by 1/9 Cav or the 1/7 Cav from their previous days battles. As a matter of fact, Solenberger later was assigned to Brigade S-3, where he learned from the S-2 that they had known there were two NVA Battalions, and possibly the 3rd NVA Regiment HQs in the area, but could not release the information yet. Tom might have deployed his company on a single axis, had he known this. Long might have employed his battalion differently, had he known this. Who knows? 5/7 Cav had yet to experience running into an NVA defensive position

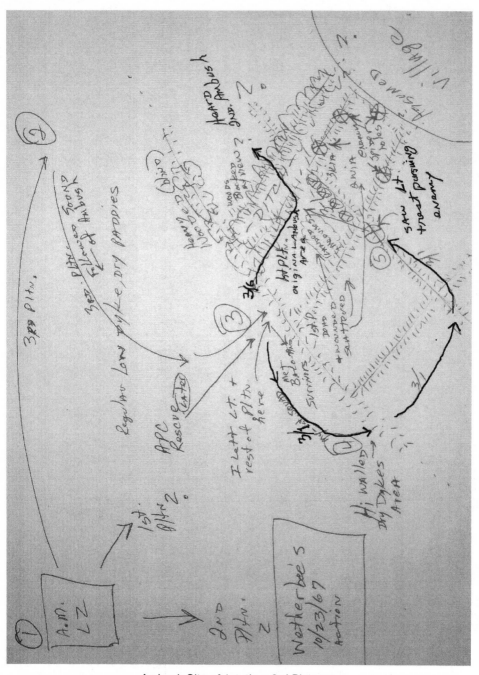

Ambush Site of 1st, then 3rd Platoons

manned by a force far too powerful for a platoon attack, or even a company attack for that matter.

B Co could not be moved to come in on Delta's flank, because Trimble states that B Company was already pinned down in a separate battle. "We air-assaulted into a hot LZ nowhere near any villages, we saw no hooches. I think it was near Van Dong." Van Dong was across the waterway on Cigar Island. The B Company objective area consisted of 75 meter square areas surrounded by sand berms. "Lt. Sime was the first platoon in, and he was hit bad. I talked to him on the radio on my way in with the final platoon, and could tell he was dying."

Bob went on to say that "the NVA had machineguns positioned to fire down the tops of the dikes. It was chaos. Guns were jamming. We called in air strikes. I took over Sime's platoon when I got there." They fought a day-long battle, and by the end of the day had "driven off the enemy, and had killed 13 to 14 NVA by body count, but the NVA took most of their dead with them. In addition to Lt. Sime, we had 10 to 12 men severely wounded and medevaced."

Without the journals for October 1967, I have no information about A Company that day. Perhaps Long elected not to commit them at some point. Maybe so as not to reinforce failure. Good tacticians reinforce success, not failure. Possibly the 1/1 ACR APCs were on the way, which was a much better idea than throwing in more light infantry against these hardened and invisible targets.

2d Platoon on the right spent several more hours on the dike exchanging fire with the enemy, trying to pull their wounded back, and putting in gunships and air strikes. Jim Mitchell continued to lie out in front of them, in a wide open area, blind and unable to move. Trujillo came back out on a helicopter a few hours later, all taped up, and bringing an M-60 machinegun with him. Messersmith was their only KIA. Sp4 Jack Stevens says "the battle lasted 6 hours, and then the APCs showed up. I don't remember tanks." It had to be 1700 hours or later by that time.

Keith Nolan in his book *Search and Destroy* about 1/1 ACR quotes the Troop commander of B Troop thusly: "Captain Staley of B Troop listened on the tactical net as a company from the 5th of the 7th Cav was ambushed on the west side of the Troung Giang. The radio traffic was desperate, and Staley didn't wait for orders before heading toward the sound of the guns."

Interestingly, the D/5/7 XO, Lt. Reinmiller, talked of "having located a platoon of Army armored personnel carriers securing a marine engineering unit, and directing them to our location."

It is more likely that Lt. Col Long, or Col. McKenna's headquarters, generated the message that got the 1/1 ACR's B Troop coming to the fight. In any event, it was late in the day, maybe 1800 hours, when they reached the 1st & 3rd Platoon contact area. Maybe they got to 2d Platoon's contact much earlier. Hank Thomas of 2d Platoon described the commander of one of the tracks of the 1/1 ACR looking down from his cupola and saying "fall back through us, we'll take care of this." Doc McBride describes the big machineguns of the APCs as "chewing up the tree lines and saving our butts." Stevens of 2d Platoon recalls that "it was dark when we withdrew back to the company perimeter."

As the afternoon wore on, the 3rd Platoon had two squads remaining after the LT was ambushed. *(We called lieutenants "LT" in the infantry.)* Platoon Sergeant Cardenas and one squad had remained on the dike facing the enemy spider holes to their front; and Wetherbee's squad held the right side of the square. They went on to fight against NVA who had sneaked back into the far dike. This one central square became the defensive position for Cardena's platoon. They had Medevac birds coming into it, taking fire as they loaded out wounded men. Their M-16s had all stopped functioning. They had one M-79, but were low on ammunition. The NVA were sensing their plight and becoming more aggressive. Wetherbee's squad was defending themselves at the end with hand grenades, and were running out of them when they heard the company of APCs rumbling in for support. B/1/1 ACR, with their awesome firepower, chewed up the far dike as they assaulted straight ahead, and onto the other enemy positions in the adjacent squares.

With the area secure, Cardenas led his men to look for their squad that got ambushed. Robert Shaw, Joseph Pink, Ed Beiber, George Colbert, Leroy Hopkins and the radio operator, Charles Mullis were KIAs. Working with the 1/1 ACR , they also helped to recover the 1st Platoon casualties. The men killed in the 1st Platoon were: Pfc Vineyard, Sgt Chappell, SFC Ford, Cpl Herrel, Pfc Tschumper, and SSG Campbell. Campbell had taken over this squad only a day or so earlier from Chief Menard, whose life may have been saved when he assumed the leadership of the squad that had remained with Cardenas.

Capt Staley of B/1/1 ACR is quoted in Chloe's book as saying that the infantry had pulled back by the time Bravo Troop arrived. He went on to say "Those enemy positions that could be identified were marked with tracers for B-Troop of 1/9 Cav. The gunships did a job on them. They just took the tree lines out." An interesting comment about 1/9 Cav gunships. They had been operating in and out of the area all day. Perhaps we were too banged up to effectively coordinate their firepower. We definitely had radio problems. Better late than never, though.

The Battle of Huong My was perhaps the first experience most of these men had fighting a hardcore NVA infantry unit. Throughout the summer of 1967 down in the Binh Dinh area, the enemy had been primarily VC units. Much smaller. Less equipped.

The NVA had been pushing its regiments down the Ho Chi Minh Trail into the northern area of South Vietnam throughout 1967, but they had not arrived in strength down in Binh Dinh.

23 October 1967 was a huge eye-opener for 5/7 Cav. They got caught in a sandy area by a large enemy unit totally hidden in the hedgerows. The initial action was

too close for effective artillery and air power. It became a battle of equals, with us in the open against skillfully concealed enemy infantrymen dug into the dikes. M-16s jammed from the swirling sand. Arguably, the battle was between less than equals, because their AK-47s worked great, while our M-16s folded up. They were invisible. We were in plain sight. They let us come right to them, too close to effectively use our big bullets — artillery, air strikes.

I remember McKenna coming into the TOC late in the day. He was hot. He ranted about the M-16 being no damn good, among other things. Mistakes were made at every level on 23 Oct, from Brigade continuing to maneuver companies separately about the checkerboard battle area in the presence of larger NVA units, to intelligence not flowing down to the company commanders on the ground. The battalion command level continued to be out of the loop, continuing to let company commanders fight the "company commander's war." A company operating with platoons too spread out, and then deploying platoons piecemeal into a strong enemy defense. Mistakes made at platoon leadership level based on headstrong but inexperienced leaders. We applied most of these hard lessons in the months to come, which held us in better stead for February 1968. Not all those days went too well either, but never like Huong My. Throughout all this chaos of this day, though, the troops fought like hell. Like they always did.

23 October 1967 was a huge defeat for us. We had lost 15 men forever. And for the survivors, lots of real PTSD was born that day. It was a big victory in Saigon, however. 1/9 Cav reported 43 NVA killed by body count. 1/1 Armored Cav reported a large number of NVA bodies after they had secured the area. Collective reports indicated up to 180 NVA had been counted as killed that day in the Huong My area. Well over Bobby MacNamara's goal of 10 to 1.

This action was very typical for the Que Son Valley dating back to the summer when the 5th Marines had the AO. You went along for several days with no action, no sight of the enemy, and then in a flash you were in a big firefight with a unit of equal or superior manpower. It was all about ambush. The NVA ambushed us when the time and conditions were right for them. We tried to pre-discover and defeat their ambush site by stealth, aerial observation, good tactics and lots of fire support. In Vietnam, they "found" us 80% of the time, and we found them the other 20%. Either way, we fired 100 rounds of all sizes at them for every one they fired at us, or so the story went in Saigon. Bobby had numbers for everything.

As time passed that fall, the enemy buildup in the northern end of the country was becoming noticeable to the higher-ups. The 3rd Brigade had been sent to the Que Son Valley so that the 5th Marines could move further north toward Hue. We had surprised an enemy not used to a sky full of helicopters, but as the weeks wore on into November, the NVA began to get more organized. They were not about to abandon the Que Son Valley. The one thing the NVA did not bring with them down the Ho Chi Minh Trail was food. They lived off the land. They depended on the VC to get them rice. The Que Son was rich with rice, and was an area worth fighting for.

The Battalion Journal recorded the words of a young NVA soldier captured by A Company on 16 November 1967.

> *"A Company had trip flare set off and engaged, results: 1 M/A NVA WIA with no weapon. Wearing web gear, carrying pack full of rice, he is 20 years old and is a member of a 40 man patrol sent down 5 days ago to get food. And he was with a rice gathering group. He is in the 1st Bn with a strength of 700 men. They left N. Vietnam one year ago and have stayed in the mountains for the last month. Dug in deep and they are prepared to stay. They have 12 MGs, 8 82mm mortars with plenty of ammo, but no food. They have one radio per battalion. When they came down from the mountains they met 12 VC in village of Guang Da, had them collect rice for the Bn. His unit has a lot of malaria, typhoid from the water, morale is low, the officers are very strict with them. The Bn is very low on medical supplies, and he says his element has never been hit with artillery or bombs. It has come close at times, but never hit. He is a rifleman in 2d Company. The enlisted men get 3 months training, the NCOs get 10 months training, and the officers 18. He states that 16 yr old is the draft age, and they are kept in for the duration of the war, reason for morale being as low as it is. Medevac was requested."*

The Que Son valley had long been dominated by the VC. And reinforced by the presence of a large NVA force, there were no hearts and minds to be won out there. Even after 23 October, our companies were spread out like checkers on a checkerboard. When one got in heavy contact, the CO and S-3 started moving the checkers. The battalion had an allocation of helicopters almost every day, and the rifle companies were dropped into separate landing zones to search for the enemy in company areas of operation. Our soldiers were sometimes called "Skytroopers", because we attacked from the sky. The pilots and crews of the 227th and 229th Combat Aviation Battalions carried us in, and never failed to pick us up when it was time to go.

In early December the Brigade Headquarters held an impressive Change of Command Ceremony. Lots of pomp and circumstance. Medals flowed like water. Rumors were that LZ Colt was the reason for a new Brigade Commander. A damn shame, actually, because the departing Brigade Commander was an Infantry Officer, a dynamic commander. And he probably got very little help from his higher headquarters, since we were attached to the Americal Division in the Que Son Valley.

December 1967 Change of Command, Col. McKenna and his Commanders (LTC Long 2d from right)

Jim Thomas and his fellow RTOs

CHAPTER 5

HAPPY NEW YEAR G.I.

In the fall of 1967, the NVA main force units were flooding into South Vietnam. Throughout November and December, the NVA units in the Que Son tried to avoid major engagements. They were hiding out and getting ready for the big push. Brigade put out two items of enemy intelligence which were recorded in the 5/7 Cav Daily Journal in the early hours of 27 December. A deserter, "Chu Hoi" in Vietnamese, had come in and revealed the NVA plan for a major offensive in the Que Son.

Chu Hoi stated that LZ Leslie, LZ Ross and LZ Baldy would be attacked by the combined forces of the 2d and 3d Regiments of the 2d NVA Division on 25-26-27 December. If not carried out on schedule, it will take place prior to the new moon period in January 68.

An additional message came through the same day *(Cronkite apparently lacked sufficient security clearance for this one:)*

A Message from the National Liberation Front: Large battle expected during winter season. A total victory is early winter and spring season.

There was a lot of tension in the 3d Brigade TOC as these three days in late December came and went. I departed on R&R on the 29th. While Nancy and I were spending blissful days at Waikiki, the first of the three predicted attacks hit LZ Ross at 0130 hours on 3 January. It was crushed, with 200 NVA soldiers killed on the wire surrounding the base. 5/7 Cav had three of their companies operating just a few kilometers northwest of LZ Ross at the time. They all had a story to tell from early January in the west end of the valley.

3 January 1968
Lanh An (2)
Coordinates YD999352

At sunrise on 3 January, after an intense battle at LZ Ross that started just after midnight, the 2/12 Cav had 200 dead NVA infantrymen scattered along the perimeter wire. At least two battalions of the NVA 2d Division had made the assault. 5/7 Cav was operating in the hills northwest of the LZ, and began moving off the high-ground, conducting separate company operations to locate enemy units.

Alpha Company was conducting a search and destroy mission southward from its base on Hill 210. 2Lt Wells commanded the lead platoon. As his point squad moved cautiously into a village area, they suddenly came under intense fire from AK-47s and machine guns, taking several casualties in the opening blast. The men began returning fire, and Sp4 David Burson and Pfc Allen Glines assaulted the nearest enemy positions. Burson took out two enemy positions before he was cut down. Glines destroyed a Distinguished Service Cross worth of enemy soldiers before he too was mortally wounded.

The lieutenant ordered the rest of his platoon forward. As they crossed the open area they came under intense fire, and a supporting helicopter gunship was shot down before it could fire a shot. The platoon was pinned down, and the point squad was still on the ground, well out in front of them. Company A maneuvered two other platoons to the left of the contact area, and they also came in contact with a large force at YD 002351.

Not long after the company commander called in the situation, Jack Long arrived over the battle area in his command and control helicopter *(a Huey with a bank of radios in the back for passengers to operate from. We called it a C&C.)* He took his assistant operations officer with him, a captain named Howard Prince. For an hour or so they circled at 1500 feet, considered safe altitude from small arms fire, while Long issued instructions to the company commander and coordinated fire support.

Suddenly there were loud explosions and a lot of smoke coming from the rear of the helicopter. Howard's first thought was that they had strayed into the gun-target line of the 105mm howitzer rounds coming in, but he quickly realized that they would have been dead already. The pilot came on the intercom and "told us we had been hit and that he was losing power, could not maintain altitude and that he was going to attempt an auto-rotation maneuver to land at LZ Ross." *(Auto-rotation: you cut off the engine, the bird falls rapidly, stabilized only by the rotating rotors, and then you turn the engine back on again near the ground. Pretty exciting, actually, even when you are pretty sure your engine is going to re-start.)*

They had been hit by a 12.75mm anti-aircraft machinegun. Some of the incoming rounds had critically wounded the door gunner hanging out the side next to Howard. He had a large visible wound in the leg, and was slumped over his machinegun mount. There was nothing to keep him from falling out of the rapidly dropping helicopter except the gun mount and a canvas belt across the open door. Howard grabbed him by his fatigue shirt, and held on until they landed. They got him medevaced from there.

In the meantime, back in the contact area, some of Wells' men had been able to cross the field and reinforce the lead squad. And the rest of the platoon behind him was also beginning to put effective fire on the enemy. Eventually, the enemy force was suppressed by artillery and small arms fire enough for the point squad to crawl back to the platoon. Much of the credit goes to John Williams' courage and M-60 firepower.

Long and Howard were picked up by another C&C Bird sent out to return them to LZ Colt. This pilot had heard about the 12.75mm anti-aircraft machineguns operating in the area, and decided to fly on the deck. Somewhere along the way they were fired on and hit by automatic weapons fire. As Howard put it, "I heard the sound of gunfire and recall that it sounded like a loud zipper being pulled open. As the red master warning light on the dash panel in front of the pilot flashed on, the pilot came on the intercom and informed us he was losing control and didn't know if he could land the helicopter safely. Somehow he managed to fly the damaged helicopter to LZ Colt where he made a rough landing, bouncing on the skids several times. Everyone was scared and thankful that we had made it back." Jack Long dismounted the bird and went back to work at LZ Colt, without saying anything. He and Howard had been forced down by enemy fire not once, but twice, on 3 January.

Alpha Company disengaged from the contact and moved to a position about 800 meters north, where they were later counter-attacked by the pursuing enemy. This attack was repulsed by our superior firepower from several sources. When the sun went down on 3 January 1968, it had been a very rough day throughout the Que Son Valley.

For several more days, there was lots of action north and west of LZ Ross.

6/7 January 1968
Hill 210
Coordinates BT001370

While Nancy and I were playing golf at the Marine Base at Kaneohe in Hawaii, Jim Mathews and his Bravo Company were sitting on Hill 210 northwest of Ross. Someone spotted enemy soldiers in his binoculars to the west in the village at the base of the highest mountain overlooking the west end of the valley — Hill 953. Captain Matthews moved his men out toward the village, Thon Ba, and they ended up engaging and killing 40 NVA, captured seven more, all without a casualty in his company. They used an ARA bird and lots of artillery in the attack. Two of the POWs revealed the entire plan of attacks by the NVA scheduled through the 7th throughout the Que Son Valley. Brigade was able to further alert all units for the night of 7 January.

That night, Bravo Company returned to its perimeter on Hill 210. It was a good defensive position, with good observation and fields of fire. At around 0140 hours, on the east side of the perimeter, two enemy soldiers were spotted through a starlight scope, and were engaged by hand grenades. The NVA quickly answered with scattered AK-47 fire, quickly becoming heavy fire, then grenades from close range, and then a flame thrower. A flame thrower! The NVA were definitely building up in the Que Son.

The 1st platoon had to withdraw backward away from the fire, leaving some of their equipment to be burned up. Soon after the flame thrower attack, mortar rounds walked across the perimeter, and were immediately followed by the assault of two NVA platoons. Bravo Company's perimeter suddenly had a platoon-sized hole in it, and Matthews barely held things together as he called for artillery, gunships and medevac. He had five wounded, three of whom needed immediate medevac. And the very popular Raul "Shorty" Gutierrez had been killed.

The battle raged in the dark until Spooky came on station with its awesome firepower and hosed the circumference of the hill. This firepower broke the enemy's attack. Hill 210 was named LZ Shorty beginning 7 January 1968, and remains so today if you are a Bravo Company man.

And five days later, on 12 January, C Company got into its previously described battle involving the loss of Bill Port and others.

In spite of the lessons of 23 October learned at Huong My, not everyone in 5/7 Cav had made the adjustment to the dramatic increase in operational tempo. Even with the presence of large NVA formations, as seen at LZ Ross on 3 January and in Alpha Company's action, we still had our companies operating in separate areas of operation, and some were sending single platoons out on separate patrols. On 12 January we were still searching for the elusive VC and NVA units with small unit operations, even when the NVA weren't being so elusive.

After 12 January when Bill Port went missing, it got quiet in the Que Son. This lull gave me time to get the S-3 Operations section organized my way. I remember talking to the troops in the TOC about the night's action of January 12th, telling them that it was not the place of the RTOs to just order up stuff like medevacs, air support, and ammo re-supply birds, without anyone's approval. "These were decisions for the officers in the command center", I said, while looking at my captain assistant operations officer. The major clearly required some training, the troops must have said to themselves.

*　*　*　*　*

It was many years later before I learned the details of all the battles the battalion had fought in the Que Son, while I was at Brigade Headquarters. In the process I learned just how screwed up the situation had been back on my first day in the battalion — on 12 January 1968. The daily journal indicated that "two platoons of Company C began receiving sniper fire at 1429 hours" at the coordinates of the ambush. And yet, it was no earlier than 1545 hours when the message from HARD HITTER 6 came in to me reporting the situation being one of heavy contact. One of our old veterans of the 1st Platoon told me that a long period of time had gone by before anyone came to their aid. He admitted that there were radio problems, but was very bitter about the entire episode. I believe at least one hour, maybe more, went by that afternoon with the battalion commander not knowing what the hell was really going on. And maybe the company commander as well. And definitely me, his new S-3, for that matter. The train had apparently left the station before I got there that day.

The battalion had been blooded by the NVA well before I got there on 12 January. I hate that expression — getting blooded. Probably invented by a British military historian, a politician, maybe one of the multitudes who are fascinated with war without having been in one. The RTOs had plenty of stories to tell, if only we hadn't been so busy. As my first week went by, I think the troops were beginning to see that I had come to this job with some good training, to include working for Jack Long back in August and September in my position of commanding the base defense at LZ Baldy. I just hadn't been blooded yet.

Jack Long could be a really hard man when it came to the defensive positions. The grenades had to be laid out just so, the claymore firing device had to be where you couldn't miss finding it in the dark. Everything had to be protected from the sand and dirt by lining the parapet with empty sandbags. Woe unto to you when he found it otherwise.

For the rest of January, it got very quiet in the Que Son. We were only a few miles in from the coast, with ready access to artillery support, medevac, and ammo re-supply. We were in supporting range of lots of artillery fire from a network of firebases. I never got comfortable with the size of the perimeter, but at least we had triple concertina all around. Every few days we got beer, two cans per man. The only thing worse than a hot Carling Black Label was a hot Utica Club — which I pointed out to my wife who was from Utica. We occasionally saw ice cream too, melted soup though it was. We even had a USO Show, although the presence of a cute girl singer in the field actually does little for morale. Her running mascara and really bad body odor mitigated the situation a little. What courage these people had who came out to the middle of the Que Son Valley to entertain us. Ignorance is bliss in the combat zone. Life was momentarily good. There was no saluting forward of Brigade, but every now and then a trooper would greet me with a hearty "Garryowen, Sir!"

LTC Jack Long & CSM Charles McQuerry, Que Son Valley 1967

Looking west from LZ Colt – Awards Formation

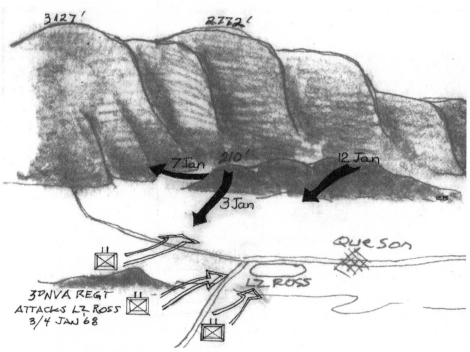

3127'

2772'

7 Jan   210'

12 Jan

3 Jan

QueSon

LZ ROSS

3D NVA REGT
ATTACKS LZ ROSS
3/4 JAN '68

Operations in LZ Ross area 3 — 12 Jan '68

CHAPTER 6

BIG JACK

I visited the squadron at Ft. Stewart a few times in the fall of 2004. In conversations with Petery and some of his officers at Ft. Stewart, I had mentioned the three battalion commanders with whom I had served in my brief six months as S-3 of the battalion, and what made the first of them so special to me. The image of Jack Long comes back to me often.

23-26 January 1968
Enroute to Quang Tri
South Vietnam

Within a week after I joined the battalion, the word came down that 3d Brigade would be moving somewhere north of Hue. The battalion had moved to the sound of the guns many times in the Que Son Valley, but we were moving to much bigger ones farther north. On 23 January I departed LZ Colt in control of our battalion's advance party. I took Bill Hussong and Jim Matthews with me. Hussong was the new S-4, after commanding A Co for six months. Jim Matthews had turned over B Co to Howard Prince, and was now the S-1.

By mid January 1968, the battalion had a totally new command team in place. We now had three captains and a 1st lieutenant in command of our four rifle companies. All three captains happened to be West Point graduates, and all of these officers had assumed command of their companies within the last few weeks. The lieutenant had been a company XO for several months, and he had also assumed command during the battle on 3 January. Some of us had not faced any fire yet. Some had, like Howard Prince and the Lieutenant. Many of the lieutenants were in the FNG phase also. FNG — fucking new guy. Over the course of the next four months we saw an endless stream of FNGs.

The advance party had an allocation of one jeep and trailer. *(Our jeep was a convertible with the top down. No armored doors. No armored bottom. No armor, period.)*

We took one RTO as driver. He made the world's best hot chocolate, along with doing many other really important jobs. We, and the advance parties from the other two battalions and the Brigade headquarters, flew by DHC-4 Caribou from LZ Baldy to Phu Bai, a big airbase south of Hue. *(The Caribou was a cargo plane belonging to the Army that looks not unlike a small C-130. It could carry a platoon of troops, or a few guys with a jeep and trailer, or an endless number of the little people being relocated away from a combat zone.)* A Caribou ride was a real hoot. It had powerful engines, very wide wings, could take off in a very short distance and climb like a rocket. It could make very sharp g-pulling turns. It could dive like a hawk and pull in to a very short landing strip. The pilots demonstrated these capabilities on every flight. One did not eat until after one's Caribou ride. It must have been one of the few planes left that was truly fun to fly, because the Air Force hated our guts for having it. Just one of countless inter-service rivalry problems in that war.

From Phu Bai, the Brigade advance party drove in convoy up Route 1 and through the city of Hue. We were headed for a place called Camp Evans, about 20 km north of Hue. Driving through New Hue on the south bank of the Perfume River toward the Nguyen Hoang Bridge, the approaching Citadel across the river was spectacular. It looked like a gigantic castle looming over the river and surrounding city. An interesting name for a river in Vietnam — Perfume. Nothing smelled good around the rivers, which constituted the primary sewage system for the country. Route 1 went across the Nguyen Hoang Bridge and immediately turned left beneath the towering wall. Between Rte 1 and the giant wall was a moat surrounding the Citadel, 2 1/2 kilometers on each side. The moat was full of inky black water that went back hundreds of years. Maybe thousands. We cut away from the moat road and drove through a giant archway called the Thoung Tu Gate, and entered the Citadel.

Hue was the imperial capital of Vietnam long before French colonialism came to Southeast Asia. In the days of Annam, before the country became Vietnam. It was the site of the historic Imperial Palace — the Forbidden City — a huge walled square within the Citadel. A castle within the castle. The Citadel of Hue was a very historic and beautiful city. In 1954, with the defeat of the French and the division of the country, Hanoi and Saigon emerged as the capital cities of the northern and southern halves, respectively, while Hue was left with being the cultural center of the old traditions. Hue was the capital of nothing. Therefore, during the war Hue was not ringed with defensive lines like Saigon. The 1st Division of the Army of the Republic of Vietnam *(South Vietnam's Army – we called them the ARVN)* had its headquarters in a compound in the northeast corner of the Citadel, otherwise the city of Hue was not an armed camp. Since anyone could come and go, the city was full of VC. So much so, one could say that Hue was the Capital of the VC and not be wrong.

The streets were very crowded as we slowly picked our way through, enjoying the sights of the ancient city and the incredibly beautiful girls in their colorful ao dais. All too soon, we left the Citadel through a gate on the western wall — the Chan Tay Gate — and were back on Rte 1 again. We crossed a final bridge and headed northward along a straight and very narrow two lane road. The road was somewhat paved and somewhat not. Potholes were plentiful. In a lot of places the tarmac was completely worn away. Route 1 ran as straight as a string for several kilometers northwestward through rice paddies and small farming villages. The surrounding countryside was incredibly beautiful. The rice paddies being farmed were the brightest of green. The small villages encased in bamboo trees looked like islands in a bright green sea.

This area just north of Hue is the subject of Bernard Fall's great book about the French War against the Vietminh in the 50s, entitled *Street Without Joy.* It was aptly named. Going east from the highway toward the ocean, the villages were increasingly rigged with booby traps. And the soil was increasingly sandy. Everyone knew by that time that the M-16 of that day would quickly malfunction in sand, one of its several drawbacks. The farmlands east of Route 1 were definitely joyless. As we drove along, I gave no thought to the possibility of any enemy ambushes or mines. It never occurred to me that I would be harmed in any way. I was so incredibly naïve at that time.

We traveled about fifteen miles north to the Marine Base called Camp Evans, and set up camp in a big open field outside the western side of the base.

The next morning, after receiving instructions about the battalion's assigned base defense sector, I took off in a C&C bird. Part of the brigade flight detachment was already up there and ready to fly for us. The four rifle companies and the battalion forward command group were coming in to the Quang Tri Airport that afternoon, where they would be met by trucks that would bring them down to Camp Evans.

Quang Tri was about 30 km north of Camp Evans, and was the northernmost city of South Vietnam. A much smaller town called Dong Ha sat right on the border, a few miles further north. *(You may have seen the famous picture of the naked girl fleeing down the road taken in 1975. She was running from Dong Ha to Quang Tri on the day the NVA began their final push to take the country in 1975.)*

I went to Quang Tri alone to meet the battalion and get them moving down the highway. The rifle companies came in to the Quang Tri Airport throughout the morning on the 26th of January, but there was no sight of any trucks. Brigade strung us along about the trucks hourly until 1700 hours, when we finally got the real story. The trucks would not be arriving, due to mines on Hwy 1. I spent the rest of the dwindling day assigning areas for company perimeters, spreading them down the length of the runway.

Each company had its own separate perimeter. The troops put up their poncho tents next to a hole to dive into. By the end of the day everyone had a hole to go to and fight from if necessary. The headquarters group created its own perimeter around the Army's operations center for the airfield. The few of us in the CO's "command group" had holes to go to just outside the door of the operations building.

Across the runway was the headquarters of the Marine Air Wing, along with a lot of their helicopters parked in sandbag revetments. Even though we were within the fence surrounding the Marines' airfield, we did all the normal precautions. The headquarters group had a perimeter, and everyone had a hole to fight from. John Seymour got plugged in with all the artillery units in the area, and I let him fire some artillery marking rounds inside the air base perimeter fence. I didn't ask for permission from the Marines. I presume he did, but didn't much care. I had a bad attitude after dealing with the 5th Marines that we replaced at LZ Baldy back in October.

Capt. John Seymour, our FSO, was attached to us from 1st Battalion, 21st Artillery. He was a West Point graduate of the Class of 1965, and his brother was an All-American football player for Notre Dame. John played pretty well himself for Army. After the work was done, John and one of the other artillery officers, a forward observer, went across the runway to get dinner in the officer's mess of the Marine Aviation Wing. The Marines were "decked out in fresh starched fatigues for the evening, looking good and smelling good." John and his pal were the center of attention attired in their rancid fatigues, mud covered boots, and day-old beards. They contrasted nicely with the white tablecloths, china, silver, and table service from the beautiful young waitresses in the finest of silk au dais.

Jack Long arrived in a C&C just before dark. He was worn out from a day of flying and briefings at Camp Evans, so he was ready to retire early. It wasn't long before everyone was settled in for the night. At 30 minutes after midnight on the 27th of January, Mr. Charlie sent approximately twenty 122mm-rocket rounds into the Quang Tri Airport, most of which landed right around the terminal building. A 122-mm rocket is a very long canister with a rocket motor and fins on the back, and a major league explosive warhead on the front. It goes off with an earsplitting crack and parallels the damage done by one of our big 155mm artillery rounds.

We had been asleep inside the wood slat terminal building when the attack started. Jack and the rest of the people were immediately up and out of their sacks, headed for the door. The RTOs slept close to the CO along the wall closest to the door. I, on the other hand, slept further down the building. I was in the middle of a nightmare about a lightning storm, with continuous bolts hitting the trees around me, and I finally woke up to see streams of dust falling from the rafters. I sat up in my sack, as another rocket landed, and my first sight was of the CO and several others in the doorway, silhouetted by the flash.

My next few seconds were spent lying back down on my side and putting on my boots, then sprinting to where the radio telephone operators had been sleeping, and of course finding all of the radios. Grabbing one, I ran out the door and jumped feet first into the hole that had been dug for the CO and me. *(I would always crawl through rocket and mortar rounds, now that I am older and wiser.)*

Asking where the CO was, the RTO across the hole said "I think you're sitting on him." I scrambled off. He wasn't breathing. Somewhere nearby Joe Begotka also lay dead in the arms of his friend Jim Thomas. Joe was from Green Bay, Wisconsin, and was a great guy. Some more wounded troopers lay around the doorway. Sp5 Scott McClaine, a senior medic, had crawled directly to the wounded men lying in the open area outside the door and administered first aid throughout the shelling. McClaine shielded the wounded men with his body as he worked on them. He was joined by SSG Fred Novak, also of the medical platoon, who left the protection of

58

his hole to assist. The actions of this group probably saved the lives of a few men.

The Operations Sergeant, an old E-8 Master Sergeant nicknamed Pappy, could see the inbound rockets and would holler out to everyone. We all hugged the sandy walls of our holes as hard as we could. Well, at least I did. It was my first experience with terror. Several more rockets came in after I had joined the group outside.

I had hardly heard a shot fired in anger until then, and I was suddenly in command. The Battalion Executive Officer (XO) was not with us at the time. The XO was a classmate of mine named Joe Arnold. He was also a brand new major like me, and was senior to me by one day. XO Joe was in command of the 3rd Brigade rear elements in a convoy somewhere south of Da Nang.

At one point, as I peeked out of the hole, a mechanical mule was on fire about twenty yards away. It was butted up against another mule loaded with ammunition. "We need to separate the mules", I yelled. Sgt. Maj. Mc Querry was in the next hole over, and without hesitation jumped up, grabbed a couple more guys, and ran out to separate the mules. McQuerry was heroic that night.

I got on the radio to the companies to see how they were doing. They had mainly been watching us get blown up over at the terminal building. Imagine the cute little Vietnamese girl who had worked all day at the flight operations desk, making that certain little phone call after she left the office for the day. Who knows? They certainly hit the target. Before we falsely accuse her, though, there are several two-story buildings right across the street from the gate. An NVA or VC observer with a radio had undoubtedly watched us the entire day.

The First Brigade had preceded us north by a couple of days, and their TOC was located on an LZ southwest of Quang Tri. I looked up their call sign and frequency in my little book, and gave them a call. My message was words to the effect, "This is Fast Flanker Three, we just received a lot of rocket rounds. We need Medevac at the terminal building. We are really pissed off. We lost a great guy." The medevac bird arrived promptly, with sporadic rounds continuing to come in, and McClaine and Novak moved the wounded onto the bird, assisted by Pappy, Chaplain King, and a couple other men.

After the medevac had come and gone, I called 1st Brigade again, and put us under their operational control for the night, but I added "just don't send us anywhere." I also think I added that anyone approaching any of our units on foot would be shot. While making these calls, the incoming rounds dried up, and Mac Querry came back to report that the troops wanted to move away from the control building. I quickly decided that we would stay put since we had taken no further casualties after everyone got in their holes.

At the Sgt. Major's suggestion, the two of us went around to each hole to reassure the troopers that we were in the best posture for the rest of the night. The SGM had already been around before me. One soldier wanted to argue about it, and I let him vent before saying, "We are ok in our holes, and we are staying in our holes the rest of the night. You'll be all right." He didn't like it, and never did take his hand off his hip, but he did get my first name right. Sir.

I was thinking that Chuck does not hit the same target twice, that he has limited resources and makes the best of them. Chuck, Charlie, Chas, every derivative of Charles. Lightning does not strike twice were the words I used. "How in the hell would he know," the troopers probably asked themselves. "He is an FNG," they probably said. Maybe even a FNGMF. And I did not know that the NVA had been stockpiling all kinds of stuff for their country-wide offensive, scheduled to start in only four days. Chuck probably could have rocketed us for hours if he had felt like it.

I issued instructions out to the company commanders. "Stay in the ground. Don't anyone move. Anyone approaching your perimeter is the enemy." Since the Quang Tri Airport is only ten feet above sea level, and was right next to the Thach Han River, many of their holes were filled with ground water. The men in the rifle companies must have had a great night; they probably ignored my orders after about an hour of quiet. I would give all the same orders today. I am convinced, based on experience, that if you get from standing up to lying down fast enough, you will most likely survive a mortar/artillery/rocket attack.

At first light we surveyed the damage. The wood-sided building was full of holes. The fins of an unexploded rocket stuck out of the tarmac about ten feet beyond the wall from my sleeping bag. I was the last to bed, and I was the last to wake up during the barrage. Maybe that saved my ass, because the entire wall of the building looked like Swiss cheese from two feet up.

Tragically, 5/7 Cav lost two great guys to one round that night — Joe Bogotka and Jack Long. Four more were seriously wounded. We learned later that there was nary a mark on Jack except for one shell fragment that went right through his heart. God works in strange ways. Jack Long was a balding, older-looking officer. If you met him in a bar in Chicago, you would not envision him as an infantry officer with Combat Infantryman's Badges from three wars. You would never imagine him as a sixteen-year old smuggling himself into the Army for WW II, winning a Silver Star and a battlefield commission to 2d Lieutenant all before he was old enough to vote or drink. Jack was a hero in the Big War, was also in the Korean War, and was doing a courageous and charismatic job in this war right up to the night he died. He always had a smile for everyone. When he left the 5/7 Cav on the 27th of January he went directly to heaven, or there is no such place. He was a fine CO and a wonderful human being.

* * * * *

From time to time, I ruefully think about my decision to put our perimeter around the operations building. The airfield was typically wide open flat ground, and they would have seen us wherever we set up. But I still think about it. In fact, I have thought a lot about all the events in the second half of 1967 and the first half of 1968, but I probably think most often about Jack Long. In 2004 I traced his name off the The Wall in Washington, and it is thumbtacked to the wall in my office.

CHAPTER 7

JB? JB WHO?

Before the 5/7 Cav left for Iraq in January of 2005, there was one more ceremony at Ft. Stewart. The Veteran's Association presented the battalion with the actual colors that had gone to Vietnam back in 1966. The 5/7 was no longer a battalion of light infantry, though. They were 5th Squadron, 7th US Cavalry. Heavy cavalry in Bradley Fighting Vehicles and Humvees. It was another memorable day, with a lot of legendary veterans in attendance. The flag that emerged from its olive drab canvas case was streaked and stained. It had one good-sized hole and numerous small ones. The soldiers in the Color Guard were greatly impressed... or maybe depressed... certainly concerned.

Major General (Retired) Maury Edmonds, the new President of the Association, had commanded the battalion in Vietnam in 1970, and had come up with the old colors and had arranged for them to be returned to the battalion. He gave a stirring speech to the troops. JB came again, and also made a few short remarks. JB, who? James B. Vaught. It reminded me all over again about the day I first met James B. Vaught.

27 January 1968
Quang Tri to Camp Evans
South Vietnam

The trucks finally showed up mid-morning on the 27th, and the troops took off for Camp Evans. John Seymour and I flew overhead until they entered Camp Evans, un-blown up by any mines, and un-ambushed. I landed at the Brigade helipad, and met the troops as they dismounted the trucks. I spent several hours putting the companies into their assigned sectors, during which time the Division Commander showed up for an impromptu awards ceremony. I was still lecturing on how to emplace machineguns in the A Company sector when SGM Mc Querry tracked me down. I could not have looked worse. Unshaven, some serious body odor, grimy fatigues, boots coated with red mud. Little sleep for two days. But I was commanding the battalion as far as I was concerned, even if I looked like a homeless person on the streets of Washington, DC.

Later that afternoon after the ceremony, I had found my gear and a shower. At about 1600 hours, I was standing in the street between the rows of dusty twelve man tents, fresh from a shower, shave, and sporting clean fatigues. The stench of burning shit in the air was good, meaning we were safe in base camp. About the time I was beginning to feel better, I spotted an officer coming down the street. He had all his shit together. Starched fatigues, pistol belt, helmet and all the right gear. I cheerily said hello as he veered right at me and asked if I was the S-3. I found myself looking at "Sgt. Rock" promoted to officer. A wide-shouldered, no-neck guy, maybe in his forties, with a huge protruding jaw, wide flat nose, big mouth full of teeth, and a helmet that came to just above his very bushy eyebrows. I started to focus on the black leaf sewn onto the man's jacket lapel. It was not brown like mine. Oops. Lieutenant Colonel. Starting over with a "Garryowen Sir", I rendered my snappiest salute.

Ignoring the formalities, "LTC Rock" reached out to shake hands while introducing himself as the new battalion commander. "Howdy. Ah'm — Jim — Vaught. Ah'm — yore — new — CO." My decent-sized hand disappeared into his huge claw. The new guy's lips continued to move. The slowest southern drawl on record spoke about hearing all about me and what a great job I had been doing, but my heart had dropped into my stomach… like they were really going to leave a kid in command of an infantry battalion.

Collecting myself, I gave the new CO a detailed briefing with my map about how I had set the companies in. We were defending the western half of Camp Evans. I offered to take him on a tour, which was declined. Not to be denied, I asked the Colonel how he liked to operate. You know… did he plan to give all the orders, or would he like me to run things and just keep him informed? I was greeted with silence and looked over from the boots up. No helmet, no weapon, no flak jacket. For the second time that day my stuff was not in one pile. Even slower yet, the new CO looked me up and down as he told me to "just be the S-3 like you have been taught." As he left, he said with a sympathetic smile that he would be out seeing the boys for the rest of the day.

I did not salute. I just stood there in shock, suddenly very tired. The events of the past two days caught up with me. I trudged back to the TOC trying to recollect just what S-3s were supposed to do — it seemed so long ago. And I was missing Big Jack something fierce.

That afternoon we got the CP up and running, and reconstructed the Daily Journal for the period 0001 on 27 Jan 68 to 2400 27 Jan 68.

ITEM	TIME		INCIDENTS, MESSAGES, ORDERS, ETC.	ACTION TAKEN	INL
NO.	IN	OUT			
1	0028		Received 122mm rocket fire; approx 20 rds,	J, S, Bde	JRT
			4 WIA's, 3 KIAs. Two companies from 2/12		
			were OPCON to the 5/7. Elements from 2/12		
			had 8 WIAs's		
2	0245		All incoming fire has stopped.	J, S, Bde	JRT

The Operations sections of all units in Vietnam used a standard form to record significant actions. We generally prepared a daily summary as well. In the actions taken column, J signified journal, S indicated Summary, and Bde meant that 3rd Brigade Operations had been informed. The initials were those of the operator who entered the item. In this case, James R. Thomas. Don't ask me why my troops in the TOC would indicate J in the J.

Bright and early the next morning, the new CO came into the TOC, plunked his map down, and said he wanted to conduct a CA into an area about 5 clicks west of Camp Evans. Nothing but scrub-brush covered hills. He called it a training run to get our procedures down. A couple hours later, we were in the sky over the objective wearing flight helmets, looking like real 1st Cav commanders and S-3s.

Seymour brought the artillery prep fires in perfectly. We circled the objective while John splashed in a smoke round, hitting the target on the first try. At the perfect time, he had the real stuff coming. We then preceded the v-formation of slicks towards the LZ. As the last artillery rounds hit the ground, the gunships raced by and peeled off to the spray the flanks. The slicks started touching down right at about twenty seconds after the last artillery round. The troopers of B Co came out of the birds and fanned out to the flanks as we pulled up in the C&C Bird to view the scene from above. *(We called the Huey helicopters that carried the troops into battle "slicks," because the doors and rear seats were removed. The troops sat on the floor and could quickly scoot out of the bird when it landed, or when it hovered a few feet off the ground on a red LZ.)*

The first company commander on the ground gave the status of the LZ. "Green" in this case. D Co came in thirty minutes later on a separate air-assault about a click away. These two companies swept the terrain back to Camp Evans. I had never coordinated full scale air-assaults before, but Seymour obviously had been on a lot of them. It went like clockwork. In reality, John Seymour and the aviators made it happen. The pilots of the 1st Cav had done this very routine over and over since 1965 throughout the central area of South Vietnam. The CO had no adverse comments to make. Practice over.

Late that afternoon our new CO held a meeting with all the company commanders, staff officers, the Sergeant Major, and other key people. He started talking. People started taking notes. He picked up speed. We wrote faster. He addressed a lot of stuff we knew, and a lot more stuff that no one had thought of or had heard about. It was Combat 101. He told the company commanders they would see a lot of action because the commanding general knew him well. Rather than "yeah, sure", they just nodded and wrote it down. The man had been with us for just over twenty-four hours, but he sounded like he had been there for several months. He talked about names, saying that he had already met every soldier in the battalion — "yeah, sure" — but over time he might have trouble remembering a name or two. He directed that every soldier write his last name on the elastic band that holds the camouflage cover on the helmet. Everyone just wrote that note down too. *(Today the troops have their blood type on the left side of their camouflage band — good idea. No name on the front, but on the right is six digits— two for their unit and the last four of their SSN. The troopers of today's Volunteer Army are far from being just numbers though. The officers seem to know all of them by their first names. And vice versa. You get close when units stick together — maybe too close at times.)*

At the start of the meeting, he was Lt. Col. Vaught. After the meeting he was JB. Not to his face, of course. His name is James B. Vaught. James B. JB. Sorta like Jeb Stewart, if you know what I mean. I did not find out until many years later that I was the only man on the planet who ever refers to him as JB. Among the best, many die young. The best who survive get nicknames.

Jim Vaught was from South Carolina. After Plebe Year at The Citadel, he enlisted in the Army in 1945 trying to make sure he did not miss World War II. Five years later, as a company grade officer in Korea, he earned his Combat Infantryman's Badge, the "CIB", the most treasured decoration of most infantrymen. With us in 1968, Vaught was on the way to earning a star on top of his CIB. He was not humble. How could he be with his experience? The facts are that he was just honest. Ok, he sometimes came across a tad boastful, but true warriors get that way. We loved him just the same.

I Corps was the name for the northernmost of four areas of operations in South Vietnam. The country had been divided into four AOs, further defined as "Corps Areas". The four areas were I Corps in the north, II Corps in the central highlands, III Corps down around Saigon, and the Mekong Delta was IV Corps. In military organizational terms, a corps is a group of divisions, commanded by a three-star general. Roman numerals have been used to identify US Army Corps dating back to the Civil War. French Corps before that. Military organizational doctrine of today dates back to Napolean. Make no mistake about it though, up in the I Corps AO the "Corps" was the "Marine Corps."

The 5/7 Cav had arrived in I Corps, and we did not feel welcome, certainly not by the NVA or even the Marine Corps. So, we wasted no time in painting the big yellow and black patch all over the place. We also wasted no time adapting the few good ideas of our hosts. For example, we were anxious to get our flak jackets. All the Marines wore flak jackets. Until the 1st Cav got to Camp Evans, only our aviators had flak jackets, which they sat on in their cockpits. Jack could have used a flak jacket. *(He could have really used one of these Kevlar vests we have today. The flak jackets of Vietnam were made of a multi-layered fabric. An AK-47 round would go right through our flak jackets, as would a large piece of shrapnel like the one that got Jack.)*

CHAPTER 8

PLANTING TREES

Throughout January and February of 2005 I traded e-mails with the new battalion commander. Jody Petery. JP. Class of 1986 from West Point. JP's battalion trained in Kuwait for a few weeks, and closed into their area of operations north of Baghdad during the first week of February — in the middle of the short but nasty rainy season.

On Valentine's Day, 2005, the dreaded message came. 5/7 Cav's first losses in Iraq. Three men had died a few nights earlier. All the more tragic because it was the result of an accident. Their HUMVEE vehicle went into a canal on a dark and rainy night, and they all drowned. Several others damn near drowned in the sub 50 degree current trying to save the men trapped inside. Nothing has changed. Bad things happen in the Combat Zone.

Clarissa Petery, the commander's wonderful wife, informed me about the memorial ceremony to be held on Cottrell Field on 17 March 2005 at Ft. Stewart. The same field where this all started back in July. The word went out to the key people in the Association. Over in Iraq, JP took it in stride, like any good commander. "We are driving on" were his words. For Nam Vets it was "keep on keepin' on." We fought on foot as light infantry, whereas today's battalion is true cavalry with vehicles, and they can "drive on" literally.

I drove up to Ft. Stewart on the morning of March 17, 2005. Just the night before, we had celebrated West Point's Founders Day at a lavish dinner. Dress Blues and tennis shoes. Full regalia for the ladies. We had listened to a general's patriotic speech, after which one of the elderly ladies asked him point blank, "what is the timetable for our bringing the boys home?" Vietnam left an indelible image in the minds of many of the older people connected with West Point — terrible loss being in the wrong place at the wrong time. How large is the group that now thinks of the fall of the Berlin Wall as the long-term reward for the sacrifice in Korea and Vietnam? Not too large. I wondered if we were maybe now on the right track, attacking the last major bastion of monarchism? What an idealist I can be.

At the ceremony I sat with Michael Sprayberry, one of our many heroes, under the VIP tent with the families and other dignitaries. It was a gray and lightly raining day. Infantry weather. The 3rd Infantry Division Color Guard stood at attention midway down the tree-lined sidewalk. The nearest trees were small, recently planted and just beginning to flower. A hundred people looked on from underneath the canopy. Another two hundred soldiers and dependents stood or sat in the bleachers flanking the area. It was a huge ceremony from my perspective.

This type of remembrance was all new to us Vietnam Vets. We never quite knew what happened back in the world after a family got the dreaded knock on the door.

We went to the war for a year *(or less)*, but the unit was there for the duration. The Battalion Flag and campaign streamers had to survive the heat, humidity and mildew of Vietnam from 1966 through 1971. There was not really a division rear back in the states. Most of the families did not stick together, living at or just outside their division rear base. There was no such thing as the Family Readiness Group. In essence, there was no unit beyond the men fighting together in a far-off place. The colonel's wife of 1965 Ia Drang fame may have kept watch over her flock of 1/7 Cav families back at Ft. Benning, but it is unlikely that her replacement did. By 1966 everyone in 1/7 Cav was an FNG from just about anywhere in the US Army — just like us.

The units rotate together these days - a dream talked about with my classmate Mike Plummer many years ago. It is like the old regimental days before Vietnam. The units are teams now. They become close. They are seeing the benefits of this closeness on the battlefields of today. But with the closeness, comes the pain. For every lost man, tears fall like rain.

The ceremony honored ten men, from three different units, who had been killed during the previous two months. During the ceremony, each name was called out over the loudspeaker by a powerful and precise voice. At the reading of the first name, a soldier standing at attention in front of the first soldier's tree bent down, removed and folded the small flag covering the plaque at the tree's base. He returned to attention, turned, and marched to the next tree. The audience sat or stood in silence. After two more names rang out in the cool, misty air, "Sgt Renee Knox, Jr.!" exploded like a mortar round.

As the soldier finished with his work and returned to attention, young Mrs. Knox began to quake. Before long she was weeping in the comforting arms of one of the wives. About that time "Sgt Dakotah Gooding" came at us like a canon shot. Across the aisle, the very young Mrs. Gooding went straight to sobbing. "SSG Chad Lake!" went off like a 122mm rocket round. The Lake family was there in force, three generations filling two rows. They were older, more experienced with life. Not a peep out of them. They wept on the inside.

I didn't hear the remaining four names from the other units. All I knew was that my battalion was in tears. The Post Commander had given a speech at the outset, in which he spoke about the dedication and care by the man who built this brick lined sidewalk, with its rows of new trees. "With the precision of a Mason," he said. And he had spoken of "the children who would be playing youth football on the immediately adjacent field."

I sat there for the rest of the Tree Ceremony — too many new trees — thinking about those little army brats running the ball into the nearby end zone, just as I had done as an army brat in Germany back in 1949. They will be running just a little harder, and just a bit faster — showing off for these ghost soldiers cheering them on from their treetop bleachers.

The Tree Ceremony was an emotional affair. I could not stay long after it was over. I had to get away. Knox, Gooding and Lake were our first casualties since 5/7 Cav arrived in Iraq; the first since leaving Vietnam thirty-four years earlier.

Lt. General Vaught with two broken wrists at reactivation parade — 21 July 2004

Presenting Vietnam War Colors to 5/7 Cav – January 5, 2005

CHAPTER 9

To Earth's Edge

I didn't look back after retiring in 1983. Couldn't get far enough fast enough from the US Army. But by the end of the Tree Ceremony in 2005, I was back in the Army. I had to go to Iraq. I had been invited — how do you say no? On the 30th of March, 2005, I boarded a commercial plane in Jacksonville headed for Kuwait. Military air would take me into Iraq from there.

Many of my family, friends and neighbors were concerned. A little dangerous, perhaps? They were too polite to call me crazy. Maybe I was, but this was not the first time I had gone in search of 5/7 Cav.

My final destination was a place called Paliwoda, which I could not find on any map of Iraq. One day I was an old retired soldier - the next morning I was a yet-to-be-published cub reporter for a local newspaper. I was sixty-seven, and would be embedded with the 5/7 Cav. They were located fifty-five miles north of Baghdad near a city called Balad, on the west side of the Tigris River. Paliwoda turned out to be another place like LZ Colt — a grease pencil mark on an acetate covered 1:50,000 military map.

It was ironic that I was going to Iraq in 2005. One could assume by this act that I was a total hawk about the Iraq War. But, actually, the skepticism I had felt about our going to Vietnam in the sixties had graduated to cynicism about Iraq. So why go? I wanted to see for myself what they would be doing over there. And to do so with my old outfit — frankly, I couldn't wait to get there.

Wouldn't right after 9/11 have been a good time for a summit of the world's real players? Golf in Barcelona, perhaps, followed by intense debate. The subject — uniting ourselves against the forces of terrorism. The real players, not the UN that had been compromised for years. Not the State Department either. One needs to talk to "The Man" when things aren't going so hot. But no, we did it the American way. Do something, and do it now. Do something, even if it is wrong. Before you can whistle "The Eyes of Texas are Upon Us" we branded North Korea as being in league with Iraq and Iran. An apple and two oranges.

Is he serious, I asked myself? Just as the North Koreans are finally warming up to talk, after years of diplomatic effort, Mr. President calls them part of the Axis of Evil — like they are in cahoots with the Wahabis. On a religious scale, the North Koreans are impaled on the opposite point of the bell curve — total atheists by this time. The Islamic fundamentalists are totally immersed in religious fervor. Which Ivy League speechwriter had handed him that 3 X 5 card, I wanted to know? Surely they teach the bell curve in Ivy League schools?

In my mind it was all downhill from there. The Europeans, not being invited to talk things over, began wondering out loud about the stability of our leadership.

Cost 'em a lot of tourist dollars, it did. And on our side of the Atlantic, paranoia gained momentum. It was all about the WMDs. Weapons of Mass Destruction. What if these dirty rats set off a dirty bomb in the Lincoln Tunnel? North Korea is working on one. Iraq is working on one. Iran is working on one. The Axis of Evil is teaming up to bomb NYC. It doesn't seem to matter that we have more than enough ICBMs to end civilization as we know it. What mattered was that the Wahabis, long sworn to kill the Israelis, have added the Americans to their list. If they get hold of even one of those WMDs floating around the Russian boondocks, well . . . so, as quick as we could get it together, we crossed the Line of Departure *the "LD"*, headed for Baghdad. Back in my day it was called "crossing the LD." As the troopers of today will say, we "went through the berm." *(Kuwait was surrounded by a big sand berm.)* Gonna find those WMDs and stamp them out, so we said. I was shocked that we actually went into Iraq in 2003. I was not shocked that we didn't find the WMDs.

And since we were in a hurry, we went with about one-fourth of the power that we sent to the Gulf War. And no one else in the Free World really wanted to go with us this time. And as we hurried through Iraq, no one at the White House saw that Saddam had immediately opted for his only real option, insurgency and guerilla war.

To be sure, the Marines met very stiff resistance getting across the river at Nasiriyah. And the 3d ID had some stiff fights in Najaf. But any thinking veteran of the Vietnam War knew what was happening within a week, watching the 3/7 Cav race halfway to Baghdad in three days, opposed mainly by groups of silly guys in pickup trucks armed with AK 47s and supported by rusted-out mortars. Half the cab business between Kuwait and Baghdad was destroyed. And there was no North Vietnamese Army just across the border this time to bail out the failing insurgency. Only incompetent Arabs. They haven't cleaned a weapon since Peter O'Toole *(Lawrence of Arabia.)*

The hard corps of the Iraqi Army had obviously been told to go home, bury their Kalashnikovs, and wait for instructions. Had the Iraqis read the Chairman Mao's *Little Red Book* after all?

I   Dismay & Discontent

II   Dissent & Dissidence

III   Subversion & terrorism

IV   Active Insurrection

V   Guerilla War

VI   Conventional Military Action

VII   Final Offensive

Chairman Mao

In April of 2003 we cruised into Baghdad, killed more cab drivers and a whole lot of future guerilla soldiers, and knocked down the statue. DOD and the White House got their dander up at the mere suggestion of an emerging insurgency or guerilla war. Why is it that people in power are never wrong? In an increasingly complex world, this is a dangerous trait.

Within five weeks after going through the berm, the whiz kids took the Office of the Presidency down the path again. Their man declares that the war is won, while Bin Laden is still sending out cassettes over in Afghanistan. And, no sign of the alleged WMDs either. Iraq was apparently going to be a long-term struggle, in more ways than one.

Norman Lloyd, a fellow member of our veteran's association, had completed his own arrangements to go over and shoot film of the battalion, and he put me in touch with the right public affairs officer at the Central Command Headquarters. No cub reporter, he. Norman had retired from a career with CBS as a combat photographer. It didn't take long before I was past the point of no return.

I began e-mailing more frequently with the Battalion Commander, initials JP. In one such communication we talked about roadside bombs.

> **JP:** Interesting day here. We had no fewer than 5 IEDs *incendiary explosive device* all on one stretch of the MSR *main supply route*. We found and defused three; one blew on us with no injuries or damage, and one blew on the Engineer element and seriously hurt three of their guys. We got probed tonight with drive by shootings. No injuries, but the bastards got away.
>
> **FF3:** Are these "IEDs on the MSR" in town?
>
> **JP:** No. They are along a major highway, and in some places there are a few mom-and-pop produce stands lining the highway. Our stretch is over 25 miles long.
>
> **FF3:** I was wondering if blowing them in place was an option.
>
> **JP:** Yes, that is what we do. The problem is that they are remotely detonated. They use such things as cell phones, garage door openers, little Motorola radios, to set off the explosive.

I learned a little bit about their operations in these e-mail communications. Working with the District Council, the battalion had already sponsored the opening of its first school in February — the Tedmur Primary School for Girls. A week or so later they opened the Rafaee Boys Secondary School. These two schools were the first of many planned for their area of operations.

JP told his men, "we're fighting two wars here — the first is against the terrorists who'll never trust us due to their upbringing and the only way to win that one is to kill them. The second is against letting that perception of distrust sink into the kids, and if we don't fight that one right now we'll fight them later. To that end, we pass out school supplies every chance we get, we also pass out soccer balls."

Even with these increasing email communications, I continued to vacillate until the three lads drowned in February. After that, JP put me in touch with the Public Affairs Officers of the 3d Division, and the 42d Division to which the battalion was attached in Iraq, and that was all it took. By the time I attended the Tree Ceremony at Ft. Stewart in March, the wheels were in motion.

I dared not make concrete plans until I got officially invited by the Pentagon, so it was full court press during the two weeks prior to departure. I had so much to do: passport, inoculations, prescription goggles were a must — Wiley's sunglasses were recommended. Layers of lightweight clothing were suggested. A backpack. A digital camera. Streamline the laptop, and get a couple memory sticks. I planned to hang my sticks on my old dog tags chain, along with my trusty C-ration can opener. The old can opener was called a P-38; not to be confused with the fighter plane, although it will flat-out open a can of beans. I wondered if I would meet a C-Ration can in Iraq. Probably not.

They said plan on drinking bottled water, or bring your own camelback. And, by the way, you need to bring your own Kevlar vest and helmet. I was surprised by that one. Check the will and insurance. Organize the finances. Reassure everyone of my indestructibility. Get in even better shape. You would think I was going to the moon.

The last week was hectic. Several requirements came together only at the last minute. The officer from the Public Affairs office of CENTCOM told me to fly to Kuwait City, and he would schedule me on an Air Force C-130 destined for Baghdad. My instructions were to check in to the Kuwait Hilton Resort, and they would meet me there. But a call to the Hilton resulted in "no room." Subsequent calls would not go through. I had bought my ticket. It was panic time. I envisioned living in a tent with Bedouins while waiting for the C-130 to Baghdad. Whatever happened, I was supposed to be with my battalion somewhere north of Baghdad by Friday, and suspected I would go through some culture shock along the way.

The trip to Kuwait was a long one. Lots of time to think. Two hours to Philadelphia, nine hours to Frankfurt, and six hours to Kuwait, with long layovers at every stop. *(Not the eighteen hours of almost continuous flying to Vietnam on a rickety "Tiger Airlines" plane, but almost.)*

While flying to Philadelphia, I read an article in USA Today entitled "Tanks take a beating in Iraq — Not designed for insurgent attacks." The author reported that one of several modifications underway was to install an "external telephone so that foot soldiers working alongside the tank can talk to the crew inside." I was stunned. Are you there, Creighton? *(There is no external phone on the rear of the Abrams Tank! Abrams was rolling over in his grave, and didn't bother to reply.)*

A general interviewed by Komarow for the article said that "our doctrine has been to avoid taking tanks into cities." Not such a good concept, since that is where the war is in Iraq. He went on to say "we are also working on more armor plating on the sides and rear." *(Okay, let's spend some more money on protection, but don't think for a minute that will mean tanks can just drive into cities unaccompanied by the boys in boots.)*

In the general's defense, he went on to say that "nothing is invulnerable. The key to effective use of the Abrams is how it is used. By itself, it can be hit, but it's much less likely when the Army is fighting with a combination of tanks, artillery, aircraft, and infantry. The enemy can't handle that." *Hell no.*

In April of 1972, the North Vietnamese attacked An Loc with two infantry regiments reinforced with Soviet T-62 tanks. An Loc was just inside the Cambodian border, astride the highway only 45 miles north of Saigon. That the North Vietnamese Army had T-62 tanks down the Ho Chi Minh trail to within 45 miles of Saigon in 1972 did not bode well for South Vietnam.

A lonely Vietnamese Ranger Battalion defended the town — 400 men against 2000 NVA infantry plus their tanks. By the time the NVA tanks had penetrated into the middle of An Loc, their infantry had been shredded - first by B-52 bomb runs, and finally by air-burst artillery. Left unprotected by NVA infantrymen, all of the T-62s were destroyed by the Rangers firing a small shoulder-fired anti-tank weapon called the LAW. In some cases they had to fire ten or more LAWs into the sides and rear of a tank, but in the end they killed them all. You could say the Law came to An Loc. A captain named Everngam was our man on the ground advising the Rangers. A general named Hollingsworth, Call Sign: DANGER 6, made it happen from the air. The Vietnamese Rangers supplied the determined infantrymen. I got there not too long after this battle, and Everngam worked for me. We all worked for DANGER 6.

With all the American ground forces and advisors withdrawn by the end of March 1973, the outcome was inevitable. In 1975 there were no Everngams. There was no Hollingsworth. And there were damn few Vietnamese Rangers left, even though they were the last ones fighting. The NVA had plenty of infantrymen to protect their tanks as they advanced into the heart of Saigon in 1975. I wonder if they had their infantry platoon leaders talking to the tank commanders on a phone attached to the rear of the T-62s. Probably not, since the Russians scrimped on everything.

But, it was a new day in 2005. It's not all about Vietnam, Korea, and WW II anymore. Maybe we are appropriately concerned about each and every casualty. Maybe that is the final step toward recognizing that war is a sorry-ass way to resolve international disputes. Maybe we don't want to dismount infantrymen all around our tanks, and lose a few for sure while protecting this mighty but partially blind weapons platform, when we can just send the tank out there and maybe not lose anyone against such a low grade enemy as in Iraq. In Vietnam, we killed a lot more enemy defending ourselves than we did moving toward him across the open ground. And the Iraqi insurgents, bless their hearts, are not the NVA. So, hey, let's just send an Abrams tank down the street, unprotected by any infantry to tempt an attack, and then bring in the military industrial complex on top of the enemy. Sounds good, no? No, it would most likely be against the Rules of Engagement. *(Rules of Engagement. Let's not open up that can of worms.)*

Fundamentals, being fundamental, don't change much. So, let's put the phone back on the tank before Creighton comes down here and has us crying for our mommies. Lucky for everyone that reincarnation is unlikely, because Creighton makes Vince Lombardi look like a Cub Scout. And, put the armor on the sides. And put a grill on the back. But just don't forget, no tank can survive alone against determined infantry. Infantry — The Queen of Battle. *(They are queens alright. Who dreamed that one up, I always wanted to know.)*

The flight from Philadelphia to Frankfurt started in late evening. I was still too keyed up to sleep. I sat there for the nine hour flight thinking about this assignment.

What were the similarities and differences between the two wars, Vietnam and Iraq? For one thing, the troops of 5/7 Cav who went to Vietnam in 1966 were also in great physical shape — unlike in the early days of Korea. The Battalion commander who took them over to Vietnam in 1966 on a thirty-plus day sail across the Pacific was Trevor Swett. *(He had been on the faculty at West Point during my cadet days — highly respected.)* Trevor worked the troopers out every day on the top deck of the ship, and had them in shape when they landed. Humping forty to eighty pounds up and down the central highlands of Vietnam kept them that way.

Another similarity included the enemy in Iraq being very much like the Viet Cong - in guerrilla mode, sneaking around at night, and blowing up things. And it sounded like the old hearts and minds game again. And the administration promoted their own efforts on TV — focusing on the positive. In the 60's we heard about the Communist goal of taking over the world one country at a time, like falling dominoes. In 2002 we heard about the Axis of Evil, and the dire consequences of defeat.

In the earliest days of our involvement in Vietnam, well before I went over in 1967, I believed we had inserted ourselves into the wrong war. Something didn't smell right about monks burning themselves alive in the middle of the street in Saigon. Nevertheless, by 1965 we were making dramatic progress in protecting the population from the Viet Cong *(the insurgents)*. Protecting the population is the whole deal in countering an insurgency or guerilla war. We were being so successful that the North Vietnamese Army *(NVA)* was forced to come across the border with a very capable army. This war was North Vietnam's idea to start with, so they had to do something.

North Vietnam was in fact clearly the VC's sponsor. Their goal was unification of Vietnam under communism. To us, the emphasis was communism. To them it was unification. After the NVA came in, we began to forget about the people in the villages. We began to shift our attention to chasing the elusive NVA around the jungle, turning the job of population protection over to the fledgling South Vietnamese Army. With many of the South Vietnamese soldiers playing both ways, protecting the population went straight to hell. Population protection being the whole deal, defeat was already pre-ordained. We just didn't know it in 1967 and 1968. I certainly didn't know that year.

I was shocked when I came home in July 1968 to learn that we had lost. The Cronkiters had made the announcement. I could have sworn that we had just eliminated the Viet Cong militarily, and the North Vietnamese Army had fled the country to rebuild their units from scratch. Regardless of who perpetrated this war, however, the US Army was gone from Vietnam by 1972. And the NVA certainly finished off the South Vietnamese in 1975. Ask any American on the street today who even remembers Vietnam, and most will tell you we lost the war in 1975. The final day is etched in their minds. As if the entire war ended on the roof of the US Embassy in Saigon.

CHAPTER 10

A REAL WAR

Forty years later in Iraq, brain-washed Muslims were blowing themselves up. Something didn't smell right about this one either.

When I set out for Iraq in 2005, I have to confess that I was thinking more about our losses in February 1968 than our recent losses in February 2005. The squadron had been there for three months and had lost three men in an accident. 5/7 Cav lost 27 men in combat action just in the month of February 1968, and many more seriously wounded. The road from Camp Evans southeast down to Hue was a very dangerous place. The road all the way down to Saigon was dangerous, for that matter. Throughout all of South Vietnam, 2800 men died in the month of February 1968. *(February 1968 was something else.)*

29 January 1968
Camp Evans
QL-1 north of Hue

Two days after Jim Vaught assumed command, 3rd Brigade directed him to establish an artillery firebase about 5 km southwest of Camp Evans in the scrub hills beneath the coastal mountains. The first coastal range stood like a giant escarpment looking down on the coast all the way to the ocean. From there Mr. Charles, with good binoculars, could clearly see the streets and tents of Camp Evans ten clicks to the east. This firebase would hopefully enhance the security of Camp Evans through closer observation of the mountain ridge, which by this time was aptly called "Rocket Ridge". It would also shorten the range for counter-battery fires against Rocket Ridge. Counter-battery means what it says, our artillery firing back at their artillery. I always thought of counter-battery fires as a wild-ass guess. We identified things by six digit coordinates back then, good to within 100 meters. You could easily miss all of the targets in a 100 meter circle. *(Today in Iraq, our radar equipped artillery can watch a rocket leave its launcher, and return an artillery round on the same arc. Accurate to ten meters. Computerized. Totally unfair to Ali Baba, one of the more colorful names for the enemy in Iraq.)*

Every northward move by the 3rd Brigade had carried with it some new and harder lessons. As far as JB and I were concerned, this was not going to be another LZ Colt. We had a bulldozer out there soon after our air assault. We had our command bunker dug into the ground and covered with a sandbag roof by nightfall. We received tons of concertina wire and stakes, and had one strand up right away. Digging was tough… gravelly hard soil. There were no little people hired to fill sandbags for 50 Piastre per hour, like the REMFs enjoyed out on the coast. All the RTOs and NCOs worked their asses off. Even I, boy major, filled bags. And if JB was firm about getting the wire erected, I was relentless. Within two days the battalion had a triple concertina barrier on the entire perimeter; a perimeter not too large for a dug-in rifle company. On top of that, we kept two companies defending the position until our fence was done. The firebase was ringed with claymores, and well-organized. Good fields of fire. Open ground for the enemy to cross. No nearby higher ground staring down on us. Listening posts well out from the perimeter. Lots of trip flares. The individual positions were squeaky clean and ready to go. JB had been going around most of each day talking to troopers, showing them basic stuff like how to keep their M-16s from jamming. We were in good shape. It was a defensive position that would have pleased Big Jack. So, of course, we called it LZ JACK.

31 January was the big holiday in Vietnam. Tet. Their annual religious holiday, not unlike our Christmas. Throughout the war, both sides had historically been idle during Tet. An unofficial truce. All the ARVN units let more than half of their troops go home for the holiday. Although Bravo Company had a platoon patrol trigger a mine that day, wounding four men, our operations were relatively quiet. Sadly, Sgt. Archie Burnette was killed that day. While 5/7 Cav lost only one man on the actual day of Tet, units throughout South Vietnam lost a lot more.

We started hearing traffic about wide-spread enemy activity late in the day. There were rumblings on the Brigade command net. We were hearing chatter from other battalions. No one was telling us anything directly, but something was up. The troopers on the LZ were actually the first to hear the real news about Tet by listening to "Good Morning Vietnam" on Armed Forces Network. (AFN, still going strong in Iraq and Afghanistan.)

The NVA had kicked off a country-wide offensive on the 31st of January, knowing that half or more of the ARVN soldiers would be at home. They penetrated the US Embassy in Saigon and had to be repulsed by helicopters landing 101st Airborne troops onto the roof. And most significant of all, to us anyway, the ARVN had lost all but ten percent of the Citadel of Hue. Hue was about 20 clicks as the crow flies from LZ Jack. As the sun set on Hue, the South Vietnamese held only the small area around the 1st ARVN Div compound, in the northeast corner of the Citadel. That was it. The NVA had the rest.

Battles raged all over South Vietnam on the night of the 31st and throughout the 1st of February. Just up the street, the 1st Brigade of the 1st Cavalry Division was fighting a battle to regain the city of Quang Tri. We had gotten out of Dodge just in time. All day on the 1st, we did not hear a shot fired in anger. Not at LZ Jack, and not at Camp Evans either. Maybe the big offensive would be over and we would miss the whole thing. Timing is everything, isn't it?

It was well into the 2d of February before we actually learned much. JB and I were called to a meeting at Brigade where we learned that a major portion of the Citadel of Hue had been seized by four NVA battalions… a reinforced regiment. The Citadel portion of Hue was roughly two and a half kilometers square, protected by a massive rectangular fortress wall. *(Holy shit... did they say four battalions inside a 2.5 kilometer square?)* It was just over a week since we had driven through the Citadel on the way to Camp Evans. The Citadel was still a very historical place, but maybe not so beautiful anymore.

There were reportedly three more battalions operating south of the Citadel, across the Perfume River in New Hue... that would amount to a second regiment. Lastly, we were told that 3rd Brigade had just completed the air-assault of the 2/12 Cav into a very hot LZ just north of Hue.

NVA Division seizes Hue on 31 January 1968

As it turned out, the 2/12 Cav's air-assault actually went into the rice paddies 11 clicks north of Hue next to a place called PK-17. PK-17 was an old French Army barracks just off of QL 1. QL 1 is Vietnamese for Route 1. QL 1 runs the entire length of Vietnam along the coast. Not unlike US 1 from Key West to Boston. PK-17 was the headquarters of the 3rd Regiment of the 1st ARVN Division.

Lastly, we were told that 2/12 Cav was receiving sniper fire and considerable mortar fire that afternoon, and we were alerted to join them. We still had only two companies. Our other two companies continued to be under the operational control of 1/7 Cav back at Camp Evans. *(We called this status "OPCON".)* We were to be picked up by slicks as soon as it could be organized. We waited the rest of the day for the slicks, and they did not come. While we sat waiting at LZ Jack, I penned a letter to my dad.

> *...As you probably know by now the VC have started a big offensive and it is continuing. They are concentrating on the cities and big installations and I feel fairly safe over here at LZ Jack. Camp Evans got mortared last night and Brigade Headquarters had nine casualties. I am keeping one step ahead of Chuck.*
>
> *...We are heading for a pretty dangerous period which I think will last maybe one or two months at the outside. Chuck is making a big push up here in the north, which I think will be defeated providing we get enough Army up here. If it is left to the Marines I'm afraid of what might happen. Once defeated I think the war will take a significant turn — maybe negotiations, maybe even end. I heard that Chuck lost 5800 killed from the 27th to the 31st of January.*

Information was flooding into Brigade about NVA attacks all over Vietnam. 3d Brigade was commanded by a new guy, and an armored officer at that. There were no tanks in the First Cavalry Division, but we had increasing numbers of armored officers coming to the division. Vietnam for the most part was not tank country, but no one likes a war more than a good Armored Officer. This one wasn't going to pass them by, no siree.

Earlier on the 2d of February, while 2/12 Cav was assembling to go to PK-17, Troop B of 1/9 Cav conducted aggressive aerial recon operations on the western approaches to Hue. Major George Burrow commanded Troop B dating back to

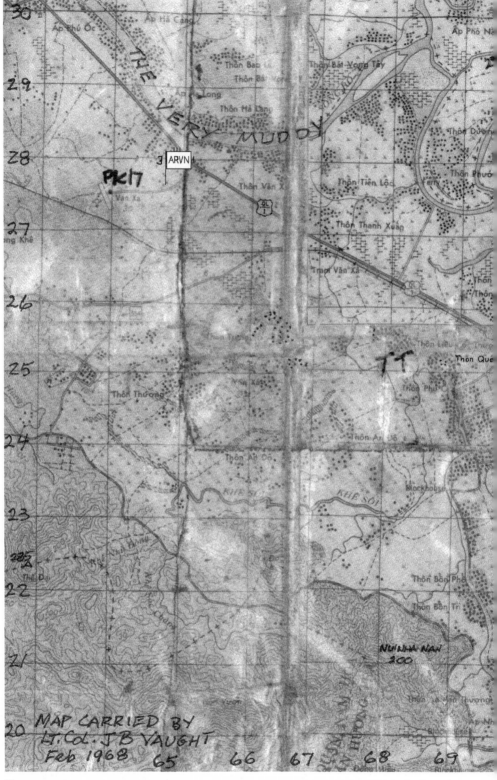

THE VERY MUDDY

PK17

3 ARVN

MAP CARRIED BY
LT. Col. JB VAUGHT
Feb 1968

82

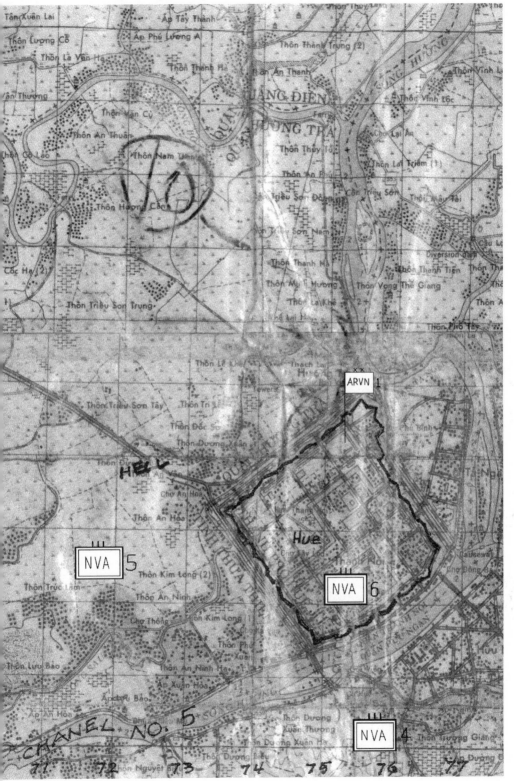

the Que Son Valley campaign. "Flashing Saber Six". George was legendary. I met him during my days at Brigade Hqs, and heard a lot more about him when I spent a day at their base in Chu Lai visiting Mike Field - a classmate. I always spoke of 1/9 Cav in glowing terms after meeting them for steaks and beer. *(Mike Field was our Mule Rider throughout our cadet days. Mike was killed soon after that visit back in October 1967, after having been a legendary 1/9 Cav hero — one of our most decorated classmates.)*

On 2 February 1968, Major Burrow's "red bird" was shot down while reconning the wooded areas north of a huge rice paddy "to be used for an air-assault by 3d Brigade units". George's co-pilot was William Neuman. The crew came under attack from an onrushing NVA force as they were dismounting from their downed aircraft. The two door gunners, Sp4 Hooker and Sgt. Laudner, were already wounded before they crashed, and the two pilots took up fire against the NVA. Fortunately, Burrow had been working in concert with Warrant Officer Roy Inman who was piloting a white bird — a small scout bird. The Reds and the Whites always operated together. Inman, using his machine guns along with a readily available air strike of napalm, drove off the platoon-sized force of NVA. This allowed George and his crew to be rescued. It was interesting how the 1/9th Cav could always get some air strikes on short notice. Pilots stick together. This action further added to Burrow's sizeable legend. It also put the kibosh to air-assaulting 2/12 Cav into this area much closer to Hue.

The birds were not available anyway. That's why we sat on our ass all day at LZ Jack. When the NVA's Tet Offensive kicked off, the Division was under extreme stress. The 2nd Brigade, with three battalions and associated support, was still down south in II Corps — the Central Highlands — so the Division was also missing one third of its helicopter and artillery resources. Throughout the previous day the 1st Brigade had been in a pitched battle with a large NVA force in Quang Tri. The city was quickly retaken, thanks in part to the heroics of the 1/12 Cav, under the command of a man called Dan French. Dan French was on the faculty at Benning the previous year and was highly respected by the men of my Advance Course class. The 1/12 Cav sort of "crossed the T" on the enemy. You could say that our French did a lot better than the previous French had done in the 50s. Fierce fighting for Quang Tri would continue for several more days.

Because TET had kicked off right in the middle of the 1st Cav Division's move to I Corps, there were significant problems in supporting operations during the first weeks of February. For one thing, the Aviation Maintenance Battalion was still at Phu Bai when Tet struck, and had little choice but to set up there. Phu Bai was a huge air base south of Hue astride QL 1. The Marine three-star in command of I Corps had his headquarters there. All our aircraft that needed maintenance had to fly out to sea, down the coast and back in to Phu Bai.

And there was a lot of maintenance going on down at Phu Bai, because our helicopters were accumulating holes on a daily basis. Additionally, there continued to be inadequate build-up of aviation gas, ammunition, water and rations to support major operations. Our helicopters had to bring everything up from Phu Bai by going east out to the sea, up the coast, and in again on every run.

The 3d Brigade Trains, commanded by our Executive Officer Joe Arnold, was in a truck convoy somewhere on QL-1 south of Hue. Joe was my classmate and one of my best friends. In other words, we would not be seeing them anytime soon. *("Trains" is the word for one's rear support base.)* So we sat at LZ JACK again all day on the 2nd, waiting for the word that never came. That night we were alerted again to move the next morning.

ITEM NO.	TIME		INCIDENTS, MESSAGES, ORDERS, ETC.	ACTION TAKEN	INL
	IN	OUT			
22	2250		Bde rpts to have entire ele of 5/7 prepared to	J, S, Bde	LCM
			move by mid morning down to Warmaster loc.		
			Also have guides determined to show 501st of		
			101st all positions which companies occupy		
			at Camp Evans & LZ Jack. Move is on a go		
			status at this time. We will go by hook unless		
			further notified. Be sure & take picks; shovels		
			and plenty of ammo.		

On the morning of 3 Feb the Brigade Commander *(or someone above him)* ordered the 2/12 Cav to move out on foot from PK-17 toward Hue. So much for being Skytroopers. Regardless of who made the decision, the Division Artillery Officer had yet to move a battery to PK 17.

That same morning, we were told that CH-47 Chinook helicopters "were on the way" to take us down to PK-17. *(The Chinook was a big lumbering cargo carrier helicopter, with a rotor on each end. It could carry a platoon of troops. 30 guys.)*

We were given back our two companies that had been OPCON to 1/7 Cav, and started talking to them on the radio. The weather was dark and dreary. As it turned out, the ceiling was too low for Chinooks. At 1011 hours that morning, C Company was picked up by slicks and carried to PK-17 to assume defense of the LZ there, so that 2/12 Cav could move out toward Hue. As for the rest of us, we sat at LZ JACK writing more letters.

If you're an old infantryman reading this, you are wondering why we didn't just go on foot down to PK 17 on the 1st or 2d of February. It would be three miles into Camp Evans — nine miles down the highway — a total of 12 miles. I can easily picture Col. Mckenna, the previous Brigade Commander, ordering us to do just that. He was a feisty old infantry officer, who had reminded me a lot of William R. Washington, my Battle Group Commander in Berlin Brigade. McKenna was an aggressive brigade commander, and even though he may have gotten a little sideways with the CG over the LZ Colt deal, we could have used him on 2 February.

So the 2/12 Cav went down the road to Hue on 3 February all by themselves, unsupported by artillery, with reports of a division's worth of North Vietnamese Army soldiers in the direction they were heading.

On the night of 3 February we started receiving intelligence about some of the NVA units we would be up against. We also read some bad news about our pals in 2/12 Cav. I hoped my classmate Bill Scudder was OK. And Captain Helvey, whom I had met and liked a lot.

0001 3 Feb - 2400 3 Feb

ITEM NO.	TIME IN	TIME OUT	INCIDENTS, MESSAGES, ORDERS, ETC.	ACTION TAKEN	INL
16	1900		Bde rpts intell estimates of enemy forces in-	J, S, Bde	JRT
			volved in hue battle. Inside Hue citadel:		
			6th NVA Regt. Consisting of 806 Bn, 35th Bn		
			6th NVA Regt and 2 unidentified bn's. west of		
			Hue 2 unident, S Hue K200 Bn, K1 Bn & Hue		
			Sapper Bn.		
20	2200		Bde rpts: The results of todays friendly cas-	J, S, Bde	LCM
			ualties at 2/12 Cav, 10 KIA (9 in contact area),		
			and 1 at PK 17, 43 WIA's around 20 of WIA's		
			at PK17. Unfriendly casualties 5 NVA KIA,		
			3 VC KIA, 1 NVA captured in contact area.		

Who knows? Some of us may be here today only because of the inability of Brigade to move us to PK 17 in time to go down the road toward Hue with 2/12 Cav. A two-battalion maneuver on foot? That would be an infantry brigade maneuver. The Brigade Commander trudging along on foot with a bevy of RTOs and other people, perhaps? Probably not. Twice as much combat power, albeit with no artillery. But it didn't happen.

We began to air-mobile to PK 17 on 4 February, leading off with Alpha Company at 1000 hours. JB and a couple RTOs went down with Alpha. Delta came in during the afternoon, giving us three companies there. JB set up his command post in a little building, and got some information on the enemy from the commander of the 3rd Regiment of the ARVN 1st Infantry Division headquartered there.

Meanwhile, 2/12 Cav was getting creamed all day a mere five clicks away. Only Bravo Company remained at LZ Jack, waiting for relief by the 101st Airborne, and I had been waiting with them to coordinate the handoff. Part of the hang-up of our deploying to PK-17 earlier had been the Division's desire to retain LZ Jack as an artillery base. Yes. Really. An easy Monday morning quarterback item, that one.

That same day the few good men of the 2nd Battalion 5th Marines were also fighting for their lives in the streets of New Hue on the south side of the Perfume River across from the Citadel. We write the Marines as 2-5 Marine, not 2/5 Marine.

The marines have dash, but we have slash. I learned years later that the Marines were laboring under rules of engagement that disallowed supporting fires of any type in the city area. In other words, their artillery was sitting at Phu Bai with lots of ammunition while their grunts were unable to use them against a determined enemy dug into a city area.

At the same time, 3d Bde was not working under any such rules of engagement, and was quite prepared to blow the crap out of anyone who fired at them. We just didn't have any artillery tubes in range to do it with on the 3d and 4th of February. I heard a few days later from Seymour, our artillery guy, that the 2/12 Cav had asked the Marines to shoot for them on 3 and 4 February, and had been turned down. Stuff like that sticks in your mind.

By the time I arrived at PK 17 late that afternoon, I vaguely understood that the 2/12 Cav was in a terrible fight in a village halfway to Hue. Only 5 clicks away. I didn't learn until later that night that they were planning to conduct a night escape from encirclement. As we were issuing orders and making final preparations to join 2/12 Cav in the battle on the morning of 5 February, the 2/12 Cav would no longer be there — they would hopefully be just arriving on top of a jungle-covered mountain six clicks out to the west of Hue. They "would observe the enemy's supply routes along the Perfume River as it came out of the mountains." Was 3rd Brigade moving to the sound of the guns or not, one might ask?

In defense of the 2/12 Cav, who had lost twenty men killed in two days, and a lot more wounded, they needed to move somewhere other than the village they were surrounded in. Backward toward PK-17 perhaps, but out to the jungle? I didn't think so.

Moving out for Hue

CHAPTER 11

MOVEMENT TO CONTACT

5 February 1968
PK 17
Coordinates YD 643246

Our orders for 5 February were to "conduct a movement to contact toward Hue: locate and destroy any enemy that got in our way." In military parlance, "movement to contact" implies that you are the lead element of a much larger force that is coming along behind you. In a sense, the point man of a rifle squad is making a movement to contact. He makes contact with an AK-47 bullet, and the rest of the squad immediately attacks forward. But the tactical term "movement to contact" was not a familiar one for our guys. Up to that point in Vietnam, battalions generally went out by themselves to find the NVA, and the only larger force coming along was in the form of various gun birds, artillery and bombs.

With the specific terms of this mission statement coming from the Brigade Commander, however, I assumed that the 1st Cavalry Division was going to the sound of the guns. Searching for the NVA was over. The enemy was in Hue in division strength, and we were all going there. That's what I thought. I apparently knew too much about tactics.

It was not unlike starting over for the 3d Brigade on 5 February. They had sent the 2/12 cav on a movement to contact without artillery, got them hammered to a point of their having to limp off to a mountain top to rebuild, and now we were doing the movement to contact with hopefully a little artillery.

JB knew all about moving in battalion formation. He had joined the Army at the time of the Big War, and was a company grade officer in Korea. He earned his second Combat Infantryman Badge in Vietnam. He seemed to know everything about the Infantry. The mission was to go toward Hue, but he decided to parallel the highway about two clicks to the west, attacking down a huge paddy area that snaked its way to the western approaches into Hue. To our right, a continuous line of trees masked the coastal mountains to the west. It also encased the village of Thon Thuong, from where the NVA or local Viet Cong 82-mm mortars had been firing on PK-17 since January 31st. The 2/12 Cav suffered the twenty WIAs at PK-17 from these mortar attacks on 2 February, even before they got underway toward Hue. Our first objective was to deal with this incessant mortar fire plaguing PK 17.

To the left of our route of advance were numerous small villages spread throughout the vast rice paddy area, each encased in bamboo thickets and trees. Thon Trang and Van Xa, Thon Lieu Coc, and on toward a big village called Thon La Chu. The highway, QL-1, was out of sight beyond those villages.

JB put us in a box formation: two companies up and two back. We were ready to fight in any direction with two companies abreast, simply by going straight ahead, or doing a right face, or a left face, or heaven forbid, even an about face. He looked forward to seeing what his company commanders could do. We put Delta Company on our right front — the side with the highest probability of an enemy force. Delta was commanded by Frank Lambert — call sign ROUGH RIDER SIX. Frank was West Point Class of 1964, was at least 6'4" and had played basketball for Bobby Knight. Chances were good that he could handle adversity. On the left was his classmate, Mike Davison commanding C Company. Call Sign: HARD HITTER SIX. Mike was even taller than Frank, and the son of a three-star general. "Knew his dad", I claimed. Hell, everyone in my class did, since his father was a tactical officer on the faculty when we were cadets.

We moved out at around 1030 hours, right after Bravo Company finally came in by slicks from LZ Jack. JB, John Seymour and I, each followed by an RTO, moved out behind Frank's Delta Company on the right. The six of us were phased into the front of Alpha Company, looking like just another rifle squad. All six of us carried M-16s, although JB had the shortened version, called the CAR-15. It fired the same dinky 5.56mm bullet as the M-16. You had to be real close to see any of our subdued rank insignia. The thing that gave us away were the three whip-antennas sticking up from the backs of our RTOs. We moved on the right side of the battalion box with Alpha Company, anticipating doing a right face and attacking into the enemy mortar position with Delta and Alpha as soon as the shooting started. Bravo Company was 200 meters across the paddy to our left.

It was overcast, damp and cold that morning, but visibility was good. I could see the whole battalion in the rice paddy when we stepped off. 475 guys in four rifle companies, plus the six of us from the Hqs. Good spacing… everything in order. It was a magnificent scene to an infantry afficionado like me.

A battery of artillery had finally arrived during the previous night, and they created a firebase on the south end of the airstrip a click or so south of PK 17. This artillery battery had been AWOL as far as 2/12 Cav was concerned. The non-existence of artillery killed them on the 3rd and 4th of February — literally. About twenty guys. 12 of them lay buried in a mass grave halfway to Hue, and we would be going to find them along the way. It would be fair to say that there is some bad blood between 2/12 Cav and all the people involved in ordering them to attack toward Hue without artillery, which will only end when everyone dies of old age. This agonizing tale has been well documented in a book entitled *The Lost Battalion*, written by their battalion S-2; a man named Krohn. A bitter tale indeed. *(Bad title — they weren't lost.)*

A rifle company from the 501st Airborne, which had just arrived in Vietnam, was flown in to provide firebase security for the artillery. Rookies. FNGs to the max. We put our Battalion CP there, with Mike Dailey, my Captain Assistant S-3, in charge. They would relay info to Brigade and keep track of everything.

Someone named this firebase LZ Sally. No self-respecting infantryman would name an LZ after a girl, so it must have been the artillery people.

Not more than two minutes after we crossed the LD, we received a report that the C&C bird normally flying for the commander of 2/12 Cav had been shot down somewhere out to the left-front of the Hard Hitters. I wondered at the time if the pilots had not gotten the word and were looking for the 2/12 Cav at the area of their big battle. JB decided, or was told by Brigade, to move toward the downed aircraft. He ordered HARD HITTER SIX to veer left and look for the bird. As soon as C Company's lead platoon approached the first village, they were hit with sniper fire and mortars, and immediately had three WIAs in need of Medevac. Mike deployed two of his platoons forward and began to develop the situation.

JB quickly ordered Bravo Company to deploy further out to the left and come in on C Company's flank to create a two-company attack toward the downed bird. The CO of Bravo Company was Howard Prince. Howard was two years ahead of Mike and Frank, a 1962 graduate of West Point. Howard Graduated 24th in his class, and only one classmate ahead of him had elected to serve in the Infantry. That man later achieved three stars for his audacity. Howard was a scholar, and Howard had been shot in the foot at LZ Colt in October. So, Howard's call sign was… LIMPING SCHOLAR SIX.

Almost immediately after Mike reported receiving fire over on the left, Delta Company came under small arms fire from the right. AK-47 sniper fire came from the trees encasing Thon Thoung. Frank skillfully deployed his company for attack and moved toward the tree line. From our position at the front of Alpha Company, the eternally long rice paddy was suddenly empty. Everyone in front of us had disappeared into the trees. The magnificence of the battalion formation disappeared in thirty seconds. We hunkered down behind a paddy dike, as AK rounds came whizzing by from Thon Thoung.

The fight was on. But because we were going on line with two companies on the left, we told Frank to develop his situation, but avoid decisive engagement. Pfc Burns, my RTO, lit two camels and handed me one. "I don't smoke, Burns, but thanks anyway." He smoked them both in nothing flat.

Howard Prince deployed Bravo Company with two platoons up, one in reserve. They ran into a strong enemy position as they came on line. Howard wasted no time sending 1Lt Bob Trimble, his XO, to coordinate the actions of his forward two platoons. Trimble crossed the open area under fire, got the artillery going, and did his customary great job. It took the rest of the day for Bravo Company and C Company to chase the enemy out of these positions in the village of Thon Trang. We had yet to find the downed aircraft.

Delta Company's exchange of small arms fire with the enemy in Thon Thoung went on all day. They were up against an equal or superior force who kept them pinned down on their initial line of deployment, and darkness was approaching.

We decided to form a perimeter for the night around the outer tree line of the village that Bravo Company and C Company had cleared, and because we were in uncharted waters against NVA forces of unknown strength, JB disengaged Delta Company and had them consolidate with the rest of us.

Our little command group found a place next to a house inside the village, while JB moved around assigning company sectors. As soon as he returned, JB began to build his hole. After several tries, his RTO gave up trying to do it for him. JB's hole was a foot longer than he was tall, three feet wide and two feet deep. Most of the dirt formed a parapet wall on the two long sides and one end. Boards from the nearest house formed the roof. The rest of the dirt went on top of the roof. He crawled into the un-walled end feet first, and had his radio antenna sticking out. It "could take a direct hit from an 82mm mortar," he explained.

My RTO and I immediately began building exact replicas, with the open end of my hole about six feet from the open end of JB's. My RTO gave up trying to dig my hole immediately. He was a quick study. As it got dark, JB said "he would be awake all night", and followed with "You get some sleep and be fresh for the next day". You didn't have to tell this boy twice; I hadn't slept in two days.

6 February 1968
YD 664251

We continued our advance the next morning with Bravo Company and C Company moving eastward to find the downed bird. They advanced 1000 meters, pushing aside sniper fire with superior firepower, until Bravo Company's lead platoon found the helicopter lying upside down in a rice paddy. Just beyond the bird was another line of bamboo encasing a small village. As the lead platoon's point squad left concealment and started to move toward the bird, intense small arms fire erupted from an estimated NVA platoon dug into the bamboo. Limping Scholar Six was as quick on the job as he was at calculus. After a brief but accurate artillery barrage on the enemy tree line, he conducted a flanking attack that drove the enemy out of their position and allowed us to secure the aircraft. No crew members were found.

0001 6 Feb - 2400 6 Feb

ITEM NO.	IN	OUT	INCIDENTS, MESSAGES, ORDERS, ETC.	ACTION TAKEN	INL
15	1005		All ele except A Co moving at this time.	J, S, Bde	LCM
17	1200		Foxhole count, A 117, B 120, C 119, D 116		
			Fwd CP 11, Cmd Gp 6		

We then turned back to the west and conducted a coordinated battalion attack to take the main objective, Thon Thoung. This may have been the first battalion-sized attack conducted by 5/7 Cav in Vietnam. We went with two companies abreast and one in reserve. We preceded the attack with 120 rounds of 105mm artillery. Seymour had his guns working great, and the enemy disappeared out the back door as we swept through. Except for the bodies the NVA left behind, there wasn't a soul — civilian or military - when we walked in. We found many fighting positions, miles of communications wire, and other signs of a strong NVA force. Food, weapons and ammunition were found in large quantities, indicating a base area for a large force. JB was convinced we had dislocated one of Chuck's major staging bases for the whole Hue operation.

A month later, we learned that our own C&C bird had swooped in and picked up the crew of the downed bird right after they had gone down. In the meantime, we had been diverted from our plan to take our main objective by a day and a half. It has always intrigued me how information is expected to flow upward, but hardly ever comes down. This was true throughout my previous years of training exercises, and it was no different in real time.

As soon as we took Thon Thoung, we turned southeast again toward Hue, which brought us back to the previous night's position at day's end. Bill Hussong sling-loaded our packs in, along with water and ammo. We even got some mail. We were feeling good. JB was gaining confidence in his company commanders, particularly the three captains. Alpha was commanded by a young lieutenant, and he had yet to be engaged. We had advanced about 4 KM towards Hue in two days, in contact most of the way. We took out quite a few enemy soldiers, in exchange for suffering no KIAs, and only 5 WIAs.

7 February 1968
YD 664251

We continued our move toward Hue on 7 February, moving in battalion formation down the big rice paddy. This time we went with three companies, leaving Frank's Rough Riders to guard the rucksacks. JB knew we had to be nimble. "You can't fight wearing a pack", he said. The sleeping bags, poncho liners, air mattresses, extra C-rations, changes of underwear, portable radios and Playboy magazines were left behind while we maneuvered against the enemy. Even without rucksacks, the troops would be carrying about forty pounds of ammunition, water, entrenching tools and weapons.

C Company was on the right, going southeastward along what turned out to be an endless tree line fronting the mountains to the west; Bravo was on the left in the rice paddy. We traveled in the midst of Alpha on the back left side of the formation.

At the same time that day, in a place called Lang Vei way up on the Laotian border west of Khe Sanh, a large NVA force with Soviet-made tanks was in the process of overrunning a 600 man South Vietnamese militia force and their contingent of 24 American Special Forces advisors. The famous Khe Sanh Combat Base, home of the 26th Marine Regiment, was only 7 clicks up the road. Only 7 clicks up the road, and the Marines sent no one to help the Army. Ten Special Forces soldiers and 400 of their South Vietnamese militia were killed or captured. Lang Vei was abandoned — in more ways than one. Things sounded serious at Khe Sanh. Not unlike in Hue.

And a few clicks to the south of us that morning, inside the Citadel of Hue, the 1st ARVN Division headquarters compound was barely hanging on against human wave attacks by the 6th NVA Regiment. Across the river in New Hue, the 2nd Battalion, 5th Marines was fighting from building to building against the 4th NVA Regiment. They were taking heavy casualties and not getting very far. See Full Metal Jacket, a good movie about the Vietnam War in general, and the battle in New Hue in specific.

A pair of 1/9 Cav helicopters — a Red and White Team — scouted ahead of our two lead companies. By noon we had gone 2600 meters. We periodically fired marking rounds of 105-mm artillery about 300 meters in front of the forward companies. That way we would have a recent round from which to quickly adjust onto any enemy that we met. The lead companies were hit with scattered sniper throughout our advance, which we silenced with 105mm artillery rounds. Our 105mm rounds against their 7.62mm rounds. Size matters. The 105 rounds were coming in overhead, right down our formation, sounding like little bees. Suddenly there was a really big bee. A bumblebee, so to speak. Everyone was already lying in the dirt when it landed right in the middle of Alpha Company's formation. No one was hurt, and we all just got up and kept moving. Stuff happens. Maybe a little more direct support than we were looking for. Not too accurate, though, because it missed its target by at least five hundred meters. Seymour was going crazy on his radio. Did someone put too small a charge in the tube? Was the charge loader dreaming about a girl named Sally perhaps? John took it personally.

It was just after the short round — or friendly fire as we call it today — that a Huey helicopter came flying down the rice paddy from the direction of LZ Sally. It was not at treetop level on the one hand, and was not above a thousand feet on the other. The pilot had to have been a rookie, flying in the wrongest possible part of the sky. Wrongest? He flew right over our heads headed toward Hue, while we frantically tried to flag him down, get his attention, and raise him on the radio. He just flew on by going south for a ways before he made a big lazy left turn which carried him toward the big tree line way off to our left. A large village called Thon La Chu over by QL-1.

When he got to the middle of the large tree line, he turned left again and flew northward up the village. He was about 200 feet above the trees at the north end when a metric ton of AK 47 and machinegun bullets came up to meet him. From 800 meters across the paddy we could hear the continuous roar of gunfire. Down went the slick, trailing smoke, making it to the edge of the next little village 300 meters across a rice paddy further north… Thon Lieu Coc. It appeared to be one more misinformed pilot looking for 2/12 Cav.

The big tree line full of NVA rifles and machineguns contained two villages called Thon Que Chu and Thon La Chu. Thon Que Chu was much smaller, and was on the northern end. It turned out to be the village in which the 2/12 Cav had been enveloped just three days earlier.

JB gave immediate instructions. "Battalion, Left Face. John, put some artillery on Thon Que Chu *(where the fire came from.)* We'll take that little village across the rice paddy from it *(Thon Lieu Coc)*, and go from there." This maneuver put Lieutenant's Alpha Company on the left. His name was still Lieutenant. Howard was on the right, Mike in reserve securing our rear and right flank. It was Alpha Company's first chance for action since JB took over.

John outdid himself collecting artillery support. The initial barrage was from 5-inch guns on a Navy Destroyer off the coast. The USS Lofberg, I think. If a 105mm round is a bee, the 5" round is an osprey. The NVA soldiers in their positions in Thon Que Chu must have been impressed. We certainly were.

John kept the stuff coming in on the known enemy position in Thon Que Chu, while we moved across the paddy toward unknown enemy positions that might be in Thon Lieu Coc. As soon as we started receiving small arms fire from our attack objective, John quickly shifted the artillery fire onto the Thon Lieu Coc tree line, and the two attacking companies continued to advance. With 150 meters to go, we lifted the artillery and the troopers moved right through the village unopposed. The Marines may have refused to part with any artillery rounds for 2/12 Cav, but the Navy shot the lights out for 5/7. *(I root for Navy's athletic teams 364 days a year.)*

During the final assault, Bravo Company spotted an NVA squad running out of Thon Lieu Coc across the paddy to Thon Que Chu, and took them under fire. Otherwise, the attack was not contested by the NVA. My RTO and I counted about forty empty fighting positions on the tree line facing us as we went through. There were a few civilians in the middle of the village who had elected to stay in their underground shelters during the artillery. A cave dug under the floor of the house was the norm in this area. From these people we learned that there had been "boo coo VC" in the village. Boo coo had been spelled beaucoup until 1963. Boo coo in this case was probably a platoon's worth.

JB had originally hoped to go further down the huge paddy well past the long continuous village of Thon Que Chu and Thon La Chu. He intended to flank this village that dominated QL 1 in plain view to the enemy, and see if this action would prompt them to withdraw toward Hue. And who knows, maybe we could have linked up with 2/12 Cav. But the second bird going down changed our plans. The NVA had also come into plain view to us, when he blasted the Huey from the sky. Everyone was in plain view.

I came to realize much later how hard it was for Captain Daily's guys back at the main CP in PK17 to present a good picture in the Daily Journal from ten kilometers away, listening only to radio traffic. This entire action was recorded thusly:

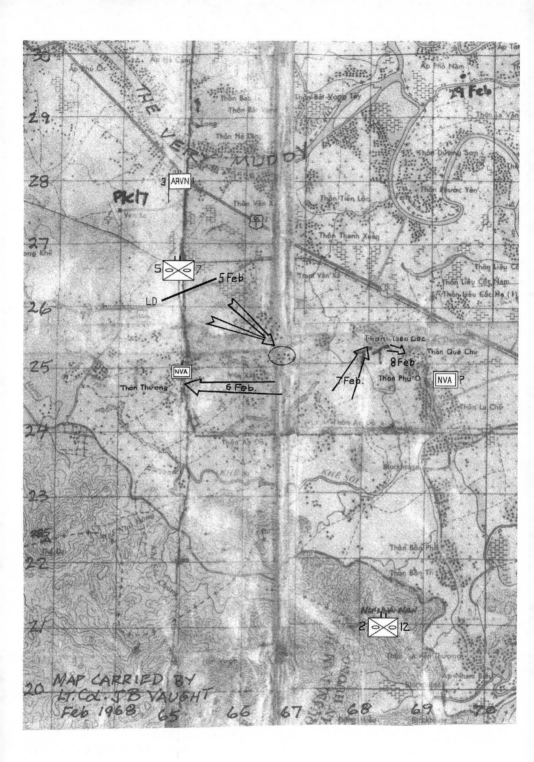

ITEM	TIME		INCIDENTS, MESSAGES, ORDERS, ETC.	ACTION TAKEN	INL
NO.	IN	OUT			
18	1145		Chopper drew fire from coor 680250	J, S, Bde	LCM
19	1145		A, B & C Co's moving to area chopper received	J, S, Bde	LCM
			fire.		
20	1305		Log Bird shot down vic 685254, crew was evaced	J, S, Bde	CRB
			safely by another log bird.		

It was late afternoon by the time we consolidated in Thon Lieu Coc, so we went into a perimeter around the tree line of the village and began to plot our course for the next day. Delta Company remained in our prior night's perimeter guarding the packs, hoping we would get a log bird in to sling-load them to us. Things were quiet until a log bird slinging ammo and water came into the open field on the northeast side of Thon Lieu Coc. NVA 82-mm mortar rounds came in right after they did, resulting in 5 WIAs requiring medevac. The medevac bird arrived fairly promptly and got mortared as well, fortunately without damage. The companies quickly dug in along the tree line. The dirt flew in the Bravo Company and C Company sectors that faced the enemy 300 meters away. Inside the village, we command group members dug some really serious holes. The rich soil was easy digging.

We were beginning to think there were a lot of NVA not too far from our little part of Vietnam. People with nothing to do spent the rest of the night thinking about the roar of all those rifles and machineguns that went up to meet that wayward log bird. JB busied himself and me thinking about a two-platoon reconnaissance in force for the next day, 8 February, to find out what we were up against.

The advance from PK 17 was a very significant three days for 5/7 Cav. It was undoubtedly the first time that these men had maneuvered as a battalion against an NVA force, yet the tactics and professionalism at every level were remarkable. This movement was a testimony to the leadership of JB, and the quality, efficiency and prior training of the company commanders, platoon leaders and the older NCOs. The abilities of our outstanding artillery captain were equally significant. All these people had plenty of training behind them that enabled us to transition so smoothly into a battalion maneuver. I had done this stuff over and over again at Wildflecken, Germany, and in the Grunewald of Berlin, both as a company commander and battalion S-3. It was like being in the real Infantry. About 70% of our troops were draftees, though, so ask many historians today and they'll tell you that our troops could not have been any good. No damn good at all. Right. Yeah, sure.

On the other hand, the NVA had confronted us with delaying actions designed to inflict casualties while they avoided decisive engagement. They had been waiting for the day when our stuff was weak, or when they had fallen back to critical ground. So far, our so-called worthless draftees had shown no weakness. They had their shit totally together. And the NVA continued to assume we could and would bring the entire western world in on their heads in a major engagement. They had grudgingly let us push them out of positions for the past three days. We had not been seriously tested up to this point.

Back at LZ Sally at 2010 hours that evening, about 40 to 50 mortar rounds came in. The NVA mortars were back up and firing from Thon Thoung, again, through which we had attacked so grandly the day before. Had we pursued that force, it would have taken us west to the mountains, away from our mission of going to Hue. They had just gotten out of our way until we passed by, and returned to go back to work. In fact, they continued to do so for several more years. Nothing was permanent in this war. No lines, no fronts, just little circles full of hearts and minds.

8 February 1968
Thon Lieu Coc
YD 682257

If the sun came up on 8 February, it was hard to tell. Very low, dark gray clouds prevailed all day. It was dank, drippy, and foggy. Visibility was so poor that we could barely see Thon Que Chu across the rice paddy. We concentrated on improving our defense perimeter. It remained quiet all morning in Thon Lieu Coc, as we made our preparations and issued our orders.

Delta Company, three clicks north of us, spotted a 30-man VC platoon and another 10-man squad between them and LZ Sally, and engaged them with artillery. But, no birds were flying in the soup we were in, so the Rough Riders continued to be alone with everyone's packs. I was getting increasingly nervous about their not being in Thon Lieu Coc with us.

By mid-afternoon, visibility started to improve, and JB decided to execute his recon-in-force maneuver across the 300 meters of open ground to Thon Que Chu. Was Charlie still there? If so, would he delay us for a bit and continue to give ground? The plan was for Bravo Company to send one platoon straight across the paddy, while C Company's platoon went in around the right flank. We preceded this advance with a short artillery preparation before the 2nd Platoon of Bravo Company went across the 300 meter open rice paddy. SSG Wilfred Solomon was in command. His platoon leader, Lt. Abraham, was on R&R.

SSG Solomon's platoon got to within a few meters of the edge of the village when their world erupted. Several machineguns and many AK 47s were fired at close range from well-concealed spider holes and trenches. Six men went down immediately. Well, actually, everyone in the platoon went down, since they were in the middle of a perfectly flat open field, but six had been hit. JB took it all in from his vantage point near the downed Huey.

As soon as the fire erupted, Howard Prince immediately began maneuvering the rest of his company. Lt Hitchcock, commanding the 3rd Platoon, was deployed to Solomon's left to develop suppressive fire against the enemy. They did not get far before they too were pinned down in the open area. Hitchcock crawled among his platoon trying to get them to return fire. His RTO, PfC Costello, dogged his every move and enabled the Lieutenant to communicate about where to put the artillery. AK and heavy machinegun fire swept the field. One of the NVA machineguns was penetrating Thon Lieu Coc all the way back through the bamboo to our makeshift command center — a deep hole at least 100 meters in from the tree line. Green tracers were coming through the trees and hitting the walls of the house behind us. All of us S-3 types dove into our holes.

SSG Solomon had gone forward right behind the lead squads, and when the firing started, he immediately took up a firing position and led by example, bringing suppressive fire on the enemy positions. Supported by Solomon's fire, Sgt Michael Elwell, one of the squad leaders, jumped up and assaulted forward against the enemy trenchline. Rifleman Daniel Meade went with him and neutralized the nearest spider hole with his rifle. While attempting to move onto the next one, Meade was mortally wounded and lay on the open ground. The combined efforts of these two troopers enabled the rest of the squad to crawl backward to less exposed positions and live to fight another day. As Elwell attempted to return to the squad, he too was shot and killed by the NVA defenders. In the heat of the battle, Solomon was also severely wounded, but not before his constant fire enabled most of the men to crawl backward to a small dike and other more tenable positions — little ruts in the rice paddy. Sp4 Pschirrer, the Platoon RTO, dashed forward and pulled Solomon back to the safety of the dike. Solomon refused to be evacuated further, and stayed with the platoon, directing the fire of the men.

Over on the right, the C Company platoon had maneuvered to a fairly prominent paddy dike between them and the village, which masked them from the action. Since this was to be a reconnaissance in force, and we had already achieved our purpose of telling us about the enemy's presence and strength, JB held the C Company platoon up on the paddy dike.

With the two platoons of Bravo Company pinned down in the open area, Prince and his artillery forward observer (FO) got artillery fire coming in almost immediately. They started it deep in Thon Que Chu and walked it back toward us. Prince then directed his reserve platoon to move up to the tree line and be prepared to support by fire. The platoon leader was a recent arrival, a Puerto Rico National Guard officer who spoke broken English and could never be raised on the radio. Instead of moving to the left side of the tree line, the new lieutenant moved his 1st Platoon directly behind Solomon's platoon. Before anyone could correct the situation, some of his men opened fire, killing Wilfred Solomon on the paddy dike in front of them. It was a tragedy of major proportions. Solomon was one of the battalion's most outstanding NCOs. Trimble, Prince, JB, everyone at the scene, went totally ballistic. The QM lieutenant was sent away on the first available bird, never to be seen again. Lt. Abrams was so bereft when he returned later from R&R and learned of his platoon sergeant's loss, he never returned to the platoon, eventually becoming our Battalion S-2.

The two pinned-down platoons began to run out of ammo. Receiving the call, one of Prince's RTOs, Dennis McGuire, ran out into the open field with as much ammo as he could carry. He was met part-way by Pfc Ballentine of Hitchcock's platoon, who assisted in carrying it forward to the men. One of the Bravo Company medics, Pfc John Williams, also did a great job dashing out and crawling among the fallen men and working on their injuries. He was joined by another Company RTO, Sp4 Bob Holland, who assisted in giving first aid. I will always remember Holland. I can see him now. He was a big man — one of the real studs in Bravo Company.

About thirty minutes into this action, we began to bring more accurate mortar and artillery on the enemy defense line. At about that time, an ARA bird came on station. The pilot was turned over to Prince, who linked him up with SSG Broom by radio. SSG Robert Broom had become the platoon sergeant when Solomon died. Supported by close in fire from this ARA bird, Broom moved with his right flank squad forward toward the enemy positions. He got to a position far enough forward where he could see the active enemy bunkers and spider holes. He was able to direct the ARA Bird so accurately that they knocked out three NVA positions, and the squad overran the enemy sector that was bringing the most fire on the men who were down.

A little earlier, JB had ordered Alpha Company to maneuver from its reserve position on the backside of our village, out into the open paddy well out to the left flank of the Bravo Company platoons. His tactic was to show a large force on the enemy's other flank that would ease the pressure on the pinned-down Bravo Company platoons. This all took some time. As Alpha Company was deploying on a line just inside the highway several hundred meters away, Broom's men were conducting their heroic charge over on the right.

The young company commander of Alpha Company moved his lead platoons forward across the open ground. About halfway across, they came under enemy fire, but they were well-deployed and spread out, and continued to move forward with good suppressive fire. He had two platoons on line and one in reserve back by the highway. *(See Diagram Opposite)*

2Lt Jessie Thomas was the right-side platoon leader of Alpha Company's advance. As his platoon came under fire, he kept his men moving forward using fire and movement technique to a position along a small rice paddy dike within a hundred yards of the enemy. 2LT Flenniken was the company's FO, and he went with them on the right to direct the artillery fire. Flenniken was able to adjust 105mm artillery rounds right into the enemy trenchlines facing Thomas' platoon. Sgt Beebe, also an FO, assisted in this effort. The weight of all this effective firepower, along with Broom's efforts over in the Bravo Company sector, finally silenced the NVA firepower. Covered by the Alpha Company fire, the 2nd Platoon of Bravo Company was able to crawl the 250 meters back to safety. Led by their new platoon sergeant SSG Robert Broom, they were able to bring four of their wounded men out, one of whom later died. It was a terrifying day for the Limping Scholars, and two of their wounded men were still out there, along with their three KIAs, Solomon, Meade and Elwell.

Fortunately, the Alpha Company "demonstration" became more. They just kept demonstrating, supported by truly awesome artillery fire *(in spite of being so-called "worthless fucking draftees")*. From the last little dike, a small group consisting of Lt Thomas, Company First Sgt Carroll, Sfc Marion Green, 2Lt Flenniken, and several other soldiers, assaulted forward and retrieved all the remaining Bravo Company dead and wounded. While under fire, Green had to administer first aid to one man before he could carry him to safety. Alpha Company also had three men wounded during this maneuver, and brought them back for medevac.

Alpha Company — the "County Lines" — were lucky that they did not lose more men when they went after the Bravo Company men in broad daylight, but I think it boiled down to their having kicked the living shit out of all the enemy in front of them. Lieutenant got recognized by the upper classmen that day. His name was Bob after that. Bob Preston. *(I haven't seen Bob since Vietnam. I hope he reads this book and surfaces. Marion Green was in my company in Berlin Brigade, which I learned forty years later.)*

By 2000 hours, everyone was back in Thon Lieu Coc putting their casualties on medevac birds. Chuck left the incoming medevac helicopters alone for once, causing us to think we had done a lot of damage with the artillery. The NVA were right. We would bring in the western world on them if they stayed to make a fight. While they had fired maybe 50 rounds of 82 mm mortar at us, along with several hours of intense rifle and machinegun fire, we responded with a phenomenal 1500 rounds of 105 mm artillery. And too many rifle and machinegun bullets to think about.

Unfortunately, we took C Battery, 21st Artillery all the way down to their self-defense load, 300 rounds. That would come back to haunt us in the subsequent days. The 1st Cav Division was not having much success moving artillery ammunition out to its batteries through the rain and fog that enveloped the area for the next week.

The platoon-sized group from Alpha Company that retrieved the Bravo Company men had observed lots of commo wire, claymore wires, and other indications of a strong position, which they excitedly reported. They were convinced that the NVA had a fortified position every bit as strong as the ones we would build. The rumors spread throughout the battalion that the enemy's position was extensive and covered with claymores. What they probably saw was a lot of stuff 2/12 Cav had left behind, but we had been told very little about 2/12 Cav's experience back on 3 — 4 February. This two-platoon reconnaissance in force operation was a rude awakening for a lot of people. Well, for me at least.

The weather never cleared up that day, and we did not get a log bird to lift our packs from Delta Company's location. They had to stay alone for another night.

And the rest of us were looking at a second night of cold drizzle with nothing but the fatigues we rode in on. I was quite worried about Delta Company being all alone two clicks away. At about 2130 hours the NVA reinforced that concern by delivering 20 to 30 rounds of 82-mm mortar on Delta Company's position. One round hit the parapet of Frank Lambert's hole. Fortunately, only two men were wounded and no one was killed in these mortar attacks.

Was Charlie measuring up the Rough Riders for a ground attack with superior numbers? JB and I worried about them all night. It didn't occur to us to worry about us. We were too busy and too tired. We learned later that the 5th Battalion of the 7th Cavalry had just met the 5th Regiment of the North Vietnamese Army. They had been at Dien Binh Phu. They had history and tradition. Three battalions is 1200 or so men, assuming all three were together.

The Gray Horse Troop was once again deep in Indian territory, with limited amounts of ammo, no wire, and an artillery battery out of bullets. It was cold and rainy. We still did not have our packs, but we had tradition too. Speaking of fifths, we could have used a couple fifths about then. I think many young NVA soldiers met their maker earlier that day. (I don't think they did the twelve virgins thing either. They just got killed for their country. They didn't really want to, but they followed the orders of their NCOs and officers.)

The Brigade Commander had told us to conduct a "Movement to Contact." We moved. We made contact… with a bunch of NVA. We had found the enemy, and they were not us. 9 February seemed like the perfect time for Brigade to start bringing up the main body.

CHAPTER 12

RAIN

9 February 1968
Thon Lieu Coc
Coordinates YD 683254

The clouds hung low over the area again when the sun came up on 9 February. The air was heavy with humidity. We stayed damp through and through all day, and it wasn't even raining.

The two platoon recon-in-force had been very enlightening. It didn't take a brain surgeon to know that a multi-company attack was in order if we were to push the enemy out of Thon Que Chu. We made our plans and issued our operation order that night for a battalion-sized attack much more powerful than the one we made into Thon Thoung two days earlier. We wanted Delta Company back up with us, though, and an attack was not going to happen until we solved that problem.

Before we even saw daylight the next morning, an attack was eliminated for the day regardless of Delta Company's location. Brigade told us before the sun came up that we would not have any artillery. Priority of fires would be shifted to 2/12 Cav for the 9th of February. Using up all their artillery rounds the previous day probably didn't set too well with the boys in the rear. Or, maybe 2/12 Cav was coming down off their mountain and moving toward the big city. In any event, there would be no attack by us for the time being. The weather was actually flyable early that morning — low ceilings but broken clouds — so we requested the C&C bird to pick us up at 1000 hours to recon our plans for taking Thon Que Chu, as well as to check out the surrounding area.

The first in a series of log birds came into the paddy just next to C Company's sector at 0835 hours. As soon as it set down, very accurate 82mm mortar fire came in to the log pad area and caused four WIAs in C Company. Ten minutes later a second bird came in, more mortar rounds came in, along with some recoilless rifle rounds, and we had more casualties. A third bird got the same treatment fifteen minutes later. B Company reported that the mortar fire was coming from about 1500 meters down the western side of Thon La Chu. We immediately called for artillery fire, and were just as quickly denied. Before we could use the log birds to bring our packs down to Thon Lieu Coc from Delta's position, Brigade cut off the log bird flights as being "too dangerous." We cancelled the aerial recon, needless to say.

Right after the third mortar attack on the log pad, we relocated it to the back side of Thon Lieu Coc. In the process, Alpha Company spotted a 70-man force of NVA far out to the west moving down the same rice paddy we had come down only two days earlier. Interestingly, Brigade saw fit to fire artillery at this target of opportunity, and a 1/9th Cav Red Bird came in to assess the strike. The Flashing Saber bird reported bodies in the rice paddy but almost immediately received heavy machinegun fire from the far tree line and had to break off. It seemed like NVA units were on the move all around us, probably heading for Hue. And that was just on our side of the highway. We put an observation post on the railroad berm over by the highway, but they were limited by the weather in how far they could see out across the vast paddies.

With no more helicopters coming into our area, Mr. Charles shifted his mortar fire to C Company's positions on the tree line, and they had ten WIAs that morning, six of whom had to be medevaced. At about 1200 hours, Charles broke for lunch, fish and rice perhaps. But they were back to work at 1345. Sporadic 82mm mortar fire came into Thon Lieu Coc for the rest of the day. Charles worked initially on our outer tree line positions, but spread his fire all around our village later in the afternoon.

I learned that a mortar round that is close enough to get you comes in with a little whisper. You have about half a second to be on your stomach. One such round came in the middle of our command post area, and my chest hit the ground just as it went off. Pieces of hot metal rattled through the trees and bushes. Whoosh... crack.

Our continuing requests for artillery against their suspected mortar position fell on deaf ears. We fired some of our own precious 81mm mortar rounds back at them, but had no exact coordinates to shoot at. PK-17 was also under mortar attack on and off all day. As was 2/12 Cav. Where were all these mortar rounds coming from all of a sudden? From lots of NVA units.

Bravo Company had nine men wounded by three very accurate mortar rounds late in the afternoon. The weather was deteriorating and it took considerable time for the medevac helicopters to arrive. In the meantime, one of the Bravo Company men had a very painful wound, and we could hear him all the way back in our CP area. By the end of 9 February we had suffered twenty-nine casualties, although none were KIAs. Almost half remained in the field sporting various bandages.

0001 9 Feb - 2400 9 Feb

ITEM NO.	TIME IN	TIME OUT	INCIDENTS, MESSAGES, ORDERS, ETC.	ACTION TAKEN	INL
11	0845		Co C has 5 Ln 2's, Ln # 56, 137, not Medevaced		
			Ln # 216, 242, 226 Medevaced on log bird.		
12	900		Co C has more wounded, req MEDEVAC. Ln # 59		
			220, 222, 242, 216, 226, 137, 204,. Tail # 455		
			Complete 0935H		
16	937		Co C had 1 more incoming mortat rd, req		
			MEDEVAC for Ln # 156		
24	1345		C Co received mortars, req MEDEVAC for Ln #		
			6, 17, 116, 134, & Sr. Medic.		

			Ln # 101, 219, 100, 148 were not medevaced.		
, 4.	1715		Received 3 mortar rds, req MEDEVAC. Ln# B Co -		
			93, 94, 133, 119, 44, 73, 102A		

The Daily Journals reflected the men as line numbers. Each company had a roster, with each man assigned a number. I have thought often about why we wrote journals using line numbers rather than real names. There must have been a reason. Security? Something. When a soldier tells you he was just a number… well, in Vietnam he was to a lot of people.

This was an unfortunate policy from a historical standpoint. We have our names on the wall. We know who our KIAs are. Without tracking down every general order for the Purple Heart, however, we now have no clue who all the wounded were. And what became of most of them — no clue. (*So… I went to the Archives, got all the general orders for twelve months starting October 1967, and made a list, even though incomplete, which is added as an appendix.*)

Late that afternoon it had started to rain, and would stay that way for several days. The temperature dropped into the forties that night, and conditions were miserable for the troops. Some of us old-timers (*"lifers" in the vernacular of the day*) had rubberized parkas, but the majority of the troops had only their fatigue shirts. Life was not pretty in Thon Lieu Coc on the night of 9-10 February.

That night we learned from Brigade that 2/12 Cav had been in a stiff firefight all day, not too far north of their mountain home. Their lead company had reportedly gotten to within 500 meters of the southern end of Thon La Chu and could go no further. I suspect they didn't get to fire 1500 rounds like we did either. The NVA missed a golden opportunity right about then. They were either too inflexible, or they were really reeling from 1500 rounds of artillery and the USS Lofberg. I learned later just how many NVA units were in close proximity to us. About a division's worth.

The 10th of February was strangely quiet after the pounding we had taken on the 9th. Maybe the NVA didn't have an endless supply of mortar rounds either. The weather was terrible. The ceiling was about 300 feet when the sun came up that morning. A cold drizzling rain had fallen all night, and continued all day. Temperatures in the 40s accompanied by rain is an infantryman's worst nightmare. I felt guilty in my rubberized parka. We sent patrols out in all directions that day, for obvious reasons, but also to hopefully keep the troops a little warmer. We also took the bull by the horns regarding the lonesome Delta Company Rough Riders. We ordered them to carry all of the other company's packs over to our perimeter in Thon Lieu Coc, a mission that they gladly performed. Hot sweaty work — they loved it.

We also sent Alpha Company by foot back up the highway to PK-17, taking more of our wounded men with them, and they returned down the highway with some re-supply vehicles, preceded by a mine-sweeper team. Along with more ammo and food, we received one precious 50 caliber machinegun. *(We simply called these guns 50s.)* We positioned the 50 next to the downed helicopter where it could fire deep into Thon Que Chu and on into Thon La Chu. We were still "light infantry", just not quite as light.

Between 2/12 Cav before us, and our actions since 8 February, Thon Que Chu had become a wasteland of blown-down houses and shredded bamboo thickets. From our observation post near the downed helicopter, we could see all the way through the Thon Que Chu to the top of a lonely three-story cinderblock building. It stuck up prominently in the center of Thon La Chu. According to JB, this building had been built by the US Army as a command post for an ARVN unit and its advisory team. His opinion was that the NVA opposing us were using it for their command post, and maybe it was even a higher headquarters for NVA operations throughout the Hue area. The enemy did not act like they were leaving anytime soon. They also took exception to our 50 cal. machinegun firing big bullets deep into their defense. Bernie Brietenbach, one of the strong and poular soldiers in B Company, was killed by a sniper round on his way back from taking a turn at the 50.

That same afternoon John Seymour and I came up with a plan to request a time-on-target attack against this cinderblock building. A time-on-target is a salvo from all the artillery units that are in range, timed to land at the same time. We planned to shoot it at dinner time, figuring there would be lots of important people milling about. Alas, we did not get to spring this barrage for two reasons. Priority of fires was still with 2/12 Cav. Additionally, most of the artillery within range was Marine Corps, and the Marines refused to participate. John and I were very disappointed. It appeared more and more that the Marines hated our guts, and it was becoming mutual.

The weather was terrible again that night, but everyone finally had their packs, along with their ponchos, poncho liners, and steak sauce for the c-rations. We had our four companies together again. Frank was full of stories. Life was good. Or as some famous writer once said, "life is enough." Walt Whitman? Thoreau? Maybe Longfellow.

We woke up on the 11th feeling a little less vulnerable. About the time I was thinking maybe we had weathered the storm, three 82mm mortar rounds slammed into Bravo Company. Fifteen men were wounded, to include Lt. Bob Trimble, Howard's fine executive officer. He had to be medevaced, along with twelve others. Charles had us dialed in. Our perimeter was in plain view to the enemy across the 300 meters of open ground. Our shit was not together. It was raining. It was miserable. It was the last straw for the Bravo Company troopers, one of whom asked his company commander a question: "Sir, why don't they just move the fucking defense line back inside the village?"

"Duh," as the young people of today would say.

We spent the rest of the day conducting a "night withdrawal" back to our new perimeter. A night withdrawal is a tactic, not a time of day. We slipped a few men from each squad back 50 meters inside the village to begin digging our new perimeter. Every hour or so another pair would slip back into the trees to build their own two-man position. We were on radio silence throughout. By day's end, we had only a few well-placed observation positions remaining on the tree line, and the main defense line was well inside the village. We had trip flares everywhere. Machine gun fields of fire were cut through the undergrowth. We also had a much smaller and tighter perimeter as a result. Even though Charles continued his sporadic mortar attacks all day, there were no more mortar casualties that day. I didn't hear a single officer bragging about this being his idea. I suspect SSG George Klein had a hand in this. George was a smart one. More importantly, though, George would speak up. We had our shit back together after that move.

But it kept raining. It kept raining for three days. With all the villages around us starting with a "T", the area was aptly named by the troops that day. "Tough Titty Woods." Later we shortened it to a more politically sensitive "TT Woods." (*Thon La Chu is a beautiful suburb of Hue today, but will always be TT Woods if you are a 5/7 Cav man.*)

Charles suspected something had happened though, because he sent patrols across the paddy in the dark to see if we were still there. Our new perimeter got probed by multiple enemy patrols that night. Several trip flares went off, and we responded only with our M-79s. The M-79 was a simply marvelous little weapon in the dark. It could accurately lob 40mm grenades with no muzzle flash and not much sound. We responded to every trip flare with only our M-79s. No direct fire giving our positions away. No one called for illumination. "The dark is your friend," said JB. It was all very effective, because Charles did not come and get us in the wee small hours. We heard a few cries of distress. We found some blood trails next morning. And we also killed a pig deader than shit.

Years later I still occasionally stop to thank the Lord above that the NVA did not round up about three of those battalions they had moving through the area toward Hue on one of nights of 8, 9 or 10 February, and have them jog through Thon Lieu Coc at about 0400 hours, firing from the hip and throwing hand grenades. They knew right where we were. They probably knew how many of us there were. In that weather, they could have jogged across the open rice paddies, with no bushes to trip over, and been on us before we could react. Without our packs we had no extra claymores and not much extra ammo. Everyone was chilled to the bone. Weather precluded air support. There would be no Puff the Magic Dragon raining down bullets from a C-130. We learned much later that two regiments, the 29th Regiment of the 324C Division, and the 510th Regiment of the 324B Division, had marched all the way from the Khe Sanh area to reinforce the seizure of Hue. They arrived on 9 or 10 February in the jungle covered hills just 4 kilometers west of our lonely perimeter. The NVA had a perfect opportunity for a successful infantry attack.

The NVA Commander apparently had bigger issues to deal with, or could not vary from his assigned mission, or lacked aggressiveness and imagination, or simply did not have the balls. Or perhaps it was the limited amount of radio equipment with which to make it happen. Word was that they had one radio per company, if it still worked. Down at battalion and below, one of our biggest advantages in that war was radio communications. By the night of 11 February the NVA Commander's opportunity was probably gone. We were alive and well, with our stuff back in one pile. Artillery air bursts in the trees would have shredded half of them and we would have mowed down the rest.

We also reissued our operations order that night for a coordinated battalion attack to seize Thon Que Chu bright and early the next morning — 12 February. We took great pains to organize this attack just right. Five paragraph field order. Lines of Departure. Phase Lines. Objectives. All the stuff we had created back on the night of 8 February for our attack planned for the morning of 9th. Some of us were beginning to think that the big village complex of Thon Que Chu and Thon La Chu was critical ground to the enemy. Key terrain, we call it. Maybe he had run out of room for his delaying tactics.

CHAPTER 13

TT Woods I

12 February 1968
TT Woods
Coordinates YD6825

Our plan of attack was three companies up and one in reserve. At 0600 hours, C Company would conduct a secondary attack to seize a little hamlet sitting like an island in the big rice paddies, about 300 meters out to the west. It was called Thon Phu O *(YD6832480)*, and from there one could see down the length of Thon La Chu, as well as across the paddies to the mountains. Taking Thon Phu O first was critical to securing the otherwise exposed right flank of our main effort. It would still be dark at 0600 hours, but we planned to cover Mike's advance across the open ground with an artillery smoke screen.

The main attack would be at 0630 hours to take Thon Que Chu *(YD688251)* with two companies. Alpha on the right, Delta on the left. At 0615 hours, we would commence with a 15-minute artillery rage against the enemy's defense lines in the main objective area. LD time for the main attack was 0630 hours sharp, just as it was getting light out, and the LD was the tree line of our village.

B Company, in reserve, would move up to their original defense positions on the tree line and provide supporting fires on call. They had the 50 as well. We also requested that our 106mm recoilless rifle be sling-loaded in at first light. Unrealistic, but hey. I thought we had a good plan. Simple. Easily understood.

Plans are just plans though. A starting point. Our plan wasted no time getting off the rails. Brigade called us at 0550 hours on the 12th just in time to tell us to hold up. There would be no artillery support until further notice. So, later that morning Howard Prince and I went up to the little building just inside the village from the downed helicopter to recon Bravo Company's part of the plan. We weren't too stealthy, because a sniper bullet whizzed by and plunked into the wall behind us. We didn't hang around too long.

The rest of the morning wasted away, and we were starting to think in terms of 13 February, about the time we got the order from Brigade to attack. The smoke for C Company would come in at 1230 hours. And it wouldn't be wasted since we were attacking in broad daylight across 300 meters of open ground. And half the day was shot. I really loved those guys at Brigade. Why they were suddenly giving us orders was lost on me. This attack was our fucking idea to start with. How fortuitous of us to have planned for smoke.

Right at 1230 hours the rounds came in perfectly, enveloping all of the open ground to Thon Phu O in smoke. Mike wasted no time moving his company at the jog to his objective, and had the place secured by 1245 hours. They met only light

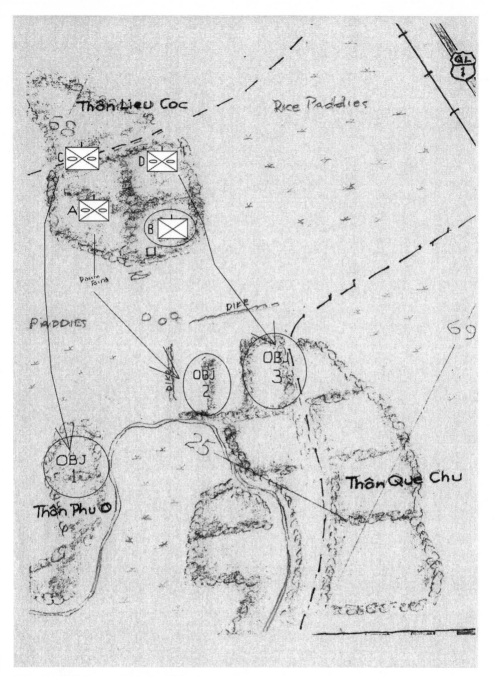

Plan for 12 February Battalion Attack

resistance, found a few blood trails, but no bodies. What a huge tactical error by Chucky Boy not to hold Thon Phu O with a dug-in company. We were winning.

The CO and I moved at the rear of Alpha Company as they moved up through the trees toward the LD. At 1245 hours the artillery was supposed to start coming into Thon Que Chu, and we would cross the LD at 1300 hours sharp. The rear of Alpha just kept moving, though. Something didn't seem right with that. JB and I arrived at the LD at about 1240 hours, a full twenty minutes before LD Time, and there stood Lieutenant and his Alpha Company about twenty meters out in the paddy, getting themselves on line and ready to go in full view of the enemy across the way. We were busted. Bob was Lieutenant again. I was ballistic. Didn't they know what LD time means? Of course not, this was the first coordinated battalion attack A Company had been in. It took no time for me to determine whose fault it was; that dumb sumbitch boy major of an S-3 Operations Officer who issued the instructions in army words instead of plain English.

We hastily got the artillery coming ahead of schedule and ordered the two companies to begin their move toward the paddy dikes just short of the Thon Que Chu village. The dike on Alpha's side paralleled the tree line, about 75 meters out in the paddy. Delta's dike was perpendicular to Alpha's about 100 meters out. As the two companies went on line and approached their dikes, JB and his RTO took off out into the paddy. My RTO and I went right behind them. We had gone about 100 meters across the open area when the troops began reaching the dikes, so I radioed to John to lift the artillery fire. As soon as the last artillery rounds splashed in, the six assaulting platoons of Delta and Alpha rose up and moved over the dikes in the assault toward their objectives. Alpha went about 20 meters when the 5th Regiment of the NVA brought in the entire eastern world. Delta out to our left had the same experience.

AK and machinegun fire raked the open grounds throughout the area. The troopers of Alpha immediately dropped into the furrows of the rice paddy, began to return fire and started to crawl forward. The enemy's fire became intense and crawling forward turned into crawling backward back to the cover of the dike.

As soon as the shooting started, JB zig-zagged forward about thirty meters to the protection of a large domed burial mound out in the middle of the field. We copied him to the letter, and everyone dove behind the mound. JB was quickly up to the top, peering out on the battlefield. It was not long before we could hear the bullets hitting the far side of the mound. Whump. I was on the radio back to brigade asking them to send the world to us, and also yelling up at the CO to get down. About the time bullets started kicking dirt up and over and landing on our helmets, I pictured the next one coming in just below JB's chin strap. I reached up and pulled him down by his pistol belt. (*Not unlike the Russian Captain who climbed up on my truck in 1963.*) Pissed him off, it did, but he softened when I described what was happening. He quickly got over it, like he always did. But he also went right back up and carried on with the war, maybe with a little more caution.

Our plan to have Bravo Company support by fire didn't work either, because the Deltas did not come in from far enough out toward the highway like they were supposed to. Instead, they went straight across the paddy on the same line used by B Company's platoon on the 8th. Not the best line to take, as it turned out. So there was no gap for Bravo to fire through. It also brought Delta under withering fire from deep inside of the village, and they had to work themselves back to their dike as well. It was a mess. From the dikes, both companies answered Charlie's fire with a lot more fire. Shooting bamboo, for the most part.

Twenty-twenty hindsight — had we attacked on the left with Alpha Company, they would have known to come in way out by the highway. We were maybe too concerned about the lieutenant's age and experience for our own damn good. It was his lieutenants and senior NCOs who were going to supervise the fighting, and he had some damn good ones.

It wasn't long before the two pinned-down companies started calling for ammo re-supply. This wasn't a western movie. Our fire began to slack off by necessity. And Charlie responded by tapering his fire to a more methodical approach. They had carried their precious rounds all the way from North Vietnam down the Ho Chi Minh Trail, and re-supply for them was a dream not likely to come true. Any time someone stuck his head up, though, Charles responded with lots of accurate fire. We were ok as long as we stayed put. We could have ordered the frontal assault with our M-16s and their teeny little 5.52 mm bullets, getting a lot of guys in the wrong uniform killed in the process, but instead we began working on bringing in the big bullets. Artillery. Gunships. Air power. The military industrial complex.

0001 12 Feb - 2400 12 Feb

ITEM NO.	TIME		INCIDENTS, MESSAGES, ORDERS, ETC.	ACTION TAKEN	INL
	IN	OUT			
8	820		The 5/7 S3 received two incoming rds of sniper		
			fire from coor YD686254, engaged with artillery,		
			Neg casualties or assessment.		
11	1305		Co D receiving incoming small arms fire at this time.		
12	1310		Co A & D pinned down at loc YD685253, request		
			ARA & Trail Blazer		
13	1320		Co C receiving sniper rds YD682248		
15	1405		The S3 reports that the ele's cannot withdraw or		
			go forward at this time. Co A & D need emer-		
			gency resupply of small arms ammo.		

About an hour into the fight one of our log bird pilots came in and hovered right behind our burial mound forward CP, while the crew chief kicked out boxes of ammo. 1st Cav pilots were truly awesome. He also circled Thon Lieu Coc and came right back in to the same spot a couple minutes later to pick up wounded men. We picked up fire all across the front while the bird came in and hovered a foot off the ground until a couple wounded men were loaded aboard. I will always remember a giant of an Italian guy crawling past me, holding up his bloody arm, and shouting obscenities at me and everyone else. He didn't like our plan of attack at all. Neither did I, as it was unfolding. I hope he made it back to the Bronx. Nothing had gone right all day as far as I was concerned, except for C Company taking their little village so smartly. A couple mortar rounds came in where the bird had landed, but they were too slow. He had lifted off and departed for civilization only a few seconds earlier.

It took a lot longer to get artillery than it should have. I think Brigade was concerned about another 1500 round day. But we finally got support and used it to pulverize the bamboo and suspected enemy trenches until the weather improved. The weather was in and out initially, and the FAC *(forward air controller)* was unable to get air strikes through the clouds. But that changed at about 1500 hours. My plan was to put air strikes right on the tree line 75 meters in front of Alpha Company to precede the final assault. 75 meters is normally way too close for air strikes, so rather than lay that on the Lieutenant, my RTO and I made a dash forward to the dike. We worked our way down to the far right end where Bob Preston was set up. It was also good to get separation between the CO and me as well; get all our eggs out of one basket so to speak.

In spite of what we said to the FAC, the initial bombs landed well inside the village. The pilots of these fast-moving jets did not like the idea of 75 meters. Bombing was not the exact science it is today. Their bombs were not so smart. They understandably didn't want the responsibility for killing a bunch of us. While Bob Preston and I were working on moving these bombs closer to us, the 5th NVA regiment conducted a counter-attack against our right flank.

From a place about 500 meters down the western side of Thon La Chu, the NVA deployed a company on line out of the trees and wheeled them northwest toward us and Thon Phu O. Maybe they were regretting giving up Thon Phu O so easily. The 5th Regiment may have had at least two of their three battalions to do all this; defend Thon Que Chu like they were doing and have more troops to commit from farther down the village. The NVA counter-attack was out of sight for Preston and me on the dike, masked by the line of bamboo along the stream. We were blissfully ignorant, and fortunate as well, because their attack line ran right across the front of C Company.

Mike Davison had his company deployed in platoon perimeters around Thon Phu O. Lt. Lawrence was his strongest platoon leader, and his platoon was across the stream out in the overgrown reeds of the open field facing Thon La Chu. Even so, with the field overgrown by tall reeds and weeds, the left side of the NVA line was very close to Lawrence's men before they were seen. When Lawrence's men frantically opened fire, the NVA did not hesitate and immediately assaulted straight into the platoon's position. They enjoyed the element of surprise as well as superior numbers. Lawrence's platoon was forced to fight its way backward and consolidate with the rest of the company. The machinegun team of Anthony

Williams and King Prescott held off the enemy, putting out devastating fire until the M-60 jammed. Prescott grabbed an M-79 and took up the fire. While these men were fighting for survival, the company's forward observer immediately called for and adjusted mortar and artillery fire against the NVA. Lawrence, his RTO Bob Schnarre, and the machinegun team of Anthony Williams and King Prescott were the last men back. Their efforts and the indirect fire enabled Lawrence's platoon to get back with the rest of the company.

In the meantime, Captain Davison had it all working by that time. Artillery. Mortars. All his machinegun teams. It was like harvesting wheat in South Dakota. As the entire enemy counter-attack began to slow, Lt. Lawrence got some reinforcements from Platoon Sergeant Rayno's adjacent platoon and attacked back into his original position. Sp4 Denis Wright, a draftee, was at the point of this assault and killed an NVA in hand to hand combat. There were eight NVA bodies left on Lawrence's position. No telling how many more bodies littered the big open field between them and Thon La Chu. The Hard Hitters brought a lot of rain on the 5th NVA regiment that day. What remained of the 100 man attack melted back into Thon La Chu. JB and Seymour had been in touch with Davison throughout this action. Preston and I were focused on communicating with the FAC on the Alpha Company radio frequency, and we were totally unaware of the battle just a couple hundred meters behind us.

All afternoon, with the clouds coming and going, the air strikes were sporadic. And the FAC had yet to put one on the tree line where I wanted them. It was going on 1700 hours. JB was running out of patience, and came sliding into our position on the dike. As he was telling me about the failed attack by the NVA, our first accurate 250 pound bomb hit the enemy trenchline 75 meters away. Craaaaack. A big piece of red hot metal came sailing over our heads and landed in the paddy behind us. We had two more just like it yet to come, and we alerted Delta Company to get ready. Someone suggested we put in some CS for the final assault, and we did right after the last bomb splintered the line of bamboo in front of us. *(CS was high powered tear gas. It would definitely make grown men cry.)* As the last artillery CS round splashed in, JB ran out in front of the dike and yelled "charge." It was surreal.

The men of Alpha Company rose up in one long line, looking like giant insects in their gas masks as they moved up and over the berm. As soon as they were past JB, they went from the quick-step to the double-time, firing from the hip as they went. They all disappeared into the line of bamboo without a single loss, followed by JB and Mike Milligan, his RTO. The NVA on the outer line of bamboo still had their heads down when we swept in, and Alpha reported killing 25 NVA before continuing the assault toward the next interior line of bamboo. Another 50 meters across open ground.

They were initially opposed by sporadic fire, so they employed fire and movement toward the interior bamboo line. Fire and movement. Some fire to keep the enemy heads down, while others move forward. The single most important tactic for an Infantry squad. Things were going well until they got halfway across the open area and came under intense machinegun fire from their right flank. Sgt. John Dean, Pvt. Poole, and Sp4 D'Agostino anchored the right flank, and they immediately located and assaulted the enemy positions dug in perpendicular to our line. Poole took out one of the bunkers, killing its three occupants. D'Agostino killed several NVA soldiers at close range before he was killed in action. D'Agostino's family hopefully received his Silver Star in a little black box. Dean was wounded numerous times while eliminating an enemy machinegun position before intense fire forced him back. Pfc Carlson covered Dean by fire as he crawled back, probably saving his life. Hopefully Dean got to wear his Silver Star later.

When the forward platoons of Alpha became pinned down by the intense flanking fire, some hand grenades started coming at them from their rear. On the initial bamboo line, bunkers were spaced intermittingly along the trenchline, completely hidden beneath the bamboo roots. They faced inward toward the village interior, and had been missed by the initial assault. NVA soldiers came up out of these bunkers lobbing grenades. There must have been tunnels.

As it turned out, the space between the two bamboo lines was the killing zone of their entire defense. The 5th NVA Regiment unit was in a "U" shaped position, with the bottom of the U being the positions that killed D'Agostino. Alpha was caught and pinned down inside this killing zone, and was rapidly taking casualties. In short order they had two KIA and several WIA.

Over on Delta's side of the battle, things were even worse. The NVA had let Frank's right most platoon come right into the open end of the big "U" position, which extended through the village past Alpha Company. The men from Delta advanced into the open end, straight toward the same machinegun fire raking A Company in the interior open ground. When the NVA opened up, including fire from both of the flanking bamboo lines, several of Frank's men went down immediately. Frank's right platoon veered right toward the tip of the outer bamboo line and made it there, but not before four riflemen and a medic went down in the open area and were not moving. Delta could not return fire up the trenchline without hitting Alpha Company, and they couldn't maneuver in the open area. Things were not going well for them.

At the same time, Frank's left platoon had come under fire from a third parallel line of bamboo to their left. They veered left and engaged this trenchline full of enemy. When the two lead platoons split off in two different directions, Frank and his RTO, Thurman Wood, suddenly found themselves alone and exposed in the open area. They hugged the ground, receiving fire from a nearby position. Wood finally pinpointed the NVA bunker that had them zeroed in and took it under fire. As he fired, Thurman said to Frank, "you go." Frank said, "no, you go." Thurman wasn't about to leave his captain out there. Thurman fired everything he had as they both jumped up and made the dash together.

Frank's reserve platoon was positioned out on the dike, facing the open end of the big U, and they were also within easy range for the machineguns deep in the NVA defense position. The platoon leader was hit by one of these bullets, and SSG Walter Bassout took over directing the platoon's supporting fires.

The left platoon was in a face-to-face battle with a trenchline full of NVA soldiers. They duked it out at close range, quickly killing eight for sure, and maybe more. The platoon sergeant, Al Cardinal, led the assault and personally eliminated two bunkers. 1Lt Krupa commanded this platoon and moved among his men, directing their fire. One of the brightest moments inside Thon Que Chu that day was Lt. Krupa's platoon kicking the crap out of an entrenched enemy unit of equal size, with no KIAs and only a few minor wounds.

The gallant assaults by Delta and Alpha companies had been going on for about twenty minutes when JB returned to my position on the dike. It was right after Alpha had started reporting the grenades, the flanking fire, and the mounting casualties. Frank had reported about his five men down in the open area. The casualty count was accelerating. It was late, and getting dark. He asked me what I thought we should do. It was decision time.

I told JB what I knew from Delta's reports. He knew a lot more than I did about the 2/12 Cav battle on this same ground back on 4 February. And we had heard nothing about what 2/12 Cav might be doing at the other end of Thon La Chu on this particular day. As we huddled there, Lt. Preston intensely reported that his casualties had grown to twenty. Delta's report sounded even more dire. We quickly brainstormed it back and forth. What if we pushed into Thon Que Chu for the night, only to be surrounded by a large NVA force just like 2/12 Cav had been? With two machineguns in a standard NVA company, we guessed they had lots of companies. Based on our count of the numbers and types of weapons the NVA was employing, and the experiences of the day, we were convinced they had more guys than we did. And they were defending this ground like it was critical. This was no delaying action. We had already been counter-attacked once. I added that very little had gone right all day, what with Brigade sending us in broad daylight, Alpha busting the LD, difficulty getting fire support, and not really understanding the enemy's defense. But, then, I am always overly critical. My view was that things would get a lot worse in Thon Que Chu in the dark.

JB agreed, and ordered the disengagement. Easier said than done. In the Alpha sector, 2d Lt Thomas led the platoon closest to the enemy that was doing most of the damage. He was particularly valorous in regrouping his men and getting them fighting backward out of the village. They were able to extract themselves, but at high cost. As Pvt.Poole, who had been so courageous in the assault, "noticed a wounded platoon member lying exposed to the enemy weapons. Completely disregarding his safety, he moved to assist the fallen soldier. He was mortally wounded while attempting to rescue his comrade."

PFC. Leo Dunsmore was a medic supporting the platoon. His citation reads "...seeing many casualties lying fully exposed to the enemy weapons, Private Dunsmore unhesitatingly moved back into the open terrain to aid his comrades. He repeatedly crossed the bullet-swept rice paddy to skillfully treat the casualties and carry them to safety. While administering aid to one fallen soldier, Private Dunsmore was mortally wounded by the relentless enemy fire." Poole and Dunsmore were each posthumously awarded the DSC (*Distinguished Service Cross*). The DSC is a very big deal in the U.S. Army.

Lt. Thomas' platoon was covered by intense fire from Sp4 Ezel and his platoon sergeant, SFC Norwood, and they managed to get all of their wounded men back to the cover of the initial bamboo line. They eliminated a few more NVA on the outer line as they came out. It took Alpha Company more than an hour to get everyone out of Thon Que Chu and back across to Thon Lieu Coc. They brought three KIAs and more than twenty wounded with them.

Over in Thon Phu O, the Hard Hitters of C Company could not find two of their men who had gone down in the tall grass during the NVA counter-attack. It was pitch dark when they finally found them and they got back to Thon Lieu Coc after everyone else had.

The Rough Riders had the most difficult time disengaging. Their right side platoon was in the same predicament as Solomon's platoon had been in back on 8 February. They were faced with crawling back across the open area that was raked by enemy fire from deep inside the enemy position. As they started their move, the first man was hit and dropped out in the open. Frank Lambert ran out under intense fire, picked the man up, and carried him to cover behind the center bamboo line, forever endearing himself to the men of Delta Company. That platoon ended up waiting until it was pitch dark before coming out. Krupa's platoon had an easier time because his platoon had decimated the enemy over on the left side. Delta brought three seriously wounded men to the log pad for medevac at 1930 hours. Left on the battlefield were five men killed in the initial onslaught. Anderson, Dunn, Hackleman, Melish and a medic named Alley. Their location was in the open area of the killing zone, covered by several NVA machineguns. Everyone was convinced that they had been killed, but no one quite wanted to sign a statement about it. We reported them as MIA that night.

We ended the day with 370 men in the rifle companies, and the 6 of us in the command group. Down from 472 one week earlier. We had turned half of Thon Que Chu into a huge pile of rubble. It looked like Stalingrad. There was no living vegetation left in the part of the village we could see. The enemy battalion, or battalions, of the 5th NVA Regiment had been dealt a huge blow. We had confidently reported 68 KIAs for them as the day went along, and estimated a lot more, particularly out in the field in front of Thon Phu O. We conservatively estimated 100 KIA for the enemy. We, on the other hand had returned with 5 KIAs, and had 5 more lying on the ground.

ITEM NO.	TIME		INCIDENTS, MESSAGES, ORDERS, ETC.	ACTION TAKEN	INL
	IN	OUT			
18	1745		Co A & D moving in behind air strike using CS		
			gas as they move.		
19	1750		Co D receiving some incoming rds fro tree line		
			to their left flank & and now some rds coming		
			from right flank. Co D has silenced fire from left		
			flank YD683248		
21	1845		5/7 S3 request number of medevac sorties needed		
			at this time for ground control Co C & A.		
30	2300		Total of KIA's, WIA's & MIA's, also foxhole counts.		
			A - 25 WIA's, 2 KIA's FH 105. Co B - 1 WIA FH 80		
			Co C - 2 KIA, 8 WIA's, FH 101. Co D - 3 WIA		
			5 MIA, FH 84. Co A also lost 1 PRC-25.		

We had achieved that ten-to-one ratio that Bobby Mac Namara and Westy always talked about. We also had 36 men wounded, but the wounded didn't seem to count so much, statistically speaking. The kill ratio was the thing. At the rate of ten to one, we will win this war, they said down in Saigon. So 12 February in TT Woods was a victory down in Saigon. Up in Thon Lieu Coc, it was a big defeat, and the NVA still held their precious ground.

Bombarding Thon Que Chu

Gen. Tolson brings medals 13 Feb. Prince, Lambert & Broom receive Silver Stars

1LT. Bob Trimble (right) — XO of B Company — and his RTO

CHAPTER 14

REINFORCEMENTS

13 February 1968
Thon Lieu Coc
Cordinates YD683254

It was deathly quiet around Thon Lieu Coc the morning after the battalion attack. We had spent another night back in our tight perimeter. You might say we slept in. B Co had their OP at the downed bird, keeping their eye on Thon Que Chu; the other companies each had OPs out in their sectors. Nguyen slept in too.

Word came around 0900 hours that the Generals were coming. I was worried about keeping my job. JB, on the other hand, couldn't wait to talk to them. The Assistant Division Commander came first, a one-star named Oscar Davis. He brought with him our first reinforcement — a crusty old sergeant armed with an M-14 sniper rifle. We took the General up to the little building just inside the tree line from the downed bird. JB gave a full accounting of the previous day's battle and his thoughts about enemy strength. JB's opinion was that at least three battalions were required to get beyond this point to the Citadel. As they talked, I listened in. The sniper loved the little building and busied himself moving in.

Oscar left, and the two-star commanding general of the 1st Cav Division *(called the CG)* flew in an hour later. John Tolson. First off, the CG pinned some medals on the heroes of the day for both 8 and 12 of February. Tolson always brought medals, and always had a paternal smile for everyone. He was the consummate southern gentleman-type general. I could easily picture him astride his horse on the heights above Fredericksburg, wishing all the men the best of luck in the coming battle. We gave him the same dog and pony show we had rehearsed with Oscar, taking him up to the little house where you could see the battlefield. JB and the General conferred. The rest of us were definitely in "speak only if spoken to" mode.

The CG led off with a caustic comment or two, but surprisingly not about us. As they talked, you could tell he liked JB a lot. I was greatly relieved that no one was being relieved. After JB finished talking, the General talked about what had to happen: "It had to be a multi-battalion attack to get to Hue." He went on to say that he had only us at the moment, but if he could just get the 2nd Brigade up from II Corps, and if he could somehow free up 1/7 Cav from Camp Evans security, and get an armored cavalry troop and some tanks attached to us, and get the use of Marine Corps 155mm and 8 inch artillery that were within range, and if 2/12 Cav could just get involved in some way, we could take this place and roll on into Hue.

The General had a very long list of "ifs". The only ones he did not mention were his other four battalions — 2/7 Cav and the First Brigade up by Quang Tri. What were they doing, one might ask in hindsight? 1/7 Cav was guarding Camp Evans and the highway. 2/7 Cav was under operational control of the First Brigade, and it sounded like they were operating in an area of operations like the good old days — searching for the enemy. It sounded like a lot of infantry battalions guarding firebases, with a couple companies out searching for the NVA. I could be wrong about all of this. I am sure some of my friends in First Brigade will point it out. But in my view, the NVA had been found, and they were either in Hue, or were on the way there.

Right after the General departed, our new reinforcement popped an NVA soldier who had stuck his head up about 400 meters away. We were ahead one to nothing regarding snipers.

JB was not planning to wait for all of these "what if future events" to take place. Our planning began in earnest for another battalion attack. Delta Company had 5 troopers on the ground across the way. We did not want to wait. The 2/12 Cav grave site was in the same general area as our 5 men, and a skinny little kid from 2/12 Cav came in on a log bird who knew right where their troopers were. We put him with D Co.

That afternoon, Brigade indicated that support from the Marines' 155mm and 8 inch artillery would be available by 15 February. JB therefore planned to attack at first light on the morning of the 15th with or without any other battalions. It was our plan to once again have C Co cross the paddy in the dark and take Thon Phu O. A Co would be base of fire on the tree line this time. The main difference was that we would not go straight up through the killing zone of their U shaped position. The main attack would cross the LD at 0630 hours. D Co on the left would be way out to the left, to create a gap through which our base of fire company on the Thon Lieu Coc treeline could pound the enemy deep inside their position. B Co would be on the right this time. It was their turn in the barrel. I closed the briefing with "Oh, and not one swinging dick better poke his head out of the tree line before 0630 hours," or words to that effect.

We requested the Quad 50s and Twin 40s that Brigade had been bragging about sending for the past several days. They would be positioned with A Co on the tree line. These awesome weapons would have more of a clear shot into the depths of the enemy position. You might say we were going to stick it right up their "U". Brigade immediately jumped in to the planning with gusto, indicating they would CA 2/12 Cav in on our left between the highway and Thon La Chu to reinforce the attack.

The next big attack suddenly became the bigger attack. The bigger attack was also made contingent on getting air support, which meant we were not going if the weather did not improve, which meant we were not going, since the forecast was continued fog and rain. Oh, why did we ask for anything, I asked myself later. We should never have said a word. I think we could have taken them on the 15th with artillery support, and had the enemy withdrawing toward Hue a lot sooner. Failing that, we would have kicked the crapola out of a lot more boys from the 5th NVA Regiment, and retrieved our 5 fallen Rough Riders.

Predictably, the weather was awful on the morning of the 15th. And, of course, Brigade called in the middle of the night to sadly report the unavailability of the 155mm and 8 inch artillery. Oh, and no sign of any Quad 50s and Twin 40s. And by the way, we can't move 2/12 Cav either. It was the Big Attack That Wasn't.

So we kicked off "combat in cities" training on the rear side of our perimeter out of sight of the enemy in Thon Que Chu. We practiced all sorts of new techniques, like using our just-arrived flamethrower, making and firing off pole charges. We practiced taking out individual bunkers, using a base of fire and the movement of a few individuals equipped with pistols, hand grenades, and some of the aforementioned more powerful items.

The 15th was a damp, dreary and boring day. It remained that way until D Co of the 2nd Battalion, 501st Airborne stepped into the deepest of shit about five clicks north of us at the now infamous Thon Thuong west of PK 17. As they approached the village, these 101st Airborne Division troopers of course came under fire from snipers in the trees. As they deployed to assault forward, they came under intense fire from the tree line by an estimated company of NVA. As they brought in supporting artillery, they had another one of those aggravating short rounds. This one caused 3 KIAs and 7 WIAs. In short order, they were face down in the tiny furrows of the rice paddy. The 101st Airborne was definitely having their "Rendezvous With Destiny." (I used to hum to myself "Rendezvous With Destiny" when commanding Honor Guard formations and parades at Ft. Campbell.)

At 1240 hours, 5/7 Cav assumed operational control of these pinned-down paratroopers, and we put B Co and C Co in motion to go to their aid. On the way over there, C Co spotted an NVA platoon far off to the south pulling a mortar, and we blasted them with artillery. Other than that, no one got in our way, and Howard and Mike got their guys over to the battle area in reasonably short order.

We came toward the village from the flank and rear of the enemy in the tree line. B Company on the right entered the village and ran straight into NVA soldiers only 25 meters away. Their focus of attention was out toward the pinned-down paratroopers in the rice field. We had been able to cross open ground and surprise the enemy, which did not speak well of the NVA commander regarding flank security. Howard's FO brought his artillery in close. Very close. Would you believe within the bursting radius of the 105mm round? You probably don't believe that one. Howard got hit in the left arm by a small 105mm fragment that got there somehow. Everyone hugged the ground. As Howard put it, "we were scared shitless." A helicopter gunship was on the way. The enemy was deployed on the tree line facing the 101st pinned down in the rice paddy. B and C Companies were coming in beside and behind them. The NVA were between a rock and a hard place. They could only hold their ground, and they got decimated by the helicopter. The gunship "just killed them. They just killed them."

B Company and C Company stood toe to toe with the NVA well into the afternoon. The NVA finally gave up the field at about 1530 hours, leaving 58 bodies behind. 5/7 Cav had zero casualties. Zero. Not a battle for the history books. The paratroopers were able to disengage and get back to PK 17 with all their people, alive as well as not. It was a bright and shiny day of combat for the 5/7 Cav, if there is such a thing. I am always amazed by the military historian's fascination with battles in which many of our men die. Fredericksburg. Little Big Horn. I, on the other hand, am fascinated with battles in which we score 58 to zero.

Later that night, in the absence of our planned attack, Frank Lambert personally led a patrol out to get his 5 troopers back. They got right up to the edge of Thon Que Chu, and could see the five bodies lying where they had fallen three days before. The patrol could also see a camp fire about 300 more meters down the village to the south, and hear music from a radio. Just as they were making final preparations to move in and recover the bodies, an illumination round went off right over their heads. The patrol stood stock still, their hearts pounding. The tops of two NVA helmets were spotted nearby. Frank was convinced that the patrol had been compromised, and he called off the effort. The one positive thing that came out of the operation was that Frank's men were not MIA any more; they were documented as KIA. A very important distinction to their families and loved ones.

No one knew who called for illumination. JB didn't allow illumination. "The dark is your friend." It might have been some misguided fool. No one 'fessed up. Possibly it was the 5th Regt of the NVA. The enemy had not fired illumination at us in this war that I knew of, but this was their all-out offensive to take the country. Recall the flamethrower on LZ Shorty. The NVA had certainly been demonstrating a lot of capabilities lately, so why not have some illumination mortar rounds?

The Intel people back in the rear later determined that the NVA unit we crushed up in Thon Thoung that day had marched all the way from Khe Sanh to join the Hue battle. They were from the 29th or 90th NVA Regiment. They had come through that NVA forward base area that JB talked about earlier. It was fifteen days after Hue was taken over by the NVA. 80 percent of the Citadel was still firmly in their control. The NVA Commanders were reinforcing success. Going to the sound of the guns, so to speak. We, on the other hand, had gotten only one US battalion inside the Citadel, the 1-5 Marines, and it had taken until the 13th to do so. Up on the highway, it was still just us. Down to about 370 guys, by that time. It was halfway through February and there were nowhere close to enough boots on the ground. *(Not unlike in Baghdad before Petraeus showed up.)*

I remembered the 1-5 Marine guys from back in early October when we replaced them at LZ Baldy down in the Que Son Valley. They were a surly and uncooperative bunch, as I recall. Maybe they sensed where they were going. Maybe they didn't like the 1st Cav patches that my Brigade Security Platoon had painted all over the place starting on day one. Who knows? Who cares? History shows that they did a helluva job once they finally got inside the Citadel.

On the next day, 16 February, Brigade again told us to wait. The attack would have to involve three more battalions besides us, and 21 February was indicated as the big day. Our plans for the next big attack gave way to the great big attack. The main body was moving up at last. Beginning this day we started getting greatly increased artillery support, with which we began to incessantly bombard the TT Woods.

We were also beginning to feel more secure about our environment. Charles had not come over and kicked our butts, like he should have on the 9th or 10th. We had put a real hurt on him on 12 Feb. We had no trouble roaming 5 clicks away the previous afternoon to kick the shit out of yet another of his units. So, while waiting for the great big attack, we began to expand outward. We continued to "develop the battle area", as JB described it.

On the morning of 16 February, we sent C Co back across to Thon Phu O again, where they would have observation of the western side of TT Woods. Once again, Charles was not holding this good piece of ground. During the day, the Hard Hitters put accurate artillery fire on two different groups, the first one being five men, the latter was ten to fifteen men moving through the village. The NVA defense should have included Thon Phu O. It was a big tactical error on their part. We also started pounding the objective area with periodic artillery, naval gun fire, and air strikes. I made small talk with the Forward Air Controller (FAC) all day. Call sign: RASH 1. He got all of my jokes, although he liked country, not jazz. He was one of those crazy Air Force pilots in Piper Cubs who marked the targets for the fast movers.

The air strikes were awesome that day, and I took a lot of pictures. I didn't know if they were Air Force or Navy. The jets came in from the northwest, paralleling the highway, released their bombs which we could clearly see as they fell onto the target, and arced up and away down the length of Thon La Chu. Even over the roar of their afterburners, we could hear the NVA's 12.75mm anti-aircraft machinegun following them out of town, sounding like a popcorn popper.

Brigade was beginning to formulate plans for the great big attack, and our part would be to take our same objective — Thon Que Chu. I wanted to see our objective from above to formulate a better plan, and with JB's approval, I arranged to go flying with my new pal RASH 1 on 17 Feb. The C&C came in and took me up to PK-17 so I could visit my guys at our Main CP for the first time since we crossed the LD on the 5th; then we flew up to Quang Tri where the RASH birds were stationed. When I walked into my Air Force friend's quonset hut, I was not disappointed. He had the sandy hair, the freckles and the reedy voice of a crop duster. And he had the cooler full of beer. Most incredibly, there was ice in the cooler.

Visibility was good over Thon Que Chu that day, and we flew in circles at about 2000 feet while I drew pictures of the cross-hatching of bamboo tree lines that created the village. Once the artwork was completed, we made four or five dives, with RASH 1 shooting white phosphorous rockets to mark the bunkers and trenchline positions that he could see. It was great excitement, even though I should not have eaten breakfast that morning. On the third dive I was sick. On our fifth dive the NVA below were also sick - sick and tired of our foolishness. They responded with a 12.75mm machinegun making little concussions in our ears. RASH asked me if I had seen enough, and I assured him that I had. He was probably more concerned with the rancid smell of puke in the back of his plane, than the likelihood of being hit. For my part, I had figured out the weakness of their defense, and was ready to leave. The 12.75mm rounds were a little unsettling in the back seat. *(To put 12.75mm in perspective, it was the equivalent of 51 caliber. Essentially the same as our 50.)*

When we got back to his Quonset hut in Quang Tri, he gave me one of his precious cold ones before I left to go back to TT Woods. RASH 1 was simply "the grooviest cat", I reported to my fellow jazz fans at the Main CP before my return to TT Woods. I spent a little more time there, edited a few of the daily reports and generally abused my assistant S-3, Captain Mike. In retrospect, I did a very poor job of working with the rear CP while we were on the road to Hue. Out of sight, out of mind. Mike and his men did a fine job of responding to our requests and keeping Brigade informed in the absence of any help from me.

While I was gone, C Co moved across and set up in Phu O again on the morning of 17 February and had lots of activity on and off all day. They made four different sightings, engaged these targets with artillery, even used their small arms a couple times, and confirmed 3 enemy KIA. Over in the main objective area, the company FOs and the Artillery FSO continued systematically pounding the enemy's defensive positions all day. We received naval gun support as well as artillery. The 5th NVA Regiment must have been seeing the inevitability of all this right about then. *(I wonder how many of them had shell shock when they got back home, like in WW II and Korea, or did they mainly have PTSD.)*

Mike Davison left a night ambush patrol in place when they moved back across the paddy from Thon Phu O. The other three companies also put out night ambushes well out from our perimeter. Howard put his patrol across QL-1 to the north, and Frank set one up right next to QL-1. None of the ambushes had any action on the night of the 17th, so we came up with a bolder plan for the night of the 18th.

We were being told to keep pounding the objective, and to wait for the great big attack, but JB wanted to get the boys out of the perimeter. So on 18 Feb, we took the battalion on a search-and-clear operation to the east across the highway, and down to the southeast, past Thon La Chu. We had one platoon from each company stay behind in Thon Lieu Coc to assume defense of the perimeter under the command of Joe the XO. Joe and Sergeant Major McQuerry had finally gotten around Hue to Camp Evans, and they came out to join us that day in Thon Lieu Coc.

The battalion, minus the four platoons, moved out in box formation, and went all the way to a little village within 3 clicks from the wall of the Citadel. Thon Trieu Son Trung. We received a few sniper rounds but otherwise met no one. As we returned, we left ambush patrols from B Co and D Co hiding out on the far side of the highway, waiting for dark. The rest of the battalion closed back into Thon Lieu Coc for the night. It was great to see Joe and McQuerry again.

Covered by darkness, the B Co and D Co patrols moved across to the southwest side of Hwy 1 and set up by the two little roads going into the middle and south end of Thon La Chu. They were about five hundred meters apart, and could see QL-1, as well as the Thon La Chu tree line. D Co's patrol, led by ROUGH RIDER 16, was the southernmost patrol all the way down at the other end of Thon La Chu. *(16 means the leader of the first platoon. 26 was the 2d platoon leader.)* At 2100 hours things started happening. The Rough Rider patrol spotted 100 NVA through their starlight scopes, running in tight formation northwest up QL-1 away from Hue. We tried to meet them at a spot on the highway with artillery, but it took too long and the patrol could not tell if we had hit anything. By this time, I was listening to the D Co command net. I was all excited. At 2200 hours another 75 men came jogging along, this one going toward Hue, and we got the artillery in a lot faster. We worked the area up and down with artillery. I finally couldn't stand it any longer, and asked for a report in their company net directly from the patrol. The patrol leader's RTO was very polite. He asked me to please whisper.

From then until 2240 hours, ROUGH RIDER 16 reported sighting another seven smaller squad-sized groups going in the opposite direction away from Hue. At 2400 hours, another 100 man unit came along. This one was moving southeast toward Hue. By this time we had the artillery response time down to a minimum. The D Co patrol put the artillery right on target. A perfect collision in time and space. I got so excited I got involved again, whispering to the patrol for more information. This time they whispered back, "We have people running through our position, get off the fucking radio."

The D Co patrol had seen direct hits in the column. They conservatively estimated 10 killed, and continued to work the artillery up and down the road. They heard lots of moaning and yelling. Much later, at 0300 hours, the B Co patrol further north spotted a 130-man unit in indigenous uniforms, weapons and packs, moving down the road toward Hue. They appeared to be VC rather than NVA. Artillery fires were worked up and down the highway for the rest of the night. At about 0330 hours, the two patrols headed for home. The D Co patrol observed numerous blood trails and also found a communal grave in the area of their successful artillery strike on the moving target.

The enemy was moving lots of units on the night of the 18th. It was curious how they were moving in both directions. Thanks to the bravery and skill of these two patrols, we had made it a very bad night for Mr. Charles. And I never opened my mouth into a company command net again, and that was another good thing for a battalion S-3 to know.

We went on another battalion maneuver across the highway the next day, 19

February. This time we went north toward the villages along the banks of the Song Bo River, and we got into a nice little scrap when we got there. As we approached the village, we received sniper fire. The lead elements went on line; we fired a brief artillery prep, and moved forward. It was reminiscent of our attack on the 7th into Thon Lieu Coc. The enemy withdrew out the back door and turned north along the river. We walked in to find no one there but one young girl tending to her ancient father. He was too sick to travel so she had stayed with him. The young girl was attractive, so my RTO and I stood guard over them and shooed all the gawkers on through.

"Just stay with your unit, trooper."

"Yes, sir." He got my name right.

From there the two lead companies wheeled left along the river and quickly got into a firefight that went on for the rest of the afternoon. The enemy force was anchored along the riverbank. We were unable to push them further north, short of getting into a decisive engagement, so we withdrew in the late afternoon and returned to Thon Lieu Coc. As we walked back across the paddies, I gave JB my ideas about how we should attack Thon Que Chu on Feb 21.

On 20 Feb, things were falling into place. On the previous day the entire 2d Battalion, 501st Airborne, of the 101st Airborne Division, had come under Brigade control. The 1/7 Cav was relieved of Camp Evans defense. The Brigade CO now had four battalions to fight with. 2/501st Airborne would come down the big paddy and swing in from the west beyond Thon Phu O. 1/7 Cav would go further down and come in on the paratrooper's right. They would take the southern end of Thon La Chu. I think 2/12 was supposed to parallel the Perfume River toward Hue. We had yet to see the proof of any of this, however, and were carrying on with our plan to take Thon Que Chu as though it would be just us again.

My determination of the weakness of the NVA position in Thon Que Chu, gained from the ride with the FAC, was the little bamboo-lined stream that went into Thon Que Chu from Thon Phu O. The ten-meter wide bamboo thicket on our side of this stream gave us a route directly into the bottom of their U Shaped defense with good concealment and some cover. Taking the intersection of this bamboo thicket and the outer tree line of the village would allow us to then knock off one bunker at a time along the outer tree line. We would be protected by the NVA's own trenchline from fire from the other lines deeper in the village. The idea was to have one company go through the thicket, and turn left down their outer defense line. This would only take a platoon, and the rest of the company would be base of fire from the dike. As soon as the intersection was secured, a second company would go straight through the intersection and roll up the positions across the bottom of their "U". Later they would turn left and do the same thing to the interior lines. I put this plan together, got JB's blessing, and briefed it late in the afternoon to the company commanders.

I was very proud of my plan. I described it as attacking with two companies up, on a 10 meter front, but no one appreciated this little attempt at levity. The company commanders took the plan back and briefed their troops. It became apparent that the troops had a very bad feeling about Thon Que Chu. B Co would lead the attack by taking the intersection, and then clear the outer tree line. The troopers in B Co thought my plan was just about the dumbest thing they had ever heard.

Captain Frank Lambert, Rough Rider Six

Joe Arnold and SGM McQuerry at Thon Lieu Coc 20 Feb

CHAPTER 15

TT Woods — Act II

Even after receiving a few replacements, we had eighty-four fewer guys in foxholes than we started with back on 5 February. *(In Iraq it is boots on the ground, in Vietnam it was foxhole strength.)* A Co had 106 and C Co was a robust 110, but B Co was at 91, and D Co was a woeful 81. We were also missing most of the lieutenants by this time. Many of them had tried to be point men. Some out of necessity.

Manpower was the bad news. The good news was the two Twin 40mm "Dusters" that came chugging into the perimeter from PK 17 at 1820 hours on 20 February. The sniper was no longer our only reinforcement. The duster could really dust things off. *(A Duster is an 11-ton tracked vehicle with two 40mm fully automatic "Bofors" guns mounted in an open-topped turret. It fired a steady stream of explosive rounds at the rate of 240 per minute.)*

Howard had been assigned the mission of moving into my favorite little finger of bamboo to take the intersection, then turn left and roll up the NVA's outer line. Just before dark that night, Howard came to see me. He was very concerned. Some of his troopers were very upset with this mission, and some were suggesting the possibility of not going. Their complaints included the fact that they had never used pole charges before. They didn't understand the point of crawling into the objective through a bamboo thicket. They were leery about the notion of going single file down the trench and series of enemy bunkers. They started pounding Limping Scholar Six as soon as he had briefed them. Well, after all, we had encouraged them to speak up. Recalling Gregory Peck's memorable speech to the reluctant soldier in the great movie about Pork Chop Hill, I responded to Howard with the inspirational words, "I don't know what to tell you, Howard."

The 21st of February was not more than 10 minutes old when a man from C Co was killed by a misdirected artillery round that landed close to our perimeter; not the greatest omen for such an important day. A little while later, at around 0100 hours, we received an intelligence report from Brigade to the effect that the headquarters of the entire Tri Thien Front was located in Thon La Chu. We had been hearing the suggestion of this for almost a week, and JB had in fact surmised this to be the case a lot earlier than that.

The Tri Thien Front was the NVA's "Division or higher Headquarters" commanding the Hue operation. The commander would be a two or three-star general in our terms. How poetic. The **TT Front** was headquartered in **TT Woods**, and if still true, resistance should be stiff indeed.

Our plan called for everyone to move across the paddy in the dark, all the way to the paddy dike 75 meters from the enemy trenches in the tree line. Reveille comes early when you are making a great big attack, so no one got much sleep that night.

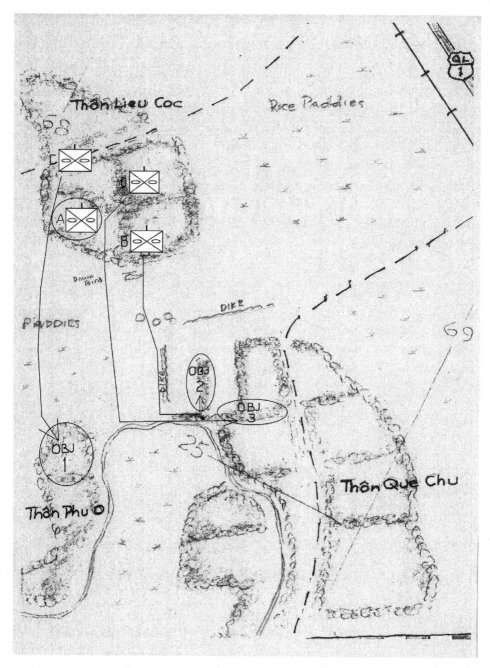

Plan for The Big Attack — 21 February 1968

At 0440 hours, A Co began moving up to the tree line in Lieu Coc to be base of fire and reserve company. I breathed a huge sigh of relief when the Limping Scholars started moving at 0450 hours. The night movement was another of the several things the troops did not like about the plan. They moved out anyway, like the good soldiers they were. I was struck by how quiet everyone was. The troops had done a great job tying everything down. Just like good Rangers.

At 0500 hours, Mike and his Hard Hitters moved silently across the open field toward Thon Phu O. Their mission would be to protect our flank again. By that time, they knew the area like the back of their hands, and could get there in the dark.

Bravo Company began moving across the open area at 0545 hours. Howard had gone back to his company the night before and explained the attack plan in much greater detail, drawing the plan in the dirt for his leaders. They understood it much better, and were ready to go. Not without fear, of course. Everyone was fearful.

Delta Co moved out at the same time from the west side of our village. Frank had the mission of following B Co through the key intersection and taking the interior lines. Both units moved with excellent noise discipline. It was eerily quiet. No one wanted to wake up Nguyen. The two companies did a fantastic job of moving across the paddy. We had gotten truly good at working in the dark. The dark is in fact your friend when you have to move around.

JB and I, accompanied by our two RTOs, followed the Rough Riders as they moved toward the LD. This took us to a position along the western tree line of Thon Lieu Coc, where we hunkered down to monitor the operation. We received a few whispered messages of progress from the company commanders. The plan went like clockwork. The Hard Hitters made it into Thon Phu O with no resistance. And at 0620 hours everyone else was also in position. B Co was spread along the dike, ready for their lead platoon to move into the finger of bamboo running along the stream. The lead platoon of D Co was hunkered down fifteen meters away along the stream bank, and the rear of their column was continuing to make its way quietly across the field. It was still dark. Everyone was in position to jump off from the paddy dike at 0630 hours, right as it began to get light. BMNT was six minutes away when the artillery began to come in. (BMNT — beginning morning nautical twilight. Sun is not up, but it's getting light.)

It was Reveille for the little people. Why wake them up, I asked myself later. It may have been the only contradiction to our plan to sneak right up on the enemy with all of our force. Nevertheless, I was feeling pretty smug about things by that time. As the last rounds splashed in, the lead platoon of the Limping Scholars entered the bamboo. Howard only had one lieutenant remaining by this time, an FNG, and he commanded the lead platoon going into the bamboo.

Seconds later, Frank reported on the radio receiving AK 47 fire. Shortly thereafter, C Co reported incoming fire in Thon Phu O from enemy positions along the tree line of Thon La Chu. And in the finger of bamboo, the B Co platoon leader's RTO frantically reported to Howard that he had explosions going off in the thicket to his front, and they were pinned down and taking casualties.

Pfc. Walter Robinson is on the Black Marble today, and may have been in the lead squad. Everything came to a stop while Howard's troops were trying to determine the enemy's exact location. Things remained stopped for altogether too long for Howard, though, so he moved forward to find the lieutenant. Howard's RTO went with him, along with the forward observer and his RTO. Just as the four of them got up to the hunkered down LT, an 82mm mortar round landed right in their midst. Everyone was wounded except the platoon leader lying on the ground. Howard was hit in several places; more places than anyone first realized. He crawled back out to the dike before he passed out.

SFC. George Klein was leading one of the other B Company platoons, and was also the senior NCO of the company. He was the "Field First Sergeant". Klein immediately took command of the situation, got the wounded back to the protection of the dike, and got the medics working on first aid. He quickly rendered a report to us on the command net radio. "The lead platoon is pinned down and a mortar round has hit the CO". Our grand plan came to a halt.

JB knew all the LTs in the battalion at all times. He spent most of his days circulating among the companies, while I spent my time attending to details. He knew that B Company was down to one officer — the new lieutenant. He turned to me and simply said, "Go over there and take command of B Co."

I handed my little NVA backpack to Burns, buttoned up my flak jacket, and took off running. The dike was about 400 meters from where I left the tree line. By this time it was light and already getting hot. As I ran across the paddy, my first thought was that I had been relieved from my coveted job as S-3, and was now the only major commanding a rifle company in all of Vietnam. But, at least there would be no more unsolicited Camels from Burns. JB had an entirely different view, of course. He knew he had no competent officer remaining in B Co. Who should he send to take command? Why, his S-3 of course. And since it was his plan, sending him over to implement it was only fair.

While I was double-timing across the rice paddy, C Co was receiving enemy mortar and 57mm recoilless rifle fire in Thon Phu O, along with receiving sniper fire from their rear. They had a few casualties. Pfc Jablonski had been killed.

When I got over to the B Co position, I was drenched with sweat and out of breath. Howard was lying in the open rice paddy behind the dike, and there appeared to be no medics working on him. They may have already patched him up best they could and it was just a matter of waiting for the medevac bird to arrive, but I didn't know that. Ever the man in charge, I dealt with my own nervousness by yelling for the nearest medic and abusing everyone about why they weren't doing something for the captain. I was still ranting and raving when the medevac bird came in right behind the dike. Howard and the other seriously wounded men were loaded up and flown away to TV Land. As it turned out, Howard came within a few drops of blood from being an etching on The Wall that day. Fortunately he is full of blood now as a retired brigadier general.

Almost immediately after the bird lifted off, in came more mortar rounds, one of which landed right where the bird had just been. Fortunately, we were all on the ground and no one was hurt. All the B Company troops were spread along the dike. ROUGH RIDER SIX was hunkered down with his guys only a few yards away along the stream that led into the village, waiting for the intersection to be taken.

One of the B Co RTOs, McDonald or Holland, handed me the handset, and I called the "pinned down LT" for a status report. I was greeted with a panicky-voiced new LT screaming about incoming fire, incoming mortars, being pinned down, and we gotta get out of here. I thought they were still in the thicket, though I had heard no small arms firing from that direction since the time I had arrived. I told him to calm down, get his facts together, and call me back. (*I think I may have heard that line from the colonel in "Thin Red Line" by James Jones.*)

I waited, and waited, and finally called him back. About that time one of the Company RTOs tapped me on the back and told me "the LT was not in the bamboo thicket. In fact he and his troops are back out of the thicket and behind the dike." Absorbing this news, I said to the RTO, "just tell the lieutenant to go back to Thon Lieu Coc and supervise the ammo re-supply point." I never met the man. I never saw him again. I do not know his name. Oh, well. Maybe he went on to make general in one of the support branches.

It was time for a meeting. "Get all the platoon leaders over here," I said to the RTO. Sfc. Klein came crawling over and introduced himself. Unlike the rest of us, Klein looked like a grownup, more like JB. Soon thereafter, three SSG E6 squad leaders crawled over; they were the acting platoon leaders. They looked like teenagers. Frank, ROUGH RIDER SIX, crawled across the twenty meters of open area and joined the meeting, which was interrupted by more mortar rounds right on our position. Everyone hugged the dirt, and again no one was hit. Dirt is good. Dirt is your friend.

I asked everyone what had happened and they all started talking. There was a bunker right at the junction where the thicket met the main tree line — the "intersection." Of course there was. From this bunker, the NVA could cover the open area between the dike and the outer tree line, as well as out through the open end of the "U" position, all the way to A Co in Thon Lieu Coc. It was the key position to their entire defense. A lot of damage had already been accomplished by this very bunker on both 8 and 12 February.

I felt stronger than ever that our plan would still work, and started selling it to the NCOs. Frank made it easy for me. The Rough Riders would handle the bunker, then B Co could come on in and take their left turn down the trench line. Klein made it even easier, recommending that we bring one of the Twin 40 Dusters across the paddy to an area behind us on the dike, from where they could shoot supporting fire over our heads into the enemy treeline. They would support the movement down the outer tree line with their awesome fire power. Fire and movement works at every level.

Turning to the three SSGs, I asked who was going to take their platoon back in to clear the tree line to their front. SSG Broom looked at the other two guys for an instant before saying he would take care of it. The CG had pinned a Silver Star on his flak jacket just a week earlier for getting his platoon back out of the paddy on the 8th. Broom seemed to take care of just about everything. In every rifle company, there always seems to be a handful of guys who do the really hard stuff. Broom and Klein were the men in B Company. And that was all it took to get back to work.

Klein said he would control the Twin 40 fire, and ran off to meet them as they came chugging out of the Thon Lieu Coc tree line. George guided them out into the open rice paddy about 100 meters behind the dike, and I ran out there to consult on how we would control the fire. As I was jogging back to the dike, an awesome event occurred. A golden stream of twin 40 fire coming from the other Duster back in Thon Lieu Coc arced across our front toward a target well down the Thon La Chu tree line. The trajectory was just like a well-struck three iron. There was a continuous rumble of exploding rounds at the target end of the shot.

C Company in Thon Phu O had reported seeing the location of the mortars when they fired at us on the dike. The NVA mortars were directly across from them in the creek bed just outside the Thon La Chu tree line. The leader of the second twin 40 crew heard the report, and spotted the mortar muzzle smoke from his observation post in the sniper's house back in Thon Lieu Coc. They let it rip, and hit the flag in the center of the green for a tap-in birdie. The mortar fire ceased, and stayed that way for the rest of the day.

When everything was set up, Frank sent his platoon forward through the bamboo thicket. Klein had the Duster firing right over our heads at the hidden bunker location in the corner until he was told to stop. Pfc. Albert Rocha, D Co's point man, located the bunker's aperture and crawled forward, dragging a ten-pound satchel charge taped to a long bamboo pole. Suddenly an NVA soldier fired at him from the bunker, hitting the hand guard of Rocha's M-16. Undeterred, Rocha kept going. His platoon leader, Lt. Fred Krupa, was right behind him as they crawled right up to the hole. Rocha took up firing his M-16 to keep the NVA's heads down, while Krupa lit the fuse and jammed the 10-pound pole charge into the firing aperture. The lieutenant could not scramble away, however, because the NVA inside were frantically trying to push it back out. Krupa had no choice but to keep pushing the end of the pole, or it was coming back to him. When the huge charge went off, it caved in the bunker, and it also caved in Krupa's and Rocha's hearing for several minutes. Out the back door hurtled a surviving NVA, and Rocha shot him dead. Thus ended the battle for the intersection.

Fred Krupa was a warrior. He returned to Vietnam in 1971 and served with distinction in the early days of Special Operations Group. SOG. Snake eaters par exellence. Unfortunately, Fred didn't make it back from that tour, and is MIA to this day.

The rest of the morning was spent with SSG Broom's guys crawling down the trench from our right to left. They would find a bunker, pop a smoke to mark their position, and Klein would direct the Duster to fire a long burst ten-to-fifteen meters in front of the smoke. Then it was rush in with the hand grenade, bunker done, on to the next one. Sgt Curtis Lentz was Broom's lead squad in most of this effort. He was wounded in the process of maneuvering his men, but stayed with the job until it was over.

As we were clearing the outer tree line, Frank's lead platoons penetrated into the village and eliminated the series of bunkers along the bottom of the U shaped position. They had their own stories to tell. While we spread out into our half of the village, Delta was meeting resistance and destroying bunkers without the benefit of a Twin 40mm Duster.

Bravo Company had cleared about five positions when they came to the end of the trench. There was one more bunker, but it was across fifteen meters of open ground, and the bunker was definitely occupied. We fired the Twin 40mm, but the bunker was protected by the thick bamboo roots, and the NVA soldier was not affected. This bunker was built to fire into the u-shaped killing zone of their defense, not out across the paddy. We needed a new idea for what turned out to be the last bunker in B Company's objective. Bring up the flame-thrower, someone said.

After a short while, a very slight young trooper wearing a big tank full of napalm on his back reported to me on the dike. He looked about 16 years old. "I can't do this", he said immediately.

"Sure you can", I replied just as fast, reminding him how he had fired it just the other day, how he had all the stuff to light it with, and so forth. All he could do is nod yes.

Totally unconvinced, the young soldier moved out for the bamboo. He looked back wistfully as he disappeared into the thicket. A few minutes later, he had moved down to the end of the trenchline, where it can be presumed that SSG Broom and Sgt. Lentz also had to persuade him to finish the job. It was about 0915 hours by that time. We all watched in awe as the young man stood right up for the whole world to see, lit his flamethrower, and it fired up just fine. As he moved forward into the open area, he sprayed a couple weak streams of flaming liquid that only reached halfway to the bunker. Then he sucked it up and sprayed a big burst that hit the target. Out popped an NVA soldier, running toward the inner bamboo line. The flamethrower man didn't swing the nozzle around to immerse the guy with napalm as he ran across the open area. (*I saw that film from Guadacanal back in the 4th grade.*) Maybe he could have. And no one fired their rifles at the NVA soldier either, because our brave little flamethrower man was in the line of fire. The equally brave NVA soldier disappeared around the corner of the bamboo rubble, running for his life. He had lived to fight another day. Well, maybe. He was also headed right toward D Company about then.

I never caught the flamethrower man's name, which I regret to this day. He was scared shitless and went anyway — the definition of courage. I hope we got him a medal. I do not know if we did. If not, I will give him one if he ever shows up.

Once we had the tree lines, and were receiving no more small arms fire from inside the village, the two Bravo Company RTOs escorted me across to the bunker at the intersection, pointing out the khaki-clad arm sticking out from the rubble. The two RTOs had been in the battalion headquarters back when I joined in January, and they had gone back down to their old company when Prince took over. It was old home week with them. They guarded me closely while we were walking about. Gunfire was still audible over on the other side of the village in Delta's area. As we moved down the trenchline, the stifling odor of death increased with each step. All the buildings in Thon Que Chu had been completely flattened. All the bamboo was shredded. The NVA had piled a lot of rubble into a line of smashed bamboo running down the center of the town, like a big wall. The destruction was beyond that of the big tornados which flatten our towns in the mid-west. There was nothing to pick through to find the family photos. There was absolutely nothing to come back to except the rich soil in the surrounding rice fields. It was simply an awful war that we were in.

The five bodies of Delta Company were down beyond the final bunker somewhere, as was the grave for the twelve men from 2/12 Cav. When we completed clearing the village of Thon Que Chu, the Limping Scholars reported a body count of five NVA that they could see, although some of the bunkers had been completely caved in by grenades and pole charges. The Rough Riders also called in another three bodies that they could see. They also caved in a lot of bunkers. It seemed that the enemy had withdrawn down through Thon La Chu, leaving a smaller force to delay us in Thon Que Chu. We modestly estimated that we had defeated a platoon-sized unit.

Less than one click south in Thon La Chu, 1/7 Cav, reinforced with a company of the 2/501 Abn, attacked from the west across a creek and into the middle of Thon La Chu. They must have come in about even with the cement block building in Thon La Chu, because they were met with intense resistance that morning. One of the 501st paratroopers won the biggest medal when his company assaulted across the stream. I read somewhere much later that this company of 501st paratroopers was practically wiped out by the NVA defending the western side of Thon La Chu. I never confirmed it. I don't want to confirm it.

We also learned later that 2/12 Cav had attacked northward toward the other end of the two kilometer long Thon La Chu. But at the time, we didn't hear much about what any of these other battalions were doing that morning. From our location we could see none of them. We thought we were going it alone again. Ignorance was bliss. We took our objective, and that was all we knew about.

The force of all three battalions advancing on Thon La Chu moved the 5th NVA Regiment and their higher headquarters out of there. In hindsight, I think the

General and some of his main force units may have begun leaving earlier, like maybe back on the night of 18 February, when we fired artillery at all sorts of people running up and down the highway. In any event, the enemy was withdrawing south toward Hue, from where hopefully they could escape into the mountains along the Perfume River. There were few if any NVA remaining in Thon La Chu when the sun went down.

The saddest moment of the campaign was watching the graves registration guys recover our five Rough Riders, and dig up the 2/12 Cav troopers nearby. After that, the skinny little guy from 2/12 Cav requested and received permission to transfer permanently to 5/7 Cav. He liked us and we liked him. I wish I remembered his name too.

That afternoon, with D Co still taking out bunkers over on the far side of the village, I had SFC. Klein assemble the B Company troops in the village. Occasional AK rounds were still coming through the trees from further down the village when Klein assembled the Limping Scholars in a perfect one mortar round circle. I started off by chastising them for not staying more spread out, and was disappointed that no one got the joke. They were some tired puppies by this time. But mainly, I wanted to express my great pride in getting to be their commander, even if for one day. I, of course, was just another FNG to those boys. Klein was "Da Man." He reminded me of all the great NCOs that I had served with in Berlin Brigade. Klein had taken command of the company when Howard went down, in the absence of an officer competent to do so, and had them organized when I got there. He was disappointed that he didn't get to command the company longer. I knew the feeling.

Not long after the company meeting in the trees, a captain by the name of Ralph Miles walked in looking for B Co. He had been sent out to assume the duty of company commander. About 6'2" and about 5' wide. Maybe 230 pounds without much body fat. Classic offensive guard or middle linebacker. He had to have been a football player, just like JB, because they hit it off immediately. Ralph always had a cheerful smile, and asked really smart questions. JB showed up a little while later and I got my job back. I was immediately on the radio, talking non-stop like always. The shooting was over so RTO Burns was not smoking.

I rendered a report to Brigade that the objective had been taken, and the Brigade S-3 immediately asked for a body count. I tactlessly reported two bodies from the bunker at the intersection. The Brigade S-3 responded irately about how there could not have been only two bodies. I commented about the smell of Thon Que Chu, invited him to come on down, and declined to conjecture further. The odor of the entire place was overwhelming until you got used to it. The facts are that the Brigade S-3 and I lacked chemistry - arrogance on my part being the main culprit. Captain Dailey had been monitoring the company nets, and reporting to Brigade throughout the day. He had reported a body count of 8 and another 15 estimated.

The County Lines also got a new commanding officer that day; a young live wire named John Taylor. John was a distinguished graduate from the ROTC program of a northeastern university. He came in to 5/7 Cav just like I had — very gung ho. John immediately began to model himself after JB, which, of course, was a good idea for any inexperienced infantry captain commanding a rifle company. He must have been lucky too, because he didn't get his ass killed in Vietnam. For the first time, we had captains commanding all four companies. A number of lieutenants joined us that day, as well. FNGs were everywhere. I had all of five weeks in the battalion. I was ancient.

The journalists arrived in early afternoon. About ten guys with cameras. We had seen no journalists since I had joined the battalion. I had just hung up on the Brigade S-3 and I didn't want to talk to journalists either. "Go talk to the soldiers" I think I said. And leave me the fuck alone, I did not say. And so they did, spending the night with our boys in Thon Que Chu, eating Cs, listening to war stories, and having a good old time.

There was a great sense of relief that the battle of TT Woods was over. "Broom is a helluva guy," I said to the B Company RTOs on 21 February — "a helluva guy."

(George Klein lived in Panama after he retired, and died in an automobile accident in 2008. SSG Broom's name is not on the Black Marble, so maybe he is still out there in TV Land.)

CHAPTER 16

FARTHER DOWN THE ROAD

22 February 1968
QL-1 Northwest of Hue

We still had five kilometers to go before reaching the giant wall around Hue, and we wanted to get the hell out of TT Woods. We assembled our leaders and briefed the plan. The LD was the Thon Que Chu tree line fronting QL-1. LD time was 0930 hours on 22 February. Route of advance — over to the highway and straight down to Hue. Objective — the railroad bridge crossing over the moat, beneath the northwest corner of the Citadel Wall. It was another movement to contact, but this time there were some other friendly units coming along.

1/7 Cav, reinforced with some of the 2/501 Abn, would be off to our right in the paddies. *(I was never quite sure if 1/7 Cav and 2/501 Abn were operating as separate battalions, or if a company of the paratroopers was OPCON to 1/7 Cav during this operation. Since this is not a history book, I am not researching it further.)* I think 2/12 Cav was supposed to come in from the west along the Perfume River. We were all headed in the same general direction, although the other battalions were pointed more toward the western approaches to Hue in order to cut off the Perfume River escape corridor.

We left B Co in TT Woods to secure one of the Dusters. It had a burned-out clutch. It was probably on its thirtieth clutch going back to WW II. I was reminded of Motor Stables in Berlin Brigade — a term for going to the motor pool and maintaining the vehicles. The essence of weekly motor stables back then was "if it ain't broke, go ahead and fix it anyway." Anyway, it gave Ralph some time to get to know his troops.

Ralph should have created a new call sign for himself, something like Linebacker. Yeah, LINEBACKER SIX. But that wasn't Ralph's style. B Co remained the Limping Scholars. For some reason I never referred to Ralph as a FNG. It was something about his size, perhaps.

The rest of us crossed the LD at the appointed time, quickly moved over to the road, and took a right. We went with two companies abreast, each in column. C Company had the road, and A Co went down the railroad tracks to our right. Alpha Company's FNG company commander did not get the chance to spend a day meeting his troopers. It was his turn in the barrel right away.

Thinking back, as we went into this campaign on 5 February we did not have as much confidence in the 1st Lt. as we did with the three captains. He looked about eighteen for one thing. It was pure prejudice, simply that. When the County Lines had been called on, their troopers totally kicked ass on February 8 and again on 12 February. Someone must have been doing something right. Bill Hussong had trained up a good outfit back in the Que Son Valley, before his time was up and he became our S-4. Bob Preston did a great job relevant to his years of experience. Two months later, on 21 February, John Taylor took command of a great company. I can't say enough about A Company in 1968.

Delta Company was in reserve behind C Company on the highway. The Rough Riders moved with one file on each shoulder of the road, ten meters between men, just like in the field manual. Just like in the movies. In front of them, C Company was deployed tactically, moving through the villages checking out everything.

The command group moved along the road near the front of Delta, along with the remaining Duster. I took the opportunity to chat with the nearest LT, Lt. Jim Bass I think, and some of his troopers as we went along. There were some smiley faces. There was a positive feeling in the air, like we had defeated all the enemy and it was just a matter of walking down to the big city.

Over on the railroad, the County Lines had their point platoon going down through the rice paddies on the far side of the railroad tracks. Their advance down the tracks had just started when a County Lineman named Jim was hit in the foot by a sniper round. He was carrying the radio for the point squad of A Co, and refused medevac because he didn't want to miss anything. He said he would catch a log bird later. Later became sooner when Jim discovered just how hurt he was, so we had a short delay while we sent him to the rear.

It was clear sailing after Alpha got moving again. By noon we had gone three clicks, reaching and clearing the village called Trieu Son Tay. It was only two clicks from the bridge into the Citadel. Coming up the highway to meet us were refugees headed north. They were bowing and smiling in typical Vietnamese fashion. Nervous... happy... scared? One could never be quite certain. And, of course, moving refugees usually means trouble ahead. One of the little old ladies told us there was an NVA Company camped in their town. "Boo-coo VC".

For the first time that month, the innocent civilians were coming our way instead of disappearing behind the bad guys... bad guys being a relative term to South Vietnamese villagers. Some of the refugees were not so innocent either. In one of the approaching clumps of women, children and old men, were two men in their twenties, at least four inches taller than everyone, wearing khaki shirts and pants. Hello. These two guys were walking right through our soldiers, whose minds were apparently on the flanks, or down at their boots, or dreaming about the girls back home, or whatever. These two men got all the way to JB before anyone noticed them as blatantly obvious NVA soldiers successfully escaping and evading through the middle of our column. I very politely asked a couple of our nearby men to please detain them. Maybe the slightest touch of sarcasm. I was in a very good mood that day.

Everything came to a temporary halt while we requested birds to pick up detainees and refugees. By 1300 hours we reported having detained 9 VCS, and a hoard of refugees. VCS was our term for enemy suspect. Not long after we reported the refugees, a CH-47 Chinook landed on the highway behind us, and all the refugees were herded up the ramp. They just kept going and going and going into the bird. Their average weight must have been about 75 pounds. Teeny little people, they were. I wonder where they went even now.

As we got closer and closer to Hue, the two lead companies took more and more time moving forward. Smoke could be seen rising beyond the far-off trees, apparently from inside the Citadel. Beyond Trieu Son Tay, the railroad was about seventy-five meters over from the highway, running down a berm that was six feet or more above the paddy fields. Capt John Taylor had the bulk of his company out of sight from the road on the other side of the railroad berm. C Company's lead platoon had reached a very small village, consisting of not more than four or five houses. The next village was big, and 300 meters across open rice fields on both sides.

About that time, we were alerted by Brigade to air-move B Co to a location way over on the north corner of the Citadel, where they would be taking control of A Troop, 3rd Squadron, 5th U.S. Cavalry. It was a good time to take a little break, coordinate with Ralph about standing by at TT Woods for pick up, and think about our next move.

The Command Group moved up to C Company's location to scope out the situation. We were just over fifteen hundred meters from the bridge into Hue. While we peered out from the edge of the trees, the troops were cooling their heels like all good infantrymen do, snacking on a c-ration, putting their future in jeopardy with a Camel, or catching a little nap.

The tree line ahead of us was the village called Thon Duc Buu. Most of the houses and trees were on the left side of the road. To the right, a huge burial yard extended well out into the rice fields. Another 300 hundred meters of open highway crossing one final rice paddy. Once there, it would only be a kilometer through continuous village areas to the bridge into the Citadel. Out to the right flank beyond the railroad berm, the only thing that broke up the endless expanse of rice paddies was a small farm out in the middle of the paddies. To our left, nothing but rice paddies for three kilometers.

Finally it was time to go. The lead elements moved out very cautiously across this open area. A Co's lead element was the 2nd Platoon, commanded by PSG. Marion Green. COUNTY LINE TWO SIX. Two was for the platoon and six meant boss man. In the 2d platoon, it was the 3rd Squad's turn to be point squad. COUNTY LINE TWO THREE.

This squad had arrived at PK 17 back on 4 February with the full complement of ten men, under the leadership of a 23-year old sergeant called Sam. Eighteen days later this squad still had seven of these men present for duty. Not bad for all we had been through. Sam was on R&R. An unlikely infantryman named Harold had been wounded in the assault into TT Woods on 12 Feb. Another trooper to remain unnamed was a reclusive and detested slacker, and had received a minor surface wound the previous day. He wasn't hurt enough to require a medic, but everyone in the squad insisted he go back to Camp Evans for treatment. He never returned, which might have saved him from a friendly-fire accident.

A wide-bodied weight lifter named Joe was the acting squad leader. When Jim the RTO was shot in the foot, the Alpha Company point squad was now down to six. Jim was a smart and good little trooper and would be sorely missed. He had joined the squad at Camp Evans, so his tour had lasted only three weeks. A man named Jacky, a tall Texan with one month in country, was the M-60 machinegunner. A short, cheerful Italian guy named John was his assistant machinegunner. John and Jacky had reported into the battalion on the same day in late January. Lee Tolley was a rifleman. He was an old timer — very experienced, very aloof, and very tall. His foxhole mate was very short, a guy named Gary. They were the Mutt and Jeff of County Line 23. Lee and Gary were also the squad slobs. Gary was a jokester, and also a dead eye with the M-79 grenade launcher. When we gave the word to continue south, this squad of six troopers moved out cautiously. They were up on the railroad berm where they had the best observation of the area.

Over on the highway, C Co's lead platoon, under the command of 1Lt John Lawrence, moved out through the rice paddies to the left of the highway. Lawrence was C Company's "go to" guy. The command group waited with D Co on the edge of the little village. After several minutes, the lead squads of C Company disappeared into the far tree line. It appeared to be more of the same — clear sailing. A few minutes later the C Company RTO reported that it was all clear, so we gave D Co the order to get on the road and move out.

A minute after the front platoon of D Company moved out on the highway, JB and our gang fell in behind them. The journalists were still with us, and maybe half of them followed our command group. As they were departing the cover of the tree line, I heard one of the older combat photographers say to the others, "we'll be okay as long as we keep close to the colonel". About ten seconds after the words were out of his mouth, AK and machinegun fire erupted all over the place.

We had gone about 100 of the 300 meters. A well-struck pitching wedge. All the Rough Riders, and everyone in our command group, swan-dived in unison off the edge of the elevated roadbed. The entire highway in front of us was empty in about one half of a second ... except for the Duster just behind us. Bullets were clanging off the armor plates and others were flying by, making their little sonic booms in our ears. It was that NVA company that Mamasan had warned us about.

The NVA had allowed the point squad of Mike's lead platoon to come right into their positions inside the village. Another crafty defense position based on ambush. The bravest of the NVA's brave were also dug into the sides of the railroad berm extending out toward us, giving them flanking fire against the men flattened in the rice paddies. They had sort of a "T" shaped defense. You could

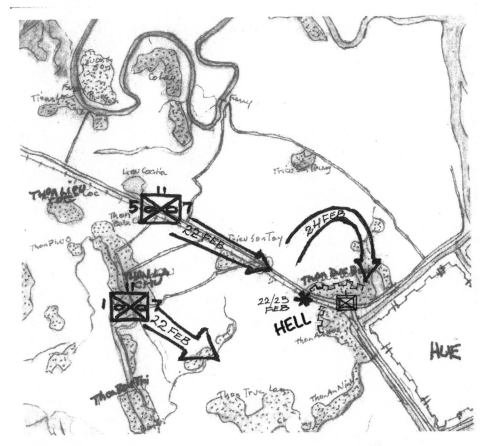

3d Bde move on Hue

say that the 5th Regiment had "Teed us up" this time. The Platoon Leader, Lt. Lawrence, along with Pfc Saunders, heroically dashed forward to pull a wounded man out of the line of fire and get his point squad back to more defensible positions. As they did so, Lawrence was shot and killed by heavy AK fire. Saunders succeeded in pulling the wounded man back. The platoon was pinned-down very close to the NVA positions, unable for the moment to do anything but see how low they could get. Things had been going too smoothly.

Up on the railroad tracks County Line 23's point man went down, and rifleman Lee Tolley moved forward and pushed him to safety off the railroad tracks. Lee then stayed up there, putting out suppressive fire against the suspected enemy positions, while the rest of the squad rolled down off the berm away from the fire that was coming from the village over on the highway. Tolley's suppressive fire suddenly stopped. Tolley lay in the tracks above them and never moved again. Lee was 20 years old and was from Arlington, Virginia.

Shortly after the fire opened up from the village, enemy fire also erupted from the burial mounds straight ahead, and from the little farm island two hundred meters

145

out in the paddies beyond the railroad. As soon as the Alpha Company point squad dived off the railroad berm, they came under intense fire coming from the farm. Jacky on the M-60, and his assistant John, had been next in line behind the point man and Lee Tolley. The other two men of the point squad, along with a medic, were behind them. Just a few meters behind them was a culvert that ran beneath the railway berm, and the three men behind John jumped up and ran through the culvert to get away from the fire. The NVA had that culvert in their sights, and all four were wounded as they went through. Wounded bad enough to be medevaced.

In the space of a minute or two, County Line 23 was two guys, Jacky and John. John had seen what happened in the culvert, and he made it back to the safer side of the railroad by climbing back up onto the berm, crawling across the tracks, and down the other side. Jacky Teakle stayed out there, in a good prone position, and could be heard from time to time pecking away with his M-60. He was the point of the spear for the County Lines at that point.

Over in the command group, we were all in the prone position in the mud off the edge of the road shoulder. A quick glance back over my shoulder revealed four or five photographers, some of them in deep mud. All that could be seen of the nearest two were big eyes and arms holding cameras aloft. After a split second of misguided mirth on my part, I heard the Duster put the pedal to the metal. He roared past us down the road toward the ambush, skidded to a stop about 100 meters from the tree line, and swung his turret to the right. Sgt. Vance Smith in command. There's something about guys in their track vehicles. They immediately sprayed a solid stream of 40mm explosive rounds back and forth across the little farm way out to the right flank of A Co. After a minute of this they traversed back to the front and did the same thing to the burial mound areas straight ahead between the railroad and the highway. The enemy fire coming into the command group area slackened noticeably, and we were able to sit up and get back to business.

The command group seemed to be protected from fire from straight ahead by a levee that ran from the highway across the paddy to the railroad. As long as we did not try to stand up we seemed to be okay. Right on schedule, RTO Burns lit two more cigarettes and offered me one.

While the Duster was taking matters into his own hands, I was on the radio reporting to Brigade and asking for a few things. Well, make that everything I could think of. JB was talking to the company commanders. The Duster was backing up and moving forward so as not to give Charles a stationary target longer than twenty seconds or so. Eventually he ran out of ammo, and withdrew back to the protection of the village behind us. In short order, he received a re-supply of ammo in the village behind us, which amazed me at the time. We put him on the C Company radio net for control, and he charged up the road to within fifty meters of the tree line and really hosed it down.

Lt. Lawrence's RTO, Pfc Trout, had quickly reported the situation to Mike Davison. SSG Pophan was the Platoon Sergeant of Lawrence's platoon, and had taken command when the LT went down. Pophan and Trout gallantly moved forward and got the rest of the point squad back to a position that offered some cover. After that, Pophan moved among the forward positions, pin-pointing enemy targets for the Duster. Trout worked on adjusting accurate artillery on the tree line. Pophan also moved among his men assisting the wounded. Saved a lot of butts, he did.

By this time, the 1st Cavalry Division appeared to be devoting its resources to taking Hue back. It was 22 February, not 4 February. But better late than never, we always say. Very soon after this enemy ambush was triggered, a Go Go Bird came on station. The Go Go Bird was a Chinook helicopter outfitted with all sorts of weaponry. I remember thanking him for coming, and after some conversation about the situation and where the enemy seemed to be, I turned him over to Hard Hitter Six for control. We had serious firepower now. I couldn't wait to see the Go Go Bird cut loose with all his mini-guns, 40mm guns, and whatever else they had on this CH-47 Chinook. Maybe things were going to be okay. Once everything was organized, everyone up forward started popping smoke to mark their positions. The Go Go Bird circled well out to the left of the highway in order to come in parallel to the front of our two pinned-down companies. The lead elements kept their smoke grenades popping as he lumbered in toward Thon Buc Duu. As soon as he got over the left end of the tree line, he was shot full of holes by boo-coo NVA gunners.

The Go Go crew never got to fire the first shot. Fortunately, the pilot was able to bank his smoking helicopter back around and head it out into the rice paddy to the left of us. He went about three hundred meters out into the paddies before he ran out of sky. The pilot sat the big bird down and got his crew out of the burning aircraft, but they were a big sitting duck out there. The crew chief came running out the back and started spraying the growing fire with an extinguisher, but it was not long before they were taking mortar and small arms fire. The incoming fire put an end to their efforts to put out the fire. Soon thereafter, a slick from their aviation battalion flew in and evacuated the crew.

The big Go Go Bird went the way of Old Dobbin, burning well into the afternoon. Helicopters have a lot of magnesium — when they burn they totally burn. By the end of the day it was a just big black spot in the mud. The Go Go Birds had been custom built for the 1st Cav, and the Division was down to only two still in service when the day started. It had some of the same technology as the Air Force C-130 gunship, and could put out a continuous stream of bullets with pin-point accuracy. The Army had decided to reserve the last one for the museum at Ft. Rucker, so that was the end of the Go Go Bird in Vietnam. They were not maneuverable enough for low level support, so it may not have been so great being a Go Go Bird crewmember dating back to 1965. *A lesson re-learned by a special operations force in Afghanistan in 2011.*

We had the Duster moving forward and backward on the highway, providing direct fire support when called for by SSG Pophan. Over on the right, COUNTY LINE SIX had done a good job of deploying the rest of A Co, and was in a stiff firefight with at least a platoon dug into the mounds well out to the right of the railroad berm. The initial effort had involved suppressive fires to help get the lead squad back out of the enemy's killing zone. Taylor did a great job moving among his elements and moving up to where he could get accurate artillery fire coming in. His days as an FNG had ended abruptly, short of twenty-four hours.

The NVA had a few stout bunkers built into the burial mounds, joined with inter-locking trenches. It was another strong defensive position protected by lots of open ground to traverse. The County Lines were able to take out most of the enemy in the nearest trenches, and at some point their RTO reported a body count of 15 NVA. A Co had crossed this open area with excellent spacing, or they would have lost a lot more people.

Over on the road, C Co continued to be confronted by the enemy positions to their front and the positions in the railroad berm to their right. We began to think that if A Company, who was having some success, could sweep through the burial mounds on the right, we could flank the enemy in the village and reduce the pressure on C Co. Just as we were about to order up a big artillery preparation for A Co's push through the burial mounds, our new Fire Support Officer's radio stopped working. He had been with us for about two hours.

Where in the hell did John Seymour go, I asked myself. His time was up. John Seymour had left us that morning to be on staff at the battalion headquarters of 1/21 Arty. I vaguely remembered it. Way too busy. Way too tired. John had wasted no time getting on a Huey right after introducing us to his replacement. The new artillery captain was doing fine until his radio gave out. He was still abusing his RTO, as the Duster moved back to where JB and I were hunkered down in the ditch beside the road.

Both of our radios were busy at the time. JB was on the command net; I was talking to various support people on other nets. There was no radio available for the artillery captain. JB started yelling for someone to get him one, and getting no response, he jumped up and ran up the road as far as the levee. There was a soldier sitting there, and JB was going to send him looking for another radio. Who should it be but young John, the assistant machinegunner from County Line 23. John Montalbano.

Montalbano was sitting there getting over his frightening experience of crawling back over the tracks. He was also was wondering where the rest of his squad was. Next to him was a man from C Company. The two soldiers had just been talking about their experiences when an AK 47 round went through the C Co man's temple. The presence of the levee was no guarantee. (*According to John years later, the man survived. Amazing.*) JB was yelling at John to run and get us a radio, and John was screaming back at JB to run and get him a medic. Surveying this scene from atop his Duster, it occurred to Sgt. Smith to offer the use of his radio to the FSO, which resolved the situation. JB returned and resumed running the war as if nothing had happened. JB only thinks about right now and what's next. (*He hasn't changed.*)

The new artillery FSO climbed up onto the Duster and hunkered down behind the radio. He had not completed his first call when a B-40 rocket came right down the road and hit the metal parapet dead center. My mind's eye saw it coming in slow motion. The blast went off right above our heads down in the ditch. The firing mechanisms of the Duster's guns did not survive. No more Duster.

And no more Fire Support Officer. He was wounded so severely in the head that no one gave him any chance of survival. It was truly ugly. He was evacuated in the C&C bird as soon as we could get him back to the village behind us. He was a goner in my mind. Ah, but the human body is tougher than steel, and the helicopter is a wonderful invention. The captain later returned to Michigan with a steel plate on top of his head and led a very productive life, so the story goes. Medical miracles happened every day in that war.

The C Co lead platoon was mostly on the left side of the highway when they entered the village. During the course of the afternoon, when the A Co effort stalled in the burial mounds, we committed D Co between the railroad berm and the road. D Co was able to move up along the base of the railroad berm and take out the spider holes dug into the berm on C Co's right flank. As a result, C Company was able to work themselves backward out of the paddy to our little village. Unfortunately, 1st Lt. John Lawrence's body lay on the ground right in front of the NVA positions. To try to recover him would have cost a lot more. We would get him later. *(This was a hard earned lesson in Vietnam, which has to be relearned in every war. Places like Mogadishu in Somalia, for example. Actually, some people are incapable of learning this lesson. Emotion takes over. It becomes very personal.)*

C Company medevaced four seriously wounded men when they got back. They had another four who stayed in the field with minor wounds, among them their captain — Mike Davison.

Most of the journalists did not seem to stick around for all this excitement. Five minutes after the fire started, the photographers behind us were gone. One of our veterans told me many years later that a few of these photographers were real troopers and stayed with us for quite a while that day. Maybe so. A picture did show up in one of the pictorial histories of the war that showed JB, me, and our two RTOs walking up the road. The Duster is on our left. The caption is "shortly after passing this road marker they were ambushed." Actually, it was the journalists who got ambushed. For us it was regaining contact with some of the same bad boys we had been fighting all month.

The Command Group worked its way back to the village. We set up a log pad in the back. Log birds were bringing ammo in and taking casualties out. Some of the journalists had been the first to be evacuated. *(I learned in a letter from home that an interview of JB appeared on TV shortly after the 22d, so some journalists must have stayed around long enough to talk to him. I would add, however, that I have not seen any additional published photos that I can recognize as being about that day.)*

149

For the first time in the Hue campaign, Jim Matthews, the S-1, was shipping up lots of replacements. Late in the day, JB was back at the log pad, meeting and greeting people while talking to a newsman or two. I stayed at the front of the village, coordinating air support resources. My RTO and I had moved back to the forward edge of the village to a position behind a stone and cement column marking the entrance. We were throwing smoke grenades of various colors as a reference point for the pilots when they first arrived in the area.

Up the street from the back of the village came a skinny little kid from the Deep South. All freckles, teeth and new fatigues. He just had to know the location of D Co. "I have to report to them right away . . sir." Delta Company was taking out bunkers in the berm one at a time, I told him, adding that he was to sit down and wait. He was determined to report for duty, and continued to pester me on and off for about five minutes, interrupting business. He just wouldn't stand still for waiting until later. I finally told him to go over to the railroad, go left, and he would find the rear end of the Rough Riders. Next thing we knew, the kid is up on the berm walking across the skyline on the railroad tracks. He went about 100 meters, with everyone screaming at him to get off the berm. He was silhouetted for the entire eastern world when a mortar round landed on the tracks, maybe ten meters in front of him. The kid never wavered. He just kept on keeping on. The second mortar round hit the tracks 100 meters behind him. Then the third round hit the base of the stone column that my RTO and I were peeking out from, knocking us backward on our butts.

I never felt a thing. I was momentarily knocked out by the concussion, and sprinkled with lots little fragments, but my RTO was hit pretty badly on his shoulder. It was a classic job of adjusting indirect fire by the NVA. They sent a round, added 100 meters, and went right 75, achieving a direct hit on the asshole throwing smoke rounds in the street.

As the day went on, we were not making much progress toward the enemy in the village or the burial mounds across the road. It was getting late. The air power had gone home. It was time to disengage and organize for tomorrow. By 1800 hours, we had most everyone back and began setting up our perimeter.

A Co had one man who could not be found, Jackie Teakle on the M-60. They brought back eleven WIAs serious enough to medevaced. The County Lines also had another four who declined medevac. It seemed like we were getting down to the hardcore troopers — guys who really wanted to visit the Imperial City. Garryowen rowdies.

D Co had one casualty who was also still out there, impossible to reach. All three companies had a man on the ground, all covered by nearby fire from yet-to-be-detected bunkers. Some of our attachments shared in the grief. A Black Hat and an engineer were also medevaced. Some members of the crew of the Go Go Bird had been hurt. It had been a very rough afternoon. We were down to 350 troopers in the four line companies. We dug in for another night in another perimeter 300 meters across open ground from a determined, well dug in NVA force of undetermined size.

The Rough Riders were able to retrieve their man once it got dark enough. A couple hours later, who should come walking in out of the dark but Jacky Teakle, sporting a big grin. A Co had found their man. Actually, he found them. John and Jacky were the only men left from their point squad. They were re-assigned to other squads, and County Line 23 no longer existed for the time being. I think this may have happened to a lot of point squads during the first half of 1968. Here today, gone tomorrow.

The next day was a little better, but not much. At 0930 hours, the Limping Scholars finally made the air movement to link up with A Troop, 3rd Squadron, 5th Cavalry, a real armored cavalry unit. Like 1/1 ACR in the Que Son, they were mounted in armored personnel carriers and M-60 tanks. They were about four clicks from us across the paddies to the east. How they got there I do not recall; it may have been by ship coming in on the Perfume River. LIMPING SCHOLAR SIX's mission was to bring them over to us on the highway and give us "firepower and shock action" — the motto of the Armored Corps.

Bravo Company moved out through the rice paddies with the track vehicles, and went about one click before they came to a stream that the tanks were unable to cross. They quickly decided to leave a few of the armored personnel carriers to protect the tanks, and forge ahead with the rest. By late morning, they made it to within 400 meters of our position before several of the APCs suddenly got mired in the mud. We could see them sitting out there in a little circle, very close to the site of the burned up Go Go Bird. There would be no firepower and shock action for today.

We decided not to wait for them any longer, and crossed the LD in the attack at 1115. A Co went farther out beyond the tracks to flank the enemy in the burial mounds. Once the burial mounds were under control, D Co would attack between the railroad and the highway, and then sweep left across the highway into the village, hoping to flank the main enemy positions. Along the way, we hoped they would recover C Co's lieutenant. B Co had encircled the APCs in the rice paddy, and we had them attack forward from this position into the far left end of Thon Duc Buu. The Hard Hitters were in reserve and provided a base of fire from the forward edge of our village.

When it was time to go, B Co deployed on line with two platoons in clear view to everyone, the NVA and us. Supported by accurate artillery prep on the tree line, they made a very brisk attack that carried them into the left end of the village. I watched them in my binoculars, and you couldn't miss their new Company Commander — Big Ralph. He looked like two guys next to everyone else. Ralph's presence was very conspicuous going across the open area, and he apparently was no less visible later during a stiff firefight that went on all afternoon inside the village. Ralph got off to a very good start. I missed Howard, but the Limping Scholars were good to go.

And Klein was his usual tough and courageous self, and he led his platoon in repulsing an NVA counter-attack later in the afternoon. He was wounded in the fight but stayed firmly in command of his platoon, along with helping his new company commander. George had the knack for helping new company commanders, and for that matter S-3s.

Over on the right, the County Lines neared their initial objective before they came under intense mortar fire, suffering sixteen wounded. This killed the momentum of John Tayor's advance, and rather than wait for A Co to clear the mounds, JB immediately committed D Co. They attacked forward between the railroad tracks and the highway, and they too came in contact with the enemy dug into the burial mounds. The two companies on the right side of the highway were quickly engaged in a stiff firefight with the enemy straight ahead of them. We had ARA birds in support, and they were taking hits. We had a Troop B White and Red Bird team bird spotting burial mounds with holes in the top. The rest of the afternoon we traded fire with the boys from the 5th NVA, trying to find and eliminate their key positions.

At about 1620 hours, a Cobra gunship came straight down the highway from the north. As it went by a hundred feet up, it was the coolest looking helicopter anyone had ever seen. Coming toward us it looked just like a big shark, and sure enough, it had a shark's mouth painted on the nose cone. For the next several minutes we had the Cobra coming straight down the highway making runs under the direction of the Alpha Company forward observers. His empty machinegun cartridges bounced noisily off the pavement all around us.

John Montalbano remembered it well. In his new squad, he was again on point for A Co. He was now a rifleman. The unmarked Cobra didn't look like a fat little Huey. It looked more like a big insect hanging under a rotor blade. It was coming right toward them in the burial mounds and John thought he was going to die right there. The Cobra began firing at the NVA targets just beyond them. Everyone was very impressed. As John put it later, it was "like going on a blind date, meeting a 300 pound girl at the door, and finding out that the fox standing behind her was your date."

At the time of the Cobra's arrival, the new squad that John had joined was leading A Co's effort against a stout bunker that had the entire attack bogged down. It was dug into the top of a domed burial mound, located inside a knee-high rectangular wall, surrounded by open ground. It contained maybe three, possibly four NVA. It was also protected by fire from other NVA riflemen in yet-to-be discovered spider-holes. John, and three other troopers named Phifer, Evans, and Bishop, crawled to the base of small wall surrounding the burial mound. They approached from what appeared to be the bunker's only blind side. The four of them hunkered at the base of the wall planning their next move, and it was getting late.

Phifer led the way, jumping up and running to the base of the burial mound under NVA fire from other positions. He was joined by Evans, while John and

Bishop covered them by fire from the little wall. They were frozen there for a while until Phifer could stand it no longer. He suddenly climbed up on top of the mound, and was silhouetted against the sky for everyone to see as he pulled the pin from his grenade. He threw it in the hole on the top of the bunker, and it flew right back out. Fortunately for everyone, the grenade rolled down the opposite side of the bunker before it went off. Phifer scrambled back down, and the four men discussed how to get a grenade in the hole that would stay in there. Phifer crawled back up on the mound again, led off with a few rounds from his M1911 Colt .45 pistol, followed with the grenade, and went back to the pistol for a couple more shots before rolling away from the hole. The grenade went off inside the bunker with Phifer still lying on the side of the dome.

After Phifer scrambled off, Jerry Evans crawled up to finish off any surviving occupants with his pistol. As he was firing into the hole, he was shot and killed by an AK 47 round fired from a concealed position. Jerry was from Holland Patent, New York.

Knocking out this bunker allowed the company to penetrate into the burial mounds. Reducing this bunker also allowed D Co to move forward and advance across the road into the village, where they got in another stiff firefight. Phifer and Evans each received the Distinguished Service Cross for their actions that day.

Meanwhile, B Co was nose-to-nose with the NVA at the other end of the village. It went on all afternoon. On the right side of the railroad, A Co advanced well into the burial mound area, but continued to meet stiff resistance from more positions they were unable to see. We were split up across a wide front, with all three companies in contact. It was getting dark. We couldn't employ our big guns — the artillery — while we were locked in with the NVA. We were right where he liked us. It became an easy decision to disengage once again and go into our same battalion perimeter location.

B Co returned to the APCs out in the paddy. They had worked to dig themselves out of the mud. 5/7 Cav was back where we had started the day. We had killed another 12 NVA by body count, and we estimated another 12. A Co had lost Sp4 Jerry Evans to The Wall, and had seven more wounded. Bishop got a Silver Star. John's medal got lost, which figures since he was the FNG in his new squad. B Co suffered five men wounded, and D Co had fifteen wounded, mostly by mortars. Another very rough day.

As we were pulling everyone back into our perimeter, my skinny little southern pal came back through, this time being carried in a litter. But he was still smiling. He had made it to the Rough Riders the previous day in one piece, but was less fortunate on his second day in combat. I thanked him for coming and told him he would be just fine. The war had lasted twenty-four hours for the kid. Hopefully he is still talking about it somewhere. That evening I wrote up Sgt. Vance Smith for a Silver Star, each of his three crewmen for the BSM(V), and sent the papers to the rear to find their way to their parent unit. We never saw those guys again, and I hope they got their medals.

"Good Morning Vietnam" greeted us again on the morning of 24 February. The enemy inside the Citadel had been pushed back to a very small enclave on the southwestern wall, and the battle was nearing its end. We got intel that night about the NVA moving out of Hue, and we figured there was only a small delaying force remaining in the burial mounds and the village. The way they were dug into the burial mounds, though, we could suffer a lot more grief while clearing them out. JB decided to bypass the village of Thon Buc Duu by circling way out to the left through the paddies and make a dash for the northwestern wall. Troop A, 3/5th Cav, had gotten their APCs unstuck during the night and were ready to go. We formed a combined arms task force consisting of B Company and Troop A, 3/5th Cav. JB made me the Task Force Commander, and my mission was to get to the moat and turn left to clear about one click of the road that paralleled the moat and wall.

JB went with two companies to sweep back to the west through the villages along the moat and get to the railroad bridge. We moved out at 1200 hours on 24 February. JB led off with D Co leading, followed by C Co. He kept A Co in reserve at the previous night's perimeter, guarding the packs.

By 1340 hours, my lead elements reached Phase Line Red, a small stream running straight north out of the moat. Resistance was non-existent. Somewhere along the way we linked up with the rest of A Troop's M-48 tanks, and became a much more powerful-looking task force. Over with JB's operation on the right, D Co found lots of abandoned positions, ammunition and other stuff in the villages.

The combined arms task force moved directly to the moat — Phase Line White. I forgot to give this task force a name. We went left up the road, as directed, and met no resistance. At least the infantry part of the Task Force met no resistance. When we arrived at a small bridge crossing the stream that fed into the moat, it was not strong enough for a tank.

The tankers had stood just about enough of being left behind and missing out. Consulting with no one, the lead tank sailed off the bank and turned left up the moat. After all, the moat was only about 30 feet wide. A piece of cake for any self-respecting M-48 tank. The driver had a maniacal gleam in his eye as he gunned the 50-ton vehicle out into space. Water went everywhere. The tank went about ten yards up the black water of the moat before churning to a halt, and started sinking into the ooze. In no time at all, the rising water came in the driver's hatch and moved upward toward the turret. The driver's eyes were even more maniacal as they disappeared beneath the water. The tank sank nose first into the rich, gooey mud that had been accumulating for somewhere beyond a thousand years. The water arrived at the top of the turret and the tank commander finally bailed out. We stood mesmerized on the bank as the gunner and the loader frantically pulled themselves out through the in-rush of water flowing into the now submerged hatch. Amazement quickly turned to grief as I started counting the seconds after the turret had disappeared beneath the inky black water. At least half a minute went by, with three guys swimming toward the tank, when the driver burst through the surface, gasping for air. He was greeted by a hearty round of applause.

The tank platoon leader was standing by me by the time the driver surfaced, and I greeted the lieutenant with some really mean spirited comments. It was the single dumbest thing I saw in the war, and I saw plenty of dumb things. The sunken tank was represented only by the tips of two radio antennas sticking up, looking like a U-Boat.

We moved on without the tanks to seize our objective. In the meantime, D Co had turned right at the moat and was moving in the opposite direction toward the battalion's primary objective on QL 1. Not long after the Rough Riders turned westward, they came under small arms fire from positions blocking the road. JB deployed C Co to their right to flank this roadblock, which resulted in a short but intense firefight. Sp4 Wilt was on point when D Co came in on the enemy positions. He was mortally wounded, but not before locating the enemy positions and directing the squad's fire against it. The NVA roadblock was anchored on a machinegun bunker. Sgt Tapia, a squad leader, along with Sp4 Kennedy, a rifleman, assaulted this bunker covered by fire from the rest of their squad. When they destroyed the bunker with grenades, the remaining NVA withdrew out of the area. The objective was seized by 1610 hours.

At 1625 hours, we were informed that the Marines and the ARVN had regained control of Hue. All units were alerted about NVA units attempting to breakout of Hue toward the mountains to the west. A little later we heard about propaganda speech material captured from NVA within the city. One document dated 16 February bragged about killing 1000 GIs, one tank, and 2 choppers. Another one of their units had supposedly killed 300 GIs north of Hue. It may have looked like that to the NVA, what with all of us lying face-down in the rice paddies on the 8th and 12th.

The rest of the afternoon, JB had Frank and Mike turn back up QL 1 toward the rear of the roadblock that we had bypassed that morning. This would complete the circle around the enemy in the burial mounds and come in on him from the rear. C Co went on the right of the road, swept unopposed through the village of Thon Duc Buu, and recovered the body of 1st Lt. John Lawrence.

D Co went on the left side of the road. They reported abandoned company-sized fortified positions as they went along. They had no contact until they came to the rear of the burial mound area, where they ran into one last defended bunker, 50 meters in from the highway, and surrounded by flat open ground in all directions. The bunker was occupied by a couple NVA soldiers intent on fighting to the death. Everyone else had withdrawn to the southwest, headed for the mountains. The NVA always seemed to have someone who would stay behind in a perfect position to take up a lot of your time, knowing full well they were going to die. Just like those boys in Thon Que Chu back on 21 Feb, and again that morning along the moat road. A major difference between eastern and western cultures. This bunker held the attention of D Co for quite some time, until our little task force of B Co and Troop A, 3/5th Cav came back down the road and rejoined the battalion.

Bring up a tank, someone said. After a brief discussion among JB, Frank, the tank commander, and various other leaders, the tank commander conducted a brazen, un-supported, frontal attack against the bunker. He drove his M-48 tank to within five yards of the bunker, lowered the muzzle of the 90-mm gun right into the rim of the hole, and let 'er rip. Firepower and Shock Action.

While this was going on, the 1/7 Cav had two companies pinned-down in the rice paddy not more than one click away to the southwest. They had been there all afternoon, having a very bad day indeed. Too bad we didn't find out about it. Too bad no one told us to move over there. There were no streams to cross in that direction, and we might have been able to move those tanks over and provide some real firepower. As it was, we ended the day with C Company continuing up the highway and joining A Co in our original perimeter. D Co & B Co, along with our armored cavalry friends, created a perimeter in the area of the railroad bridge over the moat.

When we got to the bridge we had the honor of erecting a sign sent in by Brigade. It was an 8 X 4 sheet of plywood with the patch, and was captioned "WELCOME TO HUE — compliments of Third Brigade First Cavalry Division." It was Bill Hussong's only screw up of the campaign for not sending us any yellow paint with which to add "5th Battalion 7th Cavalry". Probably a good thing.

The command group set up for the night in a little house about fifty meters from the bridge. We didn't sleep in a hole in the ground for the first time in three weeks. Unknown to us at the time, the 3rd Brigade S-3 rendered a report to Division that evening about the murdered people. In a little village 2.5 clicks out in the paddies toward the mountains the attached 501st Airborne discovered civilian bodies in open graves. The report read in part, "...several groups of women and children and old men which had apparently been murdered by enemy elements in the area. Several victims were found in ditches, some dismembered, some shot in the head. Some were found as if they had been huddled together in family groups. Some were apparently thrown into family-type protective bunkers." It was estimated to have happened two or three days earlier. This finding kicked off a thorough search of all the village areas surrounding Hue over the next several days, and resulted in the discovery of more than 3000 innocent civilians murdered by the VC and the NVA as they escaped from the Hue area.

25 February was the official end day for the Hue battle. The last NVA resistance on the south wall was crushed, and the NVA flag was replaced by the South Vietnamese colors. We consolidated the entire battalion into a perimeter by the bridge that day, from where we conducted local patrolling. It was a quiet day of rest and re-supply for us.

At about 2100 hours that evening, B Co engaged four NVA soldiers attempting to escape. They had swum across the moat, and stumbled into our perimeter. After a brief shoot-out, two were killed. The other two were captured by Sp4 Dziengowski, who ran them down, firing over their heads until they stopped. By the time we reported the capture of these two NVA soldiers, we were told that a bird would pick them up in the morning.

The US Army does a lot of training about prisoners. We use a cue word full of "S's". Seize, secure, segregate (officers from enlisted), safeguard, and speed them to the rear. It was all about S. We had arrived at the safeguard step when Sergeant Major McQuerry came to me about the prisoners, saying "It could be a problem keeping these prisoners alive tonight if we leave them in B Company."

So, we brought the two NVA soldiers into our command group's little house beside the highway. It took a little while for them to stop thinking they were going to die any second. It took a lot longer to get them to accept crackers from our C-rations. Eventually they started talking to our interrogator. They were part of a battalion that was decimated by artillery a few days earlier while attempting to enter the west wall gate. Before we learned much more, though, their total exhaustion took over. We could not keep them awake, so we tied them up with commo wire and tucked them in for the night. One slept wedged against the wall next to me, the other slept against the other wall next to someone else. We safeguarded the shit out of those boys, while higher headquarters did not exactly speed them to the rear.

Had we been aware of the 3000 murdered civilians soon to be found in the Hue area, we might have been tempted to leave the two NVA prisoners with the Limping Scholars for the night.

CHAPTER 17

PURSUIT

26 February 1968
Railroad Bridge into Hue
Coordinates YD 733233

Brigade expanded our area of operations on 26 February to include the villages along QL-1 outside the western wall of the Citadel. 1/7 Cav and 2/12 Cav were tied up with the Perfume River villages. Delta cleared the villages in the western shadow of the wall, as far south as the junction of the moat with a small river called the Song Sau. They met no resistance. Alpha and C Co searched the villages to the northwest, and Bravo Co went northeast. The three companies found all kinds of abandoned ammunition and equipment, along with many dead NVA soldiers in bunkers and trenchlines, but no evidence of murdered civilians. The atrocities of Hue happened along the Perfume River, and also in the suburbs east of Hue where some enemy units escaped toward the ocean.

That afternoon, we learned from the Huong Tra District Chief that an NVA battalion had moved into Thon Phuc Yen, about seven clicks straight north of the Citadel. Phuc Yen was a sizable village across the snake-like Song Bo River from TT Woods. Just across the river from our little scrap on the 19th of February. Our orders were to pursue the enemy in that direction starting the next morning.

We headed out early on the 27th, going northwest up QL-1 in a column of companies. Based on the way our companies had been positioned the night before, we ended up moving in alphabetical order. We did not "take turns." We always tried to move without having companies stumbling through each other. Alpha led us up QL-1 to Checkpoint 1, a road going east toward Thon Huong Can. Checkpoint 2 was the bridge crossing the Song Bo in Thon Huong Can. We had checkpoints, phase lines, and objectives. Infantry tactical doctrine the whole way. After pushing back occasional snipers along the way, Alpha crossed the bridge and secured the north side by 1200 hours. So far so good. From there we advanced northward against light resistance straight through Phase Line Green and on to Phase Line Pink. Pink? What was I thinking about? Had we run out of colors?

We consolidated on Pink as daylight began to fade, one and a half clicks from the alleged location of the NVA battalion. Thon Phouc Yen was on a peninsula formed by the river, and we sat on the open end. There was a ferry out the far side of Thon Phouc Yen, but no bridge. If Mr. Charles was still there tomorrow, we could trap him on this peninsula. There would be hell to pay. For both parties. And the real estate value for the innocent civilians would be taking a hit as well.

As the sun went down, we were back up to 389 fine young men in the four rifle companies. We had another 8 straphangers in the command group, up from the

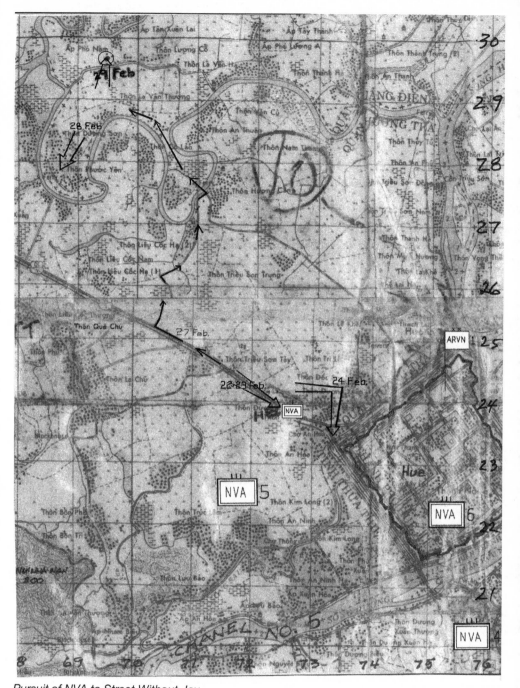

Pursuit of NVA to Street Without Joy

six we started with. We also had our normal attachments, like a squad from the 8th Engineers, and the pathfinders who always traveled with us. We had marched 8 clicks that day and no one had been hurt — amazing. The War was over. We would be home by Christmas.

That night we put the 1st Platoon of Delta Company in an ambush site on the other side of the river, in case more enemy units came along. I don't recall how they got across. The platoon must have loved being over there by themselves in the dark, picking the leeches out of their pants from crossing the stream. The Password for that night was LAST PACK. Not a happy thought for young Burns on the radio.

At first light on the 28th, our supporting 1/9 Cav white bird scouted ahead of us as we moved into the peninsula, and they reported the presence of NVA observation posts on the tree line of the village. The tree line was Phase Line Red for our move into the peninsula. A good choice of color.

As we began to deploy, B Co immediately spotted an NVA squad trying to move out of the peninsula along the Song Bo north of us. The B Company FO put 105mm artillery right on top of them. Shortly thereafter, they spotted another 40 NVA moving at the double time through the same area, and again engaged with artillery. Our favorite Air Force guy, RASH 1, came on station and reported on the results. 10 NVA were killed by body count, and another 15 KIAs were estimated. The enemy was moving out of the peninsula and heading further north, but we did not know if this was their lead element or their rear guard.

It did not take long to find out. As we neared the Phase Line Red tree line, we came under small arms fire. We responded with ground-shaking air strikes only 150 meters in front of us, then advanced across 100 meters of open rice paddy into the trees against light resistance. Delta went through the center of the tree line, and C Company extended to the river's edge on the left. It was not long before small arms fire began to build against D Co, so we maneuvered B Co to their right, giving us three companies up. We kept A Co in reserve back on Phase Line Pink securing the packs.

We dealt with increasing snipers and mortar rounds all morning, as we penetrated further into the village. A lot of support was employed all day. Scout birds. Gunships. Air Strikes. I talked non-stop on the radio. We found lots of enemy positions and abandoned stuff. We detained several people as we moved through, two of whom were on the ARVN's shit list and were sent to the rear by helicopter.

By 1700 hours we had advanced three quarters of the way through the village of Thon Phouc Yen, when Bravo came up against an NVA unit at hand grenade -throwing range. They were armed with AKs, machineguns, and determination. B Co sustained four WIAs that we later medevaced. The enemy position facing them was at least a platoon, maybe a company. About that time, we received new intel that the "K-2 Battalion" had escaped out of Hue to the village of Ap Pho Nam. This village was straight north from the peninsula we were on, across a small tributary of the Song Bo. Only one click from Alpha Company back on PL Pink. Maybe this was the same battalion we faced in the peninsula, maybe not. The NVA had an odd assortment of names for some of their units, and maybe we were sandwiched between two battalions.

Not knowing exactly what remained in front of us, and being a little concerned about getting trapped by a larger force on the peninsula during the night, we disengaged before dark and established a strong battalion perimeter back on PL Red. It was a quiet night.

The next morning, 29 February, we swept through the peninsula again. This time we were deluged with women, children and old men who had come up out of their underground bunkers. The NVA were gone. It was time to move on. 5/7 Cav swung around to the right and headed north out of the peninsula toward the supposed location of the K-2 Battalion. A Co was in the lead. For the first time since 4 February, JB employed the services of our C&C bird, and it was good to get back aloft where we could see all the terrain. It was also good to see Bob Frix and his crew again. I had not seen them since they dropped me at PK-17 back on the 4th. Bob was a 1961 graduate from West Point, and commanded the Brigade Flight Detachment. He routinely flew C&C for 5/7 Cav.

A Co moved briskly across the paddies northeast from PL Red, and arrived at the little footbridge that crossed the tributary separating us from Ap Pho Nam. As they crossed the bridge in single file, they started receiving small arms fire from their right. We also had the Brigade Aviation Platoon's scout birds working for us that afternoon, rather than 1/9 Cav teams. Their call sign was SNOOPY. They even had the little pooch painted on the bubble of their birds.

Snoopy reported receiving small arms fire every time he neared the main village 400 meters inland from the footbridge. That would be the K-2 Battalion, we figured. Or maybe more. Right after the sniper fire started we got an ARA gunship headed our way. Lots of combat power. It was time to get across the tributary and pin the enemy against the river on the north side of Ap Phu Nam.

All of A Co got across the footbridge, and began to expand outward. They quickly got into a stiff firefight a couple hundred meters eastward up the bank of the stream. The NVA's line was anchored on the thirty-meter-wide waterway and extended northward. In short order Alpha had several men hit. Pfc Groat was severely wounded, attempting to knock out a primary enemy bunker with hand grenades. A trooper named Martin was killed pulling wounded men to safety. Alpha got the artillery going. By that time half of B Co had also made it across the river, covered by a lot of artillery fire in an arc around our bridgehead. The battalion was split by the river, and it was getting late. Things were looking a little precarious.

JB dropped me off on the south side of the footbridge, and quickly went back aloft. I had my PRC-25 on my back, and was free from worry about unsolicited cigarettes. The troops were lined up, ready to go across the walking bridge, which consisted of three bamboo rails wedged between poles stuck into the river bottom. You walked on the bottom rail while holding on to the two top rails. The NVA had allowed A Co and half of B Co to cross this bridge before pinning down the lead elements. Maybe they were hoping we would be split by the river when darkness fell.

In hindsight, I got off the bird on the wrong side of the river. I needed to get over to talk with John, so I started walking across the bridge just as the helicopter gunship we had requested came on station. He asked for instructions, so I paused in the middle of the thirty-meter long bridge to introduce our collective selves and brief him on the situation. I could see the Cobra coming down the tributary toward me, and I was in mid-sentence when he fired off two rockets right at us. Time stood still. The rockets did not seem very fast. Everything was in slow motion. My life did not flash before my eyes, as I had always heard. The troops on the far bank hit the mud. I was screaming at the pilot about the time the two rocket rounds landed on the bank among the B Co troopers, slightly injuring one man and scaring the shit out of the rest. The troops were screaming at the major standing in the middle of the bridge. The major was screaming at the pilot through his handset. Everyone was screaming at everyone. The Cobra was brand new to Vietnam, and apparently so was the pilot.

Only because no one was seriously hurt was it so comical. It was not actually funny, but in the combat zone you make everything as comical as you can. A key ingredient of keepin' on keepin' on.

I eventually found John Taylor a hundred meters up the riverbank, and we discussed the situation. He was as cool as a cucumber. The message from the boss was that we had to push further out in order to get everyone across the bridge before dark. After that, John committed a second platoon to flank the enemy position.

When the troopers of County Line had charged into Thon Que Chu back on 12 February, they fought like hell. Today was no different. They put in some nice artillery, had the gunship working, and 2Lt Thomas' platoon assaulted the enemy's flank. This strong and decisive attack routed the enemy from the area along the riverbank. B Company started moving across and had the room to deploy and attack straight north up a narrow tree line extending away from the river. I went with B Company.

There was a tragic note to the Alpha Company attack, not unlike the great movie, *The Sands of Iwo Jima*. Remember that one? After seizing the top of Mount Hiribachi, Big John Wayne got shot in the back by a Jap who had feigned death. While A Company was consolidating their position, up popped a dedicated little NVA soldier who had been bypassed in the assault. Down went four troopers. Lt Watt was killed, and the other three were wounded. Watt was the leader of the initial platoon attack. He had just joined us in December.

As this setback was occurring in Alpha Company, the Bravos attacked briskly up the single line of little houses moving north away from the river. The houses were typically encased in a rectangle of bamboo, and the line of houses created a bamboo box 150 meters long and 50 meters wide. The little house halfway up the line was perfect for the battalion CP. When we entered its courtyard, and before anyone could shout a warning, one of the B Co troopers dashed through the door, setting off a booby trap that blew him backwards out into the courtyard. He was wounded severely in the thigh. Lucky he wasn't killed. His sun-tanned face went totally white before my eyes, while I was screaming for the medic. Welcome to the Street Without Joy. Back in the 50s, the French could never get past all the mines and booby traps in the VC sympathetic villages east of QL-1. We were just one more in a long line of lost learning experiences extending back to the early 50s.

We built our perimeter around this narrow little hamlet. We did put our CP in the little house, now that it was cleared of explosives. The north end of the hamlet was protected by a bamboo thicket so dense you could not crawl through it. We had clear fields of fire out into the rice paddies along both of the long sides. The river was the bottom of our rectangular position. It was a very tight defense. We presented a good mortar target, packed-in like we were, but no one was going to come walking through our position. No sir.

The enemy was just up the way. Right after all four companies had crossed the bridge and established their defense sectors, we spotted a five-man recon party of NVA sneaking down through the reeds to size us up. They were about 200 meters off when we saw them. In short order, several guys from B Company went on line and took them under fire, putting rounds on full automatic up and out over the horizon. JB and I joined in on the shooting, with JB yelling "Single Fire, goddammit!" Not one NVA soldier fell down as they disappeared into the trees. Our marksmanship was less than impressive that day, or our little bullets were too little. (*You don't see TV news film showing our soldiers in Iraq firing on full automatic. They all have little scopes, the rifle is much improved for accuracy, and the soldiers are more confident in their rifle. And in my view, the volunteer soldiers are more self-disciplined. They still bitch about the stopping power of the 5.62mm bullet, though. Of course they do, since it is too fucking small.*)

The County Lines did a great job that day. After their decisive attack, it did not take long to get everyone across the stream and into our strong position north of the river. But as the sun was going down, I felt terrible looking at four poncho wrapped bodies lying by the helicopter pad. Lt. Watt, Martin, Groat and Otis Nick. Groat had been wounded severely, but died before he could be medevaced. I thought a lot about them after the war. I still think about them.

That night JB, yet another new artillery guy, and I occupied the little house. I had talked myself hoarse that day, and JB was the night watchman as usual, so I was asleep in nothing flat. At some point I had a dream about little green bugs flying from left to right across the ceiling. The bugs turned out to be AK-47 tracers coming through the thatched roof six feet above my head. When I finally came awake and asked what was going on, JB told me to go back to sleep. "Everything is under control", he said. And it was. I lay back down and counted a few more bugs until I dozed off.

I heard the whole story the next morning. At about 2230 hours, C Co had movement to their front on the western side of the perimeter, and fired off one of their claymore mines. Thirty minutes later, Chuck was tossing grenades up and over the north-end bamboo line at B Company's guys, and Ralph's men were tossing grenades back over at Chuck. Our guys could smell the nuc mam sauce. Nuc mam is to the Vietnamese as kimshe is to the Koreans as garlic is to Italians. Their guys smelled whatever we smelled like to them. B Co had one man wounded in this exchange. At 0200 hours, B Company also saw NVA out in the open fields to the east and took them under rifle and machinegun fire. This broke our normal rules, but there was nothing about our perimeter that was concealed to the enemy. We did not fire any illumination, though. Dark was still non-negotiable. JB would get you for that one.

The NVA came down that night to check us out, found us ready and waiting, and eventually called it off. At first light, though, we were being sniped at. At 0830, ten rounds of 60mm mortar smashed into the north end of our position. The NVA were lining us up in their sights about the time that Brigade called with some magical words. "Get ready for helicopter extraction back to Camp Evans." Hallelujah! Nothing could have been more welcome.

We were coming under increasing small arms fire even before the slicks started coming into the rice paddy next to us. In preparation for an extraction from a hot LZ, we brought in continuous artillery on the tree lines to the north and east. When the slicks were on short final into the pickup zone, their supporting gunships peeled off and covered the west and south sides, staying out of the artillery gun-target lines. The fire support was terrific. The full resources of the 1st Cav Division did a heck of a job getting us out of there. It seemed like they had rounded up every flyable slick, because the operation did not take long. Everyone who greeted the day that morning came home to Camp Evans, basically in one piece, except for some nicks and bruises.

JB and I got picked up by the C&C Bird near the end of the extraction, and we ran the rest of the pickup from upstairs. Once the last troops were airborne, we headed toward the highway. As we flew over a village along the way, a man in black pajamas stood bravely in the center of a courtyard and bid us a fond farewell with his AK 47. Fortunately, we were at treetop level and went by way too fast for him. Too fast for us too — because our door gunner missed everything with a couple long bursts. In another minute, we were out of harm's way, and streaking up QL-1 toward Camp Evans.

Our involvement in the Battle of Hue was over. Our Daily Summary dated 291900H February 1968 summarized casualties for the Battle of Hue, based on reports received from the companies from 5 February forward:

> "5. © Statistical Summary:
>
> a. Friendly Casualties: Cumulative for Operation: KIA 27, WIA 203, MIA 0.
>
> b. Enemy Casualties: Cumulative for Operation: KIA (bc) 146

For the entire month of February, twenty-seven men with 5/7 Cav were killed in combat. We did not add a number for estimated enemy killed to our report. I wonder how many men of the 5th NVA Regiment died for their country that month. Somewhere north of five hundred would be my guess.

Meeting us at the Camp Evans landing zone that morning was the Division Band playing "Sgt. Flynn." The Division Commander was there too, sporting his paternal smile. And my only living military hero at the time, General Creighton Abrams, aka Akila, was there as well.

Creighton and my old man were in the same section at the Command & General Staff College at Ft. Leavenworth in 1947. Creighton served as Akila for the Cub Scout Program. The Big Chief. When Akila came down the line of Cub Scouts during the annual inspection in ranks, we were quaking in our Keds. So were our moms. Only two years before, Creighton Abrams had led his tanks into Bastogne and relieved the surrounded 101st Airborne from encirclement in the last great battle of WW II. When he greeted us at Camp Evans on 1 March 1968, wearing three stars, he had already been a legend for twenty-three years. "Sat next to his daughter in sixth grade", I remarked to anyone listening. "Where was that?" no one asked. "Bad Tolz, Germany," I replied.

It was later reported that General Abrams was very impressed with the number of walking wounded (wounded but still serving) troopers that dismounted the birds that day. We were proudly rag-tag to start with, but really looked impressive with bandages hanging off so many arms and legs.

General Abrams had begun his career in 1936 at Fort Hood, Texas. His first unit as a 2d Lieutenant — the 7th U.S. Cavalry, of course. I suspect his troops did some serious boot-and-saddle polishing back then. Just about every fellow officer I know has his own personal Creighton Abrams story. He remains the last truly great general of our times. (Powell and Petraeus were good — but they were no Creighton Abrams. No, sir.)

Welcome To Hue

Cavalrymen from the Third Brigade put up a sign on the outskirts of the Imperial Citadel of Hue depicting their part and
the division's efforts in defeating the communists there during
the Tet offensive.

Boy major at Bridge into Hue

*3dr Bde sent sign before we could
paint our own*

LTC Vaught and his commanders, Taylor, Miles, Davison & Lambert

Capt. Howard Prince in TT Woods

22 Feb — D Company on the road to Hue

CHAPTER 18

8000 MILES IN THE OPPOSITE DIRECTION

30 March 2005
Enroute to Iraq

As we flew on across the Atlantic my thoughts eventually returned to present day issues. We have been comporting with benevolent dictators for decades now. And, interestingly, the old communism has disappeared in most of the world, replaced by representative government, or sadly, no government. Somehow we have come to view Terrorism like Communism — as though terrorism is a movement rather than just a tactical method. We even call it the War on Terrorism, not the war on Islamic Fundamentalism, or some other "ism" yet to be discovered.

And somehow we linked this new enemy called Terrorism to Saddam and Iraq. Maybe they were the same, maybe not. He certainly terrorized his own citizens. The enemy is — let's not beat around the Bush — Radical Islamic Fundamentalism. We did not create this enemy. They had already targeted us before our Cold War victory over the Russians. And now their long campaign had caused a giant hole in the Bowery, haunted by three thousand ghosts forever. It is interesting how important freedom of speech is to us, while at the same time it is so difficult for the government to call things what they are.

It seemed to me that none of our great minds and decision makers were able to make the leap to the new paradigm — a non-sovereign enemy. We attacked into Afghanistan to root out the Taliban and install a new democratic government, as though that will defeat the terrorists. We attacked into Iraq to find the WMDs, but somehow that dog didn't hunt, so we switched to installing democracy there too. We seem to be stuck on installing our form of government in a sovereign land as the solution to defeating the non-sovereign terrorists. How about holding those governments responsible for what their terrorist citizens perpetrate around the globe?

During the layover in Frankfurt, I had two cold ones in a bar on the concourse. They would be my last for quite awhile. Looking around the terminal, it seemed that everyone in the world was there. In 1949 when I first went to Germany, there were two kinds of people, Caucasians in American clothes and Caucasians in European clothes. Today, Frankfurt is apparently the center of the universe. It seemed like every continent was represented. I even saw a pair of Peruvian grandparents straight out of the Andes Mountains, maybe 4'8" tall, dressed in the traditional Incan garb. Maybe the only vestige of the past - the German men still wear the most awful looking shoes on the planet. Deodorant seems to have taken hold, though.

Sitting there in Frankfurt took me back to the good old days in Berlin. As fortunate as I was to have been in Troop B, 17th Cavalry for my first two years as an officer, I was even more blessed by orders sending me to the Berlin Brigade. I reported in to 2d Battle Group, 6th Infantry in January 1963.

The struggles with Nikita had triggered a confrontation in Berlin even before the Missile Crisis. American and Soviet tanks had faced off one hundred meters apart at Checkpoint Charlie in the center of Berlin when they started building the wall. Checkpoint Charlie was on Friedrich Strasse passing through the Berlin Wall into East Berlin. During the tension-filled tank faceoff, our tank platoon was commanded by my good friend and classmate Tyler Willson, and they were locked and loaded with big bullets. John Nix, another classmate and golfing buddy, had his infantry platoon mounted in armored personnel carriers a block or so away. *(Today, the part of Friedrich Strasse that was in East Berlin is the center of the universe in unified Berlin — a fantastic street of upscale shops and restaurants.)*

Although I did not get to meet the Russians in Cuba in November 1962, I met them up close and personal less than a year later. The Cold War could be really cold in Berlin.

November 1963
East German Autobahn
West Berlin to West Germany

I was the executive officer of C Company, 2d Battalion, 6th US Infantry. Second in command, as a 1st Lieutenant. The military heritage of the 6th Infantry Regiment went back to a battle in the War of 1812 in which a British general watching our oncoming advance exclaimed, "Those are Regulars, by God."

One hundred and fifty-one years later, the Regulars were directed to travel by convoy from West Berlin to West Germany, 104 kilometers through Soviet-occupied East Germany. It was November 1963. Tensions between the Soviet Union and the United States continued to be high following the Cuban Crisis of the previous year.

Our captain was already down in West Germany, waiting for us just inside West Germany at a town called Helmstedt. I commanded the convoy as we approached the Soviet checkpoint between West Berlin and East Germany. We slowed to a halt just a few steps short of a Soviet soldier standing in the middle of the right lane. Right behind us, Charlie Company rode in the back of tarpaulin-covered 2 ½ ton trucks in full combat gear.

I got out of the jeep and approached the most impressive-looking soldier I had ever seen at that point in my service. The young Russian was six-foot-three, slender, ramrod-straight, with blonde hair and blue eyes. A Dolph Lundgren look-alike. He wore the magenta shoulder boards of the Soviet Infantry, and towered over me as he rendered a very snappy salute. The USSR had put its best foot forward at their checkpoint.

Right after we turned off our engines, an American officer and a Russian officer came out of the checkpoint building and approached the front of the convoy. The American turned out to be a full colonel.

I saluted the colonel, and he flipped an Air Force type salute back, saying, "Relax, Lieutenant. This is Captain Boronov." The colonel's shoes hadn't seen polish lately. I was taken aback by the informality of the whole thing. I was also surprised that the Russian was only a captain, even though he was at least forty-five. I had yet to hear a shot fired in anger, while the Russian probably fought the Germans across the frozen steppes of Russia right into downtown Berlin. At least he wasn't six-foot- three and ramrod straight. In fact, he was very short and very broad, with a broken nose and bad teeth. Boronov grinned and stuck his hand out. After a brief hesitation I reached out to firmly grasp what turned out to be a very dead fish. It was the Cold War, after all.

Then we moved slowly down the column of trucks, with the Soviet on my left. He would pause at the rear of each truck and try to peer into the back. He could see very little beyond the few troopers nearest to the tailgate. Halfway down the line of trucks, Boronov suddenly jumped up on a trailer hitch to get a count of the personnel inside. Holy shit. I hesitated for a split second, then reached up and grabbed the man by the back of his pistol belt and yanked him off the trailer. He stumbled backward into me. Almost falling, the Russian whirled around and we came face-to-face, a few bad-smelling inches apart. We stared into each other's eyes for several seconds before the colonel said "let's go, Lieutenant." We continued to stare each other down for another second or two, prompting the colonel to repeat himself irritably.

It was a tie about who looked away first. The inspection took on a more perfunctory air. No words were spoken until we reached the end of the column and turned to head back. The colonel and the Russian officer conferred in Russian at the end, and finally the colonel said, "You are clear to proceed, Lieutenant."

I had followed the instructions to the letter that I had received at the US Army departure Checkpoint inside the American Sector of Berlin. "Whatever happens, don't let the Russian inspectors climb up on any of your vehicles."

"Yes, sir."

As a Plebe at West Point my earliest and maybe most lasting lesson of military service was that I had three answers: "Yes sir," "No sir," and "No excuse Sir." This lesson kept me out of a lot of trouble along the way. Just not always.

We moved on down the autobahn to the checkpoint into West Germany. There was a cursory Soviet inspection down at that end, and we passed through their gate uneventfully. I went into the American checkpoint building and received brief instructions from a major about the next step of the operation. His final words were "the colonel said you did real good."

Rather than continue on to our training area in Wildflecken, we wound our way through downtown Helmstedt, a fairly large town, and set up in a wooded area on the north side of a grass-surfaced airfield. We spread the trucks throughout the woods without need of much talk. Just hand and arm signals. Charlie Company was a well-oiled machine. It helped that Tiger Lily, the First Sergeant, was 6' 7" and 300 pounds. That's right, Tiger Lily. When you are that big you can pick any name you want. And Tiger Lily took advantage of his mammoth strength from time to time. The captain was about 6' 4", and a real stud in his own right. Lamb ... John Lamb. Licensed to follow the rules of engagement. Next to them I looked like a math major in my third year of college.

Captain Lamb briefed us on the mission. It was a real mission, not training. Twenty-four hours later, the convoy moved out of the woods just as smoothly as it came in, headed back to Berlin. I brought up the rear in my jeep. This day, Charlie Company was configured into a smaller number of trucks, with one more soldier in each truck. We were in direct violation of the USSR's interpretation of the original agreement struck many years earlier about how many trucks could be in a convoy, and how many troops could be in each truck. Charlie Company was headed for an argument.

Once everyone was through the gate at the Soviet Checkpoint, the convoy was halted, and my captain walked down the column to my jeep at the rear. We waited for the inspection. And we waited. And waited some more.

Finally, the colonel and the Russian came out of the building. Surprisingly, our same colonel was there, but now dealing with a different Soviet captain I didn't get to meet — we'll call him Ivanov. Lamb moved forward to report, and there were no friendly introductions this time. There was no hand-shaking going on. They moved on up the column, and the troops sat stone-faced in the trucks. Back down the column came the two inspecting officers, looking grim, as they strode briskly past and disappeared into the guard house.

They didn't come out for some time. In fact, it was late afternoon when the colonel came out, walked up to my vehicle, and said "Well, listen. We are going to be here for quite a while. I have gotten them to agree to let you come and go from Helmstedt to bring chow."

Quite awhile turned out to be 52 hours. The second concession came almost twenty-four hours into the hold-up. The colonel came up the street to the CO's jeep to report that he had gotten Ivanov to allow the troops to get out of the trucks and sleep on the shoulder of the road. The troops had been in agony sleeping on the benches and floors of the trucks, and this was very welcome news.

All the way up the chain, maybe all the way to Washington and Moscow, people were not getting along so well. Negotiations dragged on into the evening at the joint committee building in West Berlin, with each side sending messages back and forth to the highest levels of the respective governments.

The US was getting nowhere, and elected to act. The colonel came back out to the convoy later that evening with the message, "Quietly wake your troops up at 0345 hours, have them quietly pack up and board trucks, and move out for Berlin right at 0400 hours."

At 0400 hours, the captain's driver started his engine and turned on his cat-eye lights for black out drive. On that signal, the grinding of starter motors rippled down the column. Tiger Lily was in the rear truck and radioed up to the CO. "We ready, over." The column moved off the shoulder and into the right lane, and went about two hundred meters before the Soviet Union answered back.

Out of the woods from the right came the huge black silhouette of a Soviet tank, followed immediately by a second tank. The CO came to a halt about ten meters short of the tanks, and all the trucks halted right behind him. The lead tank spun left heading down the other lane beside ours. The two tanks continued down the left hand lane toward the rear of our column, followed immediately by a bumper-to-bumper line of Soviet armored personnel carriers and a couple more intermittent tanks. They were a scary sight. When they were through, Charlie Company was pinned against the road shoulder by a Soviet force in armored vehicles, with vastly superior firepower, sitting about five meters away. We were blocked from moving in any direction.

It was getting light when I was called to go bring breakfast. When I got back, rows of Soviet soldiers were sitting at attention in their open-topped personnel carriers. They were every bit as disciplined as we were. Maybe more. You could hear a pin drop. The Soviets were so ramrod straight they looked like mannequins. While we were dishing out chow, one truck at a time, the colonel came out again and gave the CO a chilling message. "At 0800 hours, I want you to break out your ammunition from the ammo trailers. I want it to be very visible to the Soviets. At 0815 hours you will lock and load weapons. No accidents. Any questions?"

The First Sergeant briefed each of the three platoon sergeants on the way back to the rear truck. At 0800 hours sharp, the platoon sergeants dismounted a man from each of the platoon's assigned trucks to move to the platoon ammo trailer. Ammo was broken out from the boxes right on the street between the two columns. The ammo carriers took the bandoleers of M-14 ammunition and metal boxes of M-60 machinegun belts up to their squads in the trucks. Tiger Lily strode up and down the column, barking instructions to the troops in the trucks with ominous words about the result of any stupid accidents, for which there would be a lot more damage than merely having to wear sunglasses at reveille.

When all the ammo had been distributed, Tiger Lily handed the captain the buckshot rounds for his twelve-gauge pump, and the two of them sat on the hood of the CO's jeep loading their weapons and gazing indolently at the Soviets. We were Charlie Company. The "Chargin' Charlies." One hundred and thirty American Regulars, confronted by an equal number of the Soviet Union's finest soldiers. Everyone sat in silence wondering what was coming next. During the lock and load, a 90mm recoilless rocket gunner in the lead truck noisily slammed a tank killer round into the breach, not that it would have armed itself after a five-yard flight. Except for the metallic sounds of weapons being loaded and locked, there was an eerie silence throughout the two parallel columns of vehicles. Silence. More silence.

John Lamb later spoke of the intensity of the moment. Sobs suddenly burst from a young Soviet infantryman sitting in the back of the personnel carrier in front of the captain's jeep. A door opened on the far side front of the personnel carrier, and a Soviet soldier came around the back. He was no less tall than Tiger Lily, with a little less body fat. A very scary-looking guy. Probably not named after a flower either. He reached up into the back of the Soviet vehicle and literally lifted the young man out, slamming him to the ground. Picking the soldier up and dusting him off, the two of them marched past the front of the captain's jeep and disappeared into the woods. A few minutes later, the gigantic Soviet sergeant returned, and grimly nodded to Tiger Lily and the captain as he walked past.

It was a Mexican standoff. We presumed the Soviets were locked and loaded to start with. But, maybe not. In addition to four tanks, they matched us soldier for soldier, huge first sergeant for huge first sergeant.

Hours of high tension went by before the Soviet tank at the rear of our column suddenly started his engine. It was into the 52d hour of the convoy hold-up. The rest of their vehicles cranked up in turn. The column started forward, swung to the right just short of the Soviet guard shack, crossed the median and headed past us back up the highway. Once past the captain's jeep they cut back across the median and disappeared up the same dirt road from which they had come. The Soviet tracked vehicles kicked up big clods of dirt in the median and deposited it across the highway to our front — like big horse turds to bid us farewell. No pins traded. No vodkas toasted.

The colonel and Ivanov came out of the guard shack and strode up the column with big smiles. They arrived at the captain's jeep and the colonel gave the same old familiar words. "Captain, you are clear to proceed."

Company C, 2d Battalion, 6th US Infantry, Regulars by God, moved out for Berlin. I turned around, went back to Helmstedt and brought the other truck and mess truck in a separate little convoy without incident.

The rest was history. Lamb and Tiger Lily got their pictures in Newsweek as part of a full-page story. The New York Times also carried the story, which put an approximate date on this event:

> BERLIN, Tuesday, Nov. 5 — A United States troop convoy was blocked by
> Soviet armored personnel carriers late last night when it attempted to break
> through a blockade at the Marienborn checkpoint on the autobahn to West Berlin.

A few weeks earlier in October, the Soviets started all this when they held up a couple of our convoys, demanding that the troops dismount and form up to be counted. The US refused, setting the stage for this final convoy to resolve what seemed to be a test of wills between the two powers. A summary of events written later about Cold War Events said about the incident:

> "In an abrupt about-face, Soviet guards yesterday yielded to Western pressure

and allowed an American military convoy to proceed to West Berlin after holding it up for 52 hours. At the Marienborn checkpoint, the Russians suddenly dropped their demand to count the soldiers in the trucks. President Kennedy and his advisers blamed the blockade on a misunderstanding rather than on Soviet intentions to provoke an incident."

It was an interesting comment with respect to who provoked whom. Spin is not a new phenomena. This turned out to be the last American convoy held up on the East German autobahn. There were no more gray areas. Both sides had come to agreement. After the Soviets had closed the border and brought an Iron Curtain down across Europe, it took the negotiators seventeen years to agree on how many trucks we could have in a convoy, and how many guys in each truck. Grown men from the US and the USSR risked an accidental discharge potentially triggering the start of WW III, and the issue was how many guys could be in a fucking truck. Is there any wonder there are wars?

The weekend after the autobahn incident, we took the wives out to dinner in Berlin — all the officers of Charlie Company. The girls told us all about the Soviet MIGs that had been buzzing our houses in Berlin at about 200 feet, making our children cry, and the grinning faces of the pilots visible in their glass cockpits. Oh, by the way, our wives were girls back then. Good-looking girls. Real women. Midway through the meal, a middle-aged German couple came over and thanked our captain profusely for his personal courage in defending West Berlin. They had seen his face on TV or in the paper. It was quite touching.

Only a few months earlier, when JFK came to Berlin on 26 June 1963 and made his great speech, I was fortunate to be the acting company commander of the "Chargin' Charlies." Captain Lamb was on leave. An hour after his speech at City Hall, John F Kennedy stood in the back of a huge black Mercedes Benz convertible, returning our salutes as he slowly passed by Berlin Brigade's nine infantry companies. We lined Clay Allee in company formations.

The following summer I was promoted to captain, and took command of the Chargin' Charlies from John Lamb. My name was Charlie. Life was good in Berlin in 1964. Among our many adventures that year, I was honored to command half of the honor guard for the ceremony at the West Berlin City Hall to re-name the square John F Kennedy Platz. This was the site of JFK's speech a year earlier — "Ich Bin Eine Berliner." My wife gave birth to two little Berliners during this tour.

The ceremony was at night. 100,000 people stood in the small square, pressed against a rope about two paces in front of me. I had a platoon of 40 soldiers behind me, the best of the Chargin' Charlies. We had a terrible rehearsal that morning, but we sounded like one big rifle that night. "Present... Arms" WHAP! "Order... Arms!" CRACK! Candles were lit by the 100,000 citizens just at the right time, and Taps was played by two buglers in echo style from the rooftops. Tears ran down the cheeks of every Berliner in front of me. An awesome sight. A warm moment in an otherwise cold war. Afterward at the reception in City Hall the champagne flowed like water. *(Officers only in those days.)* We young officers caught a short glimpse of Berlin's high society. Willy Brandt. German aristocrats. Elegant women. People you didn't see on the streets of Berlin.

Charlie Company was also selected to guard Spandau Prison that summer, which housed Speer, Von Schirach and Hess. These three were the only Nazi bigwigs still imprisoned who had dodged the noose at Nuremberg in 1945. The Spandau Prison job was for one month. The four occupying countries rotated this duty, and the US always followed the Russians. The guard house reeked from the smell of borscht and whatever else they ate.

On a particularly bright and beautiful day, I was marching clockwise around the yard between the wall and the interior prison building, going from tower to tower and halting to receive a salute and report from each soldier. We made the hourly inspection very ceremonial. As I rounded the corner to the long side at the back of the prison, the three prisoners were coming down the walk toward me. Five and One were leading, arm in arm. Five was a big man. One was old and decrepit, holding onto Five's arm. Seven was behind them, a dark complexioned little guy. Actually, five was Albert Speer. One was Baldur von Schirach, and Seven was Rudolf Hess, but at Spandau their names were never spoken. These big cheeses were just numbers now — how ironic.

As soon as Rudolph Hess saw me coming, he left the walkway and darted through the flower garden over to the building. From there, he crept along the wall until he was past me, bent over looking like a rodent. As though I would not see him over there. He was one deranged Nazi by that time, if he had not always been so.

As I neared Five and One, Speer suddenly saluted with a big smile, and in perfect English said, "Good Morning, Captain." I totally knee-jerked it, saluting and saying "good morning" back. What was I thinking, I asked myself immediately. Where was the stone-faced grim look? I am a sucker for smiles.

By the fall of 1965, Vietnam was heating up. All of the lieutenants were leaving Berlin Brigade, headed west. Our companies were down to one officer each. There were only a few staff officers and a battalion commander at Battalion HQs. I had been the Battalion Operations Officer of 2/6 Inf for six months when I received orders to head back to Ft. Benning in 1966. Vietnam would be next. The Cold War was becoming hot.

Tyler Willson meets the Russians at Check Point Charlie - 1962

JFK reviews the troops in Berlin Brigade June 1963

Capt. Baker commanding Co C, 2d Bn, 6th Inf on parade in Berlin

US replaces USSR Guard Detail at Spandau

Marilyn in Korea 1954

CHAPTER 19

LOOKING FOR PALIWODA

1 April 2005
Frankfurt, Germany

The Lufthansa boarding gate for the flight to Kuwait was about 70% Americans heading for Iraq. The Band — Adema — was on their way to do USO shows for the troops. Hard rockers. We know they can kill plants, but can they hit the notes? Then again, who cares? It is great of entertainers to travel to the Combat Zone, like Marilyn did during the Korean War. *(Most women think that all of us older guys only love Marilyn because she was the sexiest, most beautiful girl in the world.* **Marilyn went to Korea***... and was the sexiest, most beautiful girl in the world.)*

As I came down the aisle, counting the rows and scanning ahead like one does, I could see an apparent starting NFL offensive tackle about ten rows back. A huge guy filling up the entire two seats. I started to pray, and my prayers went unanswered. The trip was not pretty in my one fourth of the two seats. I sat there, crushed and unable to move. Six hours without a pee break. I was thinking refund, but was too tired to follow through. How could anyone that obese be flying to Kuwait? To be a truck driver for KBR was a distinct possibility, I later learned.

Sleep was impossible while wedged into the fat man. As I continued to wend my way toward Operation Iraqi Freedom, more questions of the day swirled up. Questions like: Are we in a quagmire, or are we turning the corner? Do we need more boots on the ground, or is the development of the Iraqi Army moving so fast that we should write the timetable for withdrawal? Are the Iraqis in the thirteenth century, or headed for the twenty-first? In our absence will they stick with "democracy"? For that matter, should we care if they have democracy?

What more did people really want to know about our presence in Iraq? There was no shortage of information on TV and in the papers, maybe too much, and I was not confident that I would shed any new light. When I had headed for Vietnam in 1967, my only fear was that I would fail to do my job well. Now it was 2005, and my only fear was that I would fail to write anything worth reading.

Concurrent with my travel, things were happening in Lebanon. The Israelis were on the attack, and being less than successful for the first time in my memory. But it seemed that the Syrian army was being driven out anyway. I wondered if the Iraqi people would look like the Lebanese anytime soon. Well-dressed, well-fed, smiling and singing, throwing flower petals at Syrian soldiers, and raising their fists for People-Power.

1 April 2005
Kuwait City

We finally hit the tarmac at Kuwait International Airport on the 31st of March, although I didn't feel a thing nestled within the gigantic cushion sitting to my right. Feeling began to return to my lower body just in time to walk off the plane and into the nearest bathroom.

Getting the entry visa at the Kuwait airport was a snap. Very nice people. Sign said $15, but no one collected any money. Then it was through the customs, where thanks to my lovely wife I was busted for booze. Unlike the visa stamp people, the customs guys were not very nice. I had known in my heart that she should not have stuck that fifth of Jim Bean in my hiking boots, but no. It was confiscated and was probably drunk by the natives that very night. I felt like an Indian Agent corrupting the Cheyenne with whiskey in Powder River.

Once past customs, I went out into an elegantly decorated, broad marble walkway lined with beautiful people. The women were spectacular in their finery. Welcome to Kuwait City, where all the men wear identical white robes, but all the women look like they are coming down the runway on Style TV. I caught myself eye-balling a few, but quickly began to worry about having an extremity chopped off. It was eyes front the rest of the way. The Hilton Resort guy was at the end of the promenade with a roster, and my name was on it. I was home free. There would be a room after all.

The ride to the Hilton was interesting. Beautiful SUV. Beautiful highways. Beautiful decorations built around lights. Little lighted trees that look like bursting fireworks. All the buildings are cubic. Flat roofs. Asking if the huge structures along the way were office buildings, the driver laughed and said they were mansions for the rich. Golly. We finally drove through a maze of barriers and into a gate at the Hilton Compound. The Hilton Resort was an armed camp. The engine and undercarriage got inspected, and we weren't a bomb. I suddenly felt less secure, because until then I did not know we weren't.

I had spent a lot of flight time pondering the various issues, and two nights at the opulent Kuwait Hilton were a welcome rest. On the other hand, these two days exhausted any notion of profit for writing articles for my local paper, not that I expected to make a profit. The newspaper had done me a huge favor sponsoring my trip.

I met up with my friend the combat cameraman on the second day in Kuwait. His name is Norman Lloyd — a photographer who had recently retired from CBS after a long and distinguished career. As a very young cameraman, he had filmed the actions of our B Company 5/7 Cav throughout five days of continuous combat in Cambodia in 1970. This action culminated with an intense battle for what became known as Shakey's Hill, in which Norman went to the top of the hill with the lead platoon. Norman and I teamed up to make this trip. We shared a sumptuous breakfast at the Kuwait Hilton Resort before heading north. One last good meal before going to the combat zone.

The next morning we flew in a C-130 from none other than the Wyoming Air National Guard. We hit an unavoidable storm over the center of the country that scared the living shit out of the diminutive civilian contractor sitting next to me. And many of the military passengers, as well, although you could not tell it from the stoical faces they had put on. After a stop in Mosul, we flew through the storm again before spiraling sharply down and zigzagging our way to a rocky touch-down at the Baghdad airfield. I commented to my new little contractor friend that it was just another C-130 ride. He hates me yet.

It was late afternoon when we got to the US Army terminal on the north side of Baghdad International. A chaotic scene. People going out. People coming in. The Operations Building was staffed by Army as well as Marines.

Not enough phones, and everyone wanting to make a call to find out why they had not been met and picked up yet. Norman and I waded through this red tape long enough to learn that someone was coming from the Public Information Office of the big HQs that ran all of Iraq. We were waiting outside in unbearable heat, giving way to darkness and rapid cooling, when the alarm claxons went off. An attack by eighty insurgents to take Abu Ghraib Prison was taking place only a few miles to the west of the airfield. This emergency locked down the airfield tight as a Lexus. This surprise assault was defeated by the MP guards and a pair of Apache gunships. We finally got picked up by an Estonian captain and taken to Camp Victory by midnight. Welcome to the war in Iraq.

The next morning we got on a Black Hawk helicopter to fly to the historic city of Tikrit. When we stopped halfway for fuel, the crew dismounted and removed their flight helmets. The co-pilot shook out her long hair, prompting the crew chief to ask me, "Sir, did you have any pilots in Vietnam as pretty as her?"

"There were no female pilots in Vietnam, sergeant," I laughingly answered.

Trained by the finest minds in the human behavioral science field, I also quickly added "As long as she can fly, she's ok by me."

"Oh, she can definitely fly, sir," said the sergeant.

We left Baghdad bobbing and weaving across the roof tops, shaking our little tail, so to speak. She could fly like hell. 100 feet below us were endless sand-colored houses, with their millions of satellite dishes. Finally out in rich farmlands along the Tigris River, we bombed the waving children four hundred feet below with bags of toys and candy. Flying over these farmlands reminded me of flying over South Dakota, except the grid below was irrigation canals, rather than roads spaced one mile square.

Actually, the pilot was the prettiest pilot I have ever seen, up to then as well as since. She carried us to FOB Danger in Tikrit; about 100 miles north of Baghdad.

A FOB is a forwarding operating base. In 2003, the 1st Infantry Division had located their headquarters there. DANGER was the call sign of the the Big Red One dating back to my memories of going on maneuvers with my old man at Grafenwohr, West Germany in 1950. DANGER went at least back to WW II. Not sure about WW I. A lot of famous generals have been DANGER SIX over the years, to include Jim Hollingsworth, my boss in 1972 during my second tour in Vietnam.

The headquarters of the 42d Division of the New York National Guard was at FOB Danger in 2005. The FOB was located in one of Saddam Hussein's compound. It consisted of humongous marble palaces perched on a cliff overlooking the Tigris River. Saddam built this compound early in his dictatorship by demolishing the historic center of his hometown, Tikrit — only about 2000 years old. Not one for nostalgia, Saddam. Another one of those "all-about-me" national leaders.

We slept that night in Saddam's primary palace, with all its marble, gold fixtures and toilets that did not accept paper. *(No shit.)* Each john had its own little trash bag, emptied by some unfortunate person. Every combat zone seems to have its shit detail. That evening we were taken to the dining facility, a huge cafeteria that turned Morrisons into a place I would never go to again. It was steak and lobster night, so we passed on Chinese, Mexican, fix your own sub sandwich with everything, Indian, three other meat entrees if you didn't like lobster, or — heaven forbid — steak. We were so full we had to pass on dessert of Baskin Robbins, or pie, or flan, or cake, or cookies. The following morning we got up early to go to breakfast so we could get that last good meal before going to the combat zone.

We finally linked up with Jody Petery, call-sign: WARPAINT SIX. In addition to driving 50 miles north to pick us up, he and his color guard were there for a big ceremony at the headquarters of the 42d "Rainbow" Division. Before you say anything about rainbows, you need to know that Douglas MacArthur formed this division with men from across the breadth of the United States. Yes, they were a rainbow coalition, but, more importantly, they fought with distinction in World War I and World War II. The occasion for this ceremony in Tikrit was to receive the right to wear the Rainbow Division patch on the right sleeve for serving in combat with the division.

Although serving this tour under the 42d, those in 5/7 Cav who were veterans of the 1/3rd ADA in 2003 were not about to replace their 3rd ID patch on their right sleeve. Rock of the Marne, pal. Dog Face Soldiers, they were.

Norman and I took pictures and film of the impressive ceremony. All the battalion commanders were there with their color guards. Everyone's flags were all new and sparkling, and I was both disappointed and relieved that our colors from Vietnam were not the ones being carried to this event. They were safely hanging in the squadron headquarters in Balad, looking about one hundred years old.

We mounted up and moved out for Balad right after the ceremony. Norman and I were decked out in kneepads, armored vests and helmets, and nervous in anticipation of the trip southward down the highway toward Balad. Well, at least I was nervous. Norman doesn't do nervous. We traveled in a column of four heavily-armed Hummvees. The soldiers were locked and loaded, and ready for bad guys. Norman and I were unarmed, as for all journalists, but we had our fingers on the buttons of our cameras.

We drove toward the city of Balad by way of Route Tampa, a divided highway that traverses all of Iraq from south to north. The oncoming cars pulled over onto the shoulder as soon as they saw us coming. As we crossed into the battalion's area of operations, we came upon a stoppage of traffic from both directions on Route Tampa. A forlorn detainee sat in the middle of the highway, with his hands ziplocked behind him. The incoming report was that three insurgents had fired their AK-47s from a building at a passing Iraqi police patrol, and in the ensuing action one was captured. After a quick check by the CO, we continued on to the battalion's home base. We finally got to Paliwoda.

Paliwoda was the name of our forward operating base on the southwestern edge of Balad. FOB Paliwoda was named for Captain Eric Paliwoda, West Point Class of 1997, who was killed there on 2 January 2004 during a mortar attack. Another italicized one-line biography in the West Point Register of Graduates. Not unlike thirteen of my classmates. *(Everyone's biography is in the Register of Graduates. If you are killed early, it is only one, maybe two lines.)* One of Eric's good friends while at West Point was serving as the Plans Officer in the 5/7 Cav headquarters at Paliwoda. The officers corps of the Army can be an amazingly small group.

The battalion's forward operating base was 55 miles north of downtown Baghdad, a mile in from the main north-south highway running through Iraq. This highway runs all the way from Kuwait to the Turkish border north of Mosul. It was called Route Tampa. CENTCOM Headquarters is in Tampa, Florida. So there you go. This road reminded me of the infamous QL-1, which ran the length of Vietnam from Saigon all the way to Hanoi. Route Tampa was almost as dangerous as QL-1, and maybe equally dangerous around Balad. The first 100 miles north from Baghdad had roadside bombs going off every day against passing US military vehicles and KBR's truck convoys, and 5/7 Cav was stationed at the central point of that 100 mile stretch. They were deep inside the Sunni Triangle at Balad. Deep.

Paliwoda was hot, dusty and dry. It was like a lot of other places I had been years earlier. Norman and I spent the rest of the day settling in and meeting everyone. It was great to see all the young officers and soldiers again whom I had met at Ft. Stewart. The primary staff officers slept in their offices in a concrete building. The troops lived in two-man trailers called CHUs *(containerized housing unit)*, which are grouped together in big rectangles surrounded by concrete slabs, and roofed over by steel beams and three layers of sandbags. The sandbag roof system could take a hit from the biggest mortar or rocket round available to the enemy. When outside the buildings and CHUs, everyone wore all their personal armor all the time.

We went to dinner at the battalion's dining facility. In our day it was the "mess hall." Unlike Tikrit and the Rainbow Division's dining facility run by the now famous civilian contractor — KBR — this dining facility at Paliwoda was a mess hall. The battalion used its own cooks, and the food was refreshingly mediocre. The further you get from the Pentagon, the better it gets in the US Army. I knew we had finally arrived in the combat zone when we finally found Paliwoda. Life was good.

I lay awake that first night thinking about the CO managing combat operations. I finally dozed off as our resident artillery battery sent a couple rounds somewhere. I woke up in the middle of the night due to jet lag, got up, donned my Vietnam era helmet and my old Marine armored vest and walked around in the dark.

The sky was incredible — something I had not seen since the first grade in Buffalo, Wyoming. The quarter moon jumped off a page full of sharply visible stars. Millions of stars. I was approached by three different soldiers in the dark who recognized me by the silhouette of my unique helmet. One lad excitedly told me all about the training he had just completed on night driving. Jet lag wore off in a couple days and I stopped going on these midnight walks — unfortunate in hindsight. We had a lot going on at night. It may have been the best opportunity to talk to soldiers. The dark was their friend.

When the sun came up on our first full day at Paliwoda, I quickly discovered that the battalion commander spent little time managing combat operations unless there was some serious combat going on, which was rare. Instead, he was in many ways the head of government in this region called Thanna Azawi, and was spending most of his time teaching the Iraqis how to run local government. He was preparing the Iraqis to take over.

At 1030 hours we walked over to the District Joint Coordination Center (JCC) just outside the base. The chief was an ex-general in the Iraq Army. The Chief of Police, the Battalion Commander of the local Iraqi Army Battalion, and the hospital chief were also there. People of incredible courage for accepting these roles. Balad is a city of 100,000 people, almost all Shias, located on the Tigris River north of Baghdad. 40,000 more people lived in the surrounding towns and farm areas, and are mostly Sunnis. The Shias in town are surrounded by the Sunnis in the countryside villages. Saddam was a Sunni. All the officers of the Iraqi Army, now banished to their homes along the Tigris River, were Sunnis.

The goal for the meeting was to get the Iraqi Police to take over traffic control checkpoints from the Iraqi Army battalion, so that they could begin training with our battalion. One of 5/7 Cav's primary military missions this year was to turn the Iraqi battalion into a capable army unit for national defense, and pave the way for eventual US withdrawal.

JP had his translator, Tina. The JCC Chief had his translator. It was fascinating to watch and listen. JP was laudatory of the Iraqi's operations to secure the recent religious celebration, which came off free of incident. He was diplomatic but firm as he said he was withholding further funding of new projects until they hired ambulance drivers for the new clinic and teachers for a completed schoolhouse. He could award huge sums of money for projects, probably more than they could manage to spend. They got into the meat of the meeting, and he was a skillful mediator in bringing them to agreement on the transfer of checkpoint responsibility. He knew from leverage. Everyone appeared to hold JP in high esteem.

In the afternoon JP met with the District Chief, who is also a sheik of one of the largest tribes, and the Imam of the largest mosque. He wore three hats... that we knew of. They discussed JP's priorities for projects throughout the district. The goal was to get the Iraqis to also improve the mostly Sunni villages and farms through projects, rather than just focus on the mostly Shia city. At the next day's weekly District Council Meeting, all of the Iraqis we had met with the previous day sang JP's tunes as though they were their own.

JP and Tina were awesome at a job that I thought the State Department was supposed to be doing. While JP was running the government all day, his two majors were running the war against the insurgents. They made it clear that I was welcome to enter the Tactical Operations Center (the "TOC"), although at first I was sheepish. After all, I was supposed to be a "reporter." Nevertheless, as the previous Battalion S-3 from eons ago, I had special privileges. After living another life for so many years, I no longer thought of myself as "the Colonel." But everyone else in Balad apparently did.

On my first visit to the TOC, one thing that had not changed in 37 years was the two RTOs sitting in front of a board. Otherwise, the TOC was nothing that old veterans would recognize. It took getting used to. In our day we had a bunker, a couple field tables with PRC-25s hooked to 292 antennas on the roof. A map board. Two RTOs equipped only with attitude and grease pencils. Our journal was pecked out on a dust-filled Smith Corona. Lots of typos, line outs, and broken English. Whoever was on duty made entries. Today one of the RTOs listens and answers on the radio. The other man next to him types the entries into a computer. What he types concurrently prints out on a huge screen mounted on the wall above them, maybe 4' X 4'. Everyone in the TOC sees the journal as it grows, and can easily follow what has happened for about the last twenty entries. The recorder can page back on demand. The Battle Captain (Head of the TOC) and other officers go back and correct the errors even as they go along. (One thing I learned reading our journals years later was how poorly they were written. Had I to do it over again, I would have figured out who among my workers in the TOC had writing skills, and I would have made him personally responsible for the Journal. And I would have given him better guidance on what to write about.)

In the center of the TOC was a map table, with the acetate-covered Area of Operations map on the top. They used different colored pushpins to mark units. Behind on the wall was the Blue Dot Tracker, a GPS System with the map of the area on the screen. From the perspective of the TOC, a platoon patrol is a little blue dot out there in the AO. The platoons and companies have the same GPS trackers mounted in their command vehicles. As a result, you can watch the units moving along the roads in the form of little blue dots – like little pacmen moving around the map. Their coordinates can be read out to 14 digits. Our artillery can hit a target with a first round from such reference points. Were one of our units assaulted by 100 screaming Arabs, the vehicles could close their hatches and fire an air burst 155mm artillery round right on their little blue dot.

The TOC is very high tech. It was fascinating to see their operations set-up. It was amazing to me — the prospect of having a well-written and complete journal of everything that took place and getting it saved on a computer. Twenty years from now, historians will have far more information than they can absorb and summarize. But it will also be clearly written and accurate.

I learned a lot in the first day or two from JP and others in the TOC. Back in January 2004, FOB Paliwoda was a very dangerous place, with daily mortar attacks. Captain Eric Paliwoda was killed by one of these mortar attacks. But, since the fall of 2004, only one truly bad thing seemed to happen around here — IEDs on the roads. There continued to be occasional rocket or mortar rounds fired at the battalion's base, but they almost always missed.

Three rounds actually made it inside the wire on my third day, but never again during my seven week stay. Most of the rockets and mortars landed just outside the berms, and this is no small base. For one thing, the mortar was probably an old 60mm tube, with no baseplate or sight. And, let's face it — these Iraqis were not too sharp. The much bigger rocket rounds were spotted instantly by our radar, and an outgoing artillery round headed for the rocket's starting point in under two minutes. The insurgents were in a total panic to flee as soon as their rounds went up. Sometimes, the panic preceded the launch — many rounds came in with fuses that had not been armed. As harmless as these attacks had been, there can always come that sad day, and the battalion worked very hard in two areas — wearing their armor outside, and trying to find the perps.

IEDs were far more threatening. Most IEDs found in the area of operation were artillery warheads, from a single 155mm round up to three, taped together. The main counter-tactic was constant patrols along the main roads. All of the platoons of the battalion conducted patrols, in various combinations of Bradley Fighting vehicles and Humvee scout vehicles. The platoons typically did four hour patrols, twice a day. The officers in the TOC scheduled them for continuous coverage of all the main roads. These patrols ran twenty-four-seven. And their vehicles could take a hit.

I found myself wondering who would get to finish this war, us or the other people? Will we finish building the schools, nurse the children back to health, and make the parents love us enough to rat out the terrorists? I was of the mind that the radical Islamic fundamentalists started this current war. But who exactly are the "terrorists?" In 2005 no one really seemed to know, or they weren't saying, or no one listened anyway.

I learned that the IEDs were poorly hidden in the early days of the operation. Sewing them into dead dogs was popular. All dead dogs on the side of the road got blown to smithereens by the EOD squad. IEDs were hidden in trash piles, paper bags, strapped to telephone poles, dug into small piles of dirt, methods the troops quickly learned to spot. Lately, the insurgents were burying them deeper. They were getting harder to spot, but maybe less deadly by being covered with so much dirt, and they still required a hidden observer to set them off. In an IED situation, our soldiers were quickly out and looking for the detonator guy, who was also a man in a hurry.

From the outset of Operation Iraqi Freedom, there was no Hue City. There was no large city in Iraq taken over by an enemy regiment or division. In fact, there weren't any regiments or divisions in the "insurgency". For that matter, there were no battalions, or even companies, or maybe even platoons. Not even in Falluja in 2004 when the city was dominated by insurgents, many of whom were teenagers waving RPGs on TV. The enemy was just small cells of fanatics who would blow up things — just like the local VC cells in the villages of Vietnam who would mine the highway.

After the District Meeting on 5 April, I stayed home to write. I had to make deadline – a new experience for me as a wannabe writer. Norman and JP went to the opening of a new school – our third such opening within the past month.

I worked all day on my column, interrupted only by the mortar attack, the three rounds that came in on the east side of the FOB. I went over to the TOC to follow the action. Everyone was standing around the big journal screen, which I discovered doubles as a video screen. The S-2 had quickly launched his little toy airplane that looks down from 600 feet with video cameras, and feeds the pictures onto this screen in the TOC. At 600 feet, the three foot white wingspan makes it almost invisible from the ground. It was all amazing to me. Where was this plane on 8 February 1968? Or for that matter, on 3 February when 2/12 Cav went on line and ran at the double time across the 300 meter rice field and right into downtown Thon Que Chu? Just like any good Marine unit would have done.

The S-2 Intelligence Officer's unmanned airplane ("UAV") had found suspicious activity by over-flying the area from where the mortars had been fired. As we all watched, the airplane's video-cam zoomed in on a white pickup truck parked at a corner gas station. Two suspicious men jumped out of the truck bed and ran into the corner store. About that time, JP walked in and wasted no time expressing his displeasure about the response time, and the fact that the S-3 and TOC people were all just standing around being entertained by the video camera plane. Maybe he was a little stressed from an exhausting two days of diplomacy. A platoon was dispatched in HUMVEEs. (*The term combat unit commander and tact don't always go together.*)

On the other wall, blue dots were in motion. The blue dots were the platoon leaders. I could see the platoon that was moving toward the suspect area. Equally impressive, the platoon leaders could see where the other platoons were. I was stunned. As my brother-in-law would say about computers, "how do it know? How do it know?"

I went back to work, and by the end of the day I submitted my first column.

WHO ARE THE REAL BAD BOYS?

It always helps to know who the bad guys are in a combat zone. The latest line is that 10% are Islamic Extremists, and 90% are former members of Saddam's regime. How many are there? Allah only knows. The officers running the war call the 90% the Former Regime Elements ("FRE"). The media calls them the "insurgents."

We aren't in Baghdad, where the 10% segment get themselves on TV doing spectacular and inhumane terrorist acts. But we are just an hour away, living beneath the stars and listening to the dogs and frogs. The rich farmlands astride the Tigris River was home to many of Saddam's officers and special operators. Sunnis by religious preference. Now mere shadows of their former selves.

The district we operate in is like a donut, with 100,000 Shias in the city, and 45,000 Sunnis in the surrounding farms. The district is like a county, with its chairman and councilmen. But LTC Petery is the real power.

The Iraqis love their weekly meetings. For sticky issues there's always next week. Schedules are met "in sa Allah" – God willing. We prounced it imshallah. But they are moving along. Tina the interpreter is the only female at the district meeting. She is pure Iraqi, but she's there because she's from Detroit and working for the US Army. Paralleling this attempt at democracy is the tribal network. The tribes have meetings too, where they drink tea, talk things over, and the sheikh summarizes the prevailing view. There are no women at those meetings either. No sir.

In most of Iraq the tribe is where first loyalty remains. Democracy in Iraq will have to overcome, or somehow take into account, the tribal structure. There are many tribes here, small and large, rich and poor. The big agrarian tribes east of town, and along the main highway to the west, are full of Saddam loyalists. And they average 6.5 children per household. No movies. No dinner out. Nothing else to do. Lots of people by the same name. These Sunni tribes used to run things around here. Now they are just a lot of people out of work, tempted by money to set off IEDs and car bombs. The funds come in from the 10% — people like Osama Bin Laden, Syria, maybe the Saudi Arabian royalty, high up members of the Ba'ath Party. Most of the money goes to the guys in Baghdad, because they do the more spectacular stuff for CNN, Fox, BBC, et al. It takes a lot of money for that.

But the money trickles down to our district as well. Around here it goes to fat old men, maybe even a sheikh or two, still loyal to Saddam. The fat old men form the cells of country bumpkins who make IEDs, plant them along the roads, hit the clickers and run like hell. IEDs mainly flatten the tires of a Humvee and give the occupants a two-day headache. They also hire the men to fire the worn-out mortar, apparently missing a sight, and run like hell. The US commanders and intel officers seem to pursue these bad guys through the sheikhs. The sheikhs trade their bad guys in for projects funded by America, or in exchange for the merely wayward youngster who got detained — sort of like prisoner exchanges. Shades of Checkpoint Charlie. It's all about the money. It's all about the tribe. The media has softened its tone about the 90%. They call them "insurgents" since they don't strike all that much terror. Well… they aren't even insurgents. They don't have a cause, they are just out of dough.

Getting a suicide bomber to drive a car full of dynamite up to the front of a police station is in the realm of the ten percent — the "terrorists." We haven't had a suicide driver here, knock on wood. And there are the foreign fighters coming across the borders to Iraq to show their manhood against the hated Americans. Like the group that got creamed attacking a Marine camp on the Syrian Border the other day, or the 80 guys who lost half their men failing to penetrate Abu Ghraib Prison. These "military units" don't seem to be around our district either. Frankly, some of our troopers wish they were. They trained long and hard at Ft. Stewart and in the desert of California, and are still looking for payback about 9/11.

Exactly who the bad guys are, and how many of them are around, may sound confusing, but the troopers of 5/7 Cav have once again waded through the fog. Soldiers have a way of simplifying things. To the troops, all the bad guys are "Ali Baba" — criminals and thieves.

* * * * *

I inquired about how this column was received, all to no avail. I imagined a reading audience of maybe 25 residents of Jacksonville. I had so much to say, had an opinion about everything military, but it was hard to imagine that anyone really gave a shit. The US Army was at war in Iraq, but America was out to dinner followed by a movie.

With Norman Lloyd and 42d Div PIO Bob Giordano at FOB Danger

Presentation of 42d Division Combat Patch at FOB Danger

CHAPTER 20

SENIOR MAN PRESENT

It didn't take long to get into the routine of things at Paliwoda. It was hot. It was dry. It was minimal. Not unlike LZ Colt when I got there back in January 1968. But then again, not like it at all. I moved about slowly, pacing myself and getting used to drinking lots of water all day. There is more time to reflect in the combat zone than at any other time in one's life. Things move slowly. In fact, when things move too fast in combat, people get needlessly hurt. *(er, general, I mean that in tactics, if you go too fast, you will get all your best point men killed. Strategically speaking, you can't get out of this war fast enough for me.)*

The good news was that I was back with the soldiers after so many years. The main event for the rest of 6 April was planning for a big multi-site raid by Bravo Troop at dawn on 7 April. The platoons would be moving into positions in the dark. The operation would include our Special Forces unit that was located just across the street, and troops from the 203d Iraqi Army Battalion, stationed in the compound next to ours. Eight sites would be raided simultaneously. A couple of the areas were high risk. Norman had been adopted by Bravo Troop by this time, having served with them so many years earlier, and I was not about to rain on that parade.

Norman was getting ready for the operation when I returned to the hooch. He was a kid in a candy shop, polishing his new $5000 lens. I planned to say a little prayer for him that night, and get up at about 0530 so I could be drinking coffee in the TOC when things started popping.

7 April 2005
Paliwoda

The Bravo Troop raid was a big success. The results were 32 detainees and a good deal of IED materials and weapons. Eight separate houses were taken down simultaneously at 0630 hours, throughout the B Troop AO. Planning and rehearsals had taken place at B Troop's CP the night before, and the elements moved into positions during the night. Norman got three hours sleep sitting upright in the HUMVEE, not so easy for a guy of 61 years.

While this was going on I talked with the chaplain at breakfast. He does a lot of counseling. The issues were mainly family problems back home, not boredom. *(I may have tried to put the boredom word in his mouth.)* A lot of marriages breaking up. Guys get Dear Johns in this war too. A draftee went to Vietnam once, and maybe got killed. You went to Iraq over and over and over, and probably did not get killed. We talked about the nature of society today, with the increasing proclivity to bail out of the deal. And the frequent separations. He recently prepared a tutorial to equip troopers with how to go back on early R&R and negotiate. All about how to act at first, how to argue, how to get her back. He was two for two so far with soldiers who went back to save their marriages. I don't know how the two wars compare statistically. I don't want to know. It doesn't matter.

I talked to two artillerymen coming back from breakfast. They were not bored; they stayed busy all the time. I began to think this battalion kept everyone busy all the time.

Later that morning, I went with JP on a platoon-sized patrol. It was a long day, but fun talking with the troops. Burns was the driver in my HUMVEE, Sgt Hare was in the right front with the GPS, Brown was in the cupola above me, and Tina was to my left in the back. I told Burns a little about my first RTO named Burns who carried my AN/PRC 25 down the road to Hue for me in '68. This new Burns smoked too.

We had an uneventful ride on the road across the southern side of Balad and on to Anaconda. After returning briefly to Paliwoda, we continued out to the highway. Just outside the gate, JP's driver clipped the barbed wire barrier and wrapped wire around his rear bogie wheel. The crew spent 30 minutes cutting the wire out of the tracks. After that, the IED check of the highway went smoothly. It was interesting to watch all the traffic from the other direction stop when the lead Bradley wheeled across the median to u-turn our column. The Iraqis had trained themselves how to drive on Route Tampa without getting blown away by a 25mm chaingun.

8 April

A one-star general was scheduled to fly in at noon. Assistant Division Commander of the 42d Division *(ARNG)*. Norman and I scrambled to the rooftop of the headquarters building, hoping to film the bird touching down with the 5/7 Cav flag waving in the shot. They were early. Norman frantically got his camera into position just as the Black Hawk was flaring the nose for touchdown. A giant dust cloud enveloped us and practically blew us off the roof. No flag, no Black Hawk, nothing but dust in the picture. Pretty funny actually.

We went along when JP took the general on a tour of the AO. We traveled in a flying column of eight Humvees, with two Apache gunships scouting ahead and to the flanks. We were loaded for bear. I had a greatly increased feeling of security having Apaches dogging us. In fact, the odds of being attacked were zero.

We stopped first at a checkpoint on a bridge that was the target of many mortar attacks and sniper rounds. Then we went to the site on the canal where the boys had gone upside down in February. It was easy to see how it happened. The road teed right into the road that parallels the canal, on which there is no curb, no guard rail or fence. The lip of the canal is even with the road surface, making the canal invisible until you were right there. You could even do it in the daylight — and they were traveling in the dark and the rain at the time.

Our last stop was at a firing range where we met Iraqi Army personnel conducting training. I hung back and was introduced at the end. The general's opening comment was that I needed to get rid of my old helmet and get one like his. I immediately responded with "I rather like my steel pot. I'm keeping it." He instantly retorted with "it won't stop anything," at which time he was dismissed from any columns or any books I might write. *(just kidding)*

I could have gone on and on about what the helmet is actually for, but I had already done enough damage to myself. The new helmet won't stop a bullet either, but I was not about to debate that one. Helmets are not for stopping bullets. All old soldiers know that helmets are for **1)**artillery and grenade fragments, which they will stop, **2)** not getting knocked silly in the Humvee, the Bradley, the aircraft, and all other gyrating places with sharp edges, and **3)** to shave and wash in the field, as well as carry one pair of dry socks, letters from home, pictures of girlfriends, etc. Of course, we have now designed capability number 3 completely out of the new kevlar helmet. Not unlike the phone that is not on the back of the Abrams tank. My helmet was the envy of several soldiers who got the full tour of it. The new guys, of course, will tell you that the Kevlar helmet will stop a bullet. I bet when one does, it will make the Stars & Stripes. Trujillo didn't make the Stars & Stripes back on 23 October '67.

Seriously, the general turned out to be a very good guy, and we warmed up a little after that. I took pictures of everyone. How the Army became fixated on personal protection in Iraq, though, said a lot to me about the justification for this war and how the troops and their leaders really felt about it. In Vietnam, we more and more learned to disengage before losing too many guys. The war became less and less critical. It seemed like we started right off in Iraq in the "disengagement" mode.

That evening we went to a big dinner at the house of the District Chief. Again, he was the most powerful Sheik in Balad, the Imam of the Mosque, and the District Chief. He was the man in this province. Such an affair was called a "goat grab" by the troops, because you stand around a table and eat goat meat with your fingers.

Inside the dusty brown walls surrounding the sheik's house was an oasis of beauty amidst the dust and ugly buildings of Balad. We started with Cokes in the courtyard, a beautiful lawn surrounded by walls covered with rose bushes. In came his three little children for a short appearance. Little sweethearts, the eight-year old looked like my granddaughter Kelly. Once everyone had arrived, there were at least twenty Iraqis along with JP, Tina, and me. Beetle the bodyguard stood in the background in full armor, locked and loaded, scanning the crowd throughout the festivities. *(Yes, his name was Bailey.)*

Over Cokes, I asked the Iraqi battalion commander *(through Tina)* how long he had been an officer. "Twenty- eight years," she replied on his behalf. I reached my hand out, and we shook hands; no further words were exchanged. He was as shy as I was.

Being vulnerable to culture shock, I was nervous. The tables inside were piled high with all manner of foods: chicken kabobs, a big goat or lamb's leg at each end of the long table, different treatments of other meats, rice, vegetables, fruits, hummus, other sauces like hummus, and various exotic items I planned to steer clear of. The bread came in last, hot from the oven, looking like thick burrito shells. Everyone took a big piece of bread which doubled as a plate and a napkin. Bread in hand, we all just stood there. As I was staring at all the food, and beginning to wonder when we would start eating, the Iraqi Battalion Commander across the table tore off a huge hunk of lamb and plunked it down on my bread. In excellent English he exclaimed, "Sir, you are the senior man present!"

Everyone immediately dug in for an awesome feast. There was no rice with cold duck's blood sprinkled on top. Nothing smelling anywhere close to Nuc Mam. The goat grab was an incredible experience. The food would be categorized as Iraqi gourmet in NYC — with a capital Gee. Easily a $100 per person affair. We totally lambed out. It was another day in paradise. I hoped I would be ok the next morning. And I was.

Two rocket rounds were fired at Paliwoda while we were out, but missed the compound entirely. One did not go off because the fuse was missing. The Iraqis are not too technical, but they know from food.

9 April

On Saturday, JP and I went on a seven-vehicle patrol involving the 1st Platoon of A Troop. Call sign: ACE RED. The platoon was mounted in two Bradley fighting vehicles and two Humvees. The Bradley is like a small tank, with a 25mm machinegun. Actually, it is called a chaingun. Puny compared to the sixty-ton Abrams main battle tank, with its 105mm gun. But against the insurgents presently operating in the battalion's assigned area, the Bradley was all the tank anyone needed.

JP merged his three vehicles into the patrol — his Bradley and two more Humvees. The mission was to check out the area from which the mortars had been fired into the battalion base a few days earlier. The plan was to do the daily routine of checking the main highway for improvised explosive devices *(IEDs)*, and on the way back zip down the local farm road to the suspected mortar position.

Before we left, the platoon leader issued instructions about the order of the vehicles and how to react to various situations, such as being ambushed. The Battalion CO in his instructional mode elaborated about finding an IED. He pointed out that the tendency was for everyone to just stop on the road and bring out the ordnance disposal team to blow it up, but the important thing was that these roadside bombs were command-detonated by someone hiding nearby. Someone needed to be searching immediately for the detonator guy in all the good hiding and observation spots. It was decided that the lead Humvee and the platoon leader in his Bradley would immediately go left. JP, third in line in his Bradley, and another humvee would immediately go right. The rest of us would stay on the road, with the rear Bradley for additional security.

When we arrived at the farm area in question, we were greeted by a local farmer. According to him, our artillery rounds had cut a powerline, which in turn killed one of his cows, which in turn was to be compensated for, according to the farmer. We had no trouble acknowledging the artillery rounds that we sent in. We told him how to go about putting in his claim. But, on the subject of who might have fired the mortars at Paliwoda from his orchard right next to his dead cow, the farmer knew absolutely nothing. It was a total mystery to him. A search of the orchard netted two buried AK 47s and accompanying ammo.

10 April

I was picked up mid-morning by Captain Jackson, commander of A Troop, to go to a school opening. We again traveled in a patrol built around 1st Platoon. From the school opening, we would go over to Anaconda for a few days with Captain Jackson's Ace Troop. The new school was in the farmlands south of Balad, deep in Sunni territory. We left the main road halfway to Anaconda and traveled a mile south along a canal. The road was rough dirt and offered a few opportunities to slide off the bank.

Many of the adults from the area were in attendance. All the children were lined up against the wall in the courtyard. The girls in one group, the boys in another. At the beginning of the ceremony a group of three student leaders moved forward to raise the flag, conspicuously all boys. Several people spoke as we sat adjacent to the lectern enveloped in all of our armored vests, helmets and weapons.

As the speeches were winding up, it appeared that none of us would be called on to speak. So, in JB fashion but lower in rank, I removed my Kevlar and stepped up to host at the lectern. Wearing my Vietnam fatigue jacket and the 5/7 Cav baseball cap that Norman Lloyd gave me, I reached for and after some hesitation received the microphone. After all, I was the senior man present according to the commander of the 203rd Battalion of the Iraqi Army.

I directed all of my very short remarks to the children, ending by telling them to stay in school and when they grew up they would get purple ink on their finger. I then asked the Iraqi official to interpret, which caught him off guard. I presume he quoted me correctly, but then again he might have told them to disregard the crazy infidel and we will be killing him later.

The finale was for me to hand out the school supply kits donated by the 5/7 Cav Veterans Association. All the children lined up to receive a zip-lock bag full of school supplies, boys first of course. The boys were smiley. The girls were petrified. I could not get a single girl to smile, which is practically impossible for one as charming as I. One little girl had the unmistakable pattern of cigarette burns on her face. No one was fooling those little girls. They would not be seeing freedom anytime soon, or equality in their lifetime.

When I returned to the stage it was intriguing to look into the glowering eyes of the adults. I had apparently been quoted correctly on the issue of the right to vote. I returned to my seat, wondering who among them might be planting bombs beside the roads around here.

After a quick game of soccer with the boys, we mounted up and disappeared in a cloud of dust. We turned onto the main road and went about one quarter mile when I heard the boom, and a split second later felt the shockwave.

Capt. Jackson was immediately on the radio to various people, after which things went as JP had laid out on the previous day on the way to the orchards. We were quickly out and after the clicker man. That night I wrote my second column.

IMPROVISED EXPLOSIVES:
JUST ANOTHER DAY ON THE JOB

As we sped along the road, I heard the boom a split second before feeling the shock wave. My first thought was to pray for the guys in our next vehicle back. There is no rear window in an M1114 scout vehicle, so the driver slammed on the brakes and skidded sideways to a stop in the middle of the road. It was a relief to see the other M1114 all in one piece behind us. But the rear Bradley was out of sight around the curve, and not answering their radio.

Spacing between vehicles varied, but everyone was at least 100 yards apart. An insurgent had probably clicked a remote, causing the two artillery shells buried beside the road to go off – garage door opener technology. This roadside bomb missed its target, going off 50 feet behind the third vehicle. Their turret gunner, Nick Atchison, said his first thought was "to pat his arms down to see if blood came through the material." Sgt. Ducksworth, commanding the rear Bradley had the best view of the explosion 50 yards to his front. The shockwave killed his engine and radios, and by the time they braked to a stop they were enveloped by the dust cloud and falling rocks. It took several seconds to power back up.

Only minutes earlier, this patrol had been securing the area around a new school provided by the US Army.

These roadside bombs are called improvised explosive devices (IED). When an IED goes off, the patrols react with pre-planned tactics. Capt. Jackson in the second M1114 was immediately on the radio, then got out and walked back toward the third vehicle to make sure they were ok. Sgt Beau Saucier ran up to join him. They moved cautiously around the curve and were relieved to see that the Bradley was not damaged. The key to stopping IEDs is to find the guy who pushed the clicker, so they began to move into the courtyards of the houses in the blast area. Things picked up when a squad from the Iraqi Army showed up to help. Half an hour later our men came out leading two handcuffed detainees, one from Iraq and one from Sudan. They were loaded into the first Bradley. Finally the Explosive

Ordinance Demolition (EOD) people showed up. They drove a little robot truck with mounted video-cams up to the explosion site and checked the area for more bombs. They also determined the contents of the IED somehow. All very high tech. A guy in the EOD vehicle runs it with a tv screen and a toggle stick.

We finally pulled into base just before dark. I was tired from being wedged into the back seat, encased in forty pounds of armor vest. The old steel pot was still heavy after so many years. Tomorrow will be more of the same for Ace Troop. The 5/7 Cav has constant patrols like this every day throughout their area. Since arriving in January, the battalion has suffered no casualties from the frequent IEDs and the mortar rounds coming into their bases. The troops wear their protective gear religiously, and after three months on the same roads, are skillful at spotting things. The bad guys are very unsophisticated. The Sunnis in the outlying areas are very poor farmers. A rich man comes along offering to pay good money to anyone who will set off an IED. It's cash-and-carry combat. We also are looking for the rich man as well.

I sense that too much "success" has its own drawbacks. 5/7h Cavalry is a highly trained combat unit. Boredom will slowly be added to missing their wives and loved ones, and hot weather is just around the corner.

* * * * *

By this time in my trip I was beginning to figure out that the platoons were the workhorses of this war. Except for February 1968, Vietnam was mostly a company commander's war, with his 150 men in a rifle company. Iraq is a platoon leader's war, with fewer than 30 men. In Vietnam, the enemy were actual military units, and it generally took at least a company to generate combat superiority in a firefight. In Iraq, the enemy is generally a small cell that a platoon can handle. In fact, the great majority of our men and women killed in Iraq have been blown up by bombs triggered by unseen individuals, with very few following small arms attacks. The term for an IED that is combined with an additional attack is "complex IED attack." The great majority of IED attacks were not complicated… explosions followed by an eerie silence.

LTC Jody Petery Teaching Government 101 – April 2005

Meeting with Mr. Big

CHAPTER 21

ACE RED

11 April
Logistical Support Area Anaconda
East of Balad, Iraq

The 1st Platoon, call-sign ACE RED, operated under the command of Rambo. But this Rambo didn't carry an M-60 machinegun with belts of ammo across his chest. He didn't hide in rotted-out trees, or speak out of the side of his face. He didn't answer only to a mysterious old full colonel who would fly in from the Pentagon, Langley, or wherever. This was a real person named Rambo; 1st Lt. Josh Rambo in fact. He was all of 5'7" and looked about nineteen.

The history of his platoon went back to 1866 when cavalry troopers were equipped with the Spencer rifle, a saber, and a horse named Dusty, Harriet, or whatever. A lot of lieutenants had commanded this platoon over the decades. For example, my friend Vince Laurich COUNTY LINE 16, led this platoon in 1968. One of Vince's medal citations stated:

"When his unit became heavily engaged with a large enemy force and sustained several casualties, Lieutenant Laurich exposed himself to the hostile fire as he led his men through the hazardous area and directed them in placing effective suppressive fire on the enemy positions, enabling his wounded comrades to be evacuated to safety. Although he was seriously wounded in the action, Lieutenant Laurich refused to be medically evacuated until all of his injured men had been evacuated."

Over the past many reunions of the 5/7 Cav Veterans Association, Laurich always shows up accompanied by a colorful squad of veterans from the 1st Platoon, A Company, 7th Cavalry. They stay in touch to this day. Rambo was filling some really big shoes.

Rambo is a graduate of the University of Florida. He was a quiet and introspective leader. I liked him. He reminded me of me when I was a lieutenant. Throughout 2005, Rambo's all-volunteer soldiers dominated the roads and streets between Anaconda and Balad in their up-armored Humvees and 37-ton Bradley Fighting Vehicles. Rambo's troopers had rifles with night-vision scopes, night-vision goggles that snapped onto their Star Wars helmets, hand-held global positioning devices to bring in artillery with no need of adjustment, teeny little radio devices that put them all on intercom, and a myriad of other stuff that made them totally superior to the insurgent hoodlums they were fighting. They took all those things for granted, though. What Rambo's troopers really loved to show me was their personal medical kits. It seemed like they all had amassed their own personal medical kits, each with more stuff than our medics had in Vietnam. They had high tech tourniquets, drugs, and IV kits, and they knew how to use them.

In the spring of 1968, Vince Laurich's platoon patrolled on foot through the rice paddies and the jungle covered-mountains of South Vietnam, having been deposited there by the 227th Aviation Battalion's UH1B Huey Helicopters. His troopers carried the M-16, which would jam in the sand, and would not penetrate the undergrowth worth a shit. An NVA soldier, given enough opium, could advance another ten yards with five M-16 holes in his chest. No night vision scopes and goggles for Vince's boys either. No intercom, just hand and arm signals, and whispering in the dark. Laurich had a map that told him where he was within 100 meters, if he was on the coast. In the mountains where the contour lines will lie right to your face, well, that was another story. At least they had an M-60 machine gun or two. Elvis was not the King of Rock and Roll in Vietnam. The M-60 Machinegun was the King. They had a man with an M-79 grenade launcher in each squad. And they all carried the baseball-sized hand grenades. And the claymore mines for ambushes and night defense. And the 45 caliber pistols for taking out bunkers and going into tunnels. People have died from shock just by being hit in the leg by a 45 caliber round, or so the story goes.

Laurich's troopers were mostly draftees, and they hadn't volunteered for shit. These particular draftees were "airmobile infantry" in the 1st Cavalry Division, though, and they struck fear in the enemy like no others in Vietnam. The North Vietnamese soldiers were guys just like them, not rag-tag hoodlums. Draftees as well, but for the duration. They had the same basic stuff that we had, minus the artillery and air support. When the troopers of 1st Platoon collided with a unit of the NVA at a range too close for artillery, they had to fight like hell or it was sayonara. And so they did.

But that was then. This is now. Early on my first day at Anaconda, Rambo took me on their daily patrol. We went with two Bradleys and two M1114s. The patrol mission was to go to a suspected launch site for mortars, against the main road between Balad and Anaconda. We turned off the main road very near to the previous day's IED incident, and went north into a peninsula that was all farmlands, with lots of vegetation and narrow roads. This peninsula is formed by the serpentine Tigris River, and is shaped just like Michigan. Not surprisingly, 5/7 Cav designated it Michigan. As we drove up a one-lane road flanked on both sides by thick undergrowth and bamboo, I was thinking "perfect ambush country." But it was another lucky day. After checking the overall area, we visited the farmer whose land had been calculated as the launch site, telling him we were going to fire artillery into his date trees the next time a mortar came out of his property or an IED went off on the main road to the south. He stood there totally innocent, knowing nothing about anything.

Sitting back in the States, I had imagined Iraq as a desert country, all sand and palm trees. Hot. Sandstorms. Camels. Arabs. No place to hide for an enemy. Completely at our mercy from both land and air. Nothing like Vietnam, with its coastal plain full of bamboo-encased villages, surrounded by endless rice paddies.

So much for that theory. Once you navigate the desert between Kuwait and the Tigris and Euphrates Rivers, the party is over. After that Iraq is ambush country! Dikes and levees everywhere. A land where an enemy can set up U-shape ambushes, L-shape ambushes, linear ambushes, all types of ambushes against our forces, who tend to be limited by the roads. The canals, dikes, irrigation ditches, the water table not far below the crust near the river, all can stop the 35-ton Bradleys.

The lush farmlands astride the Tigris and Euphrates Rivers are ambush country, just like the Street Without Joy. Just like Houng My in October 1967. The only difference is the absence of well-equipped and well-trained ambushers.

The nearer one gets to the Tigris River, the greener it gets. Beautiful farm country for growing just about anything. Half the land is fruit tree orchards, and the other half is tilled fields. The farming is all about irrigation. From the two rivers flow the main irrigation canals. Off of the main canals flow smaller canals, and off of them flow the thousands of irrigation ditches. The farmers work hard. The women are out there working too. The pre-schoolers are out there playing. Never more than a few people in one field. Tractors are rare. Real farming equipment is rare. Their main tool is not a plow, but rather a shovel. As you drive along, you see men with their shovels, tinkering with their irrigation ditches. Redirecting the water. Growing their seedlings in little plots that they cover with plastic sheets to protect them from the sun and to hold the water in. The seedlings are transferred to the large fields when they are strong enough. Painstaking work. You look at all the fields, plowed and being farmed, and you wonder how they get all this work done with only a shovel.

All the farms are small farms. No Co-ops. If organized, the country of Iraq could feed the entire Middle East. If organized. Alas, they struck oil. Agriculture was in fact the main industry of Iraq until they started getting rich on oil. They did not modernize their farming. They let their farming go. What fools. The fertile crescent is fertile — except for the people living there. In America, we would never let our small farms go, would we? And buy all our vegetables from South America? Perish the thought.

Iraq is indeed ambush country, except for two limiting factors. There is no jungle. Once the ambush is set off, the helicopters can find them, even in the orchards. The second limiting factor is that the Iraqis are no damn good at real combat. No damn good at all. Never have been.

Our patrol in Michigan was cut short when we were called to the scene of a suspected IED up on the north side of Balad. When we got there, a Humvee from another platoon was parked on the side of the road, observing the suspect IED location, which was a white car abandoned on the curve of the road 300 meters away. EOD showed up, and ran a robot out to check things out. The robot was unable to make a clear determination, but it was decided to take no chances. The completely equipped robot was brought back, and an old stripped-down robot was sent out loaded with 6 blocks of C-4 explosive. When everything was set, we counted down the seconds to the explosion, and the car went straight up about twenty feet from the blast. There was no secondary explosion, so it wasn't an IED. I missed the shot with my camera somehow. As we carried on, I envisioned Ali Baba, or perhaps an innocent farmer, returning with his gallon of gas to find his Toyota upside down and burned to a crisp. Life in the war zone.

We then went out to patrol the main highway for IEDs, and along the way SSg Ducksworth in the rear Bradley reported noises from one of the tracks. We stopped, checked it out, found nothing wrong, and moved out again. We were going about 40 mph up Route Tampa when Ducksworth yelled into the radio, "stop, stop, goddamn, stop!" A second later he reported "my track fell off, we spun and almost tipped over."

We wheeled around and raced back. The Bradley was on the shoulder, facing against traffic, shiny bare road wheels on its left side. Further down the highway I could see the track lying on the road. My first thought was that I would have liked to see LT Rambo immediately jump out and go ask everyone if they were ok, and let them vent the story. But he knew better. The facts were that we were sitting on Route Tampa right in the middle of the area of roadside shops – perhaps the most dangerous spot in the entire battalion's AO. Rambo had other things to do before commiserating with his troopers.

Octavio, the driver, came over later and I asked him what it was like. He told me all about how it "scared him good." Sgt. Saucier had been a pinball in the back, with the world turning upside down for a second. He had his helmet on, of course. The platoon had a lot of work to do recovering all the parts and getting the Bradley back to camp. I was picked up by Captain Jackson at about 1700 hours and went on home to Anaconda.

This turned out to be the patrol from hell for the 1st Platoon. Hot, sweaty work. The crew had to take the other track off, and take both tracks apart and load all the individual pieces into the Bradley. They then towed the Bradley on its metal wheels the 25 miles to Anaconda, getting home about 2130 hours. I was beginning to draft a column about maintenance with respect to the Bradley at the time they wheeled in.

LEAVING TRACKS

"Stop! Stop! . . Stop, goddamit!" The 35 ton M6 Bradley was going 40 MPH down the divided highway when the left track snapped. The track was left lying on the highway, looking like a giant steel centipede on the tarmac. The driver's first reaction was to hit the brakes. The right side stopped, the left side kept on truckin', instantly spinning the vehicle 180 degrees and off the shoulder. The left side

bogey wheels grabbed the dirt, the right side lurched upward just shy of rolling, and slammed back to earth in a big cloud of dust.

This Bradley was the rear vehicle in the patrol. Sgt Ducksworth in command. Pfc. Octavia, the driver, had eyes like softballs when we got there. They were some pissed off guys. It's dangerous enough just being in the combat zone.

The Bradley is a good fighting vehicle, short of having enough room in the back for enough infantrymen. In the first year of the war, this unit had no such problems as they fought their way to Baghdad. Their equipment was in great shape when they departed Ft. Stewart. But now things are different. They patrol the asphalt roads daily. In Ace Troop alone, they have replaced six transmissions out of their thirteen Bradleys in three months. What's up with this? Maybe it is the extra armor. The Bradley is designed to withstand the Soviet shoulder-fired anti-tank weapon, but, the great "They" designed a 3500-pound kit of additional side armor that had to be installed on all Bradleys. One of the other Troop commanders took the initiative to remove 1500 pounds worth of the new armor kit. No robot, he. All the track pads have been replaced twice in the past month. Their third set is falling apart already. There are two kinds of track pads, the standard and the "big foot" track. The standard pad is designed for the hard surface roads, the big foot is for sand and off road. The latest replacement tracks are big feet, of course. 5/7 Cav patrols the asphalt roads up to four hours at a time, wearing off big foot pads. 5/7 Cav is quickly wearing out their Bradleys.

As the story goes, the civilian project officer from TAACOM said that the troops were not installing the tracks properly. (TAACOM - Tank Automotive and Armament Command.) Just pound the pins back in, he said. He even came down to teach them exactly what they already knew about how to install new tracks. Ace Troop's maintenance guy has eleven years experience. Bottom line. The supply system is currently out of standard pads. They are on order. They have only big feet. Why don't they just say that? And there is something wrong with the latest batch of track. The metal is failing. The TAACOM people are holding to their position that the unit doesn't tighten the pins right. Going down the road we watch the big feet flying off of the Bradley to our front. Don't ask me what TAACOM means. It's a rear support agency. I hesitate to use the term REMF, but, hey. For definition of a REMF, consult your local Vietnam veteran.

Right after the near-tragic event, I related the story to a senior maintenance NCO at battalion headquarters. His immediate response: "that's what happens when the drivers don't pull their maintenance." It took me back to my days as an officer in the Berlin Brigade so many years ago. The Battalion Motor Officer would report me to the colonel if I was not at weekly motor stables supervising my drivers. Motor stables is when we all get together with our vehicles and fix all the stuff that isn't broken yet. One day I said to him "were I the Motor Officer, my personal goal would be to keep all the battalion's vehicles rolling, instead of blaming busy company commanders." I ran into the man later in Vietnam. He brought up that story, and profusely thanked me for that advice, which he had followed ever after.

* * * * *

12 April

I went on another patrol with ACE RED. I had adopted them after a few days, as the basis for writing about operations at platoon level. This time we went in three M1114 Humvees. All of the battalion's Bradleys were grounded until they could pull maintenance on all the tracks. I rode with Sherman Reynolds, the platoon sergeant, with Tony Pace up in the turret. As much as Rambo was quiet and laid back, his platoon sergeant was unquiet and restless. He yelled and prodded the entire platoon as they mounted up. It was herding cats 101. F-bombs galore. Just like the good ole days for me. The good-guy, bad-guy routine. Works like a charm.

After covering some of the assigned routes, we drove into Paliwoda, where Rambo suggested that the rest of the patrol would be just driving around looking for IEDs. It might get boring, he suggested. I could take a hint, and took the opportunity to check back into the TOC. Maybe Ace Red needed a break from the rookie reporter with no remaining hair.

I ran into the S-2, Captain Mike Kierstead, whom I had previously thought of as somewhat aloof. Actually, he was just shy, and turned out to be very personable. He took me up on the roof of an adjacent building to see him launch the UAV. The UAV is a toy airplane — well, actually, one of the wing parts costs $3000 — but it is just like a hobby plane, with a 3' wingspan. It carries videocams on the nose and side. They crank up the propeller motor, throw it off the roof into the wind, and away it goes. After that, the captain's Intel NCO flew it with a box that has the toggle stick and a screen showing what the bird sees. They flew it out to a hot area and looked over several target houses. Mike's NCO had a special camera plugged to the system, enabling him to take still pictures of the houses. These would be used to brief the raid patrols when they prepare for a raid operation.

I tried to grab a power nap before being picked up by Ace Red on the way back to Anaconda, but couldn't sleep. A while later, when I got up and headed to the TOC, there were Apache gunships and Loach scout birds flying in circles just to the west of us. *(Reds and whites, as we called them in Vietnam.)* A visit into the TOC was illuminating. JP was there, along with many other people. The helicopters had been shadowing two black SUVs coming north up the highway from Baghdad. A civilian contractor had been kidnapped the day before, and everyone was looking for black SUVs. As it turned out, Ace Red was in position to intercept on the highway *(the real reason to leave this old guy at Paliwoda?)*. Ace Blue was hustling over there from another route. The helicopters were running out of fuel, and the S-2 was getting his toy airplane cranked up to take over.

JP got a little testy while running the situation in the TOC, and jumped on a few people as he went along. It was very educational for the LTs and Captains. This day, the screen showed "no signal" when they switched to the UAV cameras. "What's wrong with it?" asked the colonel. "It is broken," says the LT. "How long has it been broken?" asked the colonel. "Two days." "Get Juice in here," said the colonel. A Commo Sgt. came in, said he was working on it and went out. The colonel was back to scolding the battle captain for the problem's not being fixed for two days. In the meantime, the trooper typing entries on the computer moved his table back, found a yellow cable on the floor, pulled it up and plugged it into the bottom of the screen. Presto, on came the camera. The operator then grinned at me *(the old reporter)*. Who pissed off whom amongst the troopers of the TOC crew, I asked myself. Nothing has changed. Fucking RTOs know everything. In this case they were lucky it wasn't 1968.

The black SUVs never did show up in the 5/7 AO. Or they did and I didn't have a "need to know." Not long after they got the video screen back under control, another platoon reported looking at a suspect IED on Route Tampa. They put the UAV to work on this. I wrote a column that night that included among other things the prowess of the little airplane.

VIDEO GAMES IN THE COMBAT ZONE

The UAV's video-cam was focused on a white pickup truck parked on a dirt road. At 600 feet, this little white plane is invisible from the ground. Several miles away, the officers in the tactical operations center (TOC) watched the video of the truck on a big screen.

The pickup was only one hundred yards from the main supply route, out of sight behind an irrigation ditch lined with ten-foot bamboo reeds. A mounted patrol was stopped on the highway, looking at a probable improvised explosive device (IED), and the white pickup also just happened to have a view of it through a gap in the reeds. As the men in the TOC watched from several miles away, two men appeared from nowhere, got in the truck, and slowly drove away. Maybe the detonator guys. The little plane followed along, keeping them in sight as they went the wrong way up an exit ramp, cut across the four lane highway, then drove slower than normal trying to look innocent, and finally pulled into a shed beside a very nice house. The unmanned plane kept watch, while the nearest patrol of Humvees was diverted from its assigned route. Within an hour, two Iraqi men had been captured, had "tested positive for explosives," and had entered the detainee process.

The scout platoons are the workhorses of this battalion. They also perform house search missions, orchestrated by the officers in the TOC. They might just knock on doors and chat, hoping to get invited in to look around. A lot of tea gets drunk in front yards. No one ever knows anything. Tribal loyalty is paramount. If the Intel Officer indicates possible insurgents, they do "cordon and knock" operations, in which they surround the house, ask to come in, then go in regardless of the answer. With hard intel on a known insurgent, they do the "raid." In a raid, the patrol also knocks on the door -- as in knock the door off its hinges.

While poor Iraqis are being paid serious money to set off IEDs, the colonel is paying the sheiks, in the form of big money projects, to turn the bad guys in. Like almost everything in life, it's all about the money.

* * * * *

13 April
LSA Anaconda

This day started 30 minutes early, at 2330 hours on the 12th. Ace Red departed the gate in three M1114s on a night patrol. Sgt Ducksworth was in the lead. He and whoever was with him were often the point men for this platoon. LT Rambo followed, with his interpreter, driver, gunner and an artillery guy. PSG Sherman Reynolds brought up the rear. The Platoon Sergeant always brought up the rear. I rode with Reynolds. Tony Pace was up top on the gun, and Michael Sankadota drove. Reynolds is normally all four letter words, but this evening he was more jovial. Everyone was jolly and cracking funny. For one thing it wasn't hot. The sky was beautiful. The crescent moon was as clear as HDTV against the black star-filled background. Pace was a riot. They were all ridiculing the "They", and joking about "Military Intelligence — the great oxymoron."

Much to my surprise, we drove the same routes at the same spacing and speed as in the daytime, but with headlights on. It was weird. I do not know how they detect IEDs in the daylight at 20 MPH, and certainly can't imagine it at night going 40. This mystifies me still. We passed an IED crater not far from Anaconda that had been blown only an hour or so earlier. After a brief stop at Paliwoda to collect some intel papers, we continued out to the MSR. *(MSR - Main Supply Route. In this case, MSR Tampa. Iraq was crisscrossed by MSRs leading to and from Anaconda.)*

After "clearing" our zone on the MSR, we split up into three single vehicle patrols to set up night observation posts. Reynolds took us about two clicks up the highway before we cut our lights to blackout drive. A while later we turned onto a dirt roadway into an old abandoned military post. It was creepy driving in at about ½ MPH, crossing a bridge over a canal that was barely wider than the Humvee. Recalling the three men who toppled upside down off a bank into a canal while locked into one of these 11,000 pound scout cars, I was nervous at the sight of the moonlight glancing off the water below. We checked the area out, and turned back out to a parking position just off the MSR.

Michael Sankadota was talkative and we had an extensive conversation. He is a Kiowa brave from Oklahoma. His wife is Cheyenne. Michael was serving his first tour in the Army. He was friendly, earnest, and "had been discriminated against a time or two," which was amazing to me. *(Who would still be picking on an American Indian in two thousand fucking five? Someone with an 85 or less IQ, perhaps. I met some of their parents many years ago.)*

Michael was a fine young trooper on his first enlistment and trip to the CZ. He was trying to decide what to do with his life — what to be. My comment was along the lines of always just doing interesting stuff because some people never decide a final solution, not unlike myself. I think Michael liked his current job, and I predicted to myself that he would re-enlist. *(and he did)*

While we sat in the dark, I talked about Vietnam comparisons, how we operated in the dark with every two-man team having claymore mines, hand grenades, and trip flares, none of which these guys carry in their vehicles. I was surprised they did not carry grenades, the more I thought about it. I talked about using M-79 grenade launchers which had no muzzle flash, JB discouraging rifle fire in the dark, and above all not allowing illumination — and more 5/7 Cav night operations stuff from '68.

Sherman had a night scope on his rifle that turned night into day. For the next two hours we took turns looking for movement along the highway through the scope. We also listened to the dogs. There is a giant network of dogs spread across northern Iraq that relay messages among their brotherhood of dogs all night. You can hear them barking and howling in all directions, from nearby to very far away. If only these dogs would talk, we could root out the roadside bombers. Two hours went by — not a thing. No vehicles. No nothing. Just dogs.

The time went by fast, and it was time to go. We went back down the deserted highway, a lone M1114 driving down a dangerous road. We married up with the others at 0230 hours, and drove unscathed through the twenty miles back to Anaconda. It was another milk run. I was on the internet by 0330 hours checking for messages from home before hitting the sack after a very long day.

While I slept, Ace Red went back out the gate the next morning at 1130 hours on yet another patrol. No rest for those boys. They were young, and they seemed to be tireless.

I finally woke up around midday after the night patrol and decided to have an easy day around Anaconda. After lunch at the nearest DFAC, I went to the pool to collect my thoughts and just chill out.

By the time I had ridden with ACE RED for a few days I began to see beneath all their high tech gear, and the highly disciplined appearance of their uniforms. I began to see fewer differences between them and our troopers of 1968. There were no sweat-stained jungle fatigues with the crotch rotted out on these guys, but nineteen is nineteen. Once you become a 5/7 Cav trooper, it doesn't seem to matter when it is, or how you got there. Perhaps the unit is a living thing. The people come and go, but the troops and platoons live on. Going on 140 years now.

Josh Rambo had eighteen men under his command, and many of them had gone through the berm back in March 2003. The veterans of '03 seemed to be uniformly "disappointed to return to Iraq after only eighteen months at home, but they were soldiering on." They were also uniformly surprised by the relative dearth of enemy activity compared with 2003. Other than the roadside bombs, nothing was going on. Nothing for days on end. This was good for some and bad for others.

By their Table of Operating Equipment, Ace Red was supposed to be mounted in four Bradleys: thirty-seven ton tracked vehicles with a 25mm chaingun in the turret. Four men to a Bradley: the track commander, the gunner, the driver and the dismount scout. The driver mainly drove, of course. Either the track commander or the gunner could dismount along with the lonely rifle scout in the back, giving the platoon the potential for an eight-man dismounted squad collected from the four Bradleys. The platoon also had one Humvee scout car for the platoon leader. It was amazing to me how the Army put that much equipment on the road, and could not afford to put more than nineteen guys in it. There should have been no fewer than three guys in the back of each Bradley. A twenty-seven man platoon. *(Those personnel costs do add up, though, don't they.)*

A Humvee can accommodate up to five guys crammed in like sardines, and the platoon seldom patrolled with more than two Bradleys, for a variety of reasons. They generally patrolled in two Bradleys, and two HUMVEEs, one of which they borrowed from somewhere.

Out of nineteen men, mustering about thirteen to fourteen was a good day, what with perimeter guard, detail, sick call and R&R. In short, ACE RED didn't begin to have enough guys to catch the Hajis hiding in the bushes with their cell phones or garage door openers.

Life in Ace Red was routinely un-routine. One day a week they were on maintenance. Most days they were on patrol in Ace Troop's area of operation. Some days they conducted special operations, such as raids or less intrusive forms of house searches. They generally went on two patrols a day, one of four hours and one of three hours. The four hours always turned out to be a six. Any time they discovered or were hit by an IED attack, they could count on at least two more hours. On one occasion they were the battalion Quick Reaction Force *(QRF)* for a week, and moved to the battalion FOB. They often got called off of their patrol route to react to sightings by the un-manned camera plane, IEDs or small arms fire against other platoons, and other similar actions. Every day on QRF was different, which was a good thing.

The nineteen guys in Ace Red were the same "characters" found in all combat platoons. Everyone in America was in this platoon. Some were quiet and shy, some were gregarious. Some were religious, and some were the opposite. Pranksters and victims. Slackers and gung-ho tigers. The Platoon Sergeant was the oldest man present and cussed a blue streak. Every third word started with F and ended with ucking. He was old Army. When it came time to mount up, everyone just wanted to jump into the vehicles and get away from his harangue. The platoon sergeant always rode in the trail vehicle. I hate to admit it, but he was my kind of guy when it came to being a platoon sergeant. He enabled Rambo to be like me. Quiet. Kind. A dignity and respect kind of fellow.

Hard as I have tried not to, I have tended to have favorites. I was not a good officer in that regard. And maybe my favorite guy in ACE RED was SSgt Beau Saucier. Beau was designated as the dismount Squad Leader. When four to eight men dismounted to search out an area or react to a contact situation, Beau was in charge. Beau was a stud. He was better at everything. He was right up there with the best sergeants I had back in my 101st Airborne days, my Berlin Brigade days, and my 5/7 Cav days. Beau was also a highly trained rifle marksman, one of three designated snipers for the battalion. As of April of 2005, he had yet to be utilized in the sniper role, which pissed him off, particularly with the IEDs being dug in every other night along the main highway. He was dying to be lying in the buffalo reeds in the middle of the night, with one other guy for security, when the bomb droppers came sneaking out to the edge of the highway. *(I can say from experience that if he had been allowed to pop someone after curfew out near the shops, it would have put an end to IEDs there for awhile.)*

And I liked SSG Ducksworth a lot too. And Sankadota. And Tony Pace. And Brandon Godenschwager. And Joe Lucas. Nick Atchison. Big Anderson. Patrick O'Kane. Octavio. Well, I liked all of them, actually. It occurred to me from time to time how crazy it must have been for these young troopers to have a relic from the Vietnam War riding around with them on patrol, and a retired colonel at that. I didn't see myself as an old guy most of the time, but I figured they did, so I tried not to overstay my welcome.

Of all the early information I gleaned from this trip, I was most surprised to learn that the 1st Brigade Combat Team, of which we were a part, had not "task organized." I wasn't alone in this regard. Task organizing is swapping some units among battalions to give everyone the right capabilities to fight their area of operations. Two of the Brigade's three maneuver battalions consisted of Abrams Tank companies and Bradley mounted infantry companies. Before I got to Iraq, I fully expected that the two heavy battalions would each have a scout platoon from 5/7 Cav, in exchange for the 5/7 Cav having at least a platoon of tanks and a platoon or two of infantry. The infantry battalion across the river had up to eight riflemen in the back of their roomier version of the Bradleys. Our guys had one lonely scout in theirs. Both units were performing the same mission in their separate areas. True, the infantry across the river had Sunni-dominated Samarra, while 5/7 had a mostly Shia-dominated city. But any way you cut the cookie, 1/15 Inf could search their off-road areas, but over on our side of the river the 5/7 Cav could not.

A couple weeks into my stay with the battalion, I had the occasion to meet the Brigade Commander of the 1st Brigade Combat Team. I was tempted to ask him why they had not cross-organized some tanks and infantry into this AO, but I held my tongue. Instead, I spent my precious minute with him extolling the virtues of the battalion. In response to my complimentary remarks, he proudly replied "Yeah, we have the best soldiers in the history of the US Army." Being a direct descendant of a captain who died at Valley Forge, and having grown up on Army Posts starting in 1942, I was momentarily rendered speechless.

I had served under some of the heroes of World War II and Korea, and had served two tours in Vietnam well forward of higher headquarters, so I just went right on into silent mode, as I usually do when a senior officer pisses me off. Harkening back to 1964 in Berlin, when I was a newly- promoted captain taking command of C Company, 2d Battalion, 6th U.S. Infantry, Jim "Tiger Lily" Key said it all. "Sir, troops are troops, it's the leadership that makes the difference." Less than impressed was I with the colonel, in spite of his "soldiers being the best in the history of the US Army." Being hell on brigade commanders was nothing new to me though. He was a good guy doing a hard job, and I can be overly critical.

Nevertheless, I didn't get it. Maybe I was having a senior moment. Or a delusional moment about being the "senior man present." 5/7 Cav had a mission they could not totally accomplish by themselves, and they served in a Brigade HQs that didn't seem to employ its units for best results. Where had I heard this story before? Oh, yes. On the road to Hue in February 1968. There were not enough boots headed for Hue in February 1968 either. Not until late in February. Not until too late for a lot of soldiers in 2/12 Cav and maybe some in the 5/7 Cav. And maybe too late for a lot of innocent civilians in Hue.

It was great traveling with ACE RED. I hope they enjoyed it too.

1st Platoon, A Troop, 5/7 Cav. ACE RED — successors of COUNTY LINE 16.

CHAPTER 22

LOOKING FOR ALI BABA

I did a lot of writing over the next few days at Anaconda, completing several columns and trying to get ahead. On the afternoon of the 22d, I sat around the Olympic swimming pool at Anaconda, thinking about what I knew so far, particularly about the similarities between Iraq and Vietnam.

There were lots of little comparisons, they just didn't seem relevant. I was here looking for meaningful similarities, backed by two tours in Vietnam, and I was not finding many.

Yes, the enemy is invisible, as were the Viet Cong. But the Viet Cong were of single purpose. They were part of the grand plan to unify Vietnam and rid themselves of the white man's rule. They had been fighting the French before us, and were the main force units through the guerilla war phase. They were the supporting network for the NVA in the conventional war phase, mining the highways and delivering the rice to the NVA. The VC's guerilla battalions may have been decimated in the first half of 1968, but the surviving cells shared the victory on April 29, 1975. They brutalized the country for a decade or two, but they won because they had a cause specific to their country. We and the South Vietnamese government never had a discernible and unified cause. In two tours in Vietnam I never heard a cogent statement of our overall purpose. The Army was left to fight for itself, not just at rifle squad level where that is always the case, but all the way up the chain of command. In the absence of clear direction, we chased our silver stars and stars of rank. *(Now, there's a similarity.)*

I wrote a column about my view of the war in Iraq, but did not submit it for some reason. Maybe it was too much of the "big picture" for a cub reporter. Some of the words:

> *The invisible enemy In Iraq has no single cause for Iraq. The car bombers in Baghdad are the foreigners, the al Quaida, the men without a country. They are playing to the TV. The Iraqis north of Baghdad call them "the strangers." What is their cause? Their cause is self-image. Besting the white man who has looked down their noses at them for centuries. They don't care about Iraq. Their cause is revenge and hate. How many countries are going to subscribe to such a cause as that? What are they going to do for Iraq, besides blow up Baghdad? They (whoever they are) think we will fold like we did in '68. What if we do? What if we get the hell out of here by the end of the year? Beyond the central city, the men who set off IEDs are the unemployed and the ignorant. They are paid $100 to do so by the*

disenfranchised, by the old members of the Republican Guards who lost their paycheck. Their retirement is history. They are on the outs in their society for having worked for the Hitleresque Saddam Hussein. They lost friends and relatives to the Coalition Forces. Their cause is revenge and making a living the only way they know how. It's all about revenge and money.

The enemy around here is not a conventional army, or a guerilla army, or even an insurgency. The two wars between Iraq and America have marched backward up Mao's ladder. We destroyed their conventional war capability in the Gulf War. In 2003, we obliterated Saddam's guerilla war capability in thirty days. The current enemy doesn't even deserve the title of insurgent. Insurgents have a cause. All these people have is money being funneled to criminals and thieves. The enemy is "Ali Baba." The tactics against Ali Baba should be police work and job creation, not war. At this point, the Iraqi Army and the National Police are the best gigs in town. They are on salary, unheard of around here. A thousand show up for sixty new openings. It is the new IA battalion who helped defend the polling places in January. They will be doing it again in October and again in December, while we watch from even farther away. Construction of infra-structure is part of the mission. We are not rebuilding. It is from scratch. The projects get awarded to the contractors in the area of the projects. Jobs will bring the enemy down. It is we who have a clear strategy this time. Peace through prosperity. That is the cause for which the Iraqis are slowly stepping up to throw out the invisible enemy. TV will also bring the enemy down, as people begin to switch channels away from Al Jazeera. Almost everyone in Baghdad's six million live under a satellite dish.

* * * * *

A visiting CBS reporter had told me a few days earlier that in Vietnam we were "stablilzing the area", and now in Iraq we are "stabilizing the area." He, being far more studied than I, was having an easier time connecting the dots. If anything, this conflict is Vietnam in reverse. I am not even comfortable telling little vignettes about Vietnam to the troops I meet. It is just so irrelevant to them. A little history is good, but frankly, they enjoy their contacts with us 5/7 Cav veterans more for who we are today, now, in 2005, not in 1968. Truth be known, these young soldiers and officers are just like we were. They don't have much time for history, or reporters. They are plenty busy with the present, being soldiers and being the local government.

Sitting around Anaconda inspired a column about the overall issue of boots on the ground. I ate two meals a day at the huge DFAC – one of about five DFACs at the huge logistical base. Did we have enough boots on the ground? Not in 5/7 Cav. How about overall?

* * * * *

MARCHING FORWARD

On the bigger picture, do we have enough boots on the ground in Iraq? I haven't seen enough to know, but I have certainly seen lots of boots that are not on the ground. There are 15,000 people assigned to the big logistics base located in our area. I am there today, hoping for steak and lobster tail. If not, I'm choosing between Burger King and Pizza Hut. But first I will hit the 10 lane, 50 meter pool. Most of the female soldiers at the pool are getting too much to eat, but they're still tens in Iraq. Word is that at least 10,000 of these people never leave the base in their twelve month tour. They fly in on big planes, and fly back out at the end. Ace Troop, 5/7 Cav, and a company of Samoans from Pago Pago operate from this gigantic base, rumbling through the highly-guarded gate on their daily patrols. These two hundred men wear helmets, vests and weapons to the mess hall, and everywhere else. The other 14,800 people do not.

Ace Troop's marksman called the Anaconda people REMFs. I suggested that REMFs were actually good for him, because they engendered a sense of pride in not being one. He smiled. He felt better. But, so far on this tour he has not shot any bad guys. So maybe there are enough boots nationwide. Rewarding cooperation with big money projects, tutoring government officials (doing the State Department's job), and creating jobs, is what is doing most of the damage to the insurgency. More children are walking happily down the roads to their new schoolhouse every morning, looking sharp with their new backpacks, both provided by 5/7 Cav. Counter-insurgency is all about protecting the population, something we abandoned in Vietnam. In Iraq, we are thus far playing Chairman Mao's scenario in reverse. In this country of twenty six million, the few attacks you hear all about on CNN and Fox do not quite add up to "guerilla war". It is insurgency, at best and much of Iraq is only at the unrest level, headed for peace. The National Police may be bitching in Baghdad, but elsewhere their development is moving along. So is the training of the Iraqi Army. In our area, the IA battalion and 5/7 Cav are close.

The IA platoons come quickly to the sound of the guns as soon as they hear of a US platoon involved in an incident.

As long as these trends continue, my sniper-trained sergeant friend will have to cool his jets. There is no way we are going to risk his being captured or killed. If things go well, his shooting days are over.

* * * * *

At the end of the day I began to feel restless. I did not feel much closer to the truth, despite having been here three weeks. I needed to start seeing and writing about other things. Maybe the forthcoming training of the 203d Iraqi Army Battalion, the civil actions programs, and other activities. I was far from bored with A Troop, but I was also thinking about not wearing out my welcome there. Ace Red was due back about 1600 hours, and I spent the evening eating chow with Saucier, Rambo and a few others. We arranged for them to drop me back at Paliwoda the next day.

23 - 24 April
Cordon and Search

I got settled back into Paliwoda that afternoon, and learned that Combat Troop was going to be performing a "cordon and search" at dawn the following day. One of the friendly sheikhs had reported that there was a new face in his neighborhood. The Troop Commander, Captain Phil Poteet, invited me to go along, and I went to their rehearsal briefing that night.

1Lt. Lipscomb, the Troop XO, had built a big diagram on the floor, which showed all the platoon sectors, the houses, and all the streets and alleys. All the platoon leaders, platoon sergeants, section leaders, vehicle commanders, and team leaders were in attendance. The captain led off with the reason for the operation, the time schedule, the overall concept, and his areas of emphasis. Each platoon leader then walked around the diagram placing his vehicles in position, and numbering his houses one through five. They talked everyone through where each vehicle would park and set up, the order of search among their assigned houses, and sectors of fire for the covering vehicles so people would not be shooting at each other. Everyone had an aerial photo with the entire plan drawn out very clearly. *(Back in '64 when I was a rifle company commander, I used to sit next to each platoon leader in turn and draw my plan on his acetate-covered map with a grease pencil.)*

The whole rehearsal was thorough, professional, detailed. Probably like a briefing for a SWAT operation, but with one hundred guys and all kinds of armored vehicles, rather than ten guys in a black truck. The thing I liked best was how the captain invited questions. I could tell that all the men felt open to bring up anything on their minds. Even I was offered the opportunity, and I used it to give everyone a good laugh. 1Lt Lipscomb followed with admin instructions, the most important being the landing zone for medevac. First Sergeant Jones stepped up and discussed in no uncertain terms all the things each soldier had better have with him the next morning. The captain wrapped it up with the kind of stuff that good captains say. In Combat Troop it appeared that the officers do officer's work, and the sergeants do sergeant's work. I was quite impressed.

We were up and out the gate before sun up. The operation went into a small neighborhood very near to FOB Paliwoda.

"This is COMBAT RED, in position, over." The other two platoons reported the same. "Roger, this is COMBAT SIX. Move out in one minute, out."

The sixty-six men of Combat Troop departed the base just as it was getting light. Their mission was to perform a "cordon and knock" operation. Combat Six had three scout platoons and the headquarters platoon, each assigned a sector of 5 houses to search. Each platoon was reinforced with an Iraqi Army squad of about ten men. Interestingly, some of the Iraqi soldiers wore ski masks.

As an aside, the young 5/7 Cav officers I asked believe there are no insurgents in the 1100 man Iraqi battalion. As they get older, they will learn to never say "never" or "always" on any subject.

All the streets and neighboring farmlands were covered by the 25mm chainguns of the Bradleys and 7.62mm machineguns on top of the Humvees before the search teams moved in. Once in position, there were no open escape routes from this neighborhood. The Troop Commander, Capt. Phillip Poteet, led the headquarters search team. The sun was just breaking the horizon when we knocked on our first door.

Every house was enclosed by a six to eight-foot high wall, with a metal gate. For the group I went with, a very agile Iraqi soldier vaulted the seven-foot gate to open the latch. The entire group then streamed into the yard, some searching the grounds, and some going to the front door. The meanest dog on the planet woke the entire area from his position chained to a stake in the backyard.

In cordon and knock, if the person answering the door says ok, they search the house. If the person says no, they search the house anyway. This operation went exactly as it was rehearsed. The first house we went into had a tapestry in the front hall depicting George Washington and the signing of the Declaration of Independence in 1776. (I kid you not.) The only incident was when an Iraqi soldier knocked over a can of precious sugar and ticked off the lady of the house.

There was one house with nobody home, in which they found a brand new AK-47 with 60 rounds. If there was a "new face in the neighborhood", it might have belonged to the guy who owned the brand new AK, and just happened to be off somewhere when we walked in. Or, as in Vietnam, someone called him on the phone right as our first vehicle left the gate and turned left. Each male in Iraq is allowed one AK-47 and 50 rounds, which should please the NRA. Being ten rounds over, and no man to be found, this AK 47 was brought back to base. Other than that, very little was found, and no one was detained, which should please the ACLU.

As we mounted up, groups of smiling children came along with their books and backpacks. The neighborhood was safe for democracy. We were home in time for breakfast. Omelets made to order was the popular choice.

25 April — Recruiting Day
FOB Paliwoda

Not unlike JP's demands for inclusion of the rural Sunnis in the infrastructure improvement projects, he was also pushing the Iraqi leadership about adding Sunnis to the ranks of the 203d Infantry Battalion. The Minister of Defense had authorized the 203rd Battalion of the Iraqi Army an additional 60 spaces, and the battalion conducted a recruiting day on this date in the middle of April. It made for another column.

*　*　*　*　*

SIGN 'EM UP — MOVE 'EM OUT

The Minister of Defense has authorized the 203rd Battalion of the Iraqi Army an additional 60 spaces, and Monday was recruiting day. We walked over to the nearby Iraqi Army compound to see the action. The scene reminded me of teenaged girls lined up to see Paul McCartney in 1966.

Constantly jostling their way toward the door into the interview room, forty Iraqi men were draped all over each other along the wall. The Iraqi Army officers and NCOs had them penned in, and yelled and waved their arms just like cowboys do during roundup. Another line of equal length squatted along the opposite wall of the courtyard, being guarded by Iraqi soldiers. The candidates wore a wide variety outfits, from traditional white Arabic robes to the slums of East St. Louis. There was at least one Yankees baseball cap. The World's Team. For some in these lines, it was an act of patriotism, but desperation for a job was etched on the faces of most of these men and boys. LTC Petery and Tina stepped bravely into the middle of this semi-riot and called for quiet. This situation would have been a great mortar target for Charlie, the Viet Cong, but would be like hitting a needle in a haystack for the insurgents around here. The "Ali Babas" have only a general idea where that mortar round is going when it leaves the tube. Sometimes they forget to arm it.

Petery was eloquent as usual, praising their bravery and thanking them for volunteering to serve their country. He went on to say that everyone would be interviewed, and by Friday sixty would be hired. They would be checked out with their sheikhs. The sixty positions would go to men from the outlying areas, not from the city (one guy from the city got up to leave, and they wouldn't let him). They would be selected not because of tribe or position, but rather their qualifications to be a soldier. They would be selected by LTC Petery, not the Iraqi Commander, to avoid any allegations of favoritism. When he opened for questions, many pressed forward. Nervous moments for the security guys. One young man, 19 years of age looking like 15, had a letter showing he had been in the battalion earlier. He wanted to come back. "Why did you quit," asked the colonel, not unreasonably? "I quit because I got shot at," said the lad. The ensuing discussion made it apparent that an American's unreasonable can be an Iraqi's reasonable.

After letting the kid down easy, we all trooped out to the front gate, where there were another three hundred applicants in line, yet to be searched and sent into the compound. We had lots of security out there. Our troopers were every twenty yards along the line, along with a lot more IA soldiers. Two of our Bradleys and a massive tank retriever blocked the street coming in – an uninviting target for a vehicle-borne suicide bomber (VBIED). I hoped we had other vehicles farther out from the front gate to spot any vehicles propelling themselves toward the IA base. This situation was much more dangerous than the tumultuous one inside by the interview room. The rear of the line surged forward and pressed in close to LTC Petery and Tina. The Iraqis had not passed the individual pat-down search point, either. Nevertheless, the colonel stepped right up and gave the same pitch. At one point, he was interrupted by a very angry Iraqi who seemed to be verbally attacking America. It was an opportunity for Petery to tell everyone how the man had freedom of speech now that we are here. I focused on looking for bulges in his shirt. Petery almost lost his cool with the guy, who was just using the opportunity to make a political speech. We never quite understood why he was in this line to join the IA, and not out digging up mortar rounds hidden in the surrounding orchards.

The walk back to our side of the base was a relief to the Sergeant Major, who had been riding shotgun for our little group. Entering the TOC, I read a report just in about a white water truck that was suspected to be a suicide bomb. It had reportedly left Samarra headed for our area of operations. A few minutes later we heard about a gray sedan bomber coming toward us from somewhere. I immediately wrote this column, in the comfort of my mini-trailer a 200 meters

away, while waiting for the ground-shaking boom. But nothing happened.
The sun went down, we all went to dinner.

*   *   *   *   *

26 April — School Opening

Another school had been finished, this time on the edge of Balad in Shia territory. All sorts of people showed up, to include the US Army engineer unit that had supervised the building of the school. A couple female officers were there. It was great fun. The children smiled. I had a classroom full of girls beaming and giggling with glee, as only I can do with the little ones. It was a good day in the civil actions arena, but a little weird. All the teachers were delighted to see us, except one who was obviously disgusted with the whole parade of soldiers in kevlars and helmets. Who knows what her story might have been. Mrs. Baba, perhaps.

27 April

Things were going fairly well within the city of Balad, but little progress was being made in the Sunni areas on the outskirts. And no progress whatsoever was being made in the shop areas along Route Tampa, the main highway west of town.

IEDs have been positioned along Tampa daily for the last two weeks, many within a mile of these shops. Detonator devices have been found hidden in some of the stores. The target of these bombs are the US Military vehicles. The Battalion S-2 had been for some time focusing his efforts to develop intel in that area — building his "linking tree" of insurgent suspects.

It was time for a meeting with all the shiekhs and shop owners, which was held in a building out on their side of town. It made for a good column, which I wrote and submitted the next day.

*   *   *   *   *

READING THE RIOT ACT

LT. Col. Petery closed down all the shops on the national highway, and summoned all the relevant sheikhs to a meeting. When he walked in to the room, nine sheikhs, two Imams, and thirty-four shop owners were waiting for him. Forty-five glowering faces total. A tension-filled room.

These shops are in a big cluster about one quarter mile long. IEDs have been positioned along this road daily for the last two weeks. The colonel's basic message was simple, "you people in this room know who is triggering these devices. You can report the bad guys to your sheikh, or you will be living with fear the rest of your lives." My immediate thought was that they have been living with fear their whole lives so far, and it may be about who generates the most fear.

The colonel went into his "peace for prosperity" pitch. "Your area has been left behind in this district. The area east of the city is cooperating against the bad guys, and has $1.4 million in construction projects. The area southeast of the city has $1.8 million in projects. Fourteen new schools have been built, and ten are under construction. Clean water projects are ongoing. But you have not joined in. You tell us it is always strangers putting bombs on the road, that you never see them. I don't believe you. I know you see them."

Being called liars really set them off. The people were indignant. "It wasn't in our shop." "We are there twenty-four hours a day." The voices were rising when the city mayor stepped in and appeased the crowd. It was classic good guy-bad guy. The colonel went on to say, "you should also report a stranger in your neighbor's shop or fields." That went right past them. People spoke intensely about protecting their own families. Collective concern appears to be a concept further down the road than some of these folks can travel. In a much calmer tone Petery delivered what were actually much more ominous words. "You can help me get rid of these IEDs in your area, or I will have to do it as a soldier." They didn't even blink. "I don't want to drop bombs in your fields, but I have to protect the lives of my soldiers as well - they have families too." I could literally see the audience thinking: but you are soldiers, and we are not. And your soldier's families are safe in America, and ours are unsafe in Iraq.

The colonel knows all these things, of course. If the US Army was not patrolling the streets and roads, there might not be any IEDs. But the facts are that we are still here to train their police and army, and they are not trained yet. And our second mission is to bring schools and clean water into the lives of their children, since they won't. And while we are here, we have to defend ourselves. There's an indelicate term in the Army for such circular motion. Over the course of an hour they went back and forth. The crowd seemed to come around. A young Imam in the front row finally spoke, with soft words of wisdom and calm assurance. If only he was in charge of this area. The colonel immediately agreed with two of his points. There was some laughing and joking near the end. A spirit of cooperation became contagious. Some of the older people stood up and promised to start *reporting things to their sheikhs and Imams, and they encouraged others to do so as well. The shop owners moved forward in their chairs in anticipation of where this was going. When Petery announced that Captain Jackson will allow the shops to re-open, there was a spontaneous round of applause. They were back in business. The sheikhs signed letters agreeing to cooperate. They got photographed too.*

Will the IEDs go away, or will thirty year old fruit trees get wasted by artillery?

*   *   *   *   *

28 April
Route Tampa

Bright and early the morning after the big meeting with the sheikhs, there was a surface-laid IED consisting of two rounds found on the highway about three clicks north of the shops. This lent credibility to an alternate theory of the colonel and his majors about people from somewhere else driving by and dropping them off during daylight. But I still favored exhausting the conventional nighttime theory as well. Plus the troops had to be bored silly, and would relish the feeling of doing something by sneaking out to the cloverleaf and lying there all night. Additionally, having been on several patrols by this time with so few troops who could dismount, I did not see what they were going to do about finding planters of IEDs in the daylight.

At dinner, Josh Rambo, MSG Marketz, and I kicked around how to do a "sniper patrol". Marketz is a Ranger. Tough-looking guy. LT Rambo thought in terms of dropping them off a mile short of the highway along a quiet road, and driving the vehicles on up through the back streets to a place up the highway. They would set up there ready to react down the highway. The patrol, five guys, would walk in to the cloverleaf right after curfew, and set up right on the top of the overpass. Two guys on the rifle scopes looking down on Route Tampa in both directions, one patrol leader on the radio, and two guys protecting the patrol. Two 155mm Paladins would be laid in on pre-established targets just north and just south of the cloverleaf, in case the shit hits the fan.

I, on the other hand, favored dropping them off where Josh said, but then driving the vehicle patrol to the cloverleaf like always, follow the normal pattern, and return to Paliwoda to wait. Business as usual. Paliwoda was only 5 minutes away. At Paliwoda, I would have everyone stay at the vehicles all night, ready to whip down to the cloverleaf. And the ready reaction platoon would also be available to reinforce.

Had we done something like this two or three times, and nothing happened except that the IEDs still turned up, then it would be an issue of catching the perps in the daylight. A much tougher job. Or, of course, we could resort to what we did in Vietnam - hold the highway, rather than sleeping at Paliwoda or Anaconda and venturing out on 4-hour patrols. Wow. There was a novel idea.

This discussion took me back to a day late in my first tour in Vietnam. We had come out of the A Shau Valley *(more about that later)* and were on base security of Camp Evans.

13 May 1968
Outside of Camp Evans
YD 509319

In spite of all our victories of the past months, Mr. Charles was still able to rocket Camp Evans, and mine the highway. There was no question that we had some work to do regarding base security. We reinstated our grid system that we had created back in March, and began active patrolling in all the western approaches to Camp Evans

QL-1, which ran past the east gate of Camp Evans, was being mined every night by the VC. Every night a different location, but never too far north or south of Camp Evans. We began putting out ambush patrols in areas that we thought were likely avenues of approach to QL-1 for the VC sappers. One such area was the villages and farms along the Song O Lau River, about two clicks north of the base. This river came in from the mountains, crossed QL-1 under a bridge that we guarded, and continued on to the ocean.

On about our third day of base security, the County Lines searched north toward one of these villages and came across an abandoned hooch, next to a little stream that flowed north into the Song O Lau. It sat all alone in a little draw along the riverbank. They searched the area, and found lots of sandal prints. The whole place looked suspicious. The company left behind an ambush patrol hiding in the scrubby bushes on higher ground just above the little hooch. The rest of the company returned to base.

That night at about 2200 hours, well after curfew, the patrol detected movement in the area of the hooch. A couple dark shadows slipped in to check the place out. The patrol continued to wait patiently in ambush, when in walked a group of black pajama boys, carrying stuff that did not look like farm implements. When all the VC were in the kill zone, the patrol cut loose with all their weapons. They followed up with hand grenades. The VC scattered in all directions, some running close by past the patrol. When all was quiet, the patrol moved south toward Camp Evams. Artillery was brought in on the target area as soon as they were safely out of range.

The highway was not mined again through the month of June. My recollection is that as we got back to work in our grid-patrolling west of Camp Evans, the rocket attacks slacked off to a trickle as well. *(this would be how to defend against IEDs in Iraq and Afghanistan, in my humble opinion, as opposed to making stronger and stronger vehicles for the troops to not want to get out of.)*

29 April
FOB Paliwoda

The next morning, two days after the meeting with the shiekhs, another IED went off out near the shops. Ironically, the explosion set a nearby orchard on fire, negating the need for that artillery the colonel had threatened.

I was convinced more than ever that an Arab or two needed to be caught in the crosshairs at about 0430 hours one morning. War is hell, actually. I think most of the shop owners were praying for the same thing. They were scared shitless of the terrorists, be they strangers, or the guy next door they had been lying about for the past two years.

That same day, another Ace Troop Bradley threw a track. This time it rolled. One injured leg and several shaken soldiers. Remember the National Guard sergeant in a Kuwait support unit who stood up to Mr. Rumsfeld about Humvees without armored doors? Now the Humvees are strong boxes. Maybe some sergeant in a combat unit north of Baghdad should tell Mr. Rumsfeld to get the excessive armor off this fighting machine, and get some standard track over here... sir.

We also had a VBIED on the highway on 29 April. A southbound car, passing a northbound convoy, suddenly ran across the median and detonated itself next to a Humvee. The Humvee was destroyed, but the soldiers are remaining on duty. The Humvee is a strong little armored car. The troopers are lucky to be alive. The VBIED driver blew himself up for nothing, but of course went to find the twelve virgins, believing he had scored one for Islam.

A unit of 1/15 Infantry was operating along the river boundary across from Michigan this day, when they were fired on from a boat. They returned the fire, got clearance to enter our AO, and pursued the perps. One bad guy was captured. About 20 years old. There is something about 20 year olds, worldwide. They seem to do all the fighting.

That afternoon the Brigade Commander came down again, and we all went out to the oil pipeline, several clicks west of Tampa out in the desert. This pipeline is buried about two feet or more, with periodic pumping stations sticking up. The pipeline was the responsibility of the Ministry of Oil — the "MOO." The Ministry of Oil had gotten approval to form "MOO" Battalions to be employed along the Pipeline running the length of the country. Their platoon-sized positions were about every 1000 meters. But they didn't have any radios or telephones. And they slept in tents, and half of them didn't have uniforms yet. Since the MOO was not a military department, they had gotten the Minister of Defense — the MOD — to take control of their MOO Battalions. The MOO Battalion Commander was asking us for support — we said ask the MOD, who should ask the MOO for the moo-lah. The MOD was more linked to us than the MOO, and was planning on leaning on us for support of the MOOS. We, on the other hand, were leaving it entirely up to the MOO and the MOD. We only went out there to tell them to be cautious approaching our patrols, because our guys might mistake them for Ali Baba.

The biggest event on this busy day, however, was when one of the sheikhs from the area along the highway came in to talk. The sheikh put the finger on three guys, all members of linked families who have lost members to coalition forces, dating back to 2003. Some of them have missing limbs, etc. They were sworn to revenge. The S-2, S-3 and the colonel began cooking up an operation that would involve an informant, offered up by the sheikh, who would drive us by the houses of these people. The next day, there would be an operation whereby someone would call on these houses on some pretext, and if the perps were there, a platoon from Ace or Bulldog would show up and capture them. According to the sheikh, capture of these people would put an end to the IEDs.

On my way to my hooch that night, a young soldier came over to me in the dark. We traded stories for some time. All this stuff is fun, he said. He didn't know what he was going to do back in civilian life without night vision goggles, GPS tracker systems, driving in the dark, going on patrols in the clear night air, and on and on. There wasn't going to be anything fun about working for the phone company. One and a half years in the Army so far, he won't be coming up on reenlistment until they have been back in the World for some time. Were it next week, there would be no decision to be made for him.

30 April
Paliwoda

It was a day of remembrance. Thirty years ago that morning, chaos reigned in South Vietnam. People did desperate things to escape. The ocean was full of little boats. The beautiful waitresses from General Hollingsworth's mess at Plantation were probably in a prison already, or maybe were kept around to work in the new NVA general's mess *(and do other things, perhaps)*. The Vietnamese Rangers were headed for the tunnels and caves beneath the Mekong Delta, to fight on for many more years, trading places with their enemy who were now sleeping above the ground in buildings for the first time. When the sun went down on the 30th of April 1975, Saigon was Ho Chi Minh City. Ask the average American and he thinks we lost the war that day. Actually, on that fateful day in 1975, we had already been gone from Vietnam for just over two years. And we had lost it long before that. *(I went out that night to a rock and roll bar in Atlanta and had several beers. Several. At 0200 hours, a rookie cop delivered me to the Dekalb County lock-up for speeding and maybe not smelling so good. I was greeted there by a cop who was about my age. He saw my Army ID card, heard my story, and handed me a breath-o-lizer. He walked back across the room and looked at papers, while telling me to blow into the tube. "I got nothing," he said on his return. "Call your wife to come pick you up." I thought about it, but decided not to ask him what unit he was with in Vietnam.)*

Thirty-years later at FOB Paliwoda, it was a quiet night after six rounds of 155mm artillery went downrange somewhere — most likely across the river for our friends in 1/15 Infantry. I still jumped a little bit when the first round went off, because my high-frequency hearing is long gone. Incoming and outgoing all sound the same now. The "Paladin" 155mm self-propelled howitzer sounds not unlike a 120mm rocket to these impaired ears, depending on the direction they are firing. That's my story and I'm sticking with it.

It was not easy finding similarities between Iraq and Vietnam, but one commonality stood out - the young people in uniform. Our soldiers continue to be collectively wonderful, wrapped around the strong, the average and the weak of the unit. Nothing has changed about 20-year olds during my 60 years in or around the Army. If only all Americans could just stay in their 20s, America might be a better place. For that matter, if everyone in the world stayed in their 20s, who knows what the possibilities might be. I grew up impressed with the wisdom of the old people. Now that I am one, I am no longer so impressed. It is the old people, after all, who send the young off to fight their wars for personal power, greed, revenge, jealousy, ignorant biases, and all the other baggage they have collected during their adult lives.

Well, anyway... when I went back to Paliwoda I learned that we had a deal cooking in the aftermath of the CO's crazy meeting with the "Highway Robber Barons" the other day. In spite of the rhetoric, there was an IED in the Route Tampa area each day for the next two days. There continued to be one every day until the eldest of the sheikhs came in to talk about it. Today, the promised informant was driven around in one of our routine street patrols, all covered up in stuff like we wear, and he pointed out the houses.

A force from Ace Troop was going on the mission the next day. The three houses over by the highway were going to be raided at zero dark thirty, and hopefully we would make the big score. According to the informant, if we get these three guys, the IEDs will be gone from Route Tampa in the Balad area. We shall see. I hoped to be riding with the S-3, and I couldn't wait. Alas, the mission eventually got cancelled. The targeted bad guys were away at the time.

I stumbled off to breakfast the next morning and later walked back from the mess hall with Capt Bob Weeks, the S-3 Plans Officer. The sky was a beautiful blue, and the air was clear on Eric Paliwoda's this morning. Being at FOB Paliwoda must have reminded him of his friend Eric every day.

As we reached the central area, a company from the Iraqi Battalion was just marching in for training. And one of our platoons was heading out the gate on another mounted patrol of the roads and highways. But they would not be reinforced by IA soldiers if attacked. All the Iraqi soldiers would be in training over the course of the next month. General's orders. Our patrols would be operating with greater caution. There would not be any pickup trucks full of Iraqi Army infantrymen running over to assist in any big contacts.

Getting ready to jump the fence

Phil Potteet & Me at cordon and knock

LTC Petery & Tina talk to prospects

Found on wall in Iraqi Home

Passing out School Supplies

Makler, Godenschwager, Sherrer, Davis, Rambo & Saucier

CHAPTER 23

TRAINING THE IRAQI ARMY

Someone way up the line dictated that all Iraqi Army battalions receive basic training, followed by small unit training from their corresponding US Army unit. D Troop had a big role in organizing this basic individual training, and had been preparing for it for several months. They had the assistance of the nearby US Army Special Forces Team, as well as our friends from the 442d Infantry at Anaconda. C Troop would be conducting squad training. All the Iraqi companies would be rotating through the various phases.

2 May
Paliwoda

At about 1000 hours this morning, two hundred Iraqi soldiers of the 203rd IA marched in, sort of in step, in uniforms that were not exactly uniform. Major Rashad, the battalion operations officer whom I had previously met, came out of the ranks to greet me. He was wearing no insignia. "I am just a soldier today," he said with a broad grin. Everyone is taking the basic combat training program. Everyone.

A tall, weathered Iraqi first sergeant also came over to meet me — a veteran of many campaigns. Through the interpreter, I asked him, "how many years of military service do you have?" "Two hundred" he said, waving at his men.

The Iraqis were split up into groups, and I went with one to the classroom set up in the 5/7 Cav's maintenance area. The subject was disassembly, cleaning and assembly of the AK-47, which was the primary weapon for the Iraqi Army. Our instructors were from Pago Pago, on loan from the Hawaiian 442d Infantry, WW II's most decorated regiment. They were huge, Sgt. Rock-looking guys. They spoke through an interpreter, but there was no mistake on anyone's part - it was going to be the Pago Pago way or Route Tampa.

Sgt Shimasaki, one of the instructors, told me that "85% of the Iraqi soldiers have never been to school." He went on to say, "we mainly just demonstrate — it's amazing how fast they learn." I'm sure they were on to something, what with my brief exchange with the first sergeant.

One of the other groups was at the firing range in the back of Paliwoda. I was feeling poorly, but went over to see the firing. Our Special Forces friends provided the trainers. About fifteen men were on the firing line, while an equal number sat around, draped all over each other, while waiting for their turn. Not unlike in the line for recruiting day interviews. Iraqis are touchy-feely beyond the norm.

The sun got to me early this day, and I was feeling terrible by mid-afternoon. I drank a ton of Gatorade and went to bed early.

3 May
Paliwoda

I slept all night, got up at 0700, went to the internet café, got some breakfast, came back, watched some NBA on TV, but I couldn't stay awake. Phillip Poteet's company was conducting small unit training for the Iraqis starting this day, and I had promised to be there. He came by to wake me up, but I felt like crap. I was tired all over, just like the flu. Poteet said it was the dust storm the previous day. His people always feel tired the next day after a dust storm. I begged off of going to the training C Troop was running that day, and went back to the hooch to sleep. I arose at 1315, took a shower, and started to feel better. I was beginning to think it was about time to go home. The heat was wearing this old body down. But then again, I was supposed to go on the big raid with the S-3 again that night, which changed my attitude entirely.

Alas, the raid didn't come off again. Or it did and they decided not to take me along. I think the informant failed to show. In the meantime, B Troop was planning an all day IED ambush for the next day, and invited me to go. We were going to hide in the old buildings I went in on the night patrol with Ace Red earlier, and stay there until at least 2300 hours.

4 May
Paliwoda

I woke up late, feeling terrible again. I missed the B Troop operation. Interestingly there hadn't been an IED on the highway for two days now, so maybe something had happened and they just didn't tell me. I was a "reporter" after all. Maybe the heat we were bringing on that area was having some effect.

At 1000 hours Phillip came by again to get me activated. He was a little irate that he had set up small unit training of the Iraqis, and the CO and S-3 were too busy to come and see it. I felt bad about it, and got my ass in gear to go over to their area. I am glad I did.

One of the Iraqi units sat in the training area set up in Poteet's C Troop area. I sat at the back of the makeshift classroom built from ammo boxes and boards. The Iraqi trainees were from a thirty-man platoon. Coming into this training they were thirty individual soldiers, with an officer in command. The Soviet model. They could go on line, attack straight ahead, and take a bunch of casualties. Our NCO instructors subdivided them into three squads of ten men each, and had their officer appoint the three NCO squad leaders. They even had them put on our SSG(E6) rank insignia. This is the US model. Squad leaders are the whole reason we can pin the enemy down with the fire from one squad, send a squad or two through the woods to assault from the flank, and adjust plans as we go along. We work to kill the enemy with minimal casualties. If we accomplish nothing more than this, we will have revolutionized war for at least one battalion in the Iraqi Army. The rifle squad being the ultimate weapon, is this a good idea? I'm not so sure. Only time will tell.

Sgt. Hooper lectured through two interpreters about the responsibilities of a Squad Leader. Influencing, directing, motivating, planning and improving — heady stuff for men with little education and a language barrier. But, according to one man, it was also the first time in his life that anyone had ever "honored him with a class on supervision and leadership." Hooper is built like an NFL lineman. The trainees were influenced and motivated.

One man raised his hand and asked "when are we going to get helmets and vests like you Americans." His newly-appointed Iraqi squad leader, an older impressive-looking soldier in his own right, immediately jumped up and told his man in clear English, "we aren't going to wait for that stuff." My favorite guy so far.

Sgt Bess came next, smiling as usual. He taught specified, directed and implied tasks. More twenty-five cent words, but implied tasks led to interesting discussions about the things you should figure out without being told. As one example, Captain Poteet talked about how squad leaders should get to know their men. When asked if he knew his men, my new favorite guy gave a quiet command, and six men stood up in unison. I loved this guy. I shook hands with him right after the class. *(Salaam al ekum, hand over the heart.)*

5 May
Paliwoda

On the second day's training, the instructor started off by asking one of the other squad leaders what he knew about his men. The man stood up and rattled off each man's name, where he was from, if he was married, and how many kids he had. He had done his homework.

Sgt Dykes gave a great class on squad battle formations. The platoon, the instructors, and this rookie reporter then went out the gate in combat formation and marched over to a nearby soccer field. Two Bradley Fighting Vehicles secured the area. SSG Stack *(a very amusing guy)* and SSG Dykes were the main teachers, running the squads through various situations. Each squad took turns going through the maneuvers on the soccer field. The C Troop NCOs did a great job presenting this instruction through interpreters, a mentally fatiguing job. By day's end, the three Iraqi squad leaders were quite proficient at controlling their men with arm and hand signals, with my favorite guy being particularly outstanding.

It had been another interesting day with 5/7 Cavalry north of Baghdad. The young officer commanding the Iraqi Platoon looked rather pensive. He hadn't said a word all day. Some of his power may have slipped away. I shook hands with all the squad leaders right after the class.

At the end of the training, our Platoon Leader, a 2d Lt. from West Point Class of 2004, explained to the Iraqi platoon that he knew Friday was normally a holiday, but they would have to come for training. "Our soldiers are sacrificing as well by being over here," he explained. Friday. Holy Day in Iraq. Sunday for them. Definitely not Saturday. Frankly, I had a hard time understanding the wisdom of the lieutenant's plan. The Iraqis did as well, because the next day they all went to the mosque. Some of our own platoon officer's power may have slipped away as well.

It strangely reminded me of the preceding week when we flipped a Bradley. The man in the back who had his leg injured turned out to be their Iraqi interpreter. At least two people had assured me that nobody had been injured that day. The interpreter apparently was the "nobody" about whom they spoke.

I received an email this day from Jim Brigham of the 7th Cavalry Association, forwarding to me a note from Michael Sankadota's wife Maria. She had seen one of my columns on the internet about her husband on the night patrol, and was so pleased to hear about him.

That evening I was loitering in the TOC. A guy named Sutterfield worked on the artillery fire direction desk in the TOC, and we started talking for the first time. He had been very distant. He wondered what I was doing there. He didn't know I was a writer, making me wonder what I was doing over here also. It turned out that he did not like working in the TOC with 5/7 Cav. He was not reenlisting. The Army was not his cup of tea. It maybe explained why he had been so distant, since he assumed that the Army was gallons of tea for me. Actually, I had some moments of feeling like he did back in my day. Sutterfield saw civil war coming after we depart. He had bought 10 acres with a pond for $12K in the Tallahassee area, and couldn't wait to get there. I liked Sutterfield now that I had talked with him.

6 May
LSA Anaconda

There was nothing cooking for me at Paliwoda this day, and I decided to ride back over to Anaconda with Ace Red. We went on a patrol first over to the MSR — Tampa. Josh and the other platoons had just been issued their own little planes to put up and watch the highway. We parked on a dirt road behind some canal reeds, and practiced flying it around along the canals that paralleled Route Tampa for about 30 minutes. A guy named Anderson had returned that day from R&R in his hometown of Castle Rock, Colorado. I got to know him a bit on this patrol. I also mentioned to him how the Cheyenne warriors had burned Castle Rock to the ground after the nearby Cheyenne village had been attacked by the white man back in the 1860s. He had no comment. Probably didn't know anything about that.

We went to dinner at Anaconda, and Ace Red invited me to go on their night patrol that night. The sun had just disappeared when we moved out through the main gate, stopped to lock and load, and moved forward on patrol. The mission was to check out an agricultural area of about three-hundred acres, surrounded by orchards. Our counter-battery radars frequently traced rockets coming from this area, toward Anaconda to the east.

We had opened the school the previous month in this historically hostile region. This night patrol took us down the same dirt road next to a canal, and past the school, deeper into the Sunni farmlands southeast of Balad. It was very dark when we quietly pulled to a stop, and dismounted.

Beau Saucier would lead a dismount patrol to check out the suspected areas. He turned to me and said, "Are you going with us, sir?"

"Sure." What else could I have said?

We moved out silently with Michael Sankadota on point, followed by the Patrol Leader Sgt Beau Saucier. They were followed by Makler, Anderson the medic, the rookie reporter, O'Kane and Schwartz. Seven total. I was immediately struck with how quiet they could move. Their Kevlar vests and harnesses didn't rattle like ours did long ago. No metal-on-metal parts to tape down. All plastic. Imagine. Plastic is not just for cars.

We moved through the tall reeds along the edges of the orchards and paths. The men in front of me blended into the background. It was very dark when we arrived at the target area, but we had a little moonlight. The going was difficult at times. We constantly leapt over little irrigation ditches. On one occasion we stepped up onto a man-made concrete irrigation flume, and I needed what little balance I still had to step to the other wall and jump down. I was packing no weapons and ammo, which evened me out with the smaller guys in the patrol. I actually helped one of the men in front of me a couple times - he may have had the shortest legs in the Ace Red Platoon — maybe in all of 5/7 Cav.

Saucier had his men clip on their night goggles when it got really dark. My normal night vision enabled me only to see a couple men to my front. Saucier had a little palm-sized GPS device that read out our longitude and latitude to within ten meters, and he would stop to check our location from time to time. Push come to shove, we could immediately fire artillery within 50 meters with relative impunity. No adjusting. Just fire. Would have scared us shitless, though. Everyone had rifles with night scopes. Schwartz brought up the rear with a little walkman radio that was strong enough to talk to Lt. Rambo, back with the Bradley vehicles. We were seven guys alone out in the dark, but comforted by the fact that all the resources of the U.S. military in Iraq were at our beck and call.

The area was a checkerboard of grapevine trellises, lower crops such as wheat, and small orchards. It was far from being a big open field. Every little patch was surrounded by irrigation ditches. Some full of water, some full of weeds and mud. Our plan was to check out the area, then find a good observation point from which to watch and listen. There was a house diagonally across the big square area, and straight up the side that we were on was a shed. Sankadota and Makler went up and checked out the shed while the rest of us observed the house.

When they returned, we moved straight out into the field, until Sankadota literally dropped from sight into a deep irrigation ditch. We had to help him back out. It took me back to a night patrol at Ft. Campbell in 1962 when my point man fell head first into a well. He caught himself in the kudzu growing down the sides, and we were able to daisy-chain about three guys down that wall of ivy and pull him back out. It took about thirty minutes. He aged at least a year.

Saucier decided to double back and find another way into the fields. Before long, we found a trail going through an adjacent crabapple orchard. Just as we started to turn into this trail, we spotted a moving light coming toward us. Everyone hunkered down and froze. The light turned out to be a cigarette carried by one man. At the last second, Saucier could see that he carried a shovel, not a weapon, and we watched him pass by not more than ten yards from us. The farmer was heading home after a long day of farming. Or maybe from burying some rockets that had been set up earlier. Saucier had been very cool on the trigger finger.

After a bit, we found a good spot with concealment and cover to watch the field, and set up a small perimeter to wait. If we heard or saw anything we would move in from there. That would have been when I stayed close to Anderson, who carried an extra 12-gauge shotgun strapped to his back. Alas, it stayed quiet. Nothing happened.

Later, as we moved back toward the vehicles, we were confronted with a gang of barking dogs, blocking the road. Saucier decided to cut back into the orchards again and go cross-country. The vegetation was very thick. The ditches seemed to be getting bigger, or my step was getting smaller. We came to the backyard of a house, where a man smoking a cigarette stood on his rooftop. We were maybe thirty yards from him, with a big ditch to jump. That is when I fell on the far side of my jump. He had to have heard me. The frogs heard me, because they suddenly went crazy. The frogs started up, more joined in, and built to a deafening crescendo. Deep-voiced frogs, high-pitched frogs. It sounded like hundreds of frogs. We were frozen there, surrounded by frogs, while keeping the man under observation through two rifle scopes. I was wondering if he had his AK 47 with him up there on his roof. We settled down for several minutes, the frogs stopped as suddenly as they had started.

Someone said later that a single frog made all that noise. Impossible, I thought to myself. We quietly moved sideways, waded across another muddy ditch, and suddenly found ourselves back on the main road. The silhouette of a Bradley was only a few yards up the road. Saucier went up and leaned against their fender while calling them on his little radio to report our location.

Another night under the beautiful stars of the Iraqi sky. Fifty opportunities to sprain an ankle, and I survived them all. I figured that I might not get to go again, though, after triggering the frog attack. This patrol turned out to be my last escapade with Ace Red. I loved those guys.

8 May
Anaconda

I took it easy the day after the patrol. By midday I was ensconced at the Olympic Pool, reading the Stars & Stripes. I got to talking with a sergeant named Jeffrey Cunningham, assigned to the 14th QM, and working in support of 5/7 Cav. He had 20 years service, and planned to stay in for as long as they would let him. He liked to teach the young soldiers what they need to know. He told me that the 5/7 Cav was the best battalion in his memory. They had no complaints, high morale, and dedication.

Later in the day I sent a paper on IEDs to a classmate working for a think tank in Washington. My focus was that the billions of dollars worth of equipment to protect vehicle occupants was not the answer to IEDs. Soldiers on foot catching the perps in the crosshairs of sniper rifles, claymore mines, and hand grenades — those were the answers to eliminating IEDs. But then again, maybe you just can't teach this old dog new tricks.

9 May
Paliwoda

I returned to Paliwoda and hung out around the operations shop for awhile. Captain Weeks and I talked a bit about his pal Eric Paliwoda. Weeks and his senior NCO, SFC. Weisen, talked about back in 2003 on the road from Kuwait to Baghdad. The enemy had appeared to be taking farmers out of their homes and making them fight. Most of the enemy would fire with their heads in their holes, and all the incoming fire would be 10 feet up. Like they had to fire to save their families, but didn't want to hit any Americans and bring down the wrath of God on themselves.

I suggested that the mortar guys around Paliwoda were the same. Weeks described the heiarchy, with the mortar men being the lowest rung. Next up is the rocket guys, above them is the IEDs, and at the top are the VBEIDS. You get closer to the real bad guys as you go up the ladder. Like going from marijuana to cocaine moves you one step closer to the Mafia.

The mortars have dried up around here, having been ineffective, giving way to more IEDs. The IEDs seemed to have crested during last week of April and first week of May, with 10 and 9 respectively, but we only had 4 in the second week of May. There were 5 IEDs in the first week of April but we had also had a couple incoming mortar attacks. Then we had a couple more the next week, and since then nothing. We had moved up to IEDs, and they had not worked for the enemy either. The enemy was moving to VBEIDs now in north central Iraq. There had been 46 VBIEDs since 1 April, but we were sort of in a middle ground between Baghdad and Tikrit/Samarra where most of the big bombs were going off.

In the Stars & Stripes that morning, there was a report about a big battle out at Lake Tartar a day earlier, in which 80 terrorists had been killed. This lake was out beyond the MOOS from the MOD. According to Weeks, there actually had been zero bodies counted in that battle. A separate story circulating around the area was that an entire MOO unit had been wiped out by the terrorists, having all their throats slit. We never had any of these confusions over body counts back in Vietnam. Right?

Capt Weeks gave me a map of the AO, and also put a document on my stick that included copies of two relevant field manuals, and a list of the nomenclature of their equipment as well as the various acronyms. I loved the map. I didn't tell him of my disdain for acronyms. We talked about all the different weapons and vehicles some:

M-240B Machinegun – 7.62mm. Replaced the M-60

M-9 Pistol – 9mm. Replaced the 45 cal. Questionable stopping power

M-16A2 Rifle – 5.62mm. The little bullet I complain about. *Apparently they have improved the receiver since Huong My.*

M-203 Grenade Launcher. An M16A2 with the 40mm grenade launcher attached. *My project in the Weapons Committee at Ft. Benning in 1969. Demi Moore carried one in GI Jane, and looked good doing so.*

M-4 Rifle – 5.62mm. An M-16 with better rifling and "620 meter effective range." *That's a long way for that little bullet. Call me skeptical.*

M-249 Squad Automatic Weapon "SAW" – 5.62mm. A weapon like the old BAR designed for 3-round bursts, and accurate like the M60 Machinegun. *But it fires the little bullet though.*

50 caliber machinegun. Mounted on various vehicles. *Oh, yeah. Now we're talking.*

25mm Chain Machinegun. Main gun for the Bradley. "Big bullets"

M-14 Sniper rifle – 7.62mm. A real gun. Kills big animals like elk. Stops people regardless of their drug content. *This bullet will, in fact, go a very long way.*

M-6 Bradley with 25mm the Bushmaster Chain Gun, which fires at 300 rounds per minute on full automatic, or 200 rounds per minute on single fire. Also has the M-240C 7.62 Co-axial machinegun on top of the cupola.

Fister. An Armored Personnel Carrier with a 4.2" Mortar.

M-1114 Scout Car. A Humvee with turret-mounted M249. *(Should be the M240C)* The gunner also has his personal weapon up there.

UAV "Raven" The little unmanned plane with cameras.

Blue Force Tracker. A magical GPS System, with little blue pacmen running around the AO.

8 lb. Company primary radio system. *Versus 25 lbs. in our day*

Computerized Journal on large Plasma screen.

STX hand-held radio. *Replaced the huge walkie talkie that, if it worked at all, had very little range.*

Hand-held GPS locator. *Like the golfers carry.*

Infra-red Scope. For the basic rifle. *Wow.*

IR night vision goggles. Clip on the helmet. Everyone has one. *We own the night. The dark is really our friend, now.*

I came out of Vietnam years earlier dreaming of an Army that would own the night. Our ability to see the NVA through a starlight scope as they ran down QL1 on the night of 18 February 1968 represented the future to me. We had very few of these new scopes in 1968. Charlie owned the night in Vietnam.

Bottom line — Our soldiers are just as good as ever, but their equipment is a quantum leap beyond everyone else's.

Iraqis report for Training – April 2005

Iraqi Squad Leader rattling off facts about his men

CHAPTER 24

FINALLY – THE BIG OPERATION

10 – 14 May
Paliwoda

I was reading the Stars & Stripes on 10 May when I remembered that on this day in 1968 the 5/7 Cav came out of the infamous A Shau Valley after three brutal weeks of combat in very difficult conditions. My mind still vividly pictures so much of those dangerous days. More about that later.

For the next couple days I spent most of my time writing in my hooch. I was starting to get short — counting the days until my flight back to Jacksonville. Each day seemed to be five degrees hotter.

JP and I began to talk about when we would present the Combat Cavalryman Badges that the Association had purchased at my request. We have badges on top of badges now. Going into Vietnam there was the Parachute Badge, the Ranger Tab, and the Combat Infantryman's Badge, a silver musket on a blue field encased in a silver wreath. That was about it for badges.

Speaking of the Combat Infantryman Badge, it was "created during WW II in recognition of the combat service and sacrifices of the infantrymen who would likely be wounded or killed in numbers disproportionate to those of soldiers from the Army's other service branches." It was not for cavalrymen, tankers, artillerymen, signal corpsmen, or medics. It was all about being an infantryman. "General George Marshall initiated this award in response to a Medal of Honor recipient who said, 'wouldn't it be wonderful if someone could design a badge for every infantryman who faces the enemy, every day and every night, with so little recognition.'"

Things started to slide in Vietnam. Advisors were becoming KIAs. Just like my friend Konnie Lubavs. Officers and NCOs from other branches were acting as advisors to Vietnamese infantry units, and they wanted the CIB too. Through weight of numbers and political clout, the other branches got the wording changed in the criteria to "anyone serving with an infantry unit in combat." By the time the war was too far along, all kinds of non-infantrymen were being awarded the CIB. Never mind that they were going back to their branch on their next assignment, never to return to the rubber in the road. Konnie was an Infantry Officer. Had he survived his first tour as an advisor, he would have been in an Infantry unit on his second tour. He certainly earned his CIB… and a posthumous Purple Heart as well. One more instance of nothing staying the same. Nothing. Even in the Army, where customs and traditions are so important. Well… they used to be.

Now we have badges for just about everyone. But you know what? With today's technology, I wouldn't volunteer to be a tanker, a pilot, or any other kind of soldier in a metal vehicle in combat. Not when I could dig a two by six, or hide behind a tree. So, those other branches deserve some badges. I am particularly proud of the Cavalry. They didn't try to figure out how to get some other branch's badge. They simply created their own unofficial badge whether the Army liked it or not. The Combat Cavalryman Badge. A yellow bar with cross sabers superimposed. The US Army should formally authorize it. But if they don't, we in the Cavalry don't give a flip and will wear it proudly.

14 May
Paliwoda

There came to us a another informant who was well connected with the bad guys, and desired to cash in on the $50,000 reward for the capture of the "number one target" on the Brigade's target list. The target was a man named Kamel. Kamel looked like a shorter version of Osama Bin Laden. He was allegedly the head terrorist in north central Iraq. He reportedly traveled with a squad of 12 men armed with AK-47s and wearing explosive vests. If they had to go, they were taking some of us with them. He was a tailor by trade. Kamel the Tailor.

The informant and the target had been best friends for years, but the informant was sick of the constant peril his family was in. He wanted out. He wanted to come over. The plan was for him to key a satcom phone when the target showed up to meet him at a certain house between 1000 and 1400 hours on Friday. There was a mosque next door that they would be going to at some point. There was reported to be a bunker and tunnel complex in the area of this house and mosque where, if things worked out, we would also be collecting all sorts of war-making materials. Maybe we were going to be paying the $50K and sending the man and his family to some friendly Arab nation. The witness protection program, so to speak. The site was close to the river, so maybe we were heading into an ambush. Orchards, irrigation ditches and canals, dikes and levees, lots of good places to set up. So we went in force. Our first really "big operation" while I was there.

Captain Ralph Elder, BULLDOG SIX, was in command of the six platoon task force. He had his own four platoons, and two more from Combat Troop. WAR PAINT SIX had an additional force in reserve built around his PSD — "personal security detachment." *(We had a security platoon at battalion headquarters in Vietnam. It became personal when JB came along. We didn't want to lose him.)*

Lt. Vreeland and Sgt. Willis from Ace Troop were also involved to coordinate artillery support. They could drop a 155mm HE round on a fruit basket. They would be one of the observation points on the outer cordon. There was a 4.2" mortar track in the task force as well. Apache guships were laid on to be circling out beyond the horizon, ready on call to pounce. The CO was predisposed to bring in the Apaches right away if we got into a scrap. "I'll just level the place" were his words. I knew from leveling places — sounded like a good plan to me.

We headed out in the morning, doing things we always do. Business as usual. The platoon departures were phased out over several hours. But if and when the phone call came in from Agent 007, everyone had a place to go and things to do. I figured the informant actually coming in was a maybe. Kamel showing up was a possibly. The platoons moving in fast enough to catch him was somewhere between a probably not and just plain not.

The plan was simple in concept, but had lots of moving parts. The first thing to happen was that two platoons would come in from two different directions to set up the inner cordon circle. Bulldog Red had the east side of the ring, and Bulldog Green had the west. Coming along behind them in the schedule was the outer ring. Combat Blue had the west side blocking escape routes to Samarra along the canal roads, and Bulldog Red had the east side, blocking the crossing points over the river. With the inner ring in place, James Bithorn's Bulldog Blue Platoon (Norman's buddies), reinforced by two IA platoons, would come straight up the road to the objective house. The IA platoons would be mounted in dump trucks. Lt. Haugee's Combat White platoon was in reserve for the assault, positioned just beyond the inner circle.

I listened in later to 1Lt Alvin Lewis, BULLDOG RED, briefing his men. Alvin played linebacker in college. He closed with "remember, you can ride with us or collide with us." Oh, yeah. Sounded like maybe a fifteen-yard penalty, and a $50,000 fine from the commissioner.

WAR PAINT SIX would be riding in his Bradley as part of the outer cordon on the south. His PSD Platoon was mounted in Humvees. I hoped to go with them, but it turned out that there was "no room." That boy wasn't gonna put this old-timer in harm's way. I rode with the SGM.

I had a feeling it could end up being a long day in the hot sun. And it was. One of the Medic APCs blew a head gasket as soon as we got on Route Tampa, and spouted black smoke everywhere. An M88 tank retriever came and towed it away. From there, we followed JP up to Hawaii to wait for developments.

Hawaii was aptly named for the cynic that most of us soldiers are — it was devoid of everything except blowing dirt, glaring sun, and an industrial building riddled by months of target practice. The single most desolate spot in the AO. We sat and waited for the word that Kamel had showed up. And we waited, and waited. The temperature went to 114 degrees.

I had drunk water all day, but by 1330 hours I had spent too much time standing out in the sun talking to Ralph Elder and James Bithorn, and started feeling dizzy. I didn't feel right for the rest of the day, in spite of drinking endless quarts of water. The informant failed to show up, and the mission was aborted at about 1430 hours.

I was still not feeling well when we got back to Paliwoda, so I went straight to my hooch to lie down. It was late by the time I went to chow. I was supposed to depart the next day for Baghdad. Someone came and got me. I was still half out of it when we awarded the Combat Cavalrymen Badges to all the officers in the conference room. I also received my spurs for being in the Cavalry in a combat zone, which I truly cherish. I am a real cavalryman now. I got my picture taken in front of the old Vietnam battle flag hanging in the conference room. In exchange for this largesse, I gave a little talk which I delivered quite poorly in the condition I was in. I would come to miss being with them later, but it was time to go and let them get back to the war.

This was my last outing with the men of 5/7 Cav in Iraq. It was time to go visit my classmate's son in 1/69 Inf down in Baghdad.

Ace Red

15 May
Paliwoda

I spent the day packing and saying goodbye. Ace Red came through on a patrol, and we got together for a picture. That evening I got on a Black Hawk flight to Camp Victory at 2205 hours. Flying in the dark was very comforting. We could see everything on the ground, and they couldn't see us. Just the sound of a helicopter going by. We stopped for refueling along the way, dumping out two civilian females on a very remote piece of dirt. I could not really see or talk to them in the dark helicopter, so I don't know what they were doing over here, but I suspect they were contractors.

Lifting off, I could see the city lights in the distance. Before long we were flying across the eastern side of Baghdad. Twinkly lights everywhere, but no big ones. Definitely not LA, or even Jacksonville. Finally arrived at Victory Pad at 2330 hours, but there was no sign of anyone from 1/69 Infantry.

I asked the two young Marines running the operations building if anyone had been there looking for me. They knew nothing. I had a telephone number, but could not make it ring, and asked them why the phone would not work. They knew nothing. I asked them if there was a directory I could use, and they did not have one. After an hour of stewing around and periodically trying to get any number to ring, one of the Marines smugly asked me if I was getting anywhere. I think I politely said no. He had nothing to offer. I asked if there was another type phone, and before I could finish the question the answer was "no." I asked if there was an operations center at the headquarters where an Officer in Charge would be on duty. He knew nothing.

Finally they became distracted by an irate Army Lt. Col. who blew in like a hurricane, pissed off about everything to do with getting a ride to somewhere. I could understand. Amid the shouting and "yes sirs," I found a phone directory under a pile of papers just in reach over their counter. In no time at all I found the Commanding General for all of Iraq, a mere four star general, which I later pointed out to them.

"It is too late to call the General and wake him up," I said, as I leafed through the phone book. They didn't get that joke. "Knew his dad," I added, to which they just stared at me with pitying disbelief.

Luckily, I next stumbled across the telephone number for the Public Affairs Office at the main headquarters. At 25 minutes after midnight, I was incredibly fortunate to get a Marine lieutenant on the phone. He turned out to be very helpful. In fact, he hustled over and picked me up, put me up at the visiting tents where Norman and I had stayed six weeks earlier, and promised to get the 1/69 over there in the morning. As we were getting into his SUV one of the two non-helpful Marines came out of the operations building. He and the lieutenant greeted each other like long-lost relatives. Most un-Marine like. I didn't say a word. I figured that the young Marines hated civilian reporters, just as I had 45 years earlier.

The next morning my new *(and only)* Marine friend in Baghdad picked me up as promised, fed me breakfast, and took me to the big palace — headquarters for all ground forces in Iraq. It was not long before Major Charlie Crosby was outside to take me from there. His dad and I are classmates, and we were tactical Officers on the West Point faculty together in 1970. Lifelong friends.

We spent the rest of the morning at Charlie's headquarters at Camp Liberty. *(Ah, there is a difference. In this war we can call someone Charlie. Crosby's friends call him Chuck, though.)* The 1st Battalion, 69th Infantry, of the New York National Guard had been given the challenging mission of securing Airport Road. Over the past several months, they had put an end to much of the sniper fire and IEDs that had terrorized everyone dating back to 2004, particularly the media people covering it.

When I came to Iraq, I had no intention of ever seeing the infamous "Airport Road" that ran for seven miles between the airport and the "Green Zone" in downtown Baghdad. It sounded scary to me. But that was before I learned that Major Chuck Crosby was temporarily in command of the fighting Irish. I was going to go anywhere he wanted to take me. "Let's go down to the Green Zone," Chuck said. "There is a little café there and we will get some lunch."

We went out the door, and I was immediately met by Crosby's driver, a young guy named Tomb. He immediately ordered me to remove my old Marine flak jacket and put on the Kevlar vest, which he helped me into. It was the latest, complete with shoulder pads and the front groin protector *(a la baseball catcher)*. Once he had me in the vest, he produced a 9mm pistol, stating "and here is your firearm." While I was protesting that a journalist was prohibited from packing, he was plunking the pistol into the holster attached to the front of the vest, and then handing me a clip of ammo. Tomb didn't mess around. When in charge, take charge.

Before mounting up, I introduced myself to the turret gunner looking down on me from his perch. His name was Sgt. John Rogers, and like Tomb, was from Buffalo, NY. Turned out he was drafted in 1968 and was in Korea when I was in Vietnam. He was a cook in 1968, but he cooks on a M240 machinegun now. Needless to say, he was the oldest man in this battalion. Once inside the Humvee, Tomb was very much alive, paying attention to the radios and keeping the CO informed like he was supposed to. Tomb misses the snow, he said. SSG Torres sat in the back with me. He is from Queens. Tall. Quiet. Tough-looking. He was the senior NCO, and he didn't need to say anything. And he didn't.

The seven-mile ride to the Green Zone north of Camp Liberty was uneventful in terms of combat, but was very eventful for me. It was a patrol, not a milk run, and we went through some of the neighborhoods. The streets had lots of people wandering around outside during the day, unlike what I had seen in Balad. We passed one doorway filled with three young girls all decked out in lipstick and big smiles. No tents for dresses. No veils. The people in the big city were not the people up in the farmlands. No sir.

Crosby talked about his AO as we went along. They had a corridor about 1000 meters wide astride Airport Road, which was almost continuous neighborhood. In some of the areas, "sniper fire comes at our Humvees if they sit in the same place for very long." Each separate area has a distinct personality, another reflection of the "first loyalty to the tribe" that pervades Iraq. Not unlike Chicago.

Back on the highway, he also pointed out the repaired crater where a young female humanitarian worker had been blown up a month earlier. We also went by the curved on-ramp that an Italian intelligence agent had used to bring an Italian journalist back from having been kidnapped. The Italians somehow assumed that our soldiers would let them run through our checkpoint at 50 MPH, and risk being blown to smithereens by a car bomb. I got a detailed briefing later about the whole Italian journalist debacle, with the Italian intelligence operative supposedly shielding the female journalist when the bullet hit him square in the head. Pictures and all. It was not our fault, but any way you cut the cookie, it provided the Italians the excuse they needed to get their troops back out of Iraq.

It was a memorable ride, and another great day to be alive, which all of us were when we drove back through the gate into Camp Liberty that evening.

The next day Condoleeza Rice was in town for whatever Secretaries of State do nowadays, other than keeping us out of wars through statesmanship. The primary mission for the day for the 69th Infantry "Fighting Irish" was to secure the highway for the flying column of SUVs taking Ms. Rice back to the airport. It was supposed to come off sometime after 8:00 pm, and the battalion was on the highway in strength. The plan was to place observation posts at key entry points, with mobile patrols operating in between. I was struck with the professionalism of everyone at the big briefing that afternoon where the orders were issued for this operation.

One of the biggest differences between the Vietnam War and the Iraq War was the participation by the National Guard units from around the country. It blew all my theories about what would happen in the next ill-advised venture. Vietnam conditioned me to figure the National Guard would not show up for a bad idea. But the attack on the Twin Towers in NYC really pissed us off, it did. The 1/69 Inf *(ARNG)* responded immediately that day from their armory on 23d Street in New York City, setting up security around the site. And the National Guard turned out for Iraq. We remember the Alamo. We remember the Maine. We remember Pearl Harbor. Now we remember 9/11. We are really pissed off. The rest of the world should think more about this than they do.

That night I again rode with Charlie in a three vehicle patrol, all M1114 Humvees. It was still daylight when we departed. As we were driving around in the failing light, traffic on the highway was backed up behind the various 1/69 Infantry patrols. Only fools get their cars inside a three-to-four vehicle 1/69 Infantry patrol. Fear ran deep out there. The cars bunched up, then moved along at the speed of the patrol, well back a good two hundred meters. The turret gunners had spotlights. They also had miniature stop signs on handles, which they waved at cars merging in from the entrance ramps.

As we were waiting for the word about Ms. Rice, we received a report about a fallen fence on one of the overpass bridges. We went to investigate, and found that the entire chain-link fence panel above the southwest bound lane had fallen inward onto the bridge. A big truckload of explosives could have come along just at the worst time and plunged itself to the Airport Road below, sending the driver along with Ms. Rice to meet the 12 virgins. So our control plan was altered to have the battalion commander's patrol secure that bridge when Ms. Rice came by.

A while later a civilian car in front of us stopped on a bridge not far from the Green Zone. It was dark, and their emergency lights were flashing. We could see two people get out and one of them leaned against the car. We stopped about 100 meters short of them, and Sgt. Rogers used his electric bullhorn to tell them to "imshee." Imshee means get going. After a few blasts of this message, Charlie and three other men dismounted and began advancing on foot. Seeing them coming, the civilians jumped back in their car and drove off. I joined the dismount group and we walked up to check out the area thoroughly for IEDs. Nothing blew up, and we mounted back up. I imagined the Iraqis driving away on a flat tire, or with their temperature gauge going off the scale… or with an un-lit bomb in the trunk.

About that time, we saw a helicopter rise above the horizon in the Green Zone, dropping flares as it climbed to defend itself against heat-seeking missiles. The Secretary was going to the airport by air. Of course she was. We were the deception plan. Like me, she too had no intention of ever seeing the infamous Airport Road.

After two great days with the Fighting Irish on Airport Road, it was time to start wending my way back to Jacksonville. I gave Charlie my Combat Infantryman's Badge, and he gave a regimental crest of the 69th Infantry. His sergeant major gave me the coveted battalion coin. I looked forward to St. Patrick's Day in NYC, now that I had credentials.

I boarded a C-130 that night for the flight to Kuwait. Riding down to Kuwait City, I thought more about the unfriendly Marines over at the Camp Victory helipad, and how much they reminded me of our days back in 1968 when we moved into Marine Territory. 5/7 Cav entered the infamous Khe Sanh on 7 April 1968, relieving 1-9 Marines on the western perimeter. We had temporarily saved the Marines from encirclement by the North Vietnamese Army.

The Marines hated the 1st Cavalry Division for decades after that. Maybe still do. One thing that has not changed, and probably never will, is inter-service rivalry in a combat zone. From the perspective of one much older and wiser in 2005, I can say that the Marine Corps did a great job in Iraq. But in 1968 I was much younger and not wise at all. Operation Pegasus started on April Fools Day, 1968, with a brigade air-assault operation east of Khe Sanh. 5/7 Cav had a prominent role.

Charlie Crosby — St Patrick's Day on 5th Avenue in New York, 2008

Sunrise up on LZ Long — March 1968

CHAPTER 26

OPERATION PEGASUS

March 1968
Vicinity Camp Evans

When we returned from Hue on 1 March '68, we went on base defense of Camp Evans. It didn't take us long to get organized, and base defense quickly became total boredom. I sat around the TOC a lot reading and writing letters. The front page headline of the Stars & Stripes on 7 March was "KHE SANH RAID FAILS." The article went on to say "Charging through a natural camouflage of pre-dawn fog, more than 500 North Vietnamese infantrymen drove to the barbed wire ring around the US Forces base Friday… against the 500 Rangers and 5,000 US Marine defenders… the attack was launched on the eastern perimeter of the two square mile base." From our vantage point somewhere else, we could not quite understand how a force of 5,000 Marines could allow 500 NVA to walk right up to their wire. Walter might have been premature when he returned from his 24 February visit to confirm his opinion about the loss of the war to all of our moms and dads, wives and children, sisters and brothers, and friends and acquaintances back in TV Land. He could have at least waited until 7 March, when 500 NVA soldiers made it all the way to the wire at Khe Sanh against ten times their number of America's finest.

Our blissful stay at Camp Evans ended all too soon. On 11 March, 5/7 Cav conducted an air-assault onto the top of a 359 meter mountain *(BT572216)* about ten clicks west of Camp Evans. This peak was part of a long mountain ridge that rose straight up more than 1000 feet from the flat coastal plain below.

The top of the ridge was completely covered by a double-canopy jungle forest, with no place to land for even one Huey. Not to worry, though. The boys in blue dropped a "daisy cutter". The daisy cutter is a bomb that directs all its force horizontally in space. Sort of like a giant Frisbee. Or better yet, a circular saw blade. It involves some sort of chemical explosion that ignites in a big flash. When it goes off, the giant circular blast wave cuts down all the trees in a radius bigger than the rotor blade of a slick. We watched it go off while hovering out in space in the C&C Bird, about five hundred meters from the mountain top. It was a little like kids playing with M-80 firecrackers, quite exciting.

After this baby went off, our air assault remained on hold, because the circular hole in the forest was full of downed trees. We had to rappel a squad of the 8th Engineers off of the ramp of a Chinook equipped with chainsaws in order to make the LZ useable. I was very impressed watching the troopers go down the ropes from the hovering bird; you would have been too. Most of my experiences in Ranger School paled in comparison. The tense part of the operations was the extensive time that the engineers took clearing the one-helicopter-sized LZ. They were their own security. It took at least thirty minutes, if my memory serves me, before we could send in the infantry. Fortunately for all of us, Chuck was nowhere around at the time. Probably at the bottom of the hill. It was one bird at a time well into afternoon, while the engineers continued to create additional landing area with their saws.

It was the following day before we had the ridgeline cleared enough to bring in the artillery. The guns had barely enough level ground from which to operate. Someone named this firebase LZ Long. Two LZs for one guy. It was very gracious on the part of JB. LZ Long overlooked the flat lands to the east. On a clear day we could see the ocean. On just about any day you could see Camp Evans.

The most likely avenue of approach for an enemy assault was on the western slope, which was not nearly as steep as the opposite slope overlooking the coast. We built an abatee as part of our defense plan. *(Abatee, a French word. In plain English, we blew the trees down the western slope, creating a tangled mass of inter-meshed branches nearly impossible to negotiate.)* Lowering the artillery tubes and firing directly into the abatee obstacle was possible for a couple of the guns, which would provide a murderous effect. We bosses were quite proud of ourselves, as were the Engineers who got to build an abatee in a real situation.

By the second day, we had the LZ cleared, a TOC built, and an artillery battery emplaced. It was beautiful up there. When we got up the first morning, we were on an island in a vast sea of billowing white cloud tops. To the south and west we could see countless other islands sticking up in this white sea. It was all part of an interesting and very predictable weather phenomenon at that time of the year. As the air cooled at night, clouds would form at the lower elevations. At first light, the valleys would be filled with dense fog. As the temperature began to rise, the clouds would begin to rise. By about 0900 hours the tops of the clouds would reach us. By about 1030 to 1100 hours the bottoms of the clouds would go past headed for the sky, and we could see again. During the intervening two hours we couldn't see doo-doo.

The 1st Cav had the luxury of landing on the tops of the mountains and fighting downward. We did not fight up hill if we could help it, and I generally held those who did in contempt. We were snobby, not unlike the 1st Infantry Division *(Big Red One)* in WW II. The 1st Cav had a long tradition dating back to the War in the Pacific during WW II, particularly in the Phillipines, where they led the way into Manila. Like the Big Red One in Europe, they were selected to be the primary occupying force in Japan following the war. As such, they were among the first units to arrive in Korea to combat the North Korean invasion. Fresh from sleeping with Geisha girls for five years, they and everyone else got their asses kicked all the way to the Pusan at the very southern end of the peninsula before things got turned around. Later in life, guys from other divisions, or old farts from my dad's era, would jokingly remind me how the 1st Cav lost its colors in Korea.

Okay, they had a bad day. Everyone's unit was having bad days in Korea about that time. Then was then and now is now.

Sitting around the TOC one night I related the story about my battalion commander in Berlin, who had lost sixty percent of his men in three days because they couldn't outrun the North Koreans.

Our operations from LZ Long began with the rifle companies working their way down the sides of the ridgeline. 5/7 Cav was back to running separate company operations, which had been the norm until Hue. It was very difficult going through the thick jungle undergrowth down the near vertical slopes. There was no contact with Charles as one of our companies moved off the high ground. In the ensuing days we air-assaulted companies further west into the mountains. Things were quiet. Up in the TOC we were receiving and writing lots of mail, reading back issues of the Stars and Stripes, and listening to AFN.

> Dear Nancy,
>
> We are now up in the mountains with our CP and have our companies working along the river that we believe is the main supply route from Laos in this area. We assaulted three companies into the jungle today with no problems. We picked up what we thought were NVA waving a white flag, but they turned out to be ARVN officers who had been captured in Hue and had escaped just before noon today.
>
> Love, Charlie

Unfortunately, our little piece of heaven above the clouds did not last very long. We had spent considerable energy and resources building this firebase on top of the mountain, only to be told by the Brigade CO to move it to lower ground at the base of Rocket Ridge. The issue was either the range of the artillery from LZ Long being too far to help protect other firebases along the coast, or the lessening likelihood of our moving very far west from LZ Long. Or maybe it was the morning clouds. Or maybe it was the Division Artillery CO once again exercising his authority. In any event, we moved the CP and firebase to a foothill just below LZ Long.

13 March 1968
LZ Cathy
BT579227

Some artilleryman named the new LZ on lower ground after a girl named Cathy. And what a mean little bitch she was. There was no cooling ground fog that went cruising by the top of the hill every morning. Nary a tree anywhere. It was like sitting on a stove. The ground was clay and shale-like rocks, extremely hard digging for the troops. Once my work was done setting up the TOC, I dug my own hole, losing about 5 Lbs in the process. I hoped Cathy was overweight, wore braces and had terminal acne.

I no sooner got my hole dug, and was just recovering from blowing myself dizzy inflating my air mattress, when over the horizon came two Chinooks slinging a couple 155mm howitzers from the 30th Artillery. I watched in dismay as one the last 155mm gun was set down about six paces from my hole, blowing half of my dirt parapet down the hill, along with my new box of Havana Cubanas. My cherished cigars were sprinkled throughout the scrub bushes for about 30 yards down the slope. The RTOs went racing after them, since they always got their share. Fortunately, these cigars came in aluminum tubes, and we were able to find every last one draped on the bushes. It was high entertainment for the rest of the troops. Quite funny, actually.

My asking the gunnery sergeant if he could get the tube relocated cracked up his gun crew completely. Everyone roared with laughter until they noticed that I was a major. It got real quiet, and the sergeant was eventually able to explain the impossibility of moving. He went on to assure me that the likelihood of their firing was remote. They "had not had a fire mission in two weeks," he said.

Just a few minutes after midnight my air mattress and I were lifted straight up by the concussion of a 155mm round leaving the barrel. KAABOOOOM!!!!!! On the way up I collided with my descending poncho roof and about 30 lbs of dirt. The guns stopped after only one round, and I was able to scoop out my hole, replace the roof, and settle in. Just as I dozed off — KAABOOOM!!!!!! They fired on and off for the next hour. I just lay there under poncho and dirt. Infantrymen don't wear ear plugs – we don't want to miss anything. My right ear's high frequency range has never been the same. I should not have had those mean thoughts about Cathy, who was probably the artillery battalion commander's daughter. I hope she turned out just swell, and married a handsome lieutenant attending the Artillery Basic Course at Ft. Sill. And he probably hears just fine today, since he kept his ear plugs with him at all times.

We operated from this dreadful place throughout the second half of March, and conducted extensive search-and-destroy operations all along the headwaters of the Song Bo River below us. We had a lot of interesting adventures, but made no significant contact with the enemy. On one occasion A Co found a base camp hidden in the jungle on the very steep northern slope of the mountain, and moved in to find still hot cooking-fire embers. In this action, John Montalbano conducted an individual assault on an enemy bunker hidden in the bushes above him. Poised with grenade and weapon, it turned out to be a nicely constructed one-holer perched on the side of the steep slope. Shit happens, as we say today.

We conducted operations to the south across the Song Bo as well, which involved crossing a swiftly flowing river. This operation was prompted by our spotting what appeared to be radio antennae in the trees on the mountains south of the river. From our position in the C&C Bird above our companies in the jungle, we could see what appeared to be a lot of bunkers under the trees as well, and we brought in a lot of artillery on this possible NVA base camp. That night we sent a coded message to John Taylor giving him an objective across the river.

After assuring himself that the message was not an error, John put his Ranger School training to work. In the pre-dawn hours, A Co approached the riverbank. At first light, they made a river crossing with two lead swimmers taking the rope end across and securing it to a tree on the far bank. The heavily-laden troops followed, holding onto the rope. All of this was done in the best traditions of Ranger School, making the troops remove their fatigues and boots and roll them up into a ball on top of their other gear. That way if one lost hold of the rope, his wet fatigues would not impede his ability to swim for it. Unlike Ranger School, however, the A Co troopers wore no underwear under their fatigues. Some of them felt pretty stupid lying on the bank, their johnsons in the mud, waiting for the word to go.

Once the area on the far bank was clearly secure from enemy presence, we checked out the objective area with no enemy contact. The day was saved when A Company returned to the river and broke out the soap. The troops got their first bath since leaving Camp Heaven. All was well, except possibly for dysentery suffered by the little people downstream. We sent a wall of soap suds their way that morning. Even JB participated. We dropped him off in a clearing at the riverbank to get a bath and spend some time with the County Lines.

The rest of the month was spent searching for NVA units that had long since departed to their supply bases out in the A Shau Valley many clicks to the west. Life was physically demanding for the troops, but no one was being shot at. We rotated our companies around through base security frequently, giving everyone a chance to get some rest. Life was good, even at LZ Cathy in the searing heat.

Around the 23rd or 24th, we got the word that Gen. Westmoreland was to become the Chief of Staff of the Army. He would be leaving for Washington. When my troopers in the TOC expressed surprise, I explained that Westy was being "fired" up to the next job. That's politics, I added. We were also hearing that his deputy, Lt. Gen. Creighton Abrams (Akila), was already calling the shots. About the same time, we received the initial warning about the next big operation. We would be going to Khe Sanh. Beginning the last week of March, the 3d Bde started daily briefings about going to Khe Sanh. Code name — Operation Pegasus. The Winged Horse... that would be us.

On 29 March, we came back from the final briefing, assembled our leaders, and briefed them in detail about going to Khe Sanh. We would be moving our companies on the afternoon of 31 March to an assembly area out in the scrub hills west of Quang Tri. A place called LZ Pedro. D-Day was scheduled for April Fools Day. I dropped a letter in the mail.

The timetable for troop-leading-procedures called for aerial recons on the 30th, with operations orders to be issued on the morning of the 31st, leaving the rest of the 31st for the company commanders to brief their troopers and be air-lifted into Pedro. Unlike previous operations, this one involved considerable information about everything: the weather, the enemy, air lift concepts, fire support, down to what the troops would carry in their packs.

The Khe Sanh Combat Base sat in a valley looking up at much higher mountains which extended from the southwest around to the northeast. Famous hills by this time: the huge Co Roc Mountain ridge southwest across the border in Laos, Hills 680, and 881, just to the west of the base, hills 950 and 1015 directly north, and a long 800-meter-high ridgeline extending far to the northeast. Why would anyone build an operating base beneath those mountains? And worse yet, why would anyone build such a base within range of Soviet made 130mm artillery guns on Co Roc Mountain in Laos?

There was no shortage of comparisons being made between Khe Sanh in 1968 and Dien Bien Phu in 1954. David Halberstam talked about Dien Bien Phu in his great book, *The Best and the Brightest*, in which he said "With the kind of arrogance that Western generals could still retain after eight years of fighting a great infantry like the Viet Minh, the French built their positions in the valley and left the high ground to the Viet Minh. An American officer who visited the site just before the battle noticed this and asked what would happen if the Viet Minh had artillery. "Ah," he was assured by a French officer, "they have no artillery, and even if they did, they would not know how to use it." *(Like me talking about the Arabs.)*

Fourteen years later, at Khe Sanh, we had some senior officers who were every bit the equal of the French. Laos was only about ten clicks away. The NVA's 130mm howitzers shoot twice that far. It only took a couple little people, equipped with a radio and binoculars, hiding anywhere on the jungle-covered face of any of the aforementioned mountains, to employ all those guns with deadly accuracy anywhere in the Khe Sanh Combat Base.

The aerial recons were backed off to the 31st due to the weather, which led to Division's having second thoughts about recons altogether. Eventually it was decided that everyone would rely on the information from the 1/9 Cav, who were operating extensively in the area. As the higher-ups put it, we did not want the operation compromised. Surprise was critical, so the story went. Are they serious, we asked?

In preparation for this operation, the 1st Cav had been building an air strip at LZ Stud for several weeks, in plain view of the little people. LZ Stud was Operation Pegasus' jumping-off point about seventeen clicks east of Khe Sanh, coordinates YD 9949. This general area was referred to as Ca Lu, and it was chosen because it was beyond artillery range from Laos to the west as well as from across the DMZ to the north. *(Hey, there was a novel idea.)*

We went ahead and issued our final operations orders at LZ Cathy on the evening of the 30th. The CO always spoke last, after the rest of us did our thing. He seldom reiterated or amplified any of our stuff. The man always thought about the things that were really important to the troops. Cleaning and test-firing weapons. Lightening the packs. How they were going to eat. What to do if shot down. In which direction to escape and evade. He even had a mission statement for the individual soldier: "Take the initiative, do your job, and be around to fight another day."

31 March 1968
LZ Pedro

Throughout the morning, we air-lifted our companies from their operations areas along Rocket Ridge to LZ Pedro, a large open area of rolling hills similar to LZ Jack. LZ Pedro was at least a mile long and half a mile wide. It was 31 March, D minus 1. The troops were spread out in company perimeters across the area, leaving the center open for the lift birds to come in the next morning. We set up the battalion CP with one of our companies on a little hill. The other two battalions of 3d Bde were there as well.

The Garryowen Brigade would have the honor of kicking off Operation Pegasus to secure the initial objectives, which were astride Highway 9, halfway to Khe Sanh. The Brigade finally had their three 7th Cavalry battalions together again after many months. The Brigade S-3 scheduled a final flight coordination meeting for late afternoon at the west end of the LZ to work out the details with the aviation commanders, battalion S-3s, artillery people - everyone involved in the air assault.

The time for the meeting came and went. We were all standing around waiting for someone from Brigade to show up. People were getting restless. The lift battalion commanders were Lt. Cols. They were unimpressed and getting ready to leave in a huff.

Finally, a guy named Don Munson, S-3 of 2/7 Cav, waved me over to a map board. "Let's figure this out," he said.

We knew where our designated landing zones were. We had a vague idea about sequence. 5/7 Cav and 1/7 Cav were supposed to take the high ground north and south of Highway 9, respectively. After that, 2/7 Cav was supposed to come into the 1/7 Cav's LZ, which was on much lower ground and closer to the highway. From there, 2/7 Cav would move out toward the highway below, and head to Khe Sanh. It was just a matter of how to schedule the lifts with the available aviation resources to get all units to their objectives within the available hours of clear weather.

The opening day of Operation Pegasus would be a heliborne assault the size of which none of us had seen up to this point. Three infantry battalions to be air-assaulted into two separate areas in the space of a very few hours. Two hundred and forty slick loads, several phases, and lots of following Chinook loads. Don and I started bouncing ideas around. The lift commanders started coming over to listen in. Finally everyone had gathered around to put in their two cents. At the end, Don and I did a Huntley and Brinkley to sum up the plan for everyone. Clear, concise and complete.

We would take the two high ground LZs simultaneously by splitting the eighty slicks between the two lead battalions. The first two companies of each battalion would take off from LZ Pedro and head out on parallel flight routes directly to their battalion's assigned mountaintop objective. At the same time, the follow-on two companies of each of those lead battalions would go by Chinook to LZ Stud to cut in half the turn-around distance for the slicks. Once they had been picked up from Stud and delivered in Phase II, all eighty slicks would revert to 2/7 Cav for Phase III. End of meeting. Everyone was departing just as the Brigade Assistant S-3 showed up to conduct the briefing. We filled him on what he had intended to say.

Don was one of the very best officers in 3d Bde, I thought to myself as I walked back to our area. Years later, many of us went off to seminars to learn how to conduct consensus-building meetings, get things done by leaderless groups, synergy, and the like. Later in the 70s and 80s, we officers heard from many a human behavioral scientist on the subject of the "leaderless group". I suspect few of these speakers had ever been in the service. They would have loved our meeting on 31 April 1968. *(They were maybe in high school at the time.)*

Later that afternoon, the CG landed on our little hill, jumped out of his C&C Bird, and strode toward us. I instinctively ran toward him, starting to report, but the General waved me off, saying he just wanted to visit a spell with the boys. I was a little disappointed, only because it was my first time in his presence with clean fatigues, polished boots, web gear, weapon, helmet, the whole nine yards. The general wandered off, walking right by our case of C rations adorned with Miss February. Thirty minutes later, he came back through on his way to the chopper, smiling and waving at everyone. I just waved back as he walked by. Waved at him. Like he was just an old friend. At that point, I think that the CG and 5/7 Cav had become good old friends.

The sun came up on April Fools Day, but it was hidden by the clouds. The eighty slicks and a lot of Chinooks came in on schedule and set down on the LZ, but when the weather delay was announced they cut off their engines and sat. The troops were spread out in seven-man groups beside the birds. The entire center of the huge area was blanketed with helicopters. It was an awesome sight. Everyone with cameras snapped pictures. It was real nice that Mr. Charles did not rocket our ass — real nice.

We sat around waiting for the word for the better part of the morning. We also had a little letter-writing time.

Dear Nancy,

Presently sitting by my radio waiting for the latest weather decision. At 0800 hours this morning our battalion was to be the lead battalion for the 1st Cav on the biggest airmobile operation since Normandy in WW II. The weather is presently holding us up and we have had two weather delays. It is now 1000 hours and we are planning to go at 1100 hours unless it gets cancelled again. It is quite an honor for us to have been selected to be the spearhead battalion. . . .

I neglected to mention that our destination was Khe Sanh.

The weather was just like LZ Long. As the sun heated up, the clouds rose from the valley floors and cleared the mountain tops several hours later. We finally got the word for a 1330 hours assault onto the two objectives.

JB and I went airborne in the C&C to watch our forty slicks lift off, circle up, and form into ten-bird sticks for the trip westward. Birds were going in all directions. It was amazing that there were no collisions. Finally our forty birds were ready to move west. The sky was broken clouds just above the tops of the higher mountains. The visibility was excellent. We could look back and see countless strings of slicks. Ahead of us, we could see Route 9 snaking its way through a deep valley toward Khe Sanh. To the right, the jungle-covered mountain we were headed for rose straight up from the valley below. Out the left door, we could see the 1/7 Cav formations moving parallel to us across the much lower hills that ran along the south side of Route 9. Stacked above us were the various commanders in their C&C Birds. Troop B's Reds and Whites were already out in the objective areas, looking for someone to shoot. It was about a twenty-minute ride.

Our air-assault went in on a flat, grassy area just below the peak of Hill 691. The elevation of the LZ was 1950 feet above Route 9 and the Quang Tri River below — just one and a half clicks to the south. The river was ten meters above sea level. Amazing. The slope down to the river on our side of the valley seemed almost vertical. In some places it was.

There was no artillery prep, just the earlier bombs followed by the accompanying gunbirds. The lead troop ships went into an area with a lot of fresh bomb craters scattered throughout the elephant grass. As we came in on short final, all we could see was green trees, green grass, and best of all a "Green Situation". JB and I flew back with the empty slicks for the short ride to LZ Stud, where I was dropped off to supervise the next phase. JB went right back to the objective to get on the ground with the troops.

Our remaining two companies had already arrived from LZ Pedro by Chinook and were ready to mount up in the slicks. It all went like clockwork. The RTOs, the operations sergeants, and I rode back to the objective area in the slicks allocated to A Co. It was exciting riding in with the troops for a change. The clouds were thick just above the mountaintop as we approached. We were in and out of the mist. It was eerie up there, as we snaked our way at treetop level up to the LZ. Once we got out of the bird, we were in the middle of the riflemen of A Co, who were fanning out and moving off in their assigned directions. I immediately began scouting out where the CP would go, and how the LZ perimeter would be set up.

A young man named Gary Cates was one of the most heroic of the Rough Riders, when he left this world back on 12 February in Thon Que Chu. This LZ was named for Gary. LZ CATES. His name is on the black marble, and it is also on a jungle-covered mountain in Vietnam.

1/7 Cav went in on Hill 248 across the way with no resistance. They named it LZ MIKE. Probably one of their fallen heroes. We had put the two lead battalions on the ground in about an hour. The operation was as smooth as a Tu Do Street pickpocket. Well, it helped that no one saw an NVA soldier all day. Later in the afternoon, 2/7 Cav landed on LZ MIKE and got ready to move farther west along Route 9.

As the weather improved further, the Chinooks started bringing in the stuff, including metal stakes, sandbags, water, ammo, C-rations. We even got the bulldozer shortly after we got there, and began building the trench for our CP bunker. The artillery tubes came in. The stuff just kept on coming. We even got some PSP for roofing material. *(PSP — metal plating material used to make airstrips.)* I commented to myself, "Bill Hussong — a helluva S-4". We were digging holes, filling sandbags, getting set up, and talking to the company RTOs. Everyone had it together. Everyone was doing his job. Better yet, everyone was apparently going to be around to fight another day. Life was good. About then the 3d Bde forward CP group arrived.

The 3d Bde headquarters company commander, a captain responsible for setting up their CP (and my successor in that position), brought no PSP, sandbags, water, or anything else that we could see. In fact, he did not even bring himself. I was very unimpressed. I transitioned to downright disgusted when the Brigade S-3 personally came over and commandeered half of our stuff. He also commandeered the bulldozer, but fortunately we had completed our TOC trench. The things that came out of my mouth — shocking behavior for an officer and a gentleman. Hey, the Brigade S-3 was a major, and so was I.

Beginning the next morning we moved B Co south about 800 meters to an open area perched right at the edge of the almost vertical drop to the valley below. They established LZ CATES *(South)*. It would be out of the clouds that much sooner every morning and serve as the main log pad for our incoming supply helicopters. C Co also patrolled several hundred meters northward to the very top of Hill 691, and dug in up there. A Co and D Co continued to work on building the base perimeter.

Dear Nancy,

Am presently located on Hill 691 in our command bunker. We arrived on April Fool's Day after a massive air assault involving all three battalions of the 3rd Brigade. The sky was filled with helicopters. We were complimented by the CG for making the best air move by a battalion that he has seen. Negative enemy contact so far. We are 8 kilometers from Khe Sanh. Today the 2d Brigade air assaulted past us to the south of Khe Sanh, except they got screwed up and only got half of their move done. They continue tomorrow. Really little resistance so far – I think Chuck is going into Laos.

Good news on the bombing of Hanoi being ceased. I am convinced the bombing of their city doesn't accomplish anything anyway. The NVA are still able to get self-propelled artillery and well-equipped units to South Vietnam. The only problem the enemy has is eating once they get here. The Air Force has snowed everyone once again.

Don't like the sound of your taking tranquilizers. They can be addictive.

Love, Charlie

As the 2d Bde started coming in farther to the southwest, we began to conduct search and destroy operations westward along the mountain tops. Beginning on 4 April, birds became available and we air-assaulted C Co onto Hill 512 about 5 clicks west of LZ Cates. We did the whole nine yards, artillery prep and everything. This high ground was clearly visible to Khe Sanh Combat Base. KSCB for short. B Co followed into the same LZ, and began moving eastward along the long ridgeline.

Below them was a deep gorge, through which the Rao Quan River ran eastward toward the ocean. The gorge ran between our two companies on the ridgeline and

KSCB just three clicks away. This ridgeline provided a great view of the entire Khe Sanh area.

The NVA must have thought so too, because the Limping Scholars came upon a company-sized defensive position about 400 meters east of the LZ. They captured 200 lbs. of rice, 1400 AK rounds, 6500 machinegun rounds, 60 mortar rounds, and a variety of other stuff. All of this materiel had been abandoned. The Scholars did not find a living soul. It was not like the NVA to just up and leave their stuff like that. Perhaps our air-assault had scared them away, or they had been wiped out earlier by a B-52 strike while out on a mission, or something. Nowadays, a lot of Cav guys brag that ever since the Ia Drang, the NVA was afraid of the 1st Cav. I don't know about that; however, this odd incident was certainly a good basis for such a boast.

C Co moved westward along the same ridge toward Hill 504 and had nothing to report. By the end of the day on 5 April, we had two companies looking down on KSCB. War correspondent Michael Herr, in his must-read book, *Dispatches*, had some nice words about our operations. "Everywhere you went, you could see the most comforting military insignia in all of Vietnam, the yellow-and-black shoulder patch of the Cav. You were with the pros now, the elite. LZs and firebases were being established at a rate of three and four a day, and every hour brought them closer to Khe Sanh." *(Thank you, Michael for your kind words.)*

The next morning, 6 April, we air-assaulted D Co farther west along the same long ridgeline. From there, they moved northward down into a smaller gorge between the ridge and the giant Hill 1015 which loomed above everything. While down in that gorge, Frank Lambert saved one of his troopers who was drowning in an extremely hazardous river, and got himself a soldier's medal. Frank was always saving people, it seemed.

That same afternoon, we picked up C Co from Hill 504 and air-assaulted them across the Rao Quan Gorge into the open fields just a short 500 meters north of the KSCB perimeter. The landing zones were on the same ground where the NVA had done much of their trench building, bringing them ever closer to the Marine defensive positions. We next air-assaulted B Co farther to the east on ground only 300 meters from the northeast corner of KSCB. We put on a great aerial show for the Marines that day, with artillery prep, gunships, everything. Our two companies came out of the birds and began searching outward away from KSCB toward the gorge, finding all kinds of abandoned materiel and about 500 meters of trench lines.

B Co found a NVA mess hall in the jungle just over the steep drop-off into the gorge. During their encirclement of Khe Sanh, the NVA could even feed their boys that one last hot meal before going out to die.

While putting our troopers into the LZs just outside the KSCB wire on 6 April, we got a warning order about replacing 1-9 Marines on the western end of Khe Sanh. The Marines would be attacking out from the perimeter to take Hill 689 overlooking KSCB from the west. JB sent me in the C&C along with the last lift of the C Co air assault to make coordination with the Marines. We set down just outside the wire in the middle of the slicks that were off loading the C Co troops.

As I walked in to the perimeter with my RTO, the slicks continued sitting there with their rotors running, awaiting instructions from me. In my excitement I had forgotten to tell them what was next. Currrraaacck!! In came a couple artillery rounds from Laos, landing right in the midst of the idling birds. Fortunately the NVA missed everyone with their first salvo. The slicks immediately lifted up and away. On their way out, I am sure the pilots talked about me behind my back, with some choice "Army words" for emphasis. Welcome to Khe Sanh.

I found the use of the term "combat base" interesting. We called our bases "firebases". Our concept was to station our artillery firepower at the firebase, but try to do the combat at Mr. Charles' place. But the Khe Sanh Combat Base was within easy artillery range from a neighboring country that we were not allowed to visit, and 500 meters in from a river gorge big enough for an entire division to walk through. Imagine you are a 19-year-old Marine, just sitting there all day, losing friends to devilishly random artillery rounds, while Mr. Charles is marching a few good men of his own, through the gorge, right up to your doorstep.

We asked the first Marine we met for directions to the 1-9 Marines CP, and were taken to a CP tent just like the ones the Army had. We in the 5/7 Cav never used our CP tent in the forward area, operating from underground bunkers instead. It was somewhat confusing seeing a battalion CP in a tent at Khe Sanh, what with all the stories of daily artillery fire. All you can say about the tent is that Marines must be tough as nails. They really do the bravado thing well.

I introduced myself to my counterpart, a major like me who was their S-3. He was really a good guy, and told me about their mission to take Hill 689. On hearing his lament, I immediately suggested that they air-assault onto the top of the peak and fight down the slope. His eyes lit up as he made some really rude comments about the support of the Marine Air Wing.

Fueled by this reaction, I went on to offer the use of our twelve slicks. I even volunteered to coordinate the whole thing, to include artillery prep fires. The Marine S-3 thought this was a terrific idea and went to get his battalion commander. The Lt. Colonel was about JB's age, and he also agreed that it was a good plan, except "they would have to run it by Regiment". Off we went to the headquarters of the 26th Marine Regiment. Teach me to shoot my mouth off, he did.

NO FAIR LINE
13 KM

1371

1123

62

OP CHARL[...]

950

1015

881

778

861

GORGEOUS

504

918

881
5

57

LZ RAT

709

728

PANG
689

552

471

552

THE GUN-TARGET LINE

527

FORT
FRANCY

KHE
SAHN
SALOON

383

KHE
SAHN

LANG
VEI
(ABANDONED)

678

840

663

CURRAACK
MTN

585

701

HOUSE   VEET-NAM

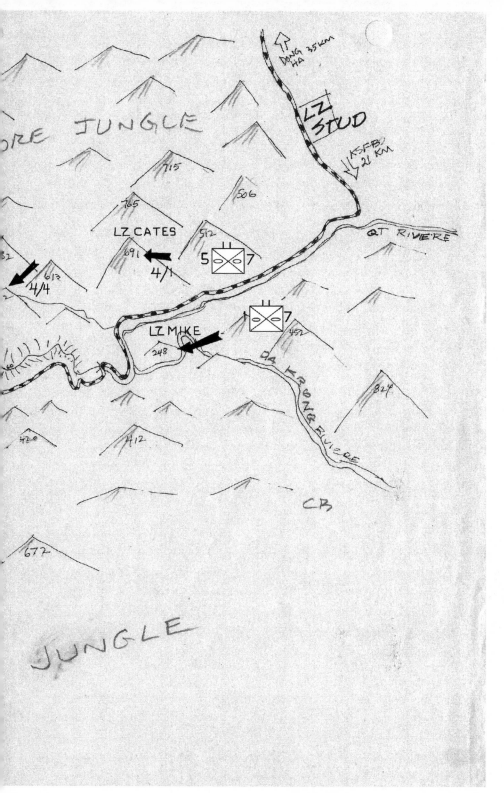

The 26th Marine CP was in a huge underground bunker off the western end of the runway, a brightly lit air- conditioned TOC that contrasted dramatically with the vast wasteland of red clay, dust and broken stuff above us. It was the most uptown place I had seen since I got to Vietnam. Soon after we walked in, a swarthy-looking guy in an olive drab t-shirt and flip-flops sauntered over, eating sardines from the can. Frankly, he looked like Pappy, our Ops Sgt. But no. The battalion CO introduced him to me as the Regimental S-3 of the 26th Marine Regiment. He was a Lieutenant Colonel in the United States Marine Corps. "Nah — couldn't be", I found myself thinking.

The CO of 1-9 Marines got about half of his next sentence out of his mouth — something about "air-assaulting onto Hill 689," when the Regimental S-3 stepped up to me and started talking. Propelling little bits of sardines from about twelve inches away, he proceeded to tell me what a moron the CG of the 1st Cav was. He said further that "our general had visited them a few days earlier and had put his big fat hand on the map east of Khe Sanh while saying that on D-Day the 3d Bde would take this area, and had put his big fat hand south of Khe Sanh while saying that by D+3 the 2d Bde would take this area, and had put his big fat hand on the map out in Lang Vei to the west while saying that on D+5 the 1st Bde would take this area, and the general had put his big fat hands on areas that would take many divisions to conquer"; all said in a high-pitched voice with his neck veins protruding. When he stopped for air, I immediately confirmed that the CG's plan had gone exactly as he had just described, at which time we were all told to get the hell out of the 26th Regimental CP. I related this story to some of the boys later, telling the tale with my own voice a little strained, and my neck veins maybe sticking out a tad. I never got the chance to check out just how fat the CG's hands were, but they were apparently a lot fatter than those of the Marine generals.

Looking back, I was totally out of my mind even suggesting that we help them conduct an air assault onto the top of some mountain. I did not consult with anyone. What would JB have said? What would the flight commanders have said? What would 3d Bde have said? What if it had gotten screwed up? I wasn't trying to needle the Marines. Honest, I wasn't. I must have been really full of myself by that time. It is even possible that the 1-9 Marines CO was having a little fun at the expense of this boy-major from the hated 1st Cav, knowing full well what would happen to me when I met Dominic, Vito, or whatever his name was up at Regiment. Remember this, boys: No one likes unsolicited advice.

I was unaware at the time that our general had ordered the 26th Regiment to move completely out of KSCB and attack the enemy in the hills. As we trudged back to the CP Tent, the 1-9 Marine Bn CO told me "it will be worth getting shot just to get to see the Marine Regimental Hqs have to put on their helmets and packs and go to the field."

The next morning, 7 April, B Co and C Co continued to scour the entire area north of the base between the wire and the gorge. They found lots of abandoned ammo and equipment. We were in essence defending the north side of KSCB by that time, even though we had not replaced the marines inside the wire.

That afternoon, the 2/7 Cav finally defeated an NVA company blocking the road just a few clicks east of KSCB, and walked into the east end of the base late in the day. It was the only major battle of the entire Operation Pegasus. By late afternoon, after a three-day contact with the NVA blocking Route 9 east of the base, they had kicked the crapola out of a battalion-sized NVA force. The last obstacle was removed that blocked the road into KSCB. 2/7 Cav captured 121 rifles, 10 machineguns, and stacked up 83 youngsters from North Vietnam. Two companies of 2/7 Cav walked in at the east end of KSCB around 1500 hours.

Eairlier that same afternoon of 7 April, while I was scouting out where our CP would go, JB and Mike Davison were walking into KSCB, with the troops of C Co, to relieve 1-9 Marines on the perimeter. B Co took over the defense of a place called the Gravel Pit. We moved our CP in from LZ Cates early the next day. And we didn't put up a tent. No, sir. We were way too skeered to do that.

Although 5/7 Cav was actually the first unit of the 1st Cav to make physical contact within the KSCB, 2/7 Cav appropriately got the "credit" for "lifting the siege". This was a good thing, because their guys had fought a gallant battle to get there. The rest of 2/7 Cav was air- lifted directly from the site of their big battle to Hill 471, just south of the base, where they relieved the rest of 1-9 Marines located there. Those marines would move on up the ridgeline in the attack to take back Hill 689.

Michael Herr aptly described the 1st Cav division's takeover of Khe Sanh in his great book *Dispatches*. "… and when the Cav sent an outfit to relieve the Marines on Hill 471, it killed off one of the last surviving romances about war left over from the movies: there was no shouting, no hard kidding, no gleeful obscenities, or the old 'Hey, where you from? No kidding! Me too!' The departing and arriving files passed one another without a single word being spoken."

Late in the day my RTO and I stood on the side of the street and watched a rifle company from 1-9 Marines move past us through the KSCB wire on the way toward Hill 689. One Marine gave me the peace sign, and I gave him our traditional "thumbs up" in acknowledgement. Otherwise, you could hear a pin drop.

When the C Co troopers started taking over the perimeter from the Marines in the late afternoon of 7 April, complaints began bubbling to the surface. The bunkers smelled terrible, they were full of huge rats, and the troops did not want to go in them. I put out the word that for the first night only, the troops could pitch their poncho tents by the doors, or sleep on top of the bunkers, or whatever, as long as they could get in the bunkers at the first sign of trouble.

The Marines were inured to the coexisting rats and incredibly foul air in the bunkers by that time. Their shit might not have stunk to them, but it did to us. In Eric Hammel's book about the siege, a Marine officer is quoted to the effect that we were "boobs and rookies for not sleeping in the bunkers that first night." *(Actually, it was just that we knew shit from shinola.)*

And the rats were huge! All those calories in C-rations had a tremendous effect on the rat population up there. The new name for Khe Sanh Combat Base was born that day. LZ RAT. Word of the name change got to the 26th Regimental headquarters in no time at all.

We started cleaning the place up as a first order of business. Michael Herr commented on this subject as well. "I went over to Hotel Company's position, but they were gone; a company of the Cav was there instead. They had cleaned out the trench floor all along the perimeter there, and the old bunker smelled now as though it had had been dug that morning. It was no wonder that the Marines called the Cav dudes and got uncomfortable whenever they were around."

Some mail and the Stars & Stripes reached us at LZ Rat. The 5 April Stars & Stripes front page was dramatic. The headline was "N. VIET DECLARES IT'S READY TO TALK". Elsewhere on the front page there was an article headed by "ALLIED FORCE PUSHES TOWARD KHE SANH". Had we kicked butt, or what? Down in the corner we read that the NYSE had broken the all-time volume record set October 29, 1929, by trading 19,200,000 shares. We should be home by July Fourth, everyone was saying. *(Many years later, General Giap was quoted as saying they were ready to quit, and had the bombing of Hanoi continued for a couple more days, they would have. Shows what I knew back then. I still maintain that bombing is overrated, though.)*

Unfortunately, things were going more smoothly on the road to Khe Sanh than in Washington, D.C. Late on 4 April, after we had commenced demonstrating how to make combat air-assaults within sight of Khe Sanh, Dr. Martin Luther King was assassinated. There was nothing in the 5 April Stars & Stripes about it. It was at least a day later when we got the word. The 7 April Stars & Stripes said that LBJ had canceled his Hawaii trip, to do with impending talks with Ho Chi Minh, in order to address a joint session of the Congress about the problems stemming from Dr. King's death. The meeting with Ho never came off after that. *(One could write an interesting piece on the impact of Martin's assassination on the war.)*

Regular troops were deployed in D.C. to quell rioting. Also mentioned was that a short, balding white man was arrested in Memphis for shooting Dr. King. In small print at the bottom it was reported that "the Khe Sanh Seige was lifted". And also on a very busy front page was a comment that General Westmoreland would fly to Washington to confer with Johnson on the forthcoming Saturday. Uh oh. Sounded like Westy might not get to be chief of Staff after all. *(He did, though.)*

On 8 April, we moved the 1st Platoon of D Co, in six slicks, to the top of Hill 950. They replaced a 1-9 Marines platoon guarding the signal station. This signal station provided radio relay throughout the area, and probably a lot of other top secret electronic missions. I led the slicks up there in the C&C. It was one slick at a time onto a tiny wooden platform, hanging out over the barbed wire and the almost vertical slope below. Each bird off-loaded Skytroopers, and on-loaded Jar Heads. I finally got to move some Marine combat troopers with our helicopters. Maybe there are a few good men out there with a fond memory of the 1st Cav after all. Not more than a platoon's worth, though.

The signal station on top of Hill 950 was legendary. It was barely big enough for a platoon. It perched on the sharp-tipped mountain, looking like a little monastery in Tibet. It was ringed with multiple concertina barriers. It sat in the shadow of the enemy-controlled Hill 1015 to the east. Hill 950 had many horror stories about daily mortar attacks and night ground attacks against the perimeter.

Adding to our problems with the 26th Marine Regiment was the issue of the patch. On 11 Feb, we began to phase out of Operation Pegasus. We pulled A Co into LZ Rat that day from Cates. That evening some of the County Lines performed basic paint duty around the area. One such 1st Cav patch appeared on the airstrip. It was huge, extending halfway across the PSP surface of the runway. The first observer of this piece of art was a B-52 pilot, who called into the Marine CP at first light, remarking how clear the 1st Cav patch looked from 35,000 feet. I had to go up to Regiment and apologize for that one, which was well worth it.

Actually, the young Marines in Vietnam were fucking great, just like the Cav. It was above battalion level that things started to deteriorate. Maybe we weren't too hot either the further up you went, but nothing like the Marines. Their men at the top were Jar Heads in the purest sense.

Eric Hammel wrote a tremendous book on the siege at Khe Sanh. It wasn't that the Marines left the mountain tops to the enemy. The Marines in the combat battalions fought with tremendous gallantry to control the tops of most of those mountains. It was just that the Khe Sanh Combat Base sat within artillery range from Laos. The Marine lieutenants, captains and majors, and all their troopers were just like us. They knew the value of offensive action, active patrolling, taking the nearby terrain away from the enemy, pushing the enemy artillery forward observers back away from accurate observation. It wasn't a young Marine officer who gave the order not to patrol more than 500 meters outside the KSCB perimeter. It was some Marine Corps general or full colonel who thought that one up. Maybe the same guy that picked this piece of terrible ground for a combat base in the first place. To the 2500 casualties suffered by the Marines at Khe Sanh, about all I can say is Garryowen to you, pal.

5/7 Cav started departing LZ Rat on 12 April. The companies flew to Phu Bai south of Hue in USAF C-123s. Joint service cooperation was epidemic. From Phu Bai, the companies convoyed up through Hue and on to Camp Evans. One wonders if there were any pretty girls in ao dais on the streets of Hue when they went through this time. The architecture and other beautiful things about the city had certainly been diminished. Traveling in deuce and half trucks up Highway 1 north of Hue must have been eerie for the old-timers. The FNGs on board must have heard some ominous war stories as they rode past Duc Buii and TT Woods that day.

I had to go back up to Rat two days later on 14 April to make sure the 2/7 Cav was taking care of the one Rough Rider Platoon we had left with them to defend the signal station up Hill 950. While standing by the entrance to the 26th Regiment CP at the west end of the runway that morning, an Air Force C-130 came in for a landing from the east. Just as the plane was getting ready to touch down, damn if a Chinook helicopter didn't lift off from the south side of the runway only to re-position itself on the north side. A huge cloud of orange dust enveloped the entire eastern end of the runway, through which came the C-130. He had zigged slightly left to avoid collision, and when he touched down he had the right strut on the PSP runway and the left one off the edge, in the red clay dirt. Down the runway he came, his brakes not working on the dirt. After repeated attempts, he could not get his left tires back up onto the PSP runway. With growing alarm, we watched the plane approaching a gasoline truck parked just off the PSP about 50 meters from us. A young marine ran out and jumped into the truck cab, immediately saw he was too late, jumped back out and ran like hell. We started to duck for cover about the time the left wing plowed into the truck, bringing everything to a sudden stop. Some of the crew members in the plane were killed. I immediately wondered if our pathfinders were in charge of air traffic control, and prayed that it was not their fault.

This accident may not have been as stupid as the tank leaping into the moat at Hue, but it was many times more tragic. Some of the things that happen in a combat zone are just dreadful. War is a damn dangerous business even before the first shot is fired. Hey, Mom and Dad, you are whistling in the dark if you think no one will be killed by friendly activities in real combat. The only alternative is to not send any troops to a war zone.

2/7 Cav completed bringing ROUGH RIDER 16 and his men off of Hill 950. We were preparing to leave for Camp Evans, when my RTO ran up to report that the Platoon had forgot to bring our two RTOs with them. We had put two RTOs from battalion operations in the radio relay bunker up on the mountain early on in our operations. Now it was mid-afternoon and the weather was clouding up. Somehow they had not gotten the word to come with the Rough Riders, and were still up there with the Marines. There was nothing else to do but jump in the C&C Bird and go up there to get our guys before the clouds descended.

As we approached the little wooden platform hanging off the side of the mountain, the clouds were right at the tips of the antennas which were sticking up from the central bunker. As we came to a hover above the platform, it seemed like the rotor was in the clouds and the skids were not. With eyes the size of grapefruits, two skytrooper RTOs launched themselves from the platform and threw themselves onto the floor of the gyrating bird, landing in a heap at my feet. We never touched the skids on the platform. With one pair of feet still sticking well out of the door, Bob Frix lifted up, put the nose down, and flew straight out into dense fog. He then did an immediate gut-wrenching 180 that sent our stomachs into our throats, and came hurtling past the wooden platform on the way out. Scared the living shit out of me, it did. As we descended towards LZ Rat, the RTOs were chattering like kids headed for Disneyland. Probably the two biggest smiles I saw in the war. Piece of cake for the pilots, of course.

As we prepared to depart for Camp Evans a while later, Oscar Davis, the charismatic Assistant Division Commander, showed up and asked me to give a lift to a journalist he had brought with him. The man's name was Wilson, and he was a writer for the Washington Post. Wilson was an older guy, apparently a long-time newspaper writer of some renown. He sat on his side of the ship, and I sat on mine. Nary a word was spoken.

As we circled up to safe altitude and looked down on LZ Rat for the last time, several NVA artillery rounds splashed in on the center of the runway two thousand feet below. It was a nice farewell touch. With the Cav departing, Khe Sanh Combat Base got its name back. It was a "combat base" again.

We dropped Mr. Wilson off at the Division Helipad at Camp Evans and went on back to the 3rd Brigade Pad. Lots of mail awaited my return.

Dear Charlie,

MLK was killed today. It is just terrible. He was the voice of reason for so many of us. Someone shot him with a rifle. JFK all over again. The black people are rioting all over the country. The National Guard is being called up. All the schools are closed here. Opening Day for baseball was just cancelled. LBJ announced April 6th as a National Day of Mourning.

Love, Nancy

If any of our men had collected together and carried on back when we got the word at LZ Rat, I do not recall. There may have been some hell raised in the bunkers, but probably not. The NCOs probably kept the lid on the troops if it had been necessary. Interestingly, we did not have that many black troopers in 5/7 Cav. Most of the ones we had won lots of medals. No one knew what to say, anyway. We were not fighting for racial equality in the Que Son Valley, Hue, or at LZ Rat. Staying alive to fight tomorrow was the main focus. 5/7 Cav fought hard and fought together, while back in the states lots of people continued to totally disgrace themselves.

The story of Operation Pegasus has been told by several writers, none better than the CG himself in his fine article in Army magazine. His work later became part of a publication by the Army called *(Airmobility)*, 1961-1971. We of the Third Brigade took great pride in the way we had led off D-Day, getting the entire brigade onto its objectives in five hours. The smoothness of the first day set the tone for the entire operation. 2d Bde was able to start one day ahead of schedule, which rippled down throughout the entire schedule. Operation Pegasus went like clockwork. It helped a great deal that the enemy got the hell out of the way as fast as they could.

Were the NVA heading for Laos even before 1 April? Possibly, maybe even probably. One thing is obvious to me now. When the 1st Cav began construction of LZ Stud over in Ca Lu long a week or so before 1 April, the little people watched that whole thing take place. We began hearing about the impending operation at least a week before going to the LZ Pedro jump-off point. I am sure the little people heard about that too. The Principle of Surprise was not involved in Operation Pegasus. The Principles of Mass and Mobility were the whole deal. It was Vince Lombardi's Green Bay Packers going off tackle on two. Starr comes up to the line and announces to the other team, "we are going off right tackle on two". And they did. And the play succeeded. One thing the little people did better than we did in that war was intelligence. They pretty much always knew what we were up to.

The NVA rifle company that blocked the road against 2/7 Cav had the mission of keeping the road closed until the main force units in the area could make their escape toward the DMZ and Laos. They held up a battalion of the 1st Cav for three days, while being pounded by lots of firepower, and served their country with extreme courage. The great majority of their unit went directly to Infantry Heaven — well, assuming they were not the ones who murdered all those innocent women and children in Hue back in February.

Even after all those Marines had died over the course of several months, 5/7 Cav had only one KIA in Operation Pegasus. The Marines had suffered 2,500 casualties at Khe Sanh up to this point. The entire 1st Cav had 64 casualties during the entire two-week operation. All the action was on Route 9 and in the hills further to the southwest.

We were proud to be in the 1st Cav. "If you ain't Cav, you ain't shit", we would say. Yellow paint sprang up everywhere. The obvious response from the Marines, of course, was "and if you are Cav, you are shit."

Operation Pegasus cemented animosity between the Marine Corps and U.S. Army, particularly the 1st Cavalry Division, that would last for several decades. On the positive side, it also prepared the 1st Cav for its next operation. Operation Pegasus was the first division-sized heliborne assault ever. It was complex. It had a lot of moving parts. Fortunately it was mostly unopposed. We now had the experience of filling the sky with slicks and Chinooks, along with all the coordination involved. It was a good rehearsal for the next operation to follow, because 5/7 Cav was again chosen to lead off a 1st Cav Division massive heliborne assault. This time it would be into the infamous A Shau Valley operation. D-Day was 19 April 1968. We had plenty of things to worry about beyond the mere scheduling of air-lifts. Oh, yeah.

CHAPTER 28

In To The Valley

Camp Evans
15 April 1968

Even before we left Khe Sanh and returned to Camp Evans, I started hearing little bits and pieces about the next big operation. JB probably knew what was up, but he wasn't talking. 5/7 Cav picked up where we left off before our visit with the 26th Marines. Three companies were air-assaulted into separate LZs on 15 April, about four clicks apart, to conduct search and destroy operations under the shadow of Rocket Ridge west of Camp Evans. All the LZs were green. The company commanders set up operations from their LZs, moved their platoons outward on patrols, and set up ambushes for the night. Delta air-assaulted in the next day, giving us the entire battalion spread across the coastal plain. We didn't go up into the mountains; Brigade wanted us easy to assemble.

These platoon-sized operations succeeded only in finding old men, women and children. The young men and women were off somewhere, as usual, but the patrols felt their influence every day. Alpha and Bravo each suffered two WIAs from booby traps on the first day. C Company had one on the third day. There were no hearts and minds out there below Rocket Ridge.

On the second day, the boredom of the situation was broken by a message from COUNTY LINE SIX.

"FLANKER 3, we have NVA in the open about six hundred meters away, over."

"FAST FLANKER 3, roger, keep me informed, out."

The first 105mm round departed LZ Cathy immediately after this brief conversation. A frantic call came in on the fire direction net over on the other side of the TOC. "Cease fire, cease fire, over!!"

Alpha Company's patrol had mistaken a group of children for enemy troops in the open. Fortunately, the adjusting round missed them entirely, and no one was hurt. *(Some woman out in California reading this would be saying, "yeah sure, all those children were wiped out".)*

On the afternoon of the second day of the operation, I received a message from Brigade S-3: "This is COLD STEEL 3, there will be a briefing for all battalion commanders and their S-2 and S-3 officers at 1830 hours today at the Brigade briefing tent. This is to include 5/7, 1/7, and 2/7."

"Roger, out." I may have talked my fool head off with the companies, but always kept it short with Brigade.

This message did not come as a surprise. By the second day under Rocket Ridge, JB started bringing me up to speed. We went off to the briefing, flew back out to our

CP location up on LZ Cathy later that night, and I immediately began formulating the operations order for another battalion air-assault.

In the middle of the night, I also sent separate encoded messages to each of the company commanders. The companies did not have secure radios like we had for the Brigade net, and we used traditional radio-telephone procedures when talking on the battalion radio net. Just like in Korea and the Big One. We encoded all unit locations. We were careful what we talked about. We didn't allow idle chatter. No personal names, call signs only. *(The officers and some of the RTOs had little pocket-sized code books that changed often, giving us a simple menu of common words, each designated by a randomly selected three-letter combination. We called it the SOI, Signal Operating Instructions.)*

The "secure" radio between Brigade and Battalion was a totally new development, first used in the Vietnam War. A scrambler was attached to the radio, creating a "secure" net. Nevertheless, old procedures lingered on, even on the Brigade Net. Everyone continued to use pretty good radio-telephone procedure, and we definitely didn't do idle chatter with Brigade. No sir.

From my SOI, I formulated a simple mission statement for each company for the following morning. I was very tired, and it took me about an hour just to encode the four separate messages. Everyone was told to move to the C Co LZ next to the village of Ap Thanh Tan on 18 April. We had a sortie of six slicks and two gunbirds to work with. Delta would move first, followed by Bravo. Alpha Co was close by and would move over on foot, checking out the surrounding area as they came over. JB moved his command group into this assembly area that afternoon.

18 April 1968
In the sky
North end of A Shau Valley

Bright and early, as the companies were beginning their moves, FLASHING SABER 6 arrived at the Bn TOC. He was followed by Bob Frix in our C&C bird. JB took off with SABER 6, and I flew in the C&C. We went around and picked up the company commanders, briefed them in the birds as we took off for the west. The Company COs put their XOs in charge for the move to the Ap Thanh Tan assembly area, and XO Joe assumed control of the battalion. JB and I took the boys on a little helicopter ride that morning.

"Where are we going?" asked Big Ralph.

"A Shau Valley", I replied with my best possible nonchalance.

"No shit?"

"No shit." *(We are going to Charlie's place this time. Damn.)*

The 1st Cav Div planned to assault the entire division into the A Shau, just like they did at Khe Sanh. 3rd Bde would start it off again on D-Day, and 5/7 Cav had once again been selected to be lead battalion. Everyone presumed it was because JB was so greatly respected by the CG. The great job we did on April 1st must have caused this decision, I told myself. These are the sort of things officers and soldiers tell themselves to "keep on keeping on" in a war. A story came out later that the Division G-3 briefed the operation to the CG with his old battalion, 2/12 Cav, as the lead unit. He was told "great plan, but switch the lead battalion to be the 5/7 Cav." It's our story, and we are sticking with it.

For this aerial recon, JB took Frank, John, and the latest FNG, a captain named Willie Gore. Willie had just replaced Mike in command of the Hard Hitters. Mike's half year in command was up *(No wonder we needed so many captains)*, and he went back to Division G-3; a not insignificant feather in that boy's hat. Ralph Miles flew with me, along with the FSO and the S-2. Additionally, a skinny freckle-faced captain who I had never seen before came out with the C&C to go with us. He mumbled something about being in S-2. Brigade? Division? I didn't clarify what he meant. Major Bob was on the stick, as usual. His co-pilot was the same young blonde-haired warrant officer who didn't like me very much. I liked him, though, because he had spunk. Major Bob and the WO had taken JB and me everywhere since January.

The two helicopters went to 8000 feet in order to cross the 4000-foot high mountains. FLASHING SABER 6 was in the lead. Bob and I were looking for a massive mountain that dominated the north end of the valley. The battalion's mission was to air-assault onto this mountain the following day, and we wanted to figure out where we could land. Ralph would have the job of taking the tip of the 1228-meter high mountain *(4015 feet)*, and hopefully they would find a big enough landing area up there for at least one slick.

The skinny visiting captain said he had arrived from TV Land only a few days earlier. He was a nervous wreck. He took one look at Ralph, who was ominous even when he was laughing, and lapsed into total shock. He chain-smoked through his entire pack, and never said another word all day. What a way to start your tour in the spring of 1968 — flying to the fucking A Shau Valley with some crazy-looking people who had serious body odor.

From Rocket Ridge out to the A Shau Valley was 30 kilometers of very steep-sloped mountains, covered by triple-canopy jungle. It was a jungle full of snakes, bugs, and strange-sounding birds, just like in the movies. It was also criss-crossed with foot trails known mainly by the NVA.

I must have been distracted or amused by all the cigarettes going down, because in no time at all we started crossing a wide area full of bomb craters and open ground. JB riding with SABER 6 was nowhere to be seen. I think they had a much faster bird, and Bob couldn't keep up. Bob thought it might be the valley, but from 8000 feet he could not tell the hills from the valleys. I had the same problem, and could not see anything that represented a massive mountain overlooking the valley. We could not make up our minds as we flew indecisively onward for several minutes. At a known distance and speed, you would think we would have figured this out sooner. When we finally concluded that we had overshot the valley, Bob wheeled the bird around and headed east.

Right as Bob was turning about, everyone on board heard and felt the shock wave of a round passing close by. Just a little thump in my earphones. The other guys without headsets probably heard it real well. "Must have been a 12.75 round," opined Bob on the intercom.

We were still at about 8000 feet, and heading back to the east. Approaching the shadow sides of the mountains made the terrain a lot easier to discern. It was a beautiful clear day. In a few minutes we could see what might be the big mountain we were looking for. Vietnam is actually quite beautiful except for the bomb craters and defoliated trees.

"Listen up. Something is wrong with the bird," said Bob, in his totally laid-back airline pilot voice. "I'm getting a warning light about the rotor blade," he added. What Bob left out was that the warning light came on right after everyone had felt that little shock wave of a round passing by, and we had been losing altitude.

(Holy shit.)

A few minutes later Bob chimed in with, "I don't think we can make it back to the coast. We are losing altitude."

(We are fucked.)

Sure enough, the huge mountain was clear as a bell as we approached from the west, since we were no longer at 8000 feet. It truly dominated the entire northern end of the A Shau Valley. By the time we were within a click, we were already below the top of the 1228 meter peak. As we flew past the southern face, which looked like a huge cliff just out the left door of the Huey, we found ourselves at the same elevation as the east-west road cut into the very steep face. Most of the trees astride the road had no foliage. Many trees were blown down, lying down the slope. Paralleling the road took us right over a barren spur coming off the mountain that would be the only good landing zone for the air assault planned for the next day.

The altimeter on the front dash was steadily spinning to lower numbers, and I was starting to think about the wife and children when Bob spoke up again. "I need to find a good place to put her down."

(Shit. Going down in the fucking A Shau Valley. Shit.)

I was the only one in the back with a headset on the intercom, so the other passengers were in the dark about the rotor blade problem. As the pilot went over the western rim of the main valley, and nosed sharply downward toward the valley floor 1500 feet below, I leaned past the skinny captain and shouted at Ralph, "We have a problem with the bird."

"What?" yelled the massive company commander of the Limping Scholars, crushing the boney little guy between us as he leaned toward me.

"We have a bad warning light," I said with a nonchalant shrug. Ralph's eyes got big for just a split second before he turned his attention back to taking in the scene. The skinny captain was out of cigarettes. He had no place left to go.

I had nothing more to say, for a change. Making matters even more intense, we seemed to be losing radio contact with FLASHING SABER 6. It was a mystery to me how and why we got separated from the Saber bird to start with, and it was becoming disappointing as well. SABER 6 and JB may have turned south down the valley in order to recon the whole area of operations. I could hear Bob talking to them. The rest of the guys back with me had the fear of the unknown going for them big time. Eyes were big on board the UH1B. SABER 6 got harder and harder to hear, and finally faded out altogether. *(If only we had cell phones back then, we could have dialed our local police department who would have called someone who would have called someone — around the world at the speed of light. Better yet, iPhones.)*

Bob was spending all of his time trying to get the message to people about his situation. After we passed the mountain, he kept the road on his left as he snaked his way down to the floor of the valley some 1,500 feet below. When we got to the base of the mountain, Bob put it right on the deck and turned left up the valley road. We came to a big wooded area in the center of the valley, and Bob lifted up and skimmed across the treetops, clipping a few branches with the skids. Back on the deck again, we continued north. There were no Troop B pilots chattering on the radio. The bird was shuddering noticeably by that time. The vibrations had spread from Bob's butt to the passenger's butts.

The northernmost end of the valley became very narrow and turned back to the west toward Laos. Coming around the bend, we found ourselves entering a large bowl area surrounded on all sides by mountains. Straight across the bowl was a hillside, maybe a click away, with all the trees cut off about 10 to 15 feet up the trunk. It looked like a giant pincushion. I was becoming very alarmed by the vibrations coming through the back seat. I wasn't looking at or talking to anyone else. Everyone had his own personal thoughts. The skinny captain was comatose. Ralph was Ralph.

Suddenly, Bob was not the laconic airline pilot talking about the weather. He showed just a trace of intensity as he said to me "we've got to land it now, we can go in on top of the canopy or try our luck with the cut-off trees. What do you think?" The top of the jungle canopy was sixty or more feet above the ground, and I quickly shot back with "yeah, the tree trunks look better than the canopy."

Bob agreed and set his course straight ahead. We made the increasingly shaky flight halfway across the bowl, and I was seeing visions of my wife on her best day, when what should appear out the left door but a beautiful little clearing, in an idyllic little draw coming off the north side of the huge mountain. The door gunner and I saw it at the same time.

"Go left… go left!" Jumping up and down, slapping Bob on the back, "Go left!" We finally got his attention. Bob banked the shuddering bird to the left, headed for the clearing, and made an elegant touch-down. Piece of cake.

(Fuck me… We've just landed deep in the NVA's home base, and have surely been observed by main force units. Troop B doesn't know where the fuck we are. We can all just kiss our collective asses goodbye.)

We were on the ground now, where I was senior man present, and I wasted no time giving orders. I sent guys out on security in all directions. I had one of the door gunners dismount his gun and move into the tree line slightly up the slope where he could cover all of the clearing as well as the more likely approach from the lower ground. I expected that we would be coming under fire any minute. Once security was in place, I ran back up the slope, only to find Bob and the co-pilot laughing and grinning.

"What's so funny?"

"It's the Cavalry," the always smartass warrant officer co-pilot gleefully reported, as he pointed skyward.

Spiraling down toward us was a little speck of a Huey helicopter. We were truly being rescued by the Cavalry – the 1/9 Air Cavalry. I immediately wondered if Bob and his co-pilot had been talking to this 1/9 Blue Team all along, and just wanted to pull a prank on me. *(Nah, Bob would never do that. His co-pilot would, though.)*

The warrant officer considered me to be a chicken-shit jerk dating back to our days together at Brigade Headquarters. Perhaps it went back to the day that this young pilot took off in a Bell scout bird without disconnecting his gas hose. It was a short and costly flight. I was his company commander at the time, and we had a subsequent discussion about the cost of Bell helicopters in general, and how many months it was going to take to pay for the damage to this one. Did I start off with "I'm so glad you weren't hurt?" Hell no. Was I an asshole back then? Apparently. The facts were that the kid was supporting a firefight out on the coast, and was in a huge hurry to get back in the fight, and this rear area motherfucker of a captain at Brigade was only interested in chewing his ass.

Well, anyway, as the 1/9 bird was on short final into the clearing, Bob was intent on staying behind to get his bird lifted out. I expected everyone to get on the Troop B slick and kiss the C & C goodbye. The relative values of men and machine were astronomically far apart, and not just because the pilot went on to make two stars. The young door gunner's mom was just as proud of him. But I let Bob talk me into leaving on the 1/9 slick. I had a couple tons of work to do before tomorrow getting the operations orders prepared and briefed.

Major Bob, his wise-ass warrant officer, and his senior door gunner stayed behind with their beloved C&C bird. She probably even had a name. There were too many people for the Troop B slick anyway, and someone had to stay. The Blue Team had nine and we 5/7 guys added five more. We crammed ourselves in like college kids in a VW Bug. The pilot was an Italian kid from Brooklyn who turned and told me right up front, "relax, I am the greatest pilot in Vietnam."

Those were his exact words. I loved this guy immediately. To prove it, he climbed up over the 4000 foot mountains, overloaded and on a very hot day, and took us home on the smoothest ride anyone had been on lately. He had amazing touch with that bird. He later made the silkiest landing in the history of helicopter landings at Bill Hussong's log pad. The young Italian was the Cassius Clay of all Huey pilots. I wrote down the pilot's name and address, but later lost it in the rain. I said I was gonna write the kid's mom, like I was Omar Bradley or somebody important. *(Actually, that would be Omar's much younger wife who traveled everywhere with the old man, and probably wrote the letters.)*

It turned out to be a smooth ride for everyone except Ralph. Ralph Miles was the last one on, and sat on the floor between my legs with his feet hanging out. I held onto the back of Ralph's harness straps. This worked well until my new best Italian friend leveled off and picked up speed. The wind started pushing Ralph down the floor toward the door gunner. It took me and two other guys to pull him back up the ship. He kept sliding back, though, and halfway home my arms gave out. I was a skinny guy, Ralph was an ox. He must have been scary-looking in pads and helmet, particularly to the wide receivers and the other guys who were skinny like me. In retrospect, we should have had positions reversed. Actually, we should have put the skinny freckled-faced FNG captain out there, with no remaining cigarettes, and really introduced him to the war... give him a story to tell his grandchildren.

Midway home, the fast-talking Italian had to slow his airspeed so we could pull Ralph back up the floor of the ship. After two such slow downs, everyone's arms gave out, and we just left Ralph pinned against the door gunner's legs the rest of the way. The door gunner looked like a fallen cavalryman pinned under his dead horse. Ralph's eyes were as big as the rest of him for the entire ride.

When we got back to Camp Heaven, the visiting captain disappeared. Maybe he went to the PX for more cigs, and could not find his way back. No one in 5/7 Cav ever saw him again. Maybe he was newly assigned to the Brigade S-2 section, and they thought someone should go out on the recon. So they sent the guy with one day's service in the combat zone.

By late afternoon, I was back out to the battalion assembly area where our battalion S-2 and I briefed the operations order for the air-assault into the A Shau Valley. The S-2, a 1Lt named Tom Abraham, began by scaring everyone half to death.

"The A Shau Valley — Indian Country — home base of the NVA. The valley was lost to the NVA back in 1965. The Special Forces and their Montagnard forces were wiped out to a man. Hardly anyone has been out there since. There is an NVA anti-aircraft unit and three tanks reported to be in our immediate objective area. The terrain is horrendous. 70 to 80 degree slopes. Triple canopy jungle. The weather tomorrow will be marginal. Fog until 0900 hours. Fog and rain are predicted for D-Day beginning at 1700 hours."

Tom was an English citizen serving in our army, and he was an interesting chap. I took a liking to him, and very much enjoyed his company. He had been a damn good platoon leader before Solomon, his Platoon Sergeant, got killed. After that, he became difficult for the people around him in B Company. We moved him to Delta. That lasted about two days. Finally we brought him back to the headquarters. *(His emotional problems may have foretold the bigger problems to come later in his life, but that is another story. A lot of Nam Vets had problems later in life. That war fucked up thousands of heads over the years.)*

I followed the S-2 to issue the operating instructions, saying with pride that we were again the lead battalion for the entire division. My operations order was paragraph 5 all the way. I talked and pointed at the wall map behind me, starting with:

1) FRIENDLY FORCES. 3rd Bde will secure three mountains overlooking the northern third of the valley. 5/7 will take Hill 1228 first. The 1/7 Cav will follow us next, landing on a much lower mountain directly across the valley. 2/7 Cav will come in last about four clicks south and on the western side of the valley.

The battalions will be way beyond artillery range, so the preparatory fires are air strikes. Beginning at H-Hour minus 45 minutes, there will be four air strikes every ten minutes, putting in seventy-two bombs.

2) MISSION. Our mission is to seize Hill 1228 and the road coming across the southern face of the mountain, block any enemy tanks and infantry coming in from the west, and set up observation of the valley floor.

3) CONCEPT OF THE OPERATION. Brigade has forty slicks to work with, enough to air-assault two companies. A and B Companies will lead us in. A Co will secure the firebase location on a finger of land just below the road, and B CO will take the mountain peak looming 900 feet above. The A Co LZ will be called "LZ Tiger." The top of Hill 1228 will be called "Tiger High". After a 35-minute turn around, C and D Companies will both come in on LZ Tiger Low down on the road. C Co will take over defense of Tiger Low and A Co will move out to the east to a point where they can observe the main valley below, and block the road coming up from that direction. D Co will move out to the west along the cliffside road to block any tanks and infantry coming in from Laos. They have the most critical mission. The forward command group will come in with C Co, and begin setting up on LZ Tiger. Once we have taken the ground, the Chinooks will bring in our artillery battery, and the balance of our headquarters and support people who will be in two Chinook loads. Brigade plans to put their Forward CP with us again.

My face was probably screwed up on the last comment regarding the Brigade Headquarters colocating with us. *(Captain Willie Gore had joined the battalion only three days earlier, and wrote down everything in his little green notebook which he showed me 30 years later. His notes from the briefing that night were very close to the standard five paragraph field order format taught at Fort Benning. Hell, yeah.)*

JB had little to add, other than "Y'all know what to do." The mission for the individual soldier remained unchanged. "Take the initiative, do your job and be around to fight again tomorrow."

After the briefing, JB sent me back to Camp Evans to get the latest scoop from Brigade, telling me to "get some sleep, and come back with the C&C in time to take off for the valley." The sun was hanging low over Rocket Ridge when I got back to the Brigade heli-pad. As I was leaving the pad, in came Bob and his crew on another 1/9 Cav bird crammed full of people. They had waited all day for a Chinook to sling their precious Huey C&C Bird back, and the Chinook never came. They were some very unhappy campers, and looked like they had been through a very tough ordeal. Everyone's day was exhausting — but doubly so for them. And yet, bright and early the next morning, they were in the cockpit of a new bird when we headed back out to pick up the boss.

While I was living the good life that night (actually, I was totally asleep until woken up by an RTO from the rear TOC), the battalion was on the receiving end of a 60mm mortar barrage just after midnight. All of the FNGs must have been awake for the rest of the night, waiting for the big ground attack. I missed all this excitement, and showed up just in time to go to the valley on schedule. JB was more than a little testy.

CHAPTER 29

19 APRIL 1968

The two lead companies of 5/7 Cav began lifting off at 0830 hours on 19 April, mounted in 40 slicks from the 227th Combat Aviation Battalion. There were two aviation companies from the 227th Combat Aviation Battalion involved, commanded by majors. Major Peterson led B Co, 227th, and Major Burkhalter had C Co, 227th. I knew Burkhalter from somewhere, but couldn't remember where. Maybe Benning. Maybe a different Burkhalter. The forty slicks traveled in strings of ten, each with two gunbirds.

The weather was clear over the valley, but poor over the intervening jungle-covered mountains. The pilots had to fly on instruments for part of the way. Many of the pilots were young and inexperienced, and this was their first dose of instrument flying in a combat zone. There is always a first time for everything. Dating back to October in the Que Son Valley, the aviation platoons in the 227th were not unlike our rifle squads — lots of FNGs.

The A Shau Valley runs north to south about twenty miles long, and parallels the Laotian border only a few clicks to the west. It was the primary NVA support base for the northern half of the country, and the launching pad for the NVA assault into Hue during Tet. By 1968, the A Shau Valley was protected by a sophisticated network of anti-aircraft units, including 37mm and 57mm radar guided anti-aircraft weapons, and lots of 12.75mm machineguns. The 12.75mm equates to 51 caliber in our system. Just like our 50 caliber machinegun, no one wants to be hit by a 12.75mm bullet. The 37mm and 57mm cannons were WW II era guns that fire explosive shells, commonly referred to as flak.

The air-assault was preceded by an awesome weeklong reconnaissance and bombing campaign waged by the 1/9 Cav. More than 100 B-52 strikes were dropped in the valley area. *(Hard to imagine, if you have ever seen even one B-52 strike.)* 200 fighter-bomber sorties from the Air Force and Marine Air Wing struck targets in the north end, where we were going. The valley floor and mountain sides were blanketed with bomb craters.

The packs were heavy. As far as the troops were concerned, we were headed for Charlie's place. They wanted to have enough stuff. Plenty of ammo. Extra water. And a goody or two. The air density allowed only 6 fully combat-loaded troopers per slick. Rumors were rampant. We assumed that some of the main force units involved in Tet were out there rebuilding. There was fear in the eyes of some. We expected a fight.

The flights climbed to 6000 feet to clear the cloud tops rising up from the mountains, and then descended through holes in the clouds, one ship at a time. As we neared the eastern rim of the valley, the strings had come back together again.

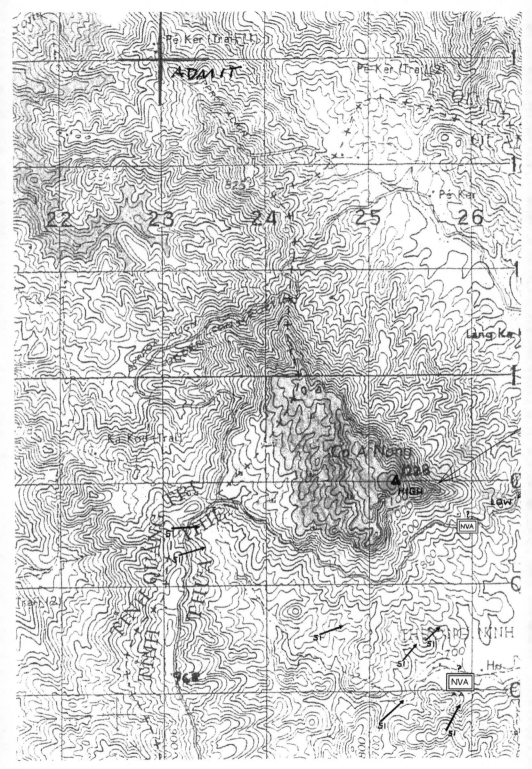

We preceded the forty-bird formation across the valley in the C&C Bird. Looking down, I saw the morning sun glancing off the hundreds of water-filled bomb craters. Everyone in the bird could see the huge mountain across the valley that we were headed for. LZ TIGER.

Looking out the back of the C&C, I could see the big armada of helicopters coming through the sky. It was an unforgettable sight. No movie about the war could begin to capture its magnitude. It was truly awesome... until the beautiful sky was suddenly marred by a little black puff of smoke. Then more. Then many. Actually, the exploding sky was every bit as awesome. Out the left door, a big puff of black smoke was instantly followed by a boom and a shockwave that shook our bird.

"37mm flak", reported Major Bob laconically, sounding like a TWA pilot announcing turbulence. Within seconds flak was everywhere. I immediately felt the same heightened anxiety of the previous day, when we had headed for the pin cushion.

In no time at all, the C&C and all the other helicopters nosed into a dive, just like a school of fish. The 37mm flak was left bursting well above the formation. By the time we leveled off we are halfway across the valley. That was when the sky in front of us erupted in a wall of red and green tracers, all going straight up past the canopy. Some eyes momentarily went shut in the back of the aircraft as we flew right into it. Mine, for example. We men in the back had a feeling of total helplessness. Chuck wasted no time adjusting his 37mm flak guns downward, and flak and tracers soon filled the air together. As soon as the flak returned, the birds just as quickly began to climb, leaving the flak on the way up. After this roller coaster maneuver it suddenly became quiet. Some eyes re-opened in the back of the bird.

It was sudden this and sudden that. Before we had even finished our various prayers and thoughts of goodbye, the formation was on the west side of the valley and spiraling down toward the landing zones. The 227th Combat Aviation Battalion was a well-oiled machine, and had saved everyone's butt yet again. Well, almost everyone. Sadly, Pfc. Clifford Sell of A Co was hit by a piece of shrapnel in the initial salvo of flak. He was sitting on the outside with his feet on the struts — ready to go like always. Before anyone could catch him, he fell to the valley below.

There were no slicks shot down by the 37mm and 12.75mm machineguns during this initial assault. Many took hits, but kept on flying the mission. It was a miracle. The Big Sky Concept was really true. The Hueys were tiny little bugs surrounded by all that sky.

Like many of the pilots, most of the Limping Scholars and the County Lines were young and inexperienced too. What the hell, everyone was young and inexperienced, except for guys like JB, McQuerry, the first sergeants and a few guys like George Klein and Marion Greene.

A Co began landing on the barren little ridge 900 feet below the mountain top. There was enough open area to land two birds at a time. LZ Tiger Low was not too Red at first, sort of Pink perhaps. AK-47 rounds were zipping through the air, coming from the cliffs above.

Up on Tiger High, B Co went in one ship at a time into a bomb crater right at the edge of the cliff. The hole in the trees was just big enough for a slick to fly in, drop his load, and back out. The men on Tiger Low could watch the bird ease into the break in the trees, then back out, spin around, and take off for the coast. There were no open landing areas up there, only defoliated and knocked over trees. The lack of air density caused loss of RPM when the birds were hovering, and the birds were very unstable as they off-loaded the heavily-laden troopers. It got Red up there real soon. The NVA 12.75mm gunners on the valley floor and out to the west shifted their attention to these birds trying to fit into the bomb crater. Tracers were floating up there from multiple directions. 12.75mm bullets were ricocheting through the surrounding trees. Tiger High was definitely a Red LZ. Even so, keeping the birds from hitting the trees may have been as scary for the pilots as seeing the enemy tracers all around them. For the troopers it was mainly about jumping off the wildly gyrating skids, wearing a sixty-pound pack, without breaking a leg.

A few more 12.75mm machine guns, located in the low ground to the south of the mountain, joined in the action against the bomb crater. About the time that half of B Co's troops were off-loaded, the flight commander would take no further chances. Having a ship shot down in the crater would be disastrous. Major Peterson directed his remaining ships to Tiger Low.

JB had approved this little ridgeline to be the main firebase and Bn CP location for several reasons. It was close enough to the rim from where we could observe the entire valley floor, but far enough in from the military crest that the fire from the valley floor would be ten feet up, and rising, by the time it went over the LZ. The artillery would also be able to fire directly at targets on the ridgelines to the south and west, including parts of the road from Laos. And, of equal importance, this ridgeline would be below the predicted morning clouds a lot earlier. JB saw and understood all of this from his recon the previous day.

Near the end of the first phase assault, enemy 12.75mm gunners from the lower ground south of the LZ, and from the ridge out to the west, had also homed in on Tiger Low. Tracers criss-crossed over the LZ from several directions. The slicks were targeted by these 12.75s, and also continued to take AK fire from the side of the mountain between the two LZs. Tiger Low became a very hot place. At the end of the assault, Ralph and his troopers from B Company were split about half-and-half between the two LZs. One of the covering gunbirds was shot down, and crash-landed in the trees, down the slope below Tiger High. Six of the birds suffered blade strikes requiring repair when they got back to the coast, and were no longer available for the later phases that day. Things were not going totally according to plan.

Some of the initial troopers on the ground from A Co moved out immediately to where they could see down to the valley floor, and it was not too long before they spotted the general location of the NVA 37mm positions. Mr. Charles appeared to be firing his flak guns from a large wooded area on the valley floor, which surrounded a little village called Lang Ka Kou. It was 1500 feet below LZ Tiger. It was the same wooded area where Bob had clipped some leaves from only twenty-four hours earlier on our way to the forced landing. The NVA had shown remarkable discipline on 18 April by not giving away their location for a lone aircraft. Ralph and the rest of our little recon group were lucky guys on the 18th. And Bob had shown fortuitous judgment coaxing the wounded bird to a more remote area up the valley.

While Burkhalter and Peterson went back for the other two companies, I was on the horn with the Flashing Sabers about the anti-aircraft positions. Before long, Troop B had scout birds and gunships streaking up the valley floor at treetop level. When they approached the suspected location, they were greeted with intense 12.75mm machinegun fire from multiple positions. It was time for the big boys to come in with some bombs.

"RASH 1, this is FAST FLANKER 3, over"

"RASH, go."

"We have the site of the 37mms spotted. In the woods on the valley floor. Need all you can get, over."

"Ahh . . roger."

"FAST FLANKER 3 here, let me know when they are inbound, over."

"Ahh . . roger."

In the meantime, JB was on the radio with the company commanders trying to get a clear picture of events. He heard all about the splitting of B Company, and was already thinking ahead.

In the second phase with C and D Companies, all the birds were to go into Tiger Low as planned. The multiple strings of UHIB slicks came across the valley through the same frightening drill with the 37 mm flak bursts and vertical red and green tracers. During this second phase, the sky was immediately hot over Tiger Low, and some birds carrying C Company troopers reverted to Tiger High. Now we had two companies split between the two LZs.

Once all four companies were on the ground, the troopers of both A Co and C Co had a good view of all the enemy fire.

"FAST FLANKER 3, this is COUNTY LINE 6, over."

"FFAST FLANKER 3, over."

"The coordinates of the 37 mike mikes is Yankee Delta 268099, over."

"Roger, out."

"RASH 1, this is FAST FLANKER 3, over."

"RASH."

I repeated to him the coordinates and went on to say "there is a big square-shaped tree line down there, and they are in that area, over."

"Ahh . . roger, I see it."

"FAST FLANKER 3, what is the inbound, over?"

"Ahh, RASH here . . have four sorties in 30 minutes, over."

"Roger, out."

Things were a lot more intense on the Tiger Low LZ during the second phase landings. With little going in on the top of the mountain, the enemy machinegunners south and west of us were concentrating on Tiger Low. The supporting gunships were returning fire against these targets. Even with all this fire, though, only two birds caught big enough bullets to go down.

A slick carrying a load of D Co troopers was hit by a 12.75 machinegun firing from the south, and crash-landed just off the road. 1Lt. Mike Sprayberry, XO of D Co, was the last man to jump from the plummeting ship before it crashed and burned. He fell about 15 feet, and made a good PLF. *(Parachute landing fall in airborne terms.)* The crew and all but two of the troopers got out okay. Tragically, Pfc. Michael Lipsius, from Santa Clara, California, was hit by one of the 12.75mm rounds coming into the bird. He was 19. And another man, from one of the attached units, was killed by the rotor blade after the bird collided with the ground.

Around the same time, one of the supporting gunships went down, while firing against the 12.75mms in the lower ground south of Tiger Low. The bird hit hard with a big explosion, followed immediately by a big fire that engulfed the ship. It didn't look like there would be any survivors.

The second phase of the air-assault was completed by 1055 hours, with only the one slick and two gunbirds lost. Amazing. An entire battalion of four rifle companies was carried across the width of Vietnam, descended on instruments through clouds, met a wall of anti-aircraft fire, and made it in with the loss of only one slick. Sometime during the morning, a 1/9 Cav gunbird also crashed up on Tiger High, and the crew was picked up by another one of their other pilots.

Soon after the end of the second phase air-assault, ROUGH RIDER 6 was reporting heavy contact with a roadblock position a few hundred meters west of the LZ. JB said, "Bob, I think I need to get on the ground now."

"Roger, sir."

The C&C was about 5000 feet above the valley floor when we started our descent. JB talked to me most of the way down.

"Stay upstairs. Keep the birds coming."

"Yes, sir."

"I doubt if the bosses will be flying around out here much. You need to keep us in commo with the coast."

"Yes, sir."

"And we need to get a fix on the damn anti-aircraft positions, and do something about it. Understand?"

"Yes, sir."

The ride across the valley toward the LZ was uneventful to JB and me because we stayed busy conferring. I kept my eyes glued to my map all the way down until I woke up to the sound of AK-47s shooting at us. The C&C pilot took us past the cliffs on the way into the LZ so JB could get a good look at the situation. Swinging around, I saw the terrain south of the mountain. I also saw the burning gunbird in the trees southwest of the LZ. *(Holy shit.)*

Going into short final, the C&C ship suddenly became visible from the main valley floor, and Bob and his co-pilot found themselves staring at fuzzy little balls of fire arching up toward them — 12.75mm machinegun fire. Rather than set down, Bob kept the bird hovering. The lack of air density was apparent as the bird bounced violently up and down, anywhere from two feet to 15 feet above the ground. JB tried to start his leap at the bottom, but the ship lurched upward. On the next try, he timed it well but was still about six to eight feet up when he cleared the struts. He made a good rolling fall and jumped right back up. He took on a look of concern, though, when I dropped him his 25 pound AN-PRC 25 radio strapped to a metal frame backpack. The bird was at least twenty feet up and climbing as the radio was launched. The AN-PRC 25 was called the "Prick 25," aptly named in this instance. JB was tough as nails, had played a lot of quarterback in his day, and made a perfect catch.

Major Bob pulled pitch, straight out over the valley, veered left and climbed with maximum power toward the big sky. We climbed for a lifetime, with 12.75mm tracers trying to catch up the entire way. Make that five lifetimes; there was a crew of four, plus me sitting all alone in the back. The enemy tracers were like curve balls as they appeared to arc away to the rear. The climb back to altitude completely overshadowed the tension of the previous day. It was terrifying, actually. Both Bob and his co-pilot were bobbing up and down in their seats, as though they could somehow get the bird to fly faster. This was the first and only visible anxiety I ever saw out of those guys dating back to January. Everyone was bobbing. We made it to the Big Sky, of course. The olive-green colored helicopter blended in nicely against the olive-green mountain behind us. *(Olive-green is a beautiful color. Quite beautiful, in fact. My favorite.)*

At first light that same morning, a twenty-man unit from the 75th Rangers air-assaulted onto the top of one of the highest mountains between the coast and the valley. This 4800-foot peak is about ten clicks southeast of Tiger on the other side of the valley, and would serve as a radio relay back to Camp Evans. When the Rangers went in at dawn, the tops of the clouds were down at 4500 feet. The mountain top was another island in a white sea, reminiscent of LZ Long. The Rangers would have to rappel from the hovering Hueys about thirty feet down into a bomb crater. When the first ship got to a hover after two tries, the pilot lost power and fell like a rock down the jungle-covered slope. Most of the passengers and crew suffered minor injuries. They were very lucky. After adjusting the approach direction, the remaining three helicopters were able to rappel their troops. The Ranger operation got off to a rough start that morning. The relay station would not be operational anytime soon.

JB, wearing a backpack radio, would be the entire forward CP until his RTO and a couple other guys came in on one of the last slicks. I would remain aloft in the C&C while communications back to the world were tenuous. I suspected that Brigadier General Oscar Davis would be up there somewhere, though. Everyone in the rest of our headquarters was back on the coast waiting for the Chinook ride into Tiger Low. *(Hooks, we called these big twin-rotor cargo helicopters. Rhymed with Chinook. And they had a big hook on a cable hanging from the bottom, on which cargo net rings could be attached. They carried the heavy stuff in to us — like artillery guns, and nets full of ammunition boxes.)*

For the next couple hours JB supervised his company commanders on the ground. Most importantly, he was there with the troops on a very scary day, as he always had been since he joined the battalion. The Hard Hitters of C Co consolidated on the LZ and moved out to their pre-assigned positions on the south and east side of Tiger Low. This freed up A Company to move up to the rim of the valley. D Co commenced their attack up the road toward Laos, clearing snipers from the cliffs above the road and to their front. They fought through this resistance for one click, with no casualties, before they ran into a strong enemy position blocking the road.

"FAST FLANKER 3, this is ROUGH RIDER 6, over."

"This is FLANKER 3, over."

"We are held up by a strong position at coordinates Yankee Delta 251085, over."

"What's it look like, over?"

"ROUGH RIDER 6. The road is cut into a real steep slope. Almost straight up on the high side, and a drop off on the other, over."

"What do they have, over?"

"The road bends around a draw coming down the mountain. They have at least one machinegun. At least a squad. They are dug into the uphill bank of the road. As soon as we step around the bend we get lots of automatic fire."

"Roger, keep working it, over."

"Roger, I am moving some guys backward and up on higher ground to give us a base."

"Roger, out."

In the meantime, Bob had us circling between 6000 and 8000 feet, maintaining communications and monitoring the following phases of the operation. I listened in on the battalion net, but much of my focus was on an alternate frequency with the

FAC, trying to coordinate a bombing effort against the 37mm anti-aircraft position on the valley floor.

As our troops on the ground began talking about gun locations, I invited the FAC and the 1/9 Cav leader to join me on the battalion's command net for a little while so that everyone concerned could listen directly to A Company and C Company describing the exact locations. It made for a little chaos, but the goal was to shut down the radar-controlled guns before the less maneuverable Hooks came in with their sling loads.

A Co had the clearest view and was giving everyone the most information. Everyone agreed about where the NVA's flak guns were firing from, but getting them eliminated was a totally different problem. After a lot of discussion between the FAC up in the sky, and the 1/9 pilots on the valley floor, we dropped a couple sorties with 250 lb. bombs into the center of the big wooded area. We got no secondary explosions. We gained no confidence.

More fast movers showed up at about 1130 hours, and began flying in circles around the C & C bird, waiting for instructions from the FAC. They were Marine and Navy jets this day, and the pilots smiled and waved as they went by. Why not? There was cold beer waiting for them when they got home. I answered with thumbs up, but not my customary smile. I had a whole new outlook about immortality after the flight into LZ Tiger. *(There is some serious shit going on out here.)*

Down on the valley floor, the 1/9 Cav still only knew generally where the guns were, but not in terms of locating the individual gun positions for the FAC. The 37 mm guns were located in deep silos, scattered throughout a fairly large wooded area. The NVA crews cranked them to the top of the silos when it was time to fire, then quickly lowered them deep into the ground. The outer tree line of the wooded area was well defended by the 12.75mm machine guns, which the enemy leveled on the Saber gunbirds as they approached on the deck. The NVA anti-aircraft position was a very tough nut to crack. The guns were in there somewhere, but no one could get close enough to pinpoint them.

"FAST FLANKER 3, this is RASH 1."

"FLANKER 3, over."

"RASH here . . We have to use em or lose em, over."

I consulted with the Flashing Sabers and County Line one more time. No one offered an opinion about exact gun locations in the wooded area the 37mms were. A decision needed to be made.

"RASH 1, FAST FLANKER 3, I guess the thing to do is put them on the south tree line where the 12.75s are firing from, over."

"Aah . . . . roger that."

"COUNTY LINE 6, did you monitor over?"

"This is COUNTY LINE 6 ALPHA, roger, over."

"Keep a sharp lookout for secondaries, over."

"COUNTY LINE 6 ALPHA, roger, over."

"FLANKER 3, Out." *(The senior man always has the last word.)*

Rash dropped the bombs as best he could, based on the collective information from A Company and the 1/9 scout birds. It was impressive watching from above, as the jets flipped over into a dive and swooped down to drop their bombs on the white phosphorous markers hitting the edge of the trees. Just like in the movies. They hit the after-burners on the way up and out, with tracers trying to catch them the whole way. None of the jets got hit that I know of. The bombs wreaked havoc with the edge of the wooded area, but there were no secondary explosions. Rash expended all of his sorties, and the 1/9 Cav scout birds and gunbirds again approached the area from the south. They were met with heavy 12.75mm fire. When it was all over, no one was very confident. Not me, or the FAC, or the 1/9 Cav, or the boys on the mountain.

Shortly after the bomb run, I got a call. "FAST FLANKER 3, this is *(Somebody)* Five Alpha, over." I don't remember the Division call sign, but I recognized the voice. It was Oscar, the Assistant Division Commander

"___ FIVE ALPHA, this is FAST FLANKER 3, over."

"This is ____ 5 ALPHA. Listen, we need to be getting the hooks in pretty soon. What can you tell me about the situation, over."

"FAST FLANKER 3 here, we have the area of the 37s located, but Flashing Saber can't get close enough to find the gun positions, over."

"_____ 5 ALPHA, what seems to be the problem?"

" The guns are at approximate coordinates YD268099. A big wooded area. It is surrounded by open ground in all directions with 12.75s guarding the tree line. We just dropped four sorties of 250s in there as best we could, before they ran out of air time, over."

"_____ 5 Alpha. I'm up above you. I see where you are talking about. . . . all right, look, I need your opinion. Should we bring in the hooks or not, over."

"Flashing Saber says they don't think we knocked out any guns. I say it is too early, over."

"Roger that, out."

Someone made the decision to start moving artillery at about noon anyway. The first Chinook load carrying one of the 105mm howitzers, along with its gun crew, lifted off at 1205 hours and headed for LZ TIGER. No one called me back to tell me anything. No one out in the A Shau ever saw this Chinook. The rest of the hooks were put on hold.

Meanwhile, the 1/7 Cav lifted off for the valley at 1230 hours, and twenty minutes later began setting down on a two-ship LZ. Initially, their slicks came down the valley from the north and swung back eastward into the LZ. This brought them in range of the anti-aircraft guns, and they took a few hits. The Aviation Battalion Commander wasted no time in redirecting the approach to straight in from the eastern high ground.

The 1/7 Cav had their own set of problems. By about 1500 hours they had closed into their position, and the terrain was totally useless. They could not see anything but trees. It was untenable for an artillery battery. Someone had picked the wrong hill. Perhaps no one did a recon the day before like we did. *(no perhaps about it.)* They immediately started planning to move to a better location lower down and closer to the valley. We didn't see any of this going on. I learned of it on the radio. While 1/7 Cav was still coming in, Rash brought in some more jets.

"Aah . . FAST FLANKER 3, RASH 1 here."

"This is FAST FLANKER 3, over."

"RASH 1 . . I have four more sorties inbound, over."

"Roger, wait."

I went on the horn to A Company and the 1/9 Cav again. The opinion was that the guns were well inside the woods.

"RASH 1, FLANKER 3 here . . let's concentrate on the center of the wooded area with these bombs, over."

"Aah . . will do, out."

And so they did. RASH 1 rolled into his dive and put in his white phosphorous markers. RASH 1 had a big pair of balls. From out of nowhere, a jet came streaking downward past the C & C bird in a beautiful upside-down arc. He was on his way back up and out before the fire balls of the exploding bombs appeared inside the trees. Four bombs later, the good news was that neither RASH 1 nor any of his buddies had been shot down. The bad news was that no big secondary explosions erupted in the target area. The 1/9 Cav, the FAC, and the fast movers continued to receive intense fire as they went about their business. They were out of bombs again, with everyone feeling that the NVA positions were still intact. *(Shit fuck piss hell damn.)*

Throughout the afternoon various people asked me on the radio if it was all clear for the hooks. They might not have taken me seriously earlier, but the first Chinook that lifted off earlier was shot down by a 57mm gun on a mountain halfway to the valley from the coast. They were taking me for my word now. First the Aviation Commander called, then someone from Division Artillery, and then the Assistant Division Commander again. Everyone below me reported no reduction of the enemy's anti-aircraft capabilities. I stuck with "negative, over."

By mid-afternoon Major Bob reported that he had to return to Camp Evans for fuel, and take a leak. Bob could have easily said, "let's put you on the ground because we have to go back to Camp Evans," and take the rest of the day off. But he didn't say that. Suddenly, everyone had to piss really bad. Some famous general back in the Crimean War was quoted as saying, "when in war, never miss an opportunity to take a piss". The instant we touched down on the pad back at Camp Evans, the door gunners and I were out of the ship and peeing right there on the fuel pad. We peed … and peed.

As soon as we returned, maybe forty minutes later, it was still not clear if any damage had been done to the 37mm positions. Rash had brought in some more sorties working directly with County Line, and still no secondaries. Troop B 1/9 Cav was sticking to their position that little had been accomplished.

About the time we got back above the valley, the Brigade Commander came up on our battalion command net. *(Hmm, I hadn't heard from him today.)*

"FAST FLANKER 3, this is COLD STEEL 6, over."

"COLD STEEL 6, this is FAST FLANKER 3, over."

"COLD STEEL 6, I have been trying to raise you for some time. You need to listen your damn radio, over!" *(Uh oh.)*

"Ahh . . I am, over."

"I couldn't even get you on your own net, over."

"Ahh . . roger. We had to go back for fuel, over."

"This is COLD STEEL 6, why aren't you monitoring the Brigade Command Net, over?"

"FLANKER 3, Ahh . . . Well, there's a lot going on out here. Everyone has been talking on my net. I am up here by myself. I've been very busy trying to get air strikes!" I said with a little of my own heat. *(Where in the fuck have you been? I was thinking.)*

"This is COLD STEEL 6, you need to do a better job keeping me informed… well, anyway, look, we need to make a decision about bringing in the hooks. It is getting late. The weather is going to deteriorate. What do you say, over?"

I had not heard from Brigade at any time that day. The Brigade commander's tone became more cordial. I looked at my watch, and it was about 1500 hours. Where had the time gone? I later regretted getting hot with the colonel, because nothing was going to be served other than screwing up my "career" some. C'est la vie. I reiterated my recommendation made to BG Davis an hour earlier. It was too early for Chinooks to fly across the valley.

It was soon after this conversation that I decided to join the troops on the ground. Rash was out of bombs and nothing was happening at 6000 feet. The pilots needed rest. And after all, the Brigade Commander was on the case now. *(Thinking back about that afternoon in the sky above the A Shau Valley, I give myself about a C plus. I didn't get any bombs on the 37s that I could tell. And I didn't answer the radio right away when called by the Brigade CO. I talked to a lot of people, though.)*

Bob and the warrant officer dropped me off with no broken bones, and they and their crew enjoyed the same thrilling escape from the 12.75mm machineguns on their way back to the big sky. The NVA continued to shoot at every bird within range. Every slick that came and went into LZ Tiger that day had the same frightening story to tell when they got home.

CHAPTER 30

INTO THE DARK

As soon as I got on the ground and got briefed by JB, he decided it was time to pay D Co a visit. He took off up the road on a mechanical mule, driven by Jim Thomas. I never heard from the Brigade CO again that day. No one saw any C&C birds way up there in the sky either.

Around 1600 hours, someone back on the coast made a command decision to send in the Hooks. Unaware of this decision, all the men of 5/7 Cav on LZ Tiger Low watched in total amazement, as a string of Chinooks towing artillery tubes and various other sling loads appeared on the horizon above the coastal range. They were on the exact path we had come in on that morning. I was screaming at the nearest RTO — "Get me on the Aviation Net!"

The Hooks were magnificent flying toward the A Shau Valley in single file. They were coming fast. The RTO had no time to look up the frequency, let alone switch the radio and get anyone. The hooks were magnificent, until the lead ship reached the center of the valley, where he was suddenly surrounded by 37mm flak, suffered some direct hits, burst into flames, and started spiraling downward. Before he was halfway to the jungle canopy, the second bird came along and got the same deal. He too spiraled downward, engulfed in flames. As the first Hook hit the jungle canopy, the third Hook was getting hit. One of my new RTOs broke into tears. Charles had gone three for three against the Hooks at that point. I was horrified and pissed off at the same time. I called that one, you dumb sons-a-bitches.

"This is terrible, Sir," said my RTO, with tears running down his face.

"That's just the way it is in war. War is terrible. Terrible things happen. All we can do is keep doing our jobs."

"Yes, Sir."

The only good thing that could be said was that the 1/9 Cav White and Red birds were in a better position to get a good look at the fire coming up out of the wooded area, and they became more effective at putting suppressive fire against the NVA gunners. They concentrated enough rocket fire into the gun position areas, that most of the remaining Hook sorties got through. But not all. They just kept coming, unable to vary their altitude like the Hueys.

The sun was starting to dip toward the western ridgeline. Five Chinooks had crashed into the sides of the mountains, mostly across the valley. Everyone sat around, filling sandbags, and trading mournful comments like, "ain't nobody coming out of that one." The Hooks were sitting ducks. (*What incredible courage by the Chinook pilots, watching their company mates going down in front of them, yet still flying west to get critical artillery tubes in before the weather closed us off.*)

5/7 Cav received four of the hoped-for six artillery tubes. Captain Fred Pope, the battery commander, got his remaining guns in position and ready to fire. All they needed was artillery ammo. At that point, they had just a little over what they called their emergency load. Artillerymen save their emergency loads for when they have to lower their guns against an enemy assault on the firebase. A battery didn't like to be below 300 rounds.

The command post group, along with other supporting attachments, arrived in two Hooks. Joe was on the first of the two birds. Our cook, Gary Nordstrom, came in on the second bird, telling anyone who would listen about the 12.75 round that came up through the floor, through his legs, and scored a perfect bullseye in his cooking pot. He showed his pot to everyone, and sure enough — dead center. When it isn't your time, it isn't your time.

It was getting late into the day. The valley floor was cloaked in shadow as the sun went lower in the western sky. Over the horizon the men in County Line saw two giant bugs coming toward them. CH-54 "Flying Cranes" from the 228th were flying the mission. One was slinging a bulldozer, the other had the backhoe. A Crane had two pilot compartments, one on each end, connected by a span of steel below which hangs the carrying hook. It was the world's most powerful helicopter. It could lift a Chinook helicopter or maybe even a tank. It was built like a dragster, no body, just frame. The lead Crane overshot the LZ and circled back out over the valley for a second try. The troops of A Co watched in horror as it got snapped in half by 37mm fire, and fall like a big pile of scrap iron to the valley floor.

A few minutes later, the other Crane came to a hover above Tiger Low and slowly inch down, landing the bulldozer upright, enabling the awaiting engineer bulldozer driver to scramble up and disengage the load. The Crane pilot had 12.75 tracers coming at him from several directions while he was off-loading the dozer, so he slid westward and dropped down below the little ridge we were on, right behind our command post area. He needed to think about his plan for departure. As he hovered in the draw with the little green balls going just over his rotor blades, I jumped up and ran over to just in front of the bubble of the Crane, and talked to the pilot on my back pack radio while waving instructions with my arms.

"This is FAST FLANKER 3, recommend you circle back over your right shoulder and climb straight up over the mountain top, Over."

"Aah .. roger."

"This is FAST FLANKER 3, I repeat, do not go straight out over the valley, understand?"

"Aah .. roger."

And with a nod of his head, the pilot lifted straight up, and flew right over my head straight out over the valley. He also climbed at an almost vertical angle all the way to 8000 feet. I did a pirouette watching them leave the area. *(So much for my advice. The pilot sensed that most of the 12.75 fire was coming at him from the bowl to the west. I had not been there very long and still had the notion that all the fire was from the valley floor to the east. Sometimes you should just keep your mouth shut, even when you are a major.)*

An unencumbered CH-54 can climb straight up faster than any helicopter in the world, and the pilot took his chances on that. He won his bet, got to the Big Sky, and returned to Camp Evans. There was no joy in the Flying Crane platoon that night. Their fallen comrades were the first Crane pilots lost to enemy fire in the war. *(And they remain Missing in Action to this day: Arthur Lord ~ Charles Millard ~ Phillip Shafer ~ Michael Werdehoff)*

Out in the 5/7 Cav corner of the globe, everyone worked to get the TOC underground as the sun was almost down to the ridgeline that loomed in the west. The last people came in and got themselves sorted out. The battalion had four of its six 105mm artillery tubes in direct support, with a limited amount of ammunition. The sky was clouding up and it was getting cold. AK rounds continued to whiz by, as the operations sergeants and RTOs worked to set up the TOC. There was no Carling Black Label coming in tonight. In fact, there was no water beyond the canteens we wore on our pistol belts. The water bladders that we planned to sling in by log birds failed to make the trip.

Westward up the road, D Co had been in contact all afternoon with a force large enough to hold them in place. There was an almost vertical drop on the left side of the road, and an almost vertical cliff on the right. It did not take a lot of NVA to hold up the Rough Rider advance in that direction. The NVA were in spider holes dug into the side of the road bank, in depth back up the road. Each position had to be taken one at a time, using the old covering fire, pistol, and grenade drill that the troops learned so well on the road to Hue. Fire and maneuver.

The fight began to grow in intensity. Late in the day, a Rough Rider named Curtis was killed trying to take out the next spider hole. Curtis was a 20 year old Pfc.

The final Chinook of the day came into the log pad that had been established on the next little finger west of the primary LZ. This big bird was hauling a net full of precious artillery ammunition and the battalion's re-supply of small arms ammo. XO Joe had made it in a little earlier with the CP Hook, and he and I just happened to be over at the log pad when the Hook came to a hover maybe thirty yards forward of the ridge.

The pinko-commie gunners had tracers coming right over the top of the Hook as the pilot maneuvered the sling load backwards toward the top of the narrow ridge. He was bobbing up and down, and looked like he was trying to keep his rotors below the trajectory of the little fire balls. This was no little Huey he was flying. When the Hook finally got the net onto the ground, the young trooper assigned to the log pad jumped up on the netting to remove the ring at the top of the strap from the Hook. He had to hold onto the Hook with one hand, and remove the ring with the other. He had the ring almost off the tip of the big hook when the bird lifted, taking the slack out of the cable, and barely missed catching his hand between hook and ring. Two more tries were foiled by the upward oscillation of the big bird, and he was visibly tiring. On the fourth attempt, the Chinook made a sudden and much more dramatic lurch upward. The young trooper was carried about 20 feet up, holding onto the cable, his feet dangling in mid air, his eyes as big as grapefruits. That was enough for him, and he jumped for his life, landing on top of the net, and falling from there to the ground. He landed hard, but jumped up with nothing broken, all smiles.

The Chinook slid a few feet forward of the ridge, and started bobbing up and down into the lower ground. Maybe it was the tracers coming at him. Maybe he was just losing RPM and there was nothing he could do. In either event, the rear blade came closer to the slope behind him on each drop. By this time, Joe and I were hunkered down behind a log. We were quickly up and frantically waving our arms at the pilot to go up, but it must be the loss of RPM that got him, not the machinegun bullets. It became inevitable that the rear rotor was going to hit the ground. He lost his power, if not his nerve.

The rear rotor blade finally struck the ground at the top of the narrow spine, creating a big cloud of red clay dust, and catapulting the front of the big bird downward. The nose slammed into the forward slope and caused a big cloud of dust there as well. The rear blade ground to a halt as it chewed up the surrounding dirt and threw rocks everywhere. Joe and I scampered back behind the log in the midst of the flying debris. The big helicopter settled into the ground on the 30% downward slope, with the rear ramp coming to rest on top of the sling load of 105mm artillery rounds in their wooden crates.

Almost immediately, a steady stream of aviation gas started dripping on the cargo netting from a ruptured fuel line. A few feet away a little fire began to crackle in the grass under the netting of the sling load. Joe looked at me. I looked at Joe. A fraction of a second later Joe was on his feet and running down the slope. He crawled over the net onto the lowered ramp of the bird, and disappeared into the hook. The hook was pitched steeply downward. Joe slipped and slid down to the dazed crewmembers in the front, got them up and out of their seat belts and moving back up the slippery slope of the rear cargo section. The fire was gaining momentum as they started coming out the rear end, but had not quite arrived at the dripping gasoline. Joe was the next to last man out, pushing people ahead of him, and they all came running up the slope away from the explosive situation. The last man had to jump off of the ramp sideways through the flames, and he suffered a severe burn on one of his arms.

Just as everyone arrived at the fallen tree, an artillery shell exploded on the top of the pile. A second or two later the gas tank went off. The explosion lifted the back of the bird up several feet and it came crashing back down. A box of small arms ammo started going off. It started sounding like July Fourth in the neighborhood. The 105mm high explosive rounds began exploding with increasing frequency and shrapnel was rattling through the trees. By the time everyone got away from the log pad and over to next ridge of the main LZ, the fireworks were in full glory. The exploding artillery shells and ammo went on for several hours into the dark. The final act for the big Chinook was being totally consumed by fire and melting into the hillside. It was just a big black spot the next morning.

As this was going on, JB and Thomas were on their way back from D Co, careening down the winding and narrow road in the twilight. They had been sniped at going out, and they anticipated the distinct possibility of NVA snipers waiting for them on their way back. Jim Thomas drove as fast as the conditions would allow. Suddenly, they came to a steep downhill section, and when Jim applied the brakes there were no brakes. They were gathering speed as they came to a curve, and Jim had no choice but to throw it left into the bank. The mule flipped upside down off the bank and headed toward the drop-off across the road. JB had landed on his feet and caught the full 500 pound ATV on his back. The mule was a little heavier than the radio JB had caught earlier in the day. It tore many a muscle, compressed and broke several vertebrae, and put JB out of the war for a couple years. But, only a couple.

The NVA soldiers around us had to be celebrating that night as they watched our burning ammo lighting up the night. They had certainly enjoyed a memorable day of combat. They knocked about ten helicopters out of the sky, and hit many more. *(From the 228th Aviation Battalion's hooks that went down on 19 April 1968, five men survived and nine remain missing today.)* And unbeknownst to them, they also knocked out our great leader.

> *We held the coastline,*
> *they held the highlands.*
> *And they were sharp,*
> *as sharp as knives.*
> *They heard the hum of the motors,*
> *They counted the rotors*
> *And waited for us to arrive.*
> *And we would all go down together.*
> *We said we'd all go down together.*
> *Yes we would all go down together.*
>
> **Billy Joel**

Nevertheless, we were in the middle of their famous supply base. We had their dominant mountain. We had their main supply road from Laos blocked. And we were going to kick their collective asses in the days ahead.

Joe and I learned of JB's accident while we were leaning against the roof of our new TOC watching the burning log pad. Some of the RTOs and medics rushed up the road to retrieve him, and it was dark when they brought him into the TOC. He was in intense pain, a good thing when it comes to fractures of the spine. The good news was that he had movement in all his extremities, although he wasn't waving to his many fans. A funereal silence settled over the command group. Everyone took turns holding his hand, saying their goodbyes, while waiting for a medevac bird to take him away forever. All the troopers in the area tried to get in to see him. The medevac bird was a no-show.

The medevac unit refused to fly out there because of the "weather." They said they would pick him up in the morning. Warrant Officer Al Eason was one of the informal leaders in the Brigade Aviation Platoon, along with an older guy named Rasmussen. Al routinely flew C&C for the battalion commander of 1/7 Cav, and he knew from earlier in the day where LZ Tiger was. When Major Bob Frix learned that the Medevacs wouldn't go out to pick up his colonel, Warant Officer Eason was the first to suggest that a C&C bird could go out there in the dark and pick JB up. It became one of those "I'll do it if you'll do it" kind of deals, after which Bob and Eason fired up the bird and took off for the west.

It was a very dark night, and the black ground below was obscured by broken clouds. They flew on instruments, using azimuths and time to get there, and ended up flying around for quite some time. They probably ventured into Laos; nothing new to Bob. Somewhere along the line they called.

"FAST FLANKER 65, we are overhead somewhere. I need you to key your handset on and off every few seconds." I happened to be outside the TOC with the pathfinders, listening for the sound of a helicopter when the call came, and I grabbed the pathfinder's hand mike. Bob was very faint, sounding far away. I broke in with "This is FAST FLANKER 3, roger," and keyed the hand set as requested for a good thirty seconds.

Bob called back with "FAST FLANKER 3, key it some more, over."

After another thirty seconds, Bob came in a lot louder. "FLANKER 3, I am going to turn on my lights for a second."

"There he is, sir," said the Pathfinder, pointing upward.

"Roger, SNOOPY 6, I believe we have you in sight."

Way up in the sky above Tiger High, a moving light was briefly framed by a hole in the clouds. I handed the mike back to the Pathfinder and got out of his way. He gave some quick flashes with his flashlight, which had a long cone on the front designed to throw out a very narrow beam just for night-landing situations.

"FLANKER 3 we have you in sight. We are coming down, over." The pathfinder answered and brought them in, while I ducked back into the TOC to say goodbye to JB and get everyone moving. The pilots came down through the clouds, and suddenly everyone outside the TOC saw them descending toward Tiger. Bob and Al Eason, on the other hand, saw nothing but one little pencil of light surrounded by black ink. At a point within 100 feet up, the Pathfinder gave him the signal to go with lights, and they lit up the landing pad and surrounding area. The Pathfinder guided them in to a nice landing on the pad, doing another great job, as usual.

It was an extremely courageous flight on the part of Eason and Bob Frix. It was also timely, because no one knew what daylight would bring. JB was on the ground at Camp Evans by 2310 hours, headed for the Division forward hospital. I was on the night shift from then on— my sleep pattern altered for the duration of my tour.

Shortly after the C&C departed with JB, C Company excitedly reported, "We have lots of headlights on the road below us, over."

The headlights were on the valley floor near the suspected enemy anti-aircraft positions. Lots of headlights. They counted at least 50 vehicles lined up on the road. Capt. Pope cranked up to fire some of his precious few artillery rounds. The Hard Hitters threw in some 81mm mortar rounds, although the target was at their maximum range and 1500 feet down. As soon as the rounds started landing, the vehicles wasted no time turning their lights out. It was such a great opportunity, and we had just finished watching our stock of artillery ammo explode over on the log pad. Had the goddamn hook not crashed on the ammo, we would have kicked the living shit out of the whatever anti-aircraft battalion of the whatever NVA division right then. We would have put a rectangle of hell astride the three hundred meters of the road in a matter of minutes. But we couldn't. Had our log pad man just been able to muscle that ring off that hook on the first try, which he missed by a fraction of an inch and a hundredth of a second, things would have been a lot different for Mr. Charles that night. It was one of those inches and seconds deals.

What a Hook looks like on fire

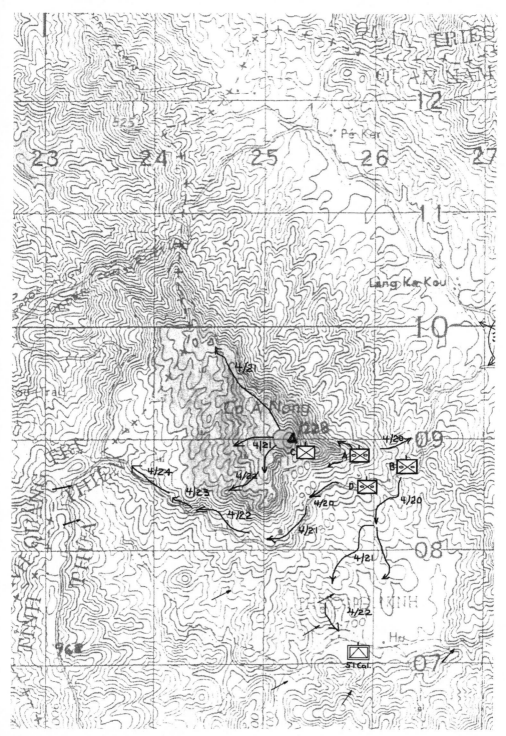

20-22 April — Developing the Battle Area

CHAPTER 31

DEVELOPING THE BATTLE AREA

When the sun came up, we were socked in by the rising ground fog. Joe and I, boy majors, sat on the roof of the TOC and talked about our situation. We concluded several things. The action was going to be along the road between Laos and the Valley. The top of the mountain had to be denied, but it was the least likely enemy approach. C Co — the Hard Hitters — had a new captain who needed some FNG time. Both Bravo and C Companies were split between Tiger Low and Tiger High, and Bravo had a very strong captain. The side of the cliff between the firebase and the mountaintop needed to be cleared of the snipers. All of these considerations led us to switch missions for Bravo Company and C Company. We wanted to get the experienced captain down on LZ Tiger. C Co would take over Tiger High, scaling the cliffs on their way up to clear out the snipers. Bravo would consolidate on Tiger Low to defend the artillery firebase and TOC. From there they would patrol southwest toward the 12.75mm machinegun positions located on the lower ground to the southwest.

After resolving our plans, Joe said, "We'll just run things together."

I said, "That sounds good to me. *(Long pause)* By the way, you are senior by one day, right?"

"Is that right? I guess you are right about that."

"We'll run it together, but you're in command. I have had some turns."

Joe and I were very good friends indeed. I was definitely used to running things by that time. Had it been anyone else regardless of dates of rank, I would have had an entirely different attitude. Plus, I knew my Principles of War. Unity of Command, for example.

In effect, things continued without missing a beat. The weather on the morning of 20 April turned from fog to marginal, and the battalion got some aviation support. A couple log birds came in from Bill Hussong, and once they had dropped their sling loads, I used them to swap troopers between the two LZs. Two of C Company's platoons scaled the cliffs, taking out some NVA along the way.

Everything went according to plan until another tragedy struck. Ralph Miles was the last man out getting his men flown down to Tiger Low. His big body was unmistakable 900 feet above. The rear boom of the slick hung off the edge of the cliff. Some of my RTOs and I were watching from the top of the TOC when Ralph suddenly fell back off of the struts. We did not know anything was wrong until the bird lifted up and backed out of the LZ, leaving Ralph behind.

I was ready for the call that came in right after the bird was safely out of the area. Ralph had been hit by a 12.75 mm round. From the day Ralph had replaced Howard on 21 February, he had done a wonderful job. It was devastating to see him go down. Major Bob Frix came into the area in the C&C, and attempted to go in to get Ralph, but he drew too much fire. A while later, Bill Hussong's other log bird came in and made a gutsy landing, picked Ralph up and carried him back to the world. *(One cannot say enough good things about the 227th and 229th pilots. Or Ralph Miles.)*

Only two days in the A Shau, and 5/7 Cav had lost two great leaders. JB was gone. Now Ralph. And Mike had rotated home — his twelve month tour was up. Company B had lost two good captains within two months. The command leadership team that got to Hue on the 24th was breaking up. We were down to Frank Lambert, and John Taylor.

RASH came on station at about 1030 hours with sorties of air strikes inbound, but he was unable to get his fighters through the clouds. The weather deteriorated as the morning went on. That same morning, the 2/7 Cav commenced their air-assault onto LZ Pepper, a ridgeline about five clicks south and on the same side of the valley as us. Things didn't go so well for them either. Their lead helicopter lost power and crashed into their bomb crater LZ. This held up the rest of the lift, and the weather worsened. The 2/7 Cav ended up with one lonely company on the ground when the weather socked in completely. After that, no one saw another helicopter in the north end of the A Shau Valley for two days. Imagine being in that lonely 2/7 Cav rifle company. One hundred twenty guys, at the most. No artillery — no shit. *(And we of the 5/7 Cav were thinking we had it rough.)*

At the end of the second day, our two companies were sorted out and everyone was working on their perimeters. The AK fire that occasionally came into LZ Tiger abated somewhat. That night, A Co again reported lots of vehicle noise, but this time without lights. We had very limited artillery ammunition, uncertain prospects for good flying weather, and could only guess the target location. Capt. Fred Pope and I decided to save our precious bullets for a truly bad day. When the sun came up on the 21st, we did not know if the 37mm unit had departed. But I was convinced that the NVA anti-aircraft unit had re-located over the course of those first two nights.

Joe and I were a committee of two, thinking through everything together. We thought exactly alike, anyway, but I always looked for that last nod from my classmate. Once decisions were made, I pretty much continued to run the operational side, and Joe did what he always did on the logistics side. I definitely deferred to him though. Even called him Sir a time or two in front of the RTOs. Habit. Respect.

We began to expand the battle area on 21 April, trying to find out what we were up against in every direction. The best defense is a good offense. All of the companies were ordered to aggressively patrol outward in all directions in platoon strength. Ordered is not the right word. Our company commanders didn't have to be ordered to do things. They just needed the plan for the day.

These outward forays resulted in several small firefights. By day's end we knew a lot. The good news was that there didn't seem to be any NVA up on the very top of the mountain with C Company. On the other hand, the County Lines did not have to go far down the steep slope toward the main valley to be taken under fire and find other evidence of the enemy's presence. They found various abandoned enemy positions that had been dug into the face of the mountain. Accurate small arms fire came up from lower ground in response to any efforts to go down the road to the valley floor.

The area south and southwest of LZ Tiger is much lower ground and is in the shape of a huge bowl. It is surrounded on all sides by higher ground. This bowl is four clicks long from east to west, and three clicks wide from north to south. The ridgeline on the western side of this bowl is just inside the Laotian border.

On 21 April, the Limping Scholars sent a platoon a click and a half southward into the bowl. They reached a point where they could see the stream that meanders through the bottom land. On the way, they came to the crashed 227th Aviation gunbird, and had the sad duty of recovering the two burned bodies on board. They also recovered the machineguns, which added to our firepower. By late in the afternoon they spotted a company-sized NVA position beyond the creek. They could see trenches, bunkers, and hooches. They also spotted several 12.75mm positions. Before returning to the perimeter, they put in artillery and mortars on all of these targets, and attained several secondary explosions. The Limping Scholars had a new company commander, a man named Blalock, and he wasted no time taking over. There was no time to waste.

To the west, we told the Rough Riders to push the NVA further away from the firebase. The NVA had abandoned their roadblock of the previous day, and D Company advanced against moderate resistance another click up the road that morning until they came up against another strong NVA position. Above and below the road, the terrain was mostly bomb craters and extensive tree blow-down. The areas along the road showed evidence of much rebuilding by the NVA utilizing heavy equipment. The tree blow-down areas afforded the NVA excellent fields of fire, along with good cover and concealment. Mr. Charles had a strong position, with fighting holes dug into the bank in depth back up the road. He also had positions on the high ground above. The Rough Riders destroyed a couple of these bunkers, one at a time, and killed an unknown number of NVA before the day ended.

Going after the last bunker of the day, a Delta trooper was badly wounded by a supporting gunbird firing too close, and they weren't able to recover him until after dark. Once they got him back to their company CP, he was treated under very austere conditions. No medevac birds could get out there through the weather.

That night, the most salient fact about the situation came clear. Mr. Charles did not like us moving westward along the road toward Laos. No sir.

All the operations conducted this day, D+2, were performed with great caution and tactics, skills honed on the road to Hue. No one was killed. 5/7 Cav took out a number of the NVA's guys. And when the sun went down, everyone had a better idea about the enemy's locations. The NVA were within a click or two from us in every direction with the possible exception of north, but maybe not in great strength on any particular axis. Tiger High was the only place that had not experienced any enemy contact. In the middle of the night, however, a B Co observer with a starlight scope reported "spotting three gooks walking up the crest toward C Co on Tiger High." The B Co guys took these silhouettes under fire, with unknown results.

When the S-3 daily journal was closed at 2400 hours on 21 April, 5/7 Cav had 504 troopers in four rifle companies, all wishing they were on R&R in Hawaii. But they weren't in Hawaii. They were in the fucking A Shau Valley, wondering what the next minute, hour and day might bring. It was scary out there at Charlie's place. And it was raining and it was cold. The troopers were missing a lot of stuff that they had planned on having: water, ammo re-supply, and more rations. The C Co men on the top of the mountain were still living on the two canteens of water that each man rode in with. There was no bubbling brook up there. There were guys up there who had been out of water for a good while.

Things were very tough in the A Co area of operations as well, so it was only natural that Ranger Taylor began planning for a night patrol to the floor of the main valley. It was his plan to send a long-range recon patrol out in the dark to the area of the 37mm positions in the village of Lang Ka Kou. He scheduled it for the following night, 22 April.

Bright and early on 22 April, the boys in blue put in an awesome B-52 strike only three clicks away. It went in on the high ground across the bowl to the south-west. The Rough Riders had the best view, and reported secondary explosions from the target area. It was curious about the B-52 strikes. They were called Arclights, and were very hush-hush operations back in those days. Brigade would plan these strikes and request them from the Air Force. It would have been useful if they asked people like us where to put them. We could have put a B-52 strike on the 37mm position on the valley floor, for example. No one ever asked us down at battalion about where to put B-52 strikes. We would just get a message about an incoming Arclight so we could get the hell out of the way.

The weather broke just enough to get a few log sorties in that day. Thankfully, a water bladder went in on the top of the mountain, and all was right with the world. B Co attacked south again, this time getting all the way into the enemy's company-sized position spotted the previous day. They found an NVA body, destroyed a number of 12.75 emplacements, and returned with one WIA back to the perimeter. The NVA left a body. Hmmm. Unusual.

D Co rested that day, limiting themselves to local patrolling from their perimeter. They had been in close contact on the road ever since the 19th, and had dug in a strong operating base position two clicks up the road.

The Hard Hitters up on the mountain patrolled a thousand meters to the west, to a point not that far from D Co's lead element below them on the road. They were close on the map, but a long way on the ground. D Company was several hundreds of feet below them, almost straight down, actually.

By this time, the helicopter pilots had gotten the word about avoiding the main valley floor, and they were coming in from the north over the western end of Hill 1228. There is a saddle linking the western end of our mountain with a very long ridgeline that forms the western side of the bowl. From the C Company patrol's position on the high ground above D Co, they could see enemy machinegun positions firing at our log birds as they flew in over the saddle. The Fire Support Officer spent some time trying to get an artillery round in there on the saddle, but couldn't do it because the saddle was in defilade behind the mountain. It would take a round coming almost straight down to get in there.

And down on the floor of the valley, the County Lines saw movement in the 37mm wood line again. Some artillery ammo had come in that day, and Capt. Pope responded. This time there were a number of secondary explosions. Things were not going so well for the little people now. In the early evening, County Line spotted vehicle movement again in the same area, and the artillery put in a little more red leg. *(The Artillery is called the Red Legs. They wore red stockings back in 1775. They no longer wear red stockings, but their champagne punch is red and is definitely the best punch for military parties.)*

It was dark when John's long-range patrol moved out toward the valley floor in the dark. 22 April had been another very good day for 5/7 Cav, as we expanded our area of control and no one was killed.

23 April was a different story. It was a score-one-for NVA kind of day. The 5/7 Cav had invaded their home court, after all. The NVA attacked the southeastern edge of our firebase perimeter in the wee small hours. Right about first light, the B Co positions on the south end of the firebase got mortared, followed by a ground attack by a small force. The attack was repulsed by small arms fire, but Pfc. Andrew McDaniel was killed. Four others were wounded in the space of twenty minutes, and Pfc. Charles Cox did not survive.

Ten minutes after the firebase started getting hit, A Co got mortared in their positions above the road. The mortar rounds were followed by the attack of a platoon-sized force. Ironically, our main effort that day was to have A Co attack down the steep side of the mountain, toward the main valley floor, and link up with their night patrol. John Taylor had already moved out with two of his platoons at 0500 hours. It was about 0535 hours when the NVA mortar attack hit his perimeter, and the NVA launched their attack at 0545 hours. By that time, Taylor's force was in position directly on the flank of the enemy, and he launched an immediate attack which caught Charlie by surprise and quickly defeated him. They killed six NVA who were left on the field, and routed the rest of the enemy force, some of whom took up positions in the rocks on the side of the mountain. Four A Company men were wounded in this action.

Throughout the rest of the morning, Taylor maneuvered his men to clear the remaining snipers off of the cliff face. His plan to link up with his patrol along the way down to the valley was delayed by the enemy attack. Well into the morning, John's long-range patrol had not returned, and wasn't answering the radio. Taylor was getting very worried about them in view of all the enemy activity. It was a big relief to everyone when the Alpha Patrol came walking into the B Co perimeter over at LZ Tiger at about 0930 hours.

In late morning, the County Lines resumed their maneuver down the mountain toward the valley floor. They did not go very far before a sniper dropped one of the A Co point men, and he had to be medevaced by a very harrowing hoist extraction. There was no stunt man playing his part in this movie. Once they resumed their advance in the afternoon, 2 more point men were wounded by AK rounds. Another time-consuming medevac used up the remainder of the day. The County Lines had a rough day, but they had decimated an NVA platoon. It appeared that Charles did not like us going down to the main valley either.

At 0830 hours that same morning, D Co resumed their attack westward up the road, and immediately began taking fire from the bowl down to their left. They responded with mortars and continued inching forward on the road, taking one position at a time. The Rough Riders accounted for six NVA by the end of the day without losing anyone.

In mid-afternoon, on the south side of the Tiger Low perimeter, B Co engaged four NVA who had apparently stayed behind after their failed attack that morning. The Limping Scholars killed three, and captured one, who was evacuated on a log bird in the late afternoon.

And last but not least, at 1415 hours, C Co up on Tiger High had two men hit by sniper fire. Uh oh. From a tactical standpoint, Joe and I did not like the sound of that one.

As a result of these probing attacks, the NVA had a better idea about where our company perimeters were. And we of the 5/7 Cav had learned more about them as well too. That night we got a call from Brigade. The POW evacuated that afternoon had been interrogated back at Camp Evans, and he was part of a 50-man force from the 1st Bn of the 559th Regiment of the 4th NVA Division. The NVA unit had been ordered to split into two groups and attack that morning, which they had done. The fools. Half of them attacked the firebase from the southeast against the B Co perimeter, while the other half came in against A Co. It was a very unsuccessful attack on their part, although the battalion sustained 12 WIAs and 2 KIAs. The NVA mortars did most of the damage. 50 guys we can handle, so this news actually relieved the tension a bit.

On 24 April the weather dramatically improved. Even before the sun came up, some ARA birds equipped with infra-red vision came out and made three different sightings in the big bowl below us to the south. We responded with artillery. Log birds started coming in bringing us more water, ammo and rations. They flew in through 12.75mm fire from the saddle area to the west. The first load of water went to the men up on Tiger High.

Bright and early, A Co was again working the cliff above the firebase, continuing to search the area of the enemy attack on the previous day. They found the mortar position and other positions where Charles had set up. We kept B Co on the LZ that day, and put the Rough Riders back to work out on the road. On the west end of the main mountain, the road goes through the previously described saddle between Hill 1228 and the western ridgeline, and continues south along that ridge toward Laos. D Co's actions of the previous day had forced the enemy to abandon another roadblock, and the Rough Riders got to within 500 meters of the saddle by noon. From this closer vantage point, they could see the NVA tracers arcing up toward the choppers. Joe and I were convinced that the saddle was extremely important ground to Mr. Charles.

The sun came out and the weather cleared up that afternoon for the first time since the operation began on 19 April. In came everyone. *(Here Comes the Sun.)* Who sang that one? The Beatles, of course. And here comes the general. In this case, Oscar, a wonderful man who was the Assistant Division Commander. Oscar paid the first visit, beaming with pride about how well everyone had done. His pal, Mr. George Wilson of the Washington Post, was still in town, and he came along. The general introduced Joe and me to Mr. Wilson in very glowing terms, and George was much more outgoing and personable than on his first contact with me back at Khe Sanh. And I actually warmed up to the man, in spite of my obsessive aversion to media types back then.

While talking to one of the operations sergeants, George asked the soldier "why are you out here?" Expecting to hear some patriotic or gung-ho response, George was caught off guard when the sergeant said, "I get paid for it," and immediately followed with "and why are you here?" After a lengthy pause to reflect, George responded "well, because I get paid for it."

Everyone had a great laugh. Truth to tell, the brilliant and legendary newspaperman did not enjoy being bested by some hick sergeant from West Virginia, and muttered words to that effect as he and I moved on to other people.

As the day went along, Joe and I briefed several groups of VIPs about the situation as it had developed, particularly about the enemy strength to the west in the saddle area. Our pitch focused on the saddle's being key terrain to the NVA for one reason or another. All these visitors treated the troopers as though they were special.

Late in the afternoon the Brigade Commander finally showed up. He didn't treat anyone special. He didn't stay for a briefing; just long enough to drop off a spanking new battalion commander for the 5/7 Cav. I can't speak for my classmate Joe, but I was disappointed once again over the arrival of yet another lieutenant colonel; this time intensely so.

LZ Tiger, as seen from Tiger High

American Fighting Men come in all sizes

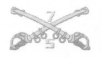

CHAPTER 32

COLONEL, SIR

The new Lt. Col. was a sandy-haired, debonair Armored Officer, with tanker boots, starched fatigues, Garryowen crests on his epaulets - the whole nine yards. He was the JEB Stewart type. Joe and I looked more like U. S. Grant fans — mud from the knees down.

I briefed the new CO on the situation. The briefing took some time, as the man began interrupting immediately with questions. He ended up hearing everything three times. I tried to tell him about where the companies were, what they were doing, and my conclusions about the enemy out to the west defending the road. As I was talking about these facts, he was interjecting his opinions about all the decisions that JB had made for the assault into the area, and all the decisions that had been made since.

"Why is the CP and the artillery down here on the road and not on top of the mountain?" he asked. "How dumb is that?" he added. *(I was momentarily speechless.)*

"Why was D Co just sitting astride the road doing nothing?" *(EXCUSE Me?)*

"Why had we not gotten to the valley floor yet?" *(No excuse, Sir . . . actually, it wasn't our mission.)*

Why this — why that? *(He was the little brother of a legendary 1st Cav leader, and he knew he was more than qualified to whip this rag-tag outfit into shape.)*

Another of my several shortcomings has always been to clam up in the face of stupidity. I went pretty much speechless by about the fourth question, and stayed that way for quite some time. Joe was speechless too, but he is my quietest friend. When JB went down on that first night in the A Shau, the entire battalion went into a state of mourning. This fucking new guy's predecessor was arguably the finest, and maybe the smartest, battalion commander to fight in that dumbass war. And in his absence for the past five days we had developed the battle area just like he had taught us. CO Joe had kept everyone's head up, and concentrating on the job. We wrote him up for a good medal for his four days in command, along with the Soldier's Medal for running into the burning Chinook. Frankly, even as young as we were, Joe and I needed this new guy like we needed a stick in the eye.

As soon as FNG turned his attention away from me and over to Joe, who unfortunately was XO Joe again, I got in the C&C and went up to the high ground to talk to Willie about building a firebase. Distraught over the loss of JB, and totally bent out of shape by the exchange with the CO, I just had to get away from the man. I actually felt nauseous. I wandered around the C Co perimeter for awhile, and was still pretty hot under the collar when some of the Hard Hitters fed me some hot chocolate, calmed me down, and brought me back to earth. I, in turn, alerted them about the CP and artillery moving up there and we walked the ground to establish the plan for the firebase perimeter. After that, I went on back to the low ground, refreshed and ready to get to work for the new CO. After all, I had worked for more than one flaming asshole in my short career. It was business as usual. It could almost be said that JB was the aberration, not this guy.

D Co continued to press their day-long attack westward on the road well into the afternoon. At about 1400 hours, they were receiving sniper fire from the cliffs above them. By 1435 hours they had reported 4 WIAs, one serious. A medevac with a hoist was required, and the lift out was accomplished by 1615 hours, about the time that the new guy arrived.

Frank had a Flashing Saber gunship in support at this point, and they could see the chopper receiving fire from NVA machineguns on the little knoll just across the saddle. But way beyond the initiative that Frank was taking, he was pushed hard by the CO on the radio. FNG wasted no time taking command. He knew his Machiavelli.

D Co stayed in contact late into the afternoon, and ended up with two men pinned down by intense enemy fire. They were still five hundred meters east of the saddle. One man was wounded, and Sgt Henry Thomas, his squad leader, had stayed out there with him. Thomas shielded the man with his body, scraped out some cover with his entrenching tool, and fired as fast as he could at the enemy bunker above him – all at the same time. Eventually he obtained enough dirt to shield them from the NVA riflemen. When it got completely dark, Thomas was able to carry the man back to civilization. D Co was fortunate to retrieve the two men by 2030 hours, and they returned to their perimeter at 2145 hours. There were several men to be medevaced when it was all over.

On July 29, 2004, Sgt. Henry Thomas was awarded his long missing Silver Star by his company Commander, Frank Lambert, and his executive officer, Mike Sprayberry, in front of four hundred attendees of the 5th Battalion 7th Cavalry Veteran's Association bi-annual reunion. I had found the orders for this medal while doing research at the National Archives. It was a significant emotional event for everyone involved.

Everything that Joe, Frank and I had concluded about the saddle was correct. Charles had it defended real well, and wasn't planning on letting it go. In the process of the battle, the pilot of the supporting 1/9 Cav Red Bird saw what he thought might be a new road intersecting the road in the saddle and running northward. They could just make out the road through holes in the jungle canopy.

It seemed to run north-northeast along the west side of the LZ Tiger mountain. If true, the NVA was building a new road circling clockwise around the mountain to enter the A Shau valley farther to the north. For the NVA, the existing road on the mountain face had long been exposed by defoliation, and was an easy target for the air force. It was easy to disrupt this road by dropping chunks of it off the side of the cliff. The boys in blue had sophisticated night-detection equipment, as well, and could see any vehicles traveling at night. And at the moment, we had it blocked. The new road would by-pass our position.

We already knew that the saddle was defended by a strong position, manned by battle-hardened NVA soldiers who had delayed our daily advance with skill, guts and determination. We also knew enough about the intersection to warrant bringing in the "western world" on it. A B-52 strike would be optimal. Failing that, lots of lesser forms of air power.

Oh, but we didn't do that. No, sir. The very next morning *(25 April)*, amid his acid comments about everyone and everything, our new CO ordered Frank to press his attack to take the saddle. They were stopped cold by intense machinegun and AK fire from the cliffs above as well as on the road, which of course Joe and I knew would happen. So, the new CO ordered Frank to outflank the enemy roadblock by climbing the cliff and moving against the saddle from the higher ground. And Rough Rider Six was a guy who would fearlessly do whatever you were dumb enough to order.

There had been brief rain showers on and off all day. Frank sent one platoon up the muddy, slippery cliff and he went with them. Frank never sent anyone to certain contact without going along. They moved out at 1038 hours. Somehow, I had the idea it was two platoons, but it was not. The CO was prescribing all the tactics directly to Frank, without any consultation with morons like me. I had told him what I thought of his intentions at the outset, and was left standing around with my thumb in my ear after that. It took considerable time for Frank and Lt Barber's 1st Platoon to scale the almost vertical cliff to the top of the mountain. The bomb craters, blown-down trees, mud, and the treacherous steepness of the slopes made movement almost impossible. They ran into several impassable obstacles, and had to retrace. At 1115 hours they reported having a man shot in the arm by AK fire, and a difficult medevac was required. It was well past noon when they reported reaching the high ground. At 1325 hours they reported reaching coordinates that put them about 500 meters northeast of the saddle.

At this point, the CO and I went airborne in the C&C and circled above Tiger High to monitor their progress. We were at about one thousand feet above the terrain, where our new man swore he could see the troops moving through the jungle. His glasses were thicker than mine, and I couldn't see shit. At 1000 feet, the big sky concept was inoperative. The treetop concept was inoperative. Given a chance to fly in combat against an enemy armed with anti-aircraft weapons, try to avoid 1000 feet. Fortunately, Frix had a very extensive knowledge about the

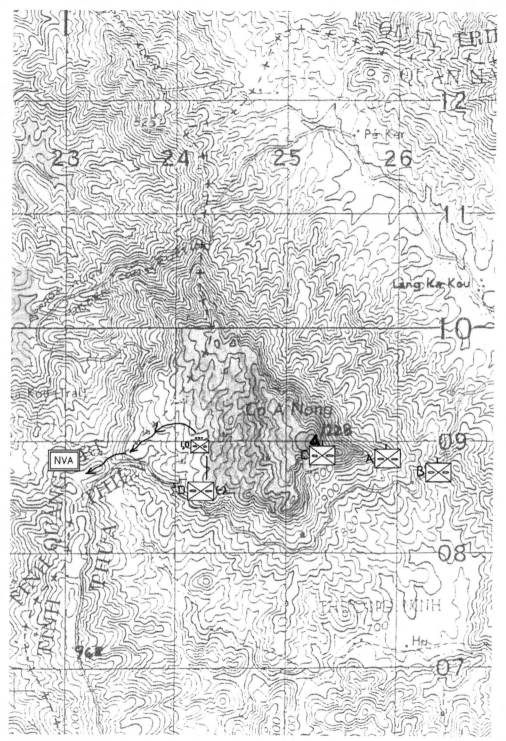

D Company Flanking Attack — 25 April

enemy's anti-372aircraft positions by this time, and we were able to keep FNG straight above the mountain and away from the 12.75s. It was loads of fun.

Throughout the next hour, we circled the area, tipping our hand to everyone for miles around. I could not see anyone on the ground, just their occasional colored smoke grenades. By the time 1st Platoon of D Co had traversed the deep ravines that could not be seen from 1000 feet, climbed over and under fallen trees and jagged rocks, and had gone down some dead ends, they probably went a thousand meters on the ground in order to go five hundred on the map. All while they were trying to sneak up on and find the enemy first, rather than be found by Mr. Charles as they came stumbling in through the bushes. It was getting late.

From his excellent observation point 1000 feet up, the CO couldn't understand why they were moving so slowly, and began abusing Frank about it constantly. At 1535 hours Frank thought they were in the objective area, but their smoke grenades were still a good 200 meters northeast of the saddle. It was getting later. The CO was getting hotter and hotter. Finally, I could stand it no longer, and reiterated my initial comments. I explained how the objective was masked from our artillery fire, that if decisively engaged in the saddle, we would not be able to reinforce any time soon, that it would be dark by the time they got there, and so forth. As I closed by recommending against pushing Frank too fast, he told me in no uncertain terms to shut the hell up, and that he was running things.

Nobody was going to rain on his parade. He couldn't wait to establish himself. He couldn't wait to get his fucking Silver Star. Probably even a Distinguished Flying Cross for being a passenger in the back of a Huey, as some non-aviators were wont to do in the 1st Air Cavalry Division. He ordered Frank to "get his ass onto the saddle and do it now."

And, so it was that Frank and his entire 1st Platoon walked into the saddle at about 1800 hours, moved up and over a little knob, and started up a second larger knob where they were promptly ambushed and surrounded just as the sun was going down. Almost all of the lead squad went down in the opening blast. Lt Barber went down, mortally wounded. In short order, half the men were casualties.

I was shocked to finally learn that Frank had gone with only one platoon. He should have had no fewer than two. The new CO had kept me so in the dark about what he and Frank had discussed. They were facing superior numbers in well-concealed bunkers and spider holes. The small-arms fire and grenades were coming at them from three directions. The enemy occupied a maze of concealed bunkers linked together by trenches and underground passageways. We had grabbed the tiger by the tail.

At 1813 hours, the RTO reported that Frank Lambert was down. Just before the ambush was triggered, Frank had been conferring with Lt. Barber. Barber took off forward and was shot down in the opening salvo. A grenade landed between Frank and his medic, Doc Mc Bride, and Frank did not get down in time. His butt and back were shredded, and Frank became Doc's first patient. Frank was arguably our strongest company commander at the time, a man who had served with distinction on the road to Hue. And Lt Barber — Rough Rider 16 — was a very promising young leader. Barber was no drugstore cowboy; he was a real cowboy from Denton, Montana. Killed almost immediately were Jerry McManus, Kelley, Hubia Guillory, and David Scott. All of these men were veterans of Hue and the move to Khe Sanh. Some of these men had been the ones who ambushed the NVA with artillery on the road to Hue back on 18 February. The break up of this platoon was a huge loss to the battalion.

SSG Billy Bayne was the platoon sergeant, and he immediately took command of the situation. He and Frank's great RTO, George Mitchell, moved about under intense fire and organized the able-bodied men of the platoon into a defensive perimeter. 1Lt Ray Townsend had also gone along with Captain Lambert as the Artillery FO, and was the only officer left standing. Although the immediate area around their position could not be reached by our artillery battery, Townsend was able to deliver artillery fire to the south and west of the position, from where any large enemy reinforcements would come.

The Battalion CO was immediately on the radio, screaming at anyone from the Rough Riders who were listening, telling them to get the rest of their company moving up the road to link up. And of course they could not go on line on a ten-yard wide shelf. And of course they ran into a stone wall of rifle and machinegun fire. Out of fuel, almost dark, Frix dropped us off at the TOC to run the rest of the war from there.

As darkness fell in the saddle, Bayne and Mitchell had organized enough suppressive fire against the NVA positions for the remaining able-bodied men to retrieve the wounded into a tight perimeter. By that time, it was pitch black. Things were not looking so hot. The bosses had returned to the TOC to think things over. What to do? FNG had no clue. I sat there wracking my brain about it, but my brain was severely distracted. I was ready to kill someone. He would remain Colonel, or Sir, for the duration. There would be no endearing nickname for him. No sir.

Fortunately, we had been operating since October under two battalion command-ers who did not tell company commanders exactly what to do, or exactly how to do it. Even during the first days on the road to Hue, JB had given his company commanders wide latitude to operate within their assigned missions. They in turn modeled his behavior. As a result, we had lots of people who knew how to do stuff. Call it trickle-down leadership. On the night of 25 April 1968, D Co had this soft-spoken, skinny little Armored Officer from Alabama serving as company executive officer. I shouldn't call him skinny. We were all skinny. Rumor had it that he was pissed off at being assigned to an infantry battalion, rather than an armored unit. But, on the night of 25 April he was the senior officer standing in D Company. His name was Michael Sprayberry, and he knew all about duty and responsibility. He immediately took command, determined to solve this problem if it took all night.

CHAPTER 33

THE DARK IS YOUR FRIEND

While I was stewing over what to do, one of the Operations Sgts tapped me on the shoulder, and quietly said that the D Co Executive Officer was proposing to lead a night patrol up the road to get to Lambert. It was Sprayberry's plan to take about a squad's worth of men, all of whom had volunteered, and see if they could fight their way along the road in the dark to link up with the platoon. I replied to the Operations Sergeant, "tell him good." I consulted with nobody.

The new Bn CO was off somewhere, maybe vomiting in the crapper. I didn't go looking for him. At some point the CO came in and got ignored. Someone other than I may have told him what was going on. Sprayberry may have even discussed it with him first, for all I know, but I did not have that impression at the time. In any event, FNG stayed the hell out of my way. I had no sense of his presence in the TOC for the rest of that night. He may have been back in the corner.

Mike Sprayberry moved out in the dark with a twelve- man patrol of volunteers, loaded down with grenades. The patrol moved cautiously in the dark up the right side of the cliffside road, with Tranchetti and Mack on point. Sprayberry and his RTO, Dave Bielski, were the next men back. They had not gone very far when machinegun fire came right down the road at them, causing everyone to hit the mud against the road bank. After Mike had ensured that everyone was ok and in covered positions, he crawled forward, armed only with his .45 and several grenades. The first enemy spider hole was a little cave dug into the side of the cliffside of the road. Mike found the forward edge of it with his fingertips. Pulling the pin on a grenade, he led off with two rounds from his pistol, and followed with the grenade.

Sprayberry crawled back to the patrol and got Tranchetti, Mack and Bielski to move up to cover him the rest of the way. Sprayberry crawled along the uphill side of the road bank. The three soldiers came along a few yards behind. Tranchetti was on the left side of the road where he could bring fire against the bank if necessary. Michael went past the first position that he had destroyed, and two Chicom grenades came out of the next hole up the road. Everyone hugged the ground and they went off with no effect. Michael again made sure that everyone was ok and in good covering positions. When they were ready, Sprayberry charged the spider hole and killed the NVA soldier with a combination of pistol and grenades. The three men along with Bielski, the RTO, continued to inch forward through the dark. Sprayberry took out a third position in the same manner.

Right after that, the rest of the patrol came under fire from above and behind. The enemy soldiers were up on the high ground above them on the road. The medic was wounded. At one point Bielski went back to the rest of the patrol to get more grenades, and was attacked by a small group of NVA. He killed one, and the rest fled back up the cliff. Bielski returned forward with more grenades, and the remainder of the men moved forward behind him.

When the patrol had gone well over halfway to the saddle, Sprayberry halted the group to reestablish radio contact with the cut-off platoon and reassure them that they were coming. In the process of whispering into the handset, he got the impression that they were not too far apart. Sprayberry then made the mistake of whistling to the isolated platoon. A little bit later he was met in the middle of the road, but not by Americans. An NVA soldier rushed right up to Sprayberry, and was dispatched at point-blank range by the ever-reliable 1911A1 45 caliber pistol. Another onrushing enemy soldier was killed by an alert Tranchetti before he could do any harm. By bayonet, actually. The point group continued to be fired at from the front and above by an unknown number of NVA. A machinegun opened up from a hole in the bank at the four lead men, at almost point-blank range, but missed everyone. A miracle. In the midst of the action at close quarters, Bielski called for indirect fire. With fighting going on around him, he manned his radio and directed the fire close into their position on the road. The panic of retreating enemy could be heard after the dust settled.

Once the attacking enemy had been either killed, or had fled, it got quiet again. Sprayberry took out another three enemy positions dug into the side of the road. Sprayberry called SSG Bayne, platoon sergeant of the cut-off platoon, and told him to begin moving some men eastward toward the patrol. He described the spider holes and instructed Bayne on how to take them out along the way. When the lead man of Bayne's platoon took out their first spider hole, the two groups knew that they were only a few yards apart. Shortly thereafter the link-up was achieved.

The S-3 RTOs and Operations Sgts sat up with me in the TOC all night, quietly listening to the D Co command net until it was over. And it took all night. Sprayberry, Tranchetti, Mack and Bielski killed NVA face to face in this fight. They had fought the enemy in the dark for seven hours. And throughout that time I never said a word into the D Co command net. I am a quick learner.

After the link-up, it was just a matter of moving enough men from the rest of the patrol up the road to organize the litter parties and bring everyone back to safety. Well — not quite. As the group was organizing for the trek out, an NVA machinegun opened up on the unit from the knoll just west of the saddle area. Sprayberry, assisted by a couple other men, went back and destroyed this bunker as well. While they were doing so, Bielski stayed back and did much of the organizing for the return of the platoon to the rest of the company. Bielski was 20 years old at the time, with only two years service. We had such great people serving as RTOs back then.

Based on after-action comments, it was estimated that a company of NVA defended the road intersection in the saddle area. The position was very strong, and in depth throughout the saddle area and surrounding high ground both south and north of the road intersection.

This action was conducted in the dark, broken only by the periodic blasts of grenades and small arms fire from the enemy soldiers. The night sky was fairly clear, and the silhouettes of the main terrain features could be seen against the sky. Seeing anything in the trees or on the ground, though, was limited to only a few feet. Five of our troopers had been killed by a hail of bullets when the initial NVA ambush was triggered. Three could not be found in the dark, and we needed to get everyone back to safety before daylight. Sp4 Kelley was 20 years old, and hailed from Dorchester, Massachusetts. Hubia Guillory was from New Orleans, and was 20 as well. David Scott was 21 and from Carlock, Illinois. We did not want to be caught on the road when light came. We would be back to get them. We always did.

Sprayberry's patrol brought the 1st Platoon back down the road to the main D Co perimeter astride the road, including Lt Barber, McManus, and all of their wounded. Eight wounded men were carried back by litter, including my friend Frank. It was 0350 hours when they reached the D Company base. The Rough Riders had suffered eleven wounded and five killed.

When the sun came up on the 26 April, I was not myself. There was no light in this boy's eyes. No more smiley face. No more jokes with the boys in the TOC, or on the radio with RASH 1. No more Mister Cool Jazz Fan. No more Mister Nice Guy. It was strictly business after that. My name was Sir. I spoke only when necessary, and most of the time when spoken to, but not always.

Sprayberry and the remnants of the 1st Platoon went back out to their forward-most point on the road, keeping their eye on the saddle area. The rest of his company was about a click back at their main operating base. He wanted to go back into the saddle to recover the three missing bodies, but didn't dare do so in broad daylight.

The new CO's plan had been to limit the companies to local patrolling from their existing perimeters that day, 26 April, so he could meet all the key people in the companies. That morning we talked about changing it. My feeling was that we had knocked out all of the positions along the road into the saddle, and this was our best opportunity to blow in there with a strong attack. The man did not think it was a good idea. Apparently Sprayberry didn't either. So, new guy stuck with his original plans to visit the other three companies that day. We were all in shock over the entire event. After the previous day I didn't argue. I should have. Sprayberry sat out there all day, making plans to take another patrol out that night to recover his men. He and his troopers observed lots of heavy machineguns firing from the saddle area at our incoming helicopters that day.

The CO spent the day visiting Alpha, Bravo and C Companies. It was a quiet day for the NVA as well. In fact, it was the first day of the operation without one shot being fired in anger by either side, other than the 12.75s shooting at the birds. I regretted not pushing for an attack at first light that morning. The enemy had been severely punished, and was vulnerable to an aggressive attack straight up the road by a fresh company. All I could think at the time, though, was how I suddenly had no influence in such matters. *(Years later Michael told me it would have been a bad idea to attack in the daylight that morning. Maybe so, but I am still not sure.)*

The CO came into the TOC late that afternoon to find me talking to Tranchetti, Mack and Bielski. I was deciphering their witness statements and extracting information for the awards recommendation. The D Co men, Tranchetti and Mack, I think, were drawing diagrams of the action for me and telling me all about it.

Colonel Sir asked what we were doing. I said, "we are writing Sprayberry up for the Congressional Medal of Honor. He turned ashen white, and impulsively blurted out, "we are doing no such thing!" I turned back to our work and we just kept writing witness statements and such.

Bayne, Tranchetti and Mack were later awarded Silver Stars for their actions. Somehow Bielski's award got lost. Sp4 George Mitchell, the RTO of the encircled platoon, said that the entire platoon and company command element owed their lives to Lt. Sprayberry, who was the first man to enter the fire-swept area, and the last man to leave. Mike Sprayberry, and the men of his twelve man patrol, had not only saved the 1st Platoon of D Co, they had saved FNG's career as well.

Procedure dictated that Scott, Guillory and Kelley be reported as MIA, pending review of the witness statements by a board of officers. Their squad mates were sure they had died, and documented it. Since Port came up missing on 12 January, we had gone to great lengths to recover all of the bodies through all the shit we had seen, and two days after whosiwhatsit took command, we had three men on the ground deep in enemy territory.

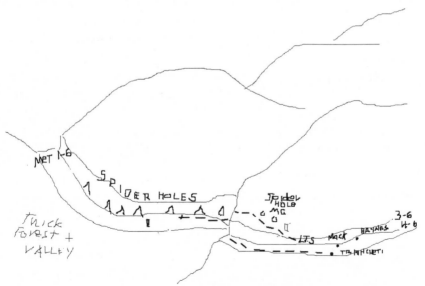

Sprayberry Night Patrol - 25 April 1968

CHAPTER 34

SPOOKY VALLEY

On 27 April, the colonel visited Sprayberry in the morning. Beginning that afternoon when he returned to the TOC, he stopped talking constantly, and actually started listening to some of the answers.

27 April was another day of local patrolling. Alpha Company got further down the mountain than previously, and without incident. C Company continued building a firebase perimeter on the top of the mountain, because the new commander was determined to follow through with his plan to move us up there. We had returned to our methodical development of the battle area, and it was definitely an away game at Charlie's gym.

Interestingly, we did not bring any yellow paint out to the valley. We didn't paint the yellow and black patch on any rocks that I can recall. We were much more interested in hiding behind the rocks. The A Shau Valley was just like the troops had predicted before we ever went out there. Spooky. The A Shau Valley was real spooky.

Late that afternoon, Sprayberry formed another patrol and led them quietly off the edge of the drop-off and down the steep slope to the creek below. Their plan was to approach the saddle from the southeast, along the stream bed. They got within sight of the knoll west of the saddle by about 1900 hours, just before it started to get dark. From the edge of the trees, they observed many NVA soldiers moving against the skyline. It became very obvious that they could not get into the objective area from that direction without being detected, uphill open ground, and Sprayberry had no choice but to call off the attempt. They moved back a safe distance before they called in an artillery barrage on the sighted enemy. It took them an hour or so to move eastward down the stream and climb back up to their roadblock position.

Starting on 28 April, we mounted our next round of actions to expand influence. D Co moved out early on a renewal of their attack toward the saddle, employing the 2d and 3d Platoons. At 0925 hours, they spotted NVA in the open on the road in the saddle and brought in artillery. As the morning progressed, they killed three NVA and moved closer to the saddle area. From this position they could observe the knoll on the far side of the saddle. At around 1100 hours they spotted numerous NVA digging in on this knoll, and they engaged the NVA for the next several hours with artillery and air strikes. At 1300 hours they also spotted an NVA 12.75 firing at the fast movers from a second larger knoll farther south along the western ridge.

Our C&C came into the LZ that afternoon, and Bob reported receiving small arms fire from the west side of the mountain throughout a stretch of 800 meters. His view was that this area was in fact a new road, being built to go around the opposite side of the mountain into the very top of the A Shau. We put in air strikes and artillery on and off the rest of the afternoon. The jets were also drawing fire from the ridgeline south of the knoll, as they made their runs. I had no more time to pout, and stayed busy on the radio all day.

We were also operating toward the valley floor, and had A Co attack eastward off the high ground. This time, they advanced about 800 meters down the mountain. Along the way, they found a mortar position with 9 rounds of 82mm mortar hidden under leaves — a happy moment for all of us. They also located an enemy complex consisting of two caves with bamboo bunks for 65 people. Inside were more mortar rounds, explosives, and associated materiel. They had most likely found the operating base for the unit that had been keeping A Company up on the mountain since Day One. The 28th of April was a productive day.

29 April was also moving day for the CP. Against my recommendation, we went to the mountaintop. At mid-morning, we received a back-hoe up on the high ground. It came in by Hook, flying in from the west side of the mountain and taking 12.75mm fire from the knoll and saddle area. I no longer recall what happened to the dozer we had on Tiger Low. At this point, all aircraft continued to avoid flying straight across the valley to come to TIGER, even though I thought that the 37mm unit was long gone by that time. It may have been just as safe, maybe safer, across the north end of the valley than around to the west and in over the saddle at this point. We had been lucky, though. The birds were past the guns in the saddle before they could range on them. We had not had any aircraft losses out there.

The Cav pilots enjoyed the beauty of the treetops in this campaign. As previously mentioned, there are two places to be in a helicopter when the enemy has anti-aircraft guns: There is way, way up in the sky, like a sand flea on a 100 meter-wide beach; the other is about six feet above the treetops — you are past them in a flash. We received two slicks at 1120 hours to shuttle the TOC people up to the high ground.

Even though we in the operations group were busy with the move, 29 April was also a busy day of combat operations. We continued to push outward, with great results. The Rough Riders maneuvered south off the road to the low ground with two platoons, and moved up the creek toward the saddle looming above them. They got to a position where they could see the enemy positions, and pounded them for another day. Sometime that day, the boys in blue brought us a 2000 lb. bomb. I did not know such a thing existed. We dropped the bomb on knoll in the middle of the saddle, and it was later described as no longer a knoll. Those Air Force guys can really spin a tale, though. (*I have wondered over the years if this air strike may have hindered our ability to find our three bodies in the post-war efforts to locate our missing troopers. But I feel almost certain they were in the low ground short of the knoll.*)

A Company got almost all the way down the mountain. By mid-afternoon, they were just above the valley floor where they came upon the enemy. After a brief but intense firefight, in which two County Linemen were killed, they pushed into a hooch area which showed signs of much recent activity. It was too late in the day to destroy what they found, however. During this action, Pfc. Billy Ford and Pfc. Henry Wunderlich gave their lives for their country. They were 22 and 19 respectively. Ford was from Mount Carbon, West Virginia. Wunderlich was from New York City.

On the southern front, B Co pushed all the way across the bowl to our south, coming in contact with a squad of NVA. They surprised this enemy unit with artillery and small arms, killing two and chasing the rest away. Moving into the area, they found 30 footprints, 35 boxes of 12.75mm armor-piercing rounds, two AKs, lots of small arms ammo, hand grenades, many fresh blood trails, and a wallet with an overlay. That would be 3,500 armor-piercing 12.75 mm bullets that we destroyed! It was a great day for the pilots. It was also a great day for the Scholars, who only had one man injured with a minor wound. Their new CO, Blalock, was off to a good start.

By the end of the day, the Battalion CP was on the mountaintop, with C Company defending the perimeter. It was cold. It was foggy. It was spooky. No one liked it — well, except for the Bn CO. He liked it a lot. That night, he ordered Bravo and Delta to switch missions. The idea was to give these two companies a new location to operate in — get some fresh blood in there, so to speak. After the initial setback, the CO was beginning to feel his oats. And, like him or not, switching the companies was probably a good idea. Get some fresh thinking on both fronts. The Deltas were stymied at recovering their three bodies, depressed about it, and were better off going on a new mission somewhere else.

The next morning, Michael and the Rough Riders relieved Bravo on Tiger Low at 0740 hours. Bravo moved out along the road to the west at 0830 hours. We also moved the artillery battery to the top of the mountain that morning. Other than Alpha having two men wounded by sniper fire from the cliffs above them, the 30th was relatively quiet as we made the switch. We had been out there ten days, and snipers would still occasionally work their way to the cliffs above Tiger.

Bravo got set up in the previous Delta base position. We had come up with a plan to seize the saddle the next day, 1 May. The B Company plan would send two platoons down off the road toward the low ground in the bowl, cross the stream, and advance westward up the western ridgeline. Their initial objective was a place on the ridgeline well south of the knolls and saddle area, from where they could turn right and attack north along the western ridge into the saddle area. We would be attacking the saddle from the left for a change. For the morning of 1 May, we had requested a gunbird from Troop B, 1/9 Cav, to support B Co's operation toward the saddle. The two platoons had moved out at first light. The rest of the company would advance along the road. It seemed like a good plan, because we could still employ our artillery on their western ridgeline objective, even though the near half of the saddle was still in defilade.

Right after first light, the 1/9 Cav White Bird landed on the Bn CP pad. I met with the young warrant officer pilot, briefed him on the situation, i.e., what Bravo was planning to do, and our prior experiences in the saddle area. Scout Bird pilots have to be fearless to get their jobs done, and this pilot was particularly eager. I then sent him on his way to operate on B Co's radio net under Blalock's control. A while later, B Co had the scout bird searching the jungle ahead of them as they moved westward, as planned.

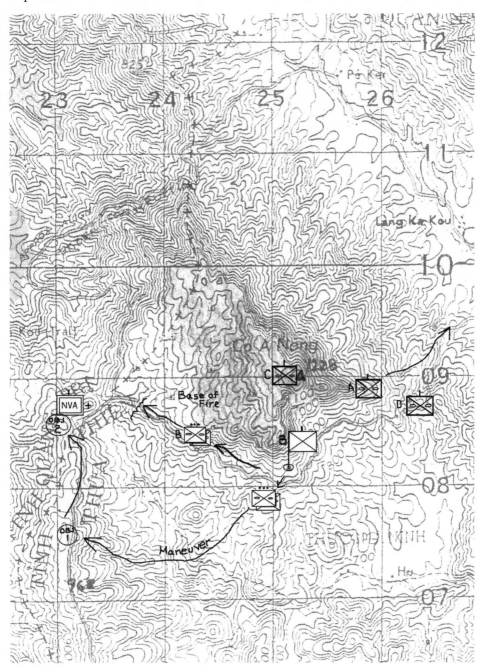

The platoon up on the road began to move forward at 0800 hours. Twenty minutes later, they could see the scout bird down in the bowl to their left front, snaking its way upward at treetop level toward the saddle. As soon as the scout bird's elevation came level with the road, it was blown out of the sky by a volley of machinegun fire. The bird crashed through the canopy on the side of the slope that leads up to the ridge just south of the saddle. The supporting Red Bird began circling the area of the downed aircraft, but was driven off by intense enemy machinegun fire.

Blalock's other two platoons had made it all the way to the base of the western ridge, and were starting upward when the bird went down. They were still a long way south of the eventual objective of the saddle, though, so Limping Scholar Six ordered his platoon that was advancing on the road to move down the cliff toward the bird. It was very arduous going down to the creek area — almost straight down initially. Now that Blalock knew the enemy in the area had significant strength, he decided to consolidate his forces. He ordered his other two platoons to stop going up the western ridge, and instead move laterally toward the crash site. All this took time. The terrain was more of the same: bomb craters, fallen trees, jagged rocks, ravines that did not show on the map. The going was very slow. It took all the morning to get the three platoons married up to a point where he could advance them into the area of the downed chopper. The lead platoon came within fifty meters of the crashed helicopter when they spotted it through the trees. It was about 1345 hours. The OH-6A scout helicopter was halfway up the steep slope toward the enemy-occupied knolls in the saddle area, and it was surrounded by several NVA soldiers. The White Bird was upside down, but seemed to be relatively intact. The three crew members could not be seen.

At the same time, the B Company CO was deploying his other two platoons to attack toward the high ground beyond the downed bird. They were spotted by the enemy when they broke out of the wood line a couple hundred meters down the slope, and an intense firefight ensued. The enemy held the high ground above them. Not good. Artillery was employed against the suspected enemy positions, as Blalock maneuvered his two platoons forward. The NVA began employing their 12.75mm machineguns with great effect. The 3rd Platoon had a couple men down right away. One man was killed, and the other had a chest wound of 12.75mm proportions.

A medevac was accomplished down in the area of the stream at 1650 hours. The firefight went on for about an hour, and it was getting dark. The slope upward to the enemy positions was extreme. It was stripped of most of the trees and undergrowth as well. The enemy strength was significant, as evidenced by all the machineguns firing at us. Because of all these factors, the Battalion CO ordered B Co to disengage and climb back up to the road. By that time, B Co had additional men to medevac.

Were we to press an uphill attack with B Co, there would have been a decisive engagement in the dark. Frankly, B Co would have gotten their asses handed to them if they had attacked up that particular piece of ground. And we would not have been able to get enough additional combat power over there to bail them out. A Co was down in the main valley. C Co was on the mountaintop guarding the colonel. And D Co on Tiger Low was in no condition to go back to that place that day. In the end, we had to assume that the three 1/9 Cav scouts had been killed, or captured and hauled off to Laos. Everyone felt terrible. *(Warren T. Whitmire ~ Donald P. Grevais ~ Richard D. Martin)*

On the other front, the County Lines of Alpha got all the way across the valley floor for the first time. They found a refueling point for vehicles at about noon. An hour later, on the far side of the valley, they found a truck and 200 rounds of 37mm anti-aircraft ammunition, all of which they destroyed. And lastly, at about 1445 hours, they reported finding three tunnels going into the side of the hill. They followed one in for 30 meters, another one for 15 meters, but they did not have sufficient lighting equipment to go further. There were numerous bloody fatigues and medical bandages in the caves; probably the medical aid station for the anti-aircraft unit. We had pounded that area on and off for days.

Interestingly, searching the valley floor had not been our mission. Perhaps Cold Steel gave the new guy different instructions on his way out to the valley. In any event, at least we were contributing to the main reason for the 1st Cavalry Division going out there to start with.

Having switched B Co and D Co on the previous day, it occurred to us in the command group that the Hard Hitters needed a new project as well. I think the C Co Commander brought it up. Willie wanted off the mountain. He was ready for some action. Aided by the good weather, we got lift birds in at about 1100 hours on 2 May, and moved D Co up to the top to take over base defense. C Co replaced them down below on the original firebase. Two moves in two days probably confused the hell out of the troopers in D Co, but it was a good thing to do. They had more than earned a base defense role by that time.

The CO also decided to move B Co back to the east to join the County Lines on the valley floor. I think at this point, Colonel-Sir had given up any notion of attacking the saddle. Nothing but trouble over there. Besides William Port on 12 January, Scott, Guillory and Kelley were the only 5/7 Cav troopers whose bodies were not recovered in the first half of 1968. At some point after the war the Army established that they were KIA, and their names are on the black marble today. So, Colonel, Sir — Fuck you and the horse you rode in on.

Our main mission, though, had always been to block the road, not to attack toward Laos. Maybe there was more to be gained down in the valley. The overall Brigade Mission, after all, was to disrupt the NVA supply base. Brigade had expanded our area of operations to include the valley floor by this time, after the fact of our operating there, directing us to join in the search for enemy support bases. I never could figure out what 1/7 Cav was doing. They were to do the valley floor job at the outset. I think their initial move further south may have put them out of range to search the northern end. I am sure they have their own story to tell. Mr. Charles seemed to be everywhere out there.

We wanted to have two full companies in the main valley, we needed to defend Tiger High, and we needed C Co to operate southward into the Bowl from Tiger Low. So, we formed a roadblock one click west of Tiger Low, using one platoon from C Co and one platoon from D Co. These two platoons would form a roadblock to stop any armor and infantry attack coming in from the saddle area. The position was a click west of TIGER LOW, and was the old D Co perimeter during the early days of the operation. From there you could see all the terrain for about 3 clicks to the west and south of the mountain; a great place to spot the enemy and call in artillery. It was also a great place to block the road, because the drop-off was sheer going both up and down.

At 1024 hours that morning, LZ Tiger High received six rounds of artillery fire. Make that ARTILLERY. Not dinky little 60mm mortars. Two men from an attached unit were killed, and five were wounded. We had two men with minor wounds in the CP Group, and they stayed in the field. These were the first casualties on Tiger High since Big Ralph back on the 20th. The top of the hill was much more magnetic now.

At the time of this artillery attack, I was down at the roadblock coordinating with the two platoons about their mission, and establishing who was to be in command. We also received three large caliber rounds down at the roadblock, resulting in two casualties — one in C Co and one in D. Not long after the enemy artillery attack ended, one of the NCOs with me pointed out a smoke ring in the trees on the western ridge. A round screamed over our heads and hit the mountain behind us. Through the binos I could see what looked like a tank on the ridgeline to the west. It may have been self-propelled artillery. It continued firing rounds that went right over our heads. Once we realized it was flat trajectory fire, we just got down in the bottom of the bomb crater that we were in. After calling in the data, and firing return artillery, we kept a man observing from the rim of the crater while the rest of us went back to eating our lunch.

We had just received a new kind of combat ration, called MRE. Meal-Ready-To-Eat. We read the instructions, heated the water, and poured it into the plastic bag. It was a miracle. We were astounded to see a bunch of crumbled up papier-mâché turn into damn good chili with beans — damn good.

The NVA tank may have been part of the "artillery" going into TIGER. Suddenly, the A Shau Valley was spookier than ever.

Late that afternoon, a couple of shiny new replacement types came out from Camp Evans, maybe from the artillery battery. They built themselves a sleeping bunker out of concertina stakes and sandbags. One guy was working on the inside while the other stacked way too many sandbags on top. Before anyone noticed what they were doing, the stakes snapped in the middle, and essentially cut the guy in half. People ran over and started tearing the sandbags off amidst his shrieks of pain. During the frantic work, he just suddenly died. All remaining morale on the LZ went down the drain for the rest of the day.

CHAPTER 35

WE GOTTA GET OUTA THIS PLACE

Later in the day, after the first NVA artillery attack, a man in C Co accidentally shot himself in the foot. Hmmmmm. It was 3 May. It was too late to medevac him, so he had to suffer through the night waiting for the log bird. The companies down in the valley continued to find all kinds of abandoned NVA gear and equipment.

The Limping Scholars moved into the woods around the village of Lang Ka Koa, and found the remains of a 57mm anti-aircraft gun that had been hit by an airstrike. This was the first physical evidence that the NVA had 57s, as well as 37s. They also found one of the Hooks that had been shot down on the 19th. It was, as always, completely burned up. Farther down the valley to the south, the County Lines found a large tunnel complex near the end of the day, and made plans to search it the following morning.

No one made any enemy contact all that day until it came time to set in for the night. B Co moved back to the west side of the valley toward a knoll that they knew to be good ground. Charles thought so as well. As the Bravos approached the knoll, one of their men suddenly went down to a sniper round. We brought in a lot of artillery while B Co deployed for the attack. Once they were ready, we lifted (*as in ceased*) the artillery, and the Limping Scholars assaulted smartly up and over the hill with two platoons abreast. Two NVA bodies and a machinegun were left behind by the retreating enemy. Jesse Carmona of Bay City, Michigan, and Billy Bridgeman of Virgie, Kentucky gave their lives for their country in the assault. Bridgeman didn't make it back after being such a distinguished medic, as far back as TT Woods.

That night, things were quiet throughout the area of operations, except the position that the Scholars had seized. At around 2000 hours, the perimeter was probed on the west side by an estimated squad of NVA — 7 to 10 men. Having already fired on the knoll just a few hours earlier, it took the artillery forward observer no time at all to bring a ton of artillery close in to the B Co positions. When the artillery was lifted, a lot of moaning and groaning was heard out in the impact area, which continued for some time into the night. For the next several hours, they reported sounds of movement on three of the four sides of their position.

It finally grew quiet, and stayed that way until 0540 hours the next morning. In came several rounds of enemy 61mm mortar. Everyone in B Co was on full alert, wondering what was coming next. The mortar rounds suddenly ceased, and to everyone's relief was not followed by the expected ground attack. One Scholar was wounded from a 61mm mortar round.

At first light, B Co explored the area around their night perimeter and found twenty-seven separate blood trails. They also found seven drag marks, meaning people who had probably been killed. Our response to the NVA squad-sized probe probably resulted in spoiling the plans of a much larger force. We kicked the crap out of another NVA unit that night, and reported an estimated seven NVA killed and twenty-seven wounded. It was a good victory. I wonder if that report became a "body count" somewhere along the way to the Pentagon. I wonder how big it got.

Up on the mountaintop that same morning, we of the headquarters and artillery were in dense clouds. It was dark, damp and dreary. We couldn't see shit. Artillery gunners were firing 105 HE rounds upward into the fog.

The Battalion Surgeon approached me, looking for help with the CO about "sending the Aid Station back to Camp Evans where it belonged". Beyond my being somewhat unsympathetic, he was unaware that I looked to speak to the Colonel only on matters of dire importance. During the conversation, the doctor noticed that I didn't look so good. He remarked that I had lost a lot of weight since he had seen me just a few weeks earlier. He observed that I wasn't talking clearly, was unsteady on my feet, and that my eyes had the dull look of a sick person. Next thing I knew, he took my temperature and it was 103. In the end, it was I, not the Surgeon and his Aid Station, who returned to Camp Evans.

I rode in on a log bird with the poor guy from C Co who had shot himself in the foot. He wanted to tell me about it. I told him to shut the fuck up. We were a sorry-looking pair.

I had been scratching an itch on the back of my ankle dating back to April 1st when we landed on Hill 691 east of Khe Sanh. I started by scratching it through my canvas boot, and we were extremely busy. When I finally had a chance to change socks about two days later, I found a red, oozing sore on the back of my leg just above my ankle. I had either been bitten by some kind of bug, or poked by a stick. Every chance I had, I would clean up the runny little sore, but there had been little chance for that since 18 April. Lets face it, I didn't have a squad leader inspecting my feet at night and watching me take my malaria pill. It was strictly do as I say, not as I do. By 4 May, it was driving me nuts. Any time I was not occupied with work, I was busy scratching. One of the RTOs must have said something to the Surgeon about it. When I got to the Division Hospital at Camp Evans, I had a black, goopy sore about the size of a quarter on the back of my left leg, just above the heel. The sore spot had eaten its way to the bone by that time, and the infection had spread into my bloodstream.

Interestingly, had it been JB who learned about this situation, he would have ordered me to go get cured immediately. As it was, the new colonel was totally pissed off to learn that I was leaving him to go have my ass filled with penicillin around-the-clock for several days. I am certain now that I had been marginally effective for several days by that time anyway. And Joe was there to hold his hand, so the CO had nothing to fear.

SGM MacQuerry visited me at the field hospital soon after I got there, to apprise me of what was going on out in the valley. Shortly after I had departed for Camp

Evans, LZ Tiger received two 122mm artillery rounds. Cuuurrrack! Mr. Charles had moved his artillery down the trail in Laos. We were well within their 23-click range at Tiger High. Two men from D Co were wounded. There would be no rest for D Co after all. At about the same time, down in the valley, B Co reported one man wounded by artillery. Things were heating up. *(The NVA had one critical superiority — the range of their howitzers. If they could get them to our vicinity, we were at a disadvantage. We corrected this situation after Vietnam.)*

It was such a great idea having the TOC and artillery up on the top of LZ Tiger. Oh, yeah. For one thing, the artillery couldn't see to put direct fire against the ridgeline to the west, where Charles was building up his forces with armored vehicles. And, in terms of being a target, if the NVA artillery could not hit the top of Hill 1228, they couldn't hit anything.

That afternoon, one of the B Co men accidentally shot himself in the foot with a 45 cal. pistol. That was two feet in two days. That same night, an illumination round fired by an artillery gun somewhere caused the untimely death of another B Co man. An illumination round involves a metal canister projectile which, at the right time, expels a little flare hanging from a parachute. The flare floats gently to earth, lighting up the scenery below, while the canister keeps on tumbling through space until it lands somewhere. This particular flare lit up the scenery for someone other than B/5/7 Cav, because our companies knew better than to light up the night. The dark was their friend. The flare may have been for the 1/7 Cav over on LZ Goodman. The somewhere for the canister was the head of one of our troopers from B Co, who was sitting on the edge of his foxhole at the time. Luck does not get worse than that. The death of young people is tragic.

A lot had transpired that day, while I received periodic penicillin shots in my ass. For me, a big benefit of going back and getting my leg fixed was to get away from the CO long enough to finalize my written recommendation for the big medal for Sprayberry. While I lay in the hospital on the afternoon of the next day, I finalized my papers and diagrams, and had them delivered to our Adjutant, Captain Jim Matthews. I also wrote an extensive letter to my Dad:

May 5, 1968

This campaign in the A Shau is the most demanding job our battalion has ever had. We weren't climbing up and down hills, we were climbing cliffs that drop 500 feet. Our battalion CP and artillery battery is on a mountain 4000 feet high and is in and out of the clouds half of the time. We never know when we will get re-supplied due to the weather. Early in the operation we had two companies with no re-supply of food or water for four days. The whole thing is ridiculous. We haven't had to go far to get in contact with the enemy. I'm afraid

the generals have gone overboard this time and are trying to conduct an
operation that they can't support logistically.

> *I've concluded that in our present configuration we are not winning the war.*
> *We are not losing either. The Vietnamese population is definitely losing, and the*
> *two outsiders (USA and North Vietnam) are breaking even. The North Vietnamese*
> *are bringing in as many supplies as ever but they will never be able to defeat us in*
> *battle because of their lack of air power. On the other hand we will never be able*
> *to stop their buildup in the country, therefore we are not going to be able to end the*
> *war by winning it. Peace talks are the only way out short of just quitting, at which*
> *time the North Vietnamese Army has the strength to take over South Vietnam in*
> *probably a few months.*

Love, Charlie

That same morning we got rocketed at Camp Evans, and one of Bill Hussong's boys was wounded on the log pad. I was in a hospital tent, not far away, at the time of the rocket attack.

One of the rocket rounds hit the sandbag roof of the emergency ward bunker just up the street, but no one was hurt. Always the take-charge guy, I made everyone in our twelve-man tent roll out of their cots, crawl across the floor, down the steps, and across the street to an underground bunker. I made everyone crawl the entire way. This included a big guy, covered with bandages and hooked up to an intravenous tube. He didn't believe me until he got screamed at in the best traditions of the Infantry. He crawled out in front of me, whimpering in pain, with me yelling at him to move faster. At one point I had to whack him on the foot to get him going. I never wanted to see a man run upright through artillery fire again. Not since 27 January 1968.

We were not a pretty sight when we got back. Everyone was covered with red clay. When Nurse Lynn returned, there was hell to pay. Everyone in the tent immediately pointed the finger at me. "These tents are surrounded by sandbag walls, and only a direct hit would have hurt you", she said. The penicillin needles seemed to get longer and fatter after that.

That afternoon, SGM MacQuerry visited me again in the hospital to cheer me up. He also let me know that "the documents had been personally delivered to the Division Sergeant Major, through the new Brigade Sergeant Major". I knew we were in good shape when McQuerry told me the new Sergeant Major was Chester Cieszak, with whom I had served in 2/6 Infantry in Berlin back in '65. He also told me that the

CG was going out to LZ Tiger on 6 May to present impact awards to the men in D Co for their actions in the saddle. Mack, Tranchetti, Mitchell and Baynes were slated for impact awards. Somehow, Bielski's recommendations had been lost in the shuffle. *(Years later I learned that Bielski's award fell totally through the cracks. He finally got his medal in 2004.)*

Later that day, the forward CP out on LZ Tiger received a message that the CG would be in on 6 May, and to add Lt. Sprayberry to the list to receive an award. It would be an "interim" Silver Star, pending submission of a higher award recommendation back to DA.

The 6th of May started off bad for me, which I related to my wife in a letter.

Dear Nancy,

I am presently suffering from the medicine that is supposed to keep the infection in my bloodstream from entering my intestines. I take four huge pills every morning, which I take on an empty stomach. I can't eat until lunch. These pills make me drunk all morning, sick all afternoon, and sleepy at night but too much in agony to sleep. I weigh 140 lbs., and am really hurting ......"

This letter writing was interrupted for a couple of hours, during which time I had reportedly passed out and was discovered by Nurse Lynn. She revived me by having me drink several glasses of water, and got the doctor over there. As it turned out, my medicine dosage had been reversed. I was supposed to take the four huge pills, one time only, back on my first day in the hospital. Thereafter I would take antibiotic pills daily for two weeks. For two straight mornings, I had taken the four big pills. The doctor commented that one more day on those pills might have been fatal. Had I pissed off Nurse Lynn, or what?

Meanwhile, out in the valley, a helicopter pilot with the call sign "Phantom Raider" had observed 37mm positions firing at our choppers, from a little draw on the west side of the main valley and a couple clicks south of us. The anti-aircraft unit that had plagued us on 19 Apr had probably set up about five kilometers farther south down the valley, and was back in business. The pilot observed at least three different positions.

Air strikes were laid on for the morning of the 6th. At 0735 hours, RASH 1 was on station, and was dropping bombs by 0740. At 0800 hours they started getting secondary explosions, creating billowing clouds of white smoke. RASH 1 brought in a total of three groups of fighter bombers over the next hour, while John and his County Lines moved out toward the smoke.

With the smoke still rising over the hills to the south, the CG flew into LZ Tiger and pinned on the medals. Too bad I missed it. I liked visits from this particular general. SGM Mac later told me in the hospital that the CG had asked about me, which made me feel good. It might have been very interesting to listen in on the conversation between the CG and FNG on the subject of what exactly happened in the saddle on the night of 25-26 April. It was probably a good thing that I was not there.

Shortly after the general departed LZ Tiger, a C Co platoon down on the road got hit with a few artillery rounds, suffering no casualties. The rest of the company was advancing up the road toward the saddle and got sniped at, and even exchanged some hand grenades with NVA soldiers on the cliff above them. Down in the valley, A Co maneuvered southward to a position opposite the bombed 37mm positions, and attacked into the draw with no resistance. Other than these actions, the day remained quiet — until 1645 hours — when all hell broke loose.

Tiger High, Tiger Low and the two-platoon roadblock position all came under a barrage of 130mm artillery fire, which continued on and off for two hours. As the artillery continued, the NVA added 82mm mortars to the mix. Of greater concern, the 4th Platoon of C Co on Tiger Low was also receiving B-40 rockets, and recoilless rifle fire. Reportedly, a 37mm anti-aircraft gun was being employed as well, lowering its barrel to fire at ground targets. From their location, the roadblock guys could see a tank or a self-propelled artillery gun on the ridge to the southwest, firing at them with their cannon. They also believed they had seen more than one such armored vehicle. A big attack against the Tiger Low position seemed imminent.

When the firing finally stopped at 1840 hours, everyone was tensed up, still fully expecting ground attacks, particularly the two platoons on the roadblock. In response to all the incoming fire, however, we had immediately responded with artillery fire from LZ Tiger, LZ Goodman, and LZ Pepper. Eight ARA birds, call sign BLUE MAX, came on station as well, and engaged the tanks, other suspected artillery positions, and probable routes of enemy attack. The ground attack from the NVA never came.

Six men in the artillery battery up on Tiger High were wounded while manning their Howitzers. Everyone else on the LZ remained in their holes and suffered no casualties. It's amazing what a little hole in the ground can do for you. Down on the low ground, C Co reported one man killed and four more men severely wounded. Medevacs were very prompt and the last lift off was at 1904 hours. Sgt. Clark, Sp4 Pennington, Sp4 Baird, Sgt Brock and a medic named Pfc Cannada are on The Wall today, dated 6 May. Some of the wounded did not make it home. Sgt Brock was the oldest at 22.

Was it our imagination, or was the NVA assembling some main force units to do something about the 1st Cav romping around in their main supply base? The fifty-man NVA unit we supposedly faced back on the 19th of April had definitely been reinforced by the first week of May.

On 7 May, I penned a letter in which I said:

> *"Still in the hospital. My leg is slowly getting better but it's still infected and runs constantly. One of our lieutenants performed a fantastic feat the other day and we are putting him in for the Medal of Honor. The Lt. Col. was against recommending it, but we went ahead and wrote it up while I was here in the hospital. This afternoon I get a message from the Lt. Col. telling me to put Lt. Sprayberry in for the Medal of Honor — like he had just thought of it."*

I guess the general had his little talk with our colonel while he was out there. It was a big laugh. I never mentioned to the CO that the award had already been submitted back on the 4th.

Out in the valley, 7 May, was another busy day. C Co spotted a twenty man force on the ridgeline to the west, and engaged them with artillery. A Co continued their attack into the draw, leading west out of the main valley, in search of the 37mm positions. They found all kinds of destroyed and abandoned gear. But, there was no enemy contact. The enemy anti-aircraft unit had limped away during the night, after our very successful bombing attack of the previous day.

In the afternoon, C Co again spotted a tank farther north along the west ridge, closer to the saddle area. Preparations were made to put in an artillery barrage for 1245 hours, in concert with air strikes inbound. Not long after RASH 1 had engaged the tank with his fighters, and our artillery barrage had ended, the NVA replied with five artillery rounds that came whistling into LZ Tiger. Three landed, and two overshot the mountain into the main valley below. No casualties resulted.

Late in the day, there were ARA Birds on station, spotting lots of activities all up and down the ridgeline to the west. They engaged several targets, including a tank and a truck. The enemy was definitely building up on the ridgeline, and a lot of air strikes were laid on that night from the saddle, southward up the ridge. An Arc Light was programmed for an area farther to the west along this main road in from Laos. *(Arc Light was the code word for a B-52 run — bombs dropped from 35,000 feet covering a 100 by 300 meter strip.)*

The Assistant Division Commander flew into LZ Tiger on 8 May and informed the CO to "get ready to leave the valley." One guy from C Co apparently did not get the good news in time, because at about 1530 hours he accidentally shot himself in the leg. Yeah, sure. It was the third self-inflicted wound in four days.

Over the course of the next two days, 5/7 Cav did an extensive job of destroying everything that could be of use to the enemy. The Engineer Squad with C Co dropped a long segment of the road off the cliff into the valley below. With construction of their new road around the north side of the mountain, the NVA probably did not repair the cliff road any too soon, since it was clearly visible from the sky and an easy target for our air assets.

Sometime during the last two or three days out there, the western ridgeline suddenly erupted in flame and smoke. Many of our men were treated to the awesomeness of an Arc Light from not too far away.

10 May was departure day, *(ironically the commencement day for the Peace Talks in Paris. I think they went with the round table.)* At 0310 hours that morning, Tiger High and Tiger Low were ringed by a close-in friendly artillery barrage meant to disrupt any NVA attack that might be coming at dawn. The 155s firing from LZ Goodman were coming so close that they immediately got called off until they could be adjusted outward. Maybe they just seemed too close, because everything does when it's pitch dark.

At 0630 hours, the first birds came in and commenced lifting C Co out to Camp Evans. The other companies and the battalion command group followed, with all elements closing Camp Evans by 1220 hours. It was another smooth air movement operation by 5/7 Cav. Everyone was on the ball that day. Motivation was high. They just had to get out of that place.

The doctor let me out of the hospital that morning, and I went outside the wire to visit with one of the incoming companies out on the scrub hills west of Camp Evans. A Co, I think. It was deathly hot, not a cloud in the sky, no shade trees, and the troops were sitting around waiting for instructions. They all looked totally exhausted. Some of the company officers and I were sitting there chatting about what they had been through since I left. As we were talking, an M-16 round cooked off right before our eyes on the little ridge about 80 yards away. The round hit its owner in the leg... another million dollar wound.

A few minutes later, the squad leader, platoon sergeant, and platoon leader were all standing there at attention while I scolded them for failure to clear weapons once they were in a secure area. I was trying my best to be stern, but as I looked into the vacantly staring eyes of those exhausted men, my heart wasn't in it. I was thinking to myself at the time: What in the hell has happened to these boys? We didn't have this kind of crap when JB was here.

* * * * *

Years later, Howard Prince said it all about Jim Vaught while recollecting the big meeting back in January 1968, a day or so after he had assumed command:

"Vaught assembled the company commanders and some staff members to introduce himself. I remember him as looking rumpled, wearing wrinkled jungle fatigues just like everyone else, wearing the steel helmet, carrying a rifle and looking in need of a shave. His voice was deep and raspy. He didn't mince words or try to feed us any fluff such as command philosophy. He simply said 'I am

LTC Vaught and I am your new battalion commander. I was a lieutenant in World War II and a captain in Korea. This is my third war. So that makes me a fugitive from the law of averages. In other words, I am scared shitless and I assume all of you are too. So let's just get that out of the way right now and do our jobs anyway.' And then he left. We all just stood there in amazement and I remember thinking to myself, this guy is going to be all right. From then on he led by example, he walked with us when we were looking for the enemy, carried his own weapon, got shot at when we were under fire, dug his own hole and heated his own rations."

James B. Vaught
3 November 1926 ~ 20 September 2013

On the Road to Hue – February 1968

Vince and His Pals
Robinson, Laurich, Hawksby, Taylor, Folden, Fredenburg, Hollaway

Platoon Leaders, 1st Platoon, A Company, 5/7th Cavalry
Vince Laurich's new pal - Josh Rambo

CHAPTER 36

COUNTING THE DAYS

I have thought much about 19 April 1968 over the years. For one thing, I am sure there was some defensiveness on my part that triggered my somewhat heated response to the Brigade Commander on the radio. The truth hurts, as we say. I had done poorly at listening to the Brigade Net, and calling in situation reports. Keeping higher headquarters informed was never one of my strong points throughout my years of service. Maybe the Brigade CO had his own defenses up as well. I did not have the impression that the man had been over the valley with me at any time, even though he had two of his three battalions on the ground. *(A guy who was on the Brigade Staff actually told me years later that they didn't need to talk to us, because they could hear everything they needed by listening to the Aviation Battalion's Command Net. No kidding, that's what he said. Can you believe that shit?)*

I had unquestionably been too focused on the anti-aircraft targets. Listening to two radios at the same time is very hard, particularly with one going a mile a minute. In retrospect, I made a big mistake not having my RTO with me in the C&C Bird when we took off on the 19th. Burns would have monitored the Brigade Net and kept me out of hot water, and maybe offered me an unwanted cigarette or two, which I probably would have smoked, since April 19th made hiding behind a burial mound look like a three-mile run at the Chattahoochee River. RTOs do a lot more than just carry the radio, the hot chocolate packs and the cream-filled cookies. Oh, yeah, a lot more.

Interestingly, all day long on 19 April, C Troop, 1/9 Cav, was operating in the south end of the valley with a huge allocation of bombing sorties. They were preparing that area for the next brigade, scheduled in later. Was consideration ever given to shifting some of these bombing sorties up to the more immediate problem? 5/7 Cav could have used a lot more sorties, and Troop C had plenty. Who knows, maybe they even had some napalm. The fastest way out of that jam would have been to burn the whole place down — take the oxygen out of those 37mm and 57mm gun silos. Now there was a reason for talking to brigade every now and then. Not to mention them maybe calling us and taking some interest in what we were going through. I totally blew it that day.

I could never get a sense of higher headquarters actually maneuvering its units during the operations in the spring of 1968. "Fighting your battalions" is the operative expression. We fought our companies. Brigade didn't seem to fight its battalions. The battalions just went out to their assigned AOs and that was the end of it. I once overheard a Brigade Commander talking about fighting his battalions, and almost broke out laughing. The 1st Cav Div and its brigades did not totally adjust to the moment when the NVA came out to fight in the spring of 1968. We did a helluva job unassisted, because our battalions were superior. But how much more could have been accomplished if the division had moved its combat power onto QL 1 to Hue within one week rather than three, even if they had to walk? How much more could have been accomplished if the Brigade Commander had come out to the battlefield early on 19 April instead of smoking his pipe and listening to the fucking Aviation Brigade Net?

One particularly amazing thing was how many of the crews from the aircraft downed on 19 April made it back to safety. As they descended, flying away from us to the east, the fire coming out of the back would appear to have consumed the entire Chinook. The fire was in the back and the people were in the front. Throughout the night, the story was that most of the downed air-crews climbed to the high ground and made it into the perimeter of the 1/7 Cav. It is amazing what people can come through. Out of this experience came an ironic twist — I no longer put any credence in estimates about the numbers of enemy we have supposedly killed in all the wars we have had. No credence whatsoever.

One of the downed Hook crews, piloted by a crusty old major many years older than I, made it into LZ Tiger early on 20 April. We had a brief conversation in which the major/pilot expressed great interest in getting the job of S-3 for the 2/7 Cav. I immediately wondered if he just wanted to get the hell out of Chinooks, or if he knew something that had happened to my friend Don. I was too busy to pursue this conversation. And I wasn't ever going to mention the Big Sky Concept to a Chinook pilot after that day.

We learned later that the first Hook that had departed the coast at 1205 hours had exploded in midair well short of the valley, and fell into the jungle. The word was that it was shot down by an estimated 57mm anti-aircraft gun. The enemy gun position was said to be on Hill 1225, one of the high points halfway to the coast from LZ Tiger. The Division Artillery Commander quickly put the artillery move on hold at that point.

The CH-54 that was shot down on 19 May was the Division's first Flying Crane lost to ground fire. 5/7 Cav brought the Division a number of significant emotional events that spring.

The aviators of the 1st Cav burned some serious calories on 19 April. Ten aircraft had been destroyed by enemy fire. At least fifteen more of their birds required major surgery. It would take several days of around-the-clock maintenance to recover from this day. Many a warm Carling Black Label went down the throats of young warrant officers that night back at Camp Evans.

One wonders if any of those little NVA anti-aircraft gunners made it back to their hometowns up north. If they did, they may still be telling the story about all the ships they brought down. And if they are, let's hope they are telling the whole truth, because by the end of the three week campaign in the A Shau, their unit was decimated by the 5/7 Cav.

Ralph Miles was a brave and charismatic leader. 5/7 Cav was blessed with such outstanding captains in the spring of 1968. Ralph went on to be a noted citizen of Fairfax County, Virginia, and went from there to Fiddler's Green a few years ago. He was buried with full honors at Arlington.

Thirty-six years later while doing research at the national archives, I was struck by how little was recorded in the Division Journal about the total debacle in the sky over the A Shau Valley on 19 April, 1968. They must have been very busy back there. It is all in the Aviation Brigade Log, I suppose. Maybe that's was where Division got all their information as well. Our battalion journal wasn't much better, since our CP Group was traveling that day.

10 May – 28 June 1968
Camp Evans

On return from the A Shau, 5/7 Cav went on base defense of Camp Evans, and remained so through June. It was a greatly deserved rest for the troopers after their experience in the A Shau Valley. A time for rebuilding the leadership as well. The Bn CO and three of the four company commanders were new in the job. The XO, S3, S4 and S1 were short-timers.

On any given day, three companies were out in the western approaches to Camp Evans, patrolling within the grid system that we had designed back in March. The other company had road duty. Road duty involved guarding a couple bridges on QL-1, providing security to the morning minesweeper teams within the Division's zone, and guarding the water point.

It was paradise for the troops, but total drudgery for the officers. Throughout the period, we received many new LTs to replace all those lost in February and April. Some of these boys weren't too sharp. There was the earlier story of the Puerto Rican 2d LT who misunderstood instructions at the expense of Platoon Sergeant Solomon. And there was the new B Co LT back on 21 February whom I have not seen since. For the most part, though, our lieutenants had been great. In June of 1968 though, I had a sense of the pipeline starting to dry up. It seemed like more of the guys coming to us in May were like the two mentioned above.

On one occasion we had a platoon with its new LT replace another platoon at one of the bridges on Hwy 1. The new LT apparently not only failed to absorb any information from the previous people, but he also put up his poncho tent and "did not come out." Soon after he took over, some of his men went down to the river to bathe. They went by way of the minefield and a couple of them were blown into little pieces. When I got there, the LT was still sitting in his tent. Rather than just shoot him right then and there, I put him in the back of the jeep, bag and baggage, and took him to Camp Evans. I never saw him again either. I don't remember his name. Don't want to. I doubt if he is still out there in TV Land. He should have killed himself by now. *(This is a cruel story.)*

After coming out of the A Shau Valley, the new colonel was much more interested in what Joe and I knew about things. He could not hear enough about what we had done, how we had done it, what we were doing now, what we should do tomorrow, and how we should do it. He would keep Joe and me up way into the night, answering the same questions over and over. I was still weak from the leg infection, and the man just kept me worn out.

One afternoon, 1st Lt. Tim Pasquerelli and I were outside the TOC having our picture taken together. Tim had been a great platoon leader for about nine months, and was still standing. We brought him in to be S-2 when Abraham left, and he was fun to work with. Just as Tim and I were walking back into the TOC, a 122mm rocket round hit the roof. It went off with an ear-splitting crack. The whole place seemed to shake, but the only thing that fell was a lot of dust from the steel rafters. After Tim and I stopped coughing, we started laughing and joking, elated that we were still alive. When the dust settled in the TOC, the colonel scrambled up from the floor behind his desk, and like all self-absorbed people assumed we were laughing at him. He "didn't think it was so goddamn funny", or words to that effect. The next morning, he requested a detailed briefing about the rocket that hit the TOC.

I could have sworn he was there at the time. Well, to be fair to the man, the whole issue for us on base defense was the 122mm rockets that were coming in from the mountains to the west, and the mines being buried in the highway every night. It was our job to do something about these things. That is what he wanted to know about. What were we going to do about it? It was a serious problem.

Back on 9 May, my last day in the hospital, Mr. Charles had fired a lucky 122mm rocket-round into the ammo dump in the center of Camp Evans. It touched off a phenomenal show that lit up the night for miles. At its peak the first night, I could hear stuff occasionally hitting the tops of our twelve-man tents. The fire eventually consumed the entire area of the ammo dump. Red hot munitions flew into the helicopter landing area not too far away and destroyed several birds. By midnight, the fire lit up the sky like it was daylight. At about 0200 hours in the morning, I decided to make everyone in the tents move outside and sleep against the sandbag walls away from the direction of the ammo dump. No one complained this time. Nurse Lynn didn't say a word the next morning. None of our tents caught on fire, but it was a "better safe than sorry" deal all the way. When we greeted the dawn, artillery rounds were lying in the streets all around our area. It was awesome. The ammunition dump cooked off for two days. Several helicopters were destroyed.

Even though we were doing a good job securing Camp Evans by early June, the exhilaration of serving under JB had been replaced by the utter despondency serving under the new guy. The Brigade CO was new, as well, and came in with a whole new set of ideas. New battalion and brigade COs every six months was such a great idea. Keep us on our toes. On 29 May, it occurred to me that I was to rotate in thirty days.

Being the consummate professional, I held in contempt any officer who openly counted the days to rotation. The troops were another matter, particularly the draftees who by that time made up at least 70% of our ranks. About the troops I understood. In fact, I was quite amused by the creativity and colorfulness with which they decorated their helmet covers and flak jackets. Calendar Art. They counted the days in every imaginable way. Just plain calendars. Number spirals leading to the final "1". Female figures made of numbers, with the "1" being somewhere real warm. Visibly counting the days was OK for the troops. But not for officers. Certainly not me — No sir… 29… 28… 27.

XO Joe had arrived in country a few weeks after I had, so he had a few more weeks longer to go. When I was looking at 30, he was in the 50s. He did not see how he was going to make it. There was nothing I could say to cheer him up. My very presence probably reminded him of how much longer he had to wait. We were a couple of dejected puppies by the middle of June.

Thoughts about my departure had to wait, however, because we had just received a mission to search the fairly large village just outside of Camp Evans on QL-1. Apparently, there were indications of VC living in this village. Actually, VC lived in every large village. We were to be reinforced by a special platoon of South Vietnamese soldiers from Hue, which was well known for searching out and interrogating the VC. They called themselves the Tiger Force, or something like that. We surrounded the village with blocking positions, covered by pre-dawn darkness. Some of our units walked in with the Tiger Force Platoon to search the village. Cordon and search, these operations were called back then.

At about 1000 hours that morning, I got a frantic call from our company RTO inside the village. There was serious trouble between the Tiger Force and the ARVN soldiers who lived in the village. Most of the men of the village were in the Third Regiment of the ARVN 1st Infantry division, headquartered at PK 17, and many had run home to defend their wives and property.

My RTO and I came tearing into the middle of the town in a jeep and slid to a stop. On one side of the street was a line of about thirty Vietnamese soldiers in tiger- striped fatigues. Mean-looking bastards. On the other side of the street were an equal number of soldiers from the ARVN 1st Division. They were meek, smiley little guys. As I stepped out of the jeep, my RTO was kind enough to point out that each side's M-16s were pointed at the other, and we were perfectly in the middle. The American Advisor to the Tiger people was also a mean-looking bastard. He was arguing with our Platoon Leader when I arrived.

Fortunately, everyone lowered their weapons when I beckoned all the leaders to meet at the jeep. In the course of the discussion, I took a real dislike to everything about the Tiger Platoon and particularly their advisor, so I told him nicely to just take a hike on back to Hue. I cancelled the operation. I recall making a call to the CO to tell him what I had done, but never heard anything about it later. It was another scary moment in Vietnam, but I was too depressed to think about it. I believe I was in single digits when this event took place… 9… 8.

I left for An Khe to out-process on 26 June. My khaki uniform was in good shape, hanging on a hanger in the supply room, but virtually all the other belongings in my suitcase were covered with a thick coat of disgusting green mold. I threw out everything that was not essential, and cleaned up the rest. I was on my way.

When I finally got on a jet plane on 29 June, 1968, Hector Santiago-Colon was on his way home as well. I was coming home standing up, and Hector was coming home in a flag-draped casket. Just the night before, Hector Santiago-Colon had jumped on a grenade to save the other men in his fireteam, along with performing many heroics in the battle leading up to his death. Sometime later, his family received his Congressional Medal of Honor. The third such decoration in 5/7 Cav in six months. Making four total in the Vietnam War, one more than any other battalion, Army or Marine. Nowadays people will correct me for not calling it simply the Medal of Honor, which is its official name. Well, stand on ceremony if you will, but we called it the CMH in 1968.

I will always remember Hector. He was always smiling. He was always saying stuff like "Garryowen, Sir". He never failed to say hello to me when he walked by. We had graduated from C-rations to B-rations when we went on base defense. The B-ration was the worst food ever devised for soldiers. God-awful stuff. Coming out of the mess tent one day with a tray heaped high with franks and beans, his comment was "this is some great chow, sir. You better get you some." Always smiling, was Hector.

CHAPTER 37

WELCOME HOME, BROTHER

So much has been said about the aftermath of the Vietnam War, and the shameful way in which returning soldiers were treated. The war was so ill-conceived. The draft was so terrorizing to so many mothers. The nation was in such a state of turmoil, not just from the military war on television every night, but from the domestic war going on in places like Detroit, Chicago, and Washington. Everyone was pissed at everyone in those days. And the threat of a much bigger war with the USSR was always there. People were crazy. My own return to the USA was pretty interesting, but apparently not as bad as it was for many.

30 June 1968
Seattle, Washington

The Tiger Airlines flight into Seattle was not unlike flying in Vietnam. Lots of warning lights. The wheel lock indicator light would not come on, the runway was foamed, and we landed bent forward at the waist with our hands laced behind our heads. Mirthful banter was the order of the moment, with people laughing about surviving combat in the jungle only to die at the Seattle fucking airport. Firetrucks lined the strip as we landed without incident – the wheels being locked after all.

As I walked through the terminal, headed for ticketing, I felt sharp in my starched khakis, newly acquired ribbons and Combat Infantryman's Badge, jump boots shined to perfection, and service cap low over the eyebrows. The khaki uniform in those days was a short-sleeved shirt with no room for shoulder patches, so I had the big yellow and black First Cavalry Division patch dangling from my shirt pocket button.

Walking down the concourse, my path was blocked by a line of bald-headed men dressed in orange-red robes. The Hari Krishnas. I approached this group without slowing pace, eyes straight ahead. Unwavering. The aspiring Tibetan Monks caved at the last second, falling back out of my way. They were for peace at any cost.

Another fifty yards down the concourse stood a group of young men, and very young women of incredible beauty. The girls wore flowing diaphanous robes and looked like angels in their curly hairdos and flower wreaths. The young men were slight of build and remarkably handsome in their flower shirts and sandals. Sorta like angels too. As I neared them, one of the young girls jumped right in my path and I had no choice but to stop. I might run over a guy in an orange robe, but a beautiful girl never. She quickly thrust a pamphlet at me, showed me a page or two with pictures of the Guru sitting in front of a tree, butterflies flitting about. She launched in on the benefits of meditation. Glancing up I found a pair of incredibly beautiful hazel-colored eyes, which I proceeded to gaze through and out the other side for at least three hundred more miles. Or perhaps a thousand yards, to coin a more familiar phrase. She blinked. She finally looked away. She slowly stepped back. I continued to march toward ticketing.

I arrived at the ticket counter with no further interference, where a middle-aged woman grimly took my ticket, processed it, and tossed it at me without a word. In fact, no one other than the little flower girl said a word to me in Seattle, all the way through ticketing and getting on a plane for San Francisco. And in the San Francisco Airport — I was the very essence of leprosy in the San Francisco Airport.

I had remembered the huge demonstration at the Oakland terminal in '65, where the returning soldiers were jeered by the crowd, so I expected the worst. There was even the unconfirmed story of a First Cav trooper who exited a plane in San Francisco and was met at the bottom of the steps by an old woman. Seeing his First Cav patch, she pulled out a .45 and shot him dead. I had heard all the stories about being spit on, shouted at, and so forth, but nothing like that happened to me on my return. But that was me. Others fared less well.

When I got home to my family in Monterrey, California, Nancy weighed about 110 lbs. She had never weighed less than 125 except on her wedding day. At least, it was nice to have been missed so. And she was off the tranquilizers. I was back up to about 160 lbs by that time, completely recovered from the infection. My two and a half year old daughter took one look at me and wanted to know "who is that man?"

* * * * *

But that all changed with the Volunteer Army. The draft was ended in 1975. People were sick of the whole military service thing. 58,000 of America's fine young men had been wiped out over a seven-year period in Vietnam, creating a big shortfall in young men coming into the service. By 1978 we were enlisting thousands of women to make up for the shortfall. The Berlin Wall came down. Russia fell by the wayside. We didn't need a big army anymore. And when the towers went down, we didn't have one. But the one we had was sharp. Impressive, and earnest. One percent of the population. Let them handle it. In the meantime, who's singing the National Anthem for the Super Bowl? Wow, have you ever seen such a huge flag? Coming home in 2005 was a lot different than in 1968.

17 May
Kuwait City

I don't remember much about the trip back out to Kuwait. I was tired all over. I caught a Blackhawk to Victory Pad in Baghdad and a C-130 out that same evening to Kuwait. It was a long day, and I fell immediately into bed at the Hilton Resort.

I woke up early at the Hilton Resort, at about 0700 hrs, because I had called in and moved my flight by one day. I had to take a cab to downtown Kuwait City to get my electronic Delta Airlines ticket changed to a paper ticket. The ride to downtown, and back out to the airport cost about $40. Not bad in their economy. But the whole deal was to milk me for another $200 for the ticket. I explained to the young Kuwaiti that I had already paid $50 to make this change, but he just looked off in space. I was over a barrel. I would be calling my travel agency as soon as I got home.

For some weird reason, I decided I didn't want to lug the helmet and steel metal jacket home, so I left it in the closet at the Hilton Resort. Imagine the maid wondering who in the hell was this masked man. I arrived at the airport that evening well ahead of time for a 2 a.m. flight, and couldn't even check my bags because the flight didn't open their check-in station until 2200 hours. So I shifted around between Starbucks upstairs, KFC downstairs, and Starbucks again. It was fun watching the arriving flights, with all the rich Kuwaiti families and their beautiful wives and daughters all dressed in just about the most elegant stuff money can buy. Even the women hidden completely behind veils were stunning.

At Starbucks, an Arab gentleman dressed in the traditional white robe struck up a conversation with me. His broken English was not that broken. He was waiting for his daughter, who comes home every week from the University in Bahrain. I thought to myself she should just go to college and stay there, but caught myself before saying anything stupid. He explained that women are generally not allowed by their families to travel alone, but he had become more enlightened. He was there to meet her at the gate every time, though, you can bet on that. She was in her 5th year of medical school, with one to go. His son was with him, about 35 to 40, a big strong-looking guy. The old man must be about 55 to 60. He explained that his son was the personal bodyguard for the Minister of Oil, or something like that, and had guarded the man for fifteen years. I could believe it. Dad had also been the Ambassador to someone at one time. Dad did all the talking. Mr. Security just listened, and I concluded that he understood English very well.

The father had lots of interesting generalizations. We started talking and he rattled off a lot of stuff. Bush is the hero of Kuwait, as far as he is concerned. (*I didn't clarify which Bush.*) The Iraqis are the most gifted in the Arab world in terms of intellectual power, but they are dishonest. Saddam's rule has ruined an entire generation. The changes in Kuwait are wonderful, but we still have a way to go. He was very proud of the fact that they had given women the vote just the previous day. The National Guardsmen can vote, but the active military cannot — makes no sense. They need to allow alcohol. He is hoping soon — tired of bootleg liquor. He likes to stay in his neck of the woods, but has been to London four times. Lebanon is a very nice place. Basra in Iraq will be the best place in the Middle East one day — the Hong Kong of the Middle East. The key to Iraq's rebirth is the children.

I told him about the 14 schools the 5/7 Cav has funded, which he thought was great. He rambled on. The US must stay involved in Iraq for a full seven years; if not with military, with funding, and economic support for building a more modern nation. Syria needs the hammer. Interesting observation looking back. Iran may change themselves from within soon, elections in Iran are coming up, and the young people are looking for change. They may need some hammer too, but he acknowledged the difficulty.

Well, these were the views of one articulate elder businessman in Kuwait. He pretty much covered everything he thought an American writer should know. His daughter showed up, dressed in the traditional flowing black gown, with beautiful embroidered art work. No veil. Maybe I should have gotten his name, although I will never see the man again.

I ran into an Army liaison girl who prowled the airport. She was a Specialist Fourth Class. Maybe 38 to 40. Very helpful — the perfect personality. She told me about the lounge for the military upstairs, called the Pearl Room, but I could not go there until I had processed in and gotten my boarding pass. At about 2000 hours, with two hours to go to check in, she came and found me and took me to the KBR Office. KBR did practically everything in Iraq that was not military. They ran the mess halls, transportation, construction, you name it. They had a receiving and departing office at the airport. I ended up hanging out with them and rebuilding battery power while I was worked on a column. The KBR people there were nice people. Very nice. All ex-military, it seemed.

Unlike the flights to Iraq, with all the trepidations and mental planning, my flights home were just long airplane rides to get the 8000 miles back. I slept most of the time. I enjoyed the same beers at the same bar in the Frankfurt Airport, but the layover was not long. It seemed like no time at all before I was in the terminal in Detroit, where everyone was friendly, starting with the guys in passport control who saw where I had been and welcomed me home.

There were groups of servicemen and women moving through in their battle dress uniforms (BDUs) and rucksacks. All of them wore their uniforms correctly. No one was drunk. It was a miracle. I said hi to several. So did other people. Later, while waiting for my flight, I sat not far from two soldiers at the bar, and people were buying them drinks. I struck up a conversation with a couple in civilian clothes next to me and they ended up thanking me for my service.

In the Vietnam War no one came home as part of a unit that could stick together as they negotiated the airports and bus stations. When you got off the plane in TV Land, you were on your own. And the average returning soldier had only his uniform as he traveled to his next duty station or home to his family. He could run, but he couldn't hide. On the other hand I had some civvies, but I still wore my uniform home back in 1968. I was a Regular Army officer. Wearing uniforms was what I did for a living. But that was back then. I returned to an entirely different country in 2005.

I arrived in Jacksonville on the 19th of May, and was greeted by a party in my honor. A big sign with Welcome Home. Everywhere I went, people wanted to know what I had done in Iraq, and what I thought about it all. It was a warm welcome, indeed.

Within a week after I got back to Jacksonville I received an e-mail from JP in which he said:

> As it turned out, we had actually captured Kamel Al Aswadi, known as Kamel the Tailor, two weeks before Operation Choctaw-Bulldog. We just didn't know it at the time. He was Value Target #1 for the 42d Infantry Division in north central Iraq. He was caught by our Iraqi Army checkpoint at the bridge to Samarra. The IA stopped his vehicle for a search, and found a compass and elevation device. He offered them $400 to let him go. He had fake teeth and a couple other minor physical alterations, and wasn't worried about being recognized. The IA soldiers not only refused the bribe but immediately zip-cuffed him, and brought him to Paliwoda on 30 April. Once there he was surprised by his treatment. He'd been detained a year earlier, had his head stepped on and other "issues." His treatment by 5/7 Cav caused him to "re-think his attitude towards Americans." While all this good spirit was going on, however, a more detailed search of his car yielded a GPS with grids of all military bases in Samarra and Tikrit, plus $6000 US.

> His cover story was that he was a muscleman and collected money from Iraqis to pay for insurgent activities. He was turned over to Brigade, and moved through the detention process at various headquarters on his way to Abu Ghraib. Apparently, over the course of three weeks, Brigade and Division S-2 personnel kept showing his picture to others who had been detained. Without prompting, multiple sources identified him as Kamel. His picture went to the Samarra City Council and they either identified him as Kamel or very nervously claimed it wasn't he. We sent our interrogator up to Division and he spent a few days grilling the man. On the 2nd day Kamel came to the session with a modified prisoner jumpsuit on. The interrogator asked him about this suit, and Kamel proudly said he had altered it with a nail and some thread to make it more comfortable, confirming his tailor skills. At this point Kamel quickly realized he had just been caught, and he confessed about everything. We had caught him on 30 April but he wasn't positively identified until 21 May. Were it not for our interrogators, he would be in Abu Ghraib under his alias, and we'd have lost the large amount of intel that was gained. Most of the Samarra City Council was in fact AIF supporters.

The informant who had come in, triggering our Operation Choctaw-Bulldog, was actually part of the cover plan for Kamel. They knew we had Kamel, and were trying to put up a smokescreen.

By the middle of June I had read and heard about many of the programs for welcoming the troops home, such as the Vietnam Veteran group that greets every troop plane landing in Bangor, Maine – an almost daily event. I visited Ryan Hollin at Walter Reed, and so did a lot of other people. And there is the Wounded Warrior Program. Lots of other foundations. Talk is cheaper than adding one to a payroll, though.

There is no shortage of flags everywhere. Patriotism is rampant. Strange behavior for a country so against this war according to various polls. And definitely in sharp contrast from the last time I had come home from the combat zone. Very sharp contrast.

Jacksonville, Florida
June 2005

Within a few weeks of my return from Iraq, the President gave a fine speech in which he summed up all the things we had accomplished so far in Iraq. It inspired me to write my last published column. The parts that are not grossly redundant were:

INCLDING THE SUNNIS

If the enemy was hard to see in the early days of Vietnam, they are invisible in Iraq. I got to Baghdad on April Fool's Day, and left in the middle of May. There was no war going on that I could see. Only a lot of endless driving around, tensing up in the back seat when going around certain curves or when seeing a lone car approaching at high speed...

...So we come now to the President's fine speech. And it was a fine speech in which he spoke of having a two track-plan. The military is fighting the war to root out the terrorists. And "we" are working on the political front to establish democracy. The "we" in this case appears to be the military also, but maybe he didn't want to hurt Condi's feelings. And he made the public aware of our accomplishments. The President said "The terrorists, both foreign and domestic, failed to prevent the transfer of sovereignty." You are correct, sir.

"They failed to stop Iraqis from signing up in large number with the police forces and the army to defend their new democracy." You are correct again, sir.

"And they failed to break our coalition and force a mass withdrawal by our allies." Well, yes sir. Estonia sent a scout platoon who patrols the streets of Baghdad, and the British, of course. But the Spaniards and Italians went home.

"They failed to stop the formation of a democratic Iraqi government that represents all of Iraq's diverse population." Almost correct, sir. Hopefully, the Sunnis will vote in October. I believe many will in Balad.

"They failed to incite an Iraqi Civil War." Sir, you might better hold up on that one.

*   *   *   *   *

The war in Iraq did not seem like a war to me in 2005, at least in our AO. It was more like being in the cops, except the SWAT Teams were huge. The perps got the same due process as a DUI outside the Sun Dog Diner in Neptune Beach, Florida. It took lots of corroborating evidence to put them away. There were no big battles.

JP and I kept in touch for the remainder of their tour. 5/7 Cav's last big operation was security for the Iraq General Election of 15 December 2005. All the efforts of the US military and emerging Iraqi military had pointed toward this day. It was a huge success. Many of the Sunni population turned out to vote, having finally recognized that it was the only way to be included. There was still violence, but the cost of violence was far less than before. Except in Ace Red.

For eleven months Ace Red was the best. They were thorough and professional, spotting the possible IEDs and taking the types of actions to minimize IED explosions. Eleven months of dodging the efforts of Arabs pushing garage door openers or similar devices. On the 15th of December 2005 while moving to position to secure the polling site, an Ace Red humvee drove over a mine with a pressure plate detonator. Not an improvised explosion device manufactured in somebody's tool shed. A real mine. The same type of mine that was deadly on QL-1 in Vietnam so many years ago. The same kind of mine that killed my friend and classmate Mike Field. The type of mine that doesn't rely on a petrified Ali Baba quaking in his sandals behind a tree. Ducksworth and Scrappy Atchison were wounded. Joey Lucas was killed. That's right. . . killed! Protecting Iraqis so that they could go to the polls and vote for a bunch of politicians who may or may not make any difference to their country; and certainly weren't going to make any difference to ours.

Joe Lucas was the only U.S. Serviceman killed in Iraq on Election Day, 15 December 2005. He went in harm's way with his platoon mates, like so many 5/7 Cav troopers have over the decades. We called and they hauled. His Ace Red mates were with him when he died. Another one line biography. Another Tree Ceremony at Ft. Stewart, Georgia. I can go to The Wall every year now. After all, it has been forty years. But the tree planted for Joe Lucas is my last tree ceremony. I can't go to any more tree ceremonies.

At the Wall 11 November 2011
Baker, Mitchell, Sprayberry, Lambert, Vaught & Florence Vaught

Joel Jackson, Beau Saucier, and Katie
2014 Reunion - Springfield, MO

CHAPTER 38

FOREVER SOLDIERS

By the end of the Iraq War in 2012, 4200 servicemen had died. In just one thirty day period around Tet of 1968, 2800 of our young men died.

Once I got home in the summer of 1968, I went back to the security of Fort Benning to help train the next wave of lieutenants and captains headed for the war. XO Joe turned up there too. Joe and I had yet to be assigned to a separate post after nine years of service, and people were beginning to talk. But we were back home again, safe and sound in Camelot.

Most of our returning draftees went back to the free-enterprise system where they got no credit for lost time in the military service. The great majority of these fine young men were emotionally strong, and they moved on with their lives. The ten percent that generally struggles anyway struggled at double time in this environment and escaped to such places as the Rocky Mountain forests, or to park benches across from the White House in Washington, DC.

For the average returning soldier, there may have been numerous short intense episodes of humiliating and hateful treatment at airports, bus stations, and back in the neighborhood, but I think the real thing was the silence. For many soldiers seeing their families and friends after the year's absence, it was an awkward and very brief "welcome home", followed by talking about the weather, kicking stones, looking off in space. "Well, hey, see ya around... keep in touch, ya hear?" Stuff like that. Even my own parents were reluctant to generate any conversation about it — and they were Regular Army. The average Veteran Vietnam was welcomed home by silence - a deafening silence that continued until midway through Ronald Reagan's presidency.

Along about 1977, I remembered the angel in the floral dress, and went to find out more about transcendental meditation. Within a year, humming away for twenty minutes a day, most of the bad memories of Vietnam disappeared into the ozone, the void, or whatever they call it. All the good memories are still there.

A lot of water has passed over the spillway, under the bridge, wherever, since those terrible days in Vietnam. Most Vietnam Veterans have started talking after so many years, getting together for reunions, and so forth. We all have our memories, both good and bad, from Vietnam. We all remember lost friends. Many of us who served in 5/7 Cav in April 1968 still agonize over the three men we were unable to bring home from the A Shau Valley. Maybe we should have massed our battalion strength and gone into the saddle, in spite of limited artillery, insufficient maneuver room, and against a steadily reinforcing enemy force. Had we done so, a lot more of our men would be etched in stone today, rather than be coming to our reunions.

Nevertheless, nothing hurts like leaving someone out there. Interestingly, in February of 1969, the 3rd Battalion, 9th Marines, was operating in the hills north and west of the saddle. Just ten months after our operations out there. India Company was patrolling into a small valley (YD228089) in the shadow of the saddle on the morning of 18 February 1969, when they came across a mass gravesite. Their daily journal read in part: "The area had been hit heavily by air strikes, and parts of decaying bodies littered the area. A sign at the site said that 185 men were buried there, and the gravesite had been closed on 11 June 1968." This burial ground is only 400 meters west of the ground where our men were cut down. Some of us think that our boys are in there, along with the many young NVA soldiers who died holding this ground. Kelly, Scott, Guillory, and probably the three crew members of the scout bird as well. To date, the Vietnamese will not let us go there. Maybe someday. Maybe not.

There are just too many stories like this from that war. Others would say that we succeeded in Vietnam, because the Berlin Wall fell in 1989, and Vietnam today is a happy, bustling, emerging country filled with beautiful little people with smiley faces. They are applying all kinds of western ideas. Some would say that these new things would have happened any way — net of 58,000 guys. So what of Iraq? What have we really accomplished? Afghanistan? What have we actually accomplished? When will we know if we succeeded? Not in my remaining lifetime. And it doesn't look good.

During the Vietnam War the "Greatest Generation", as Brokaw has dubbed them, were in their most productive years. As young men they had been victorious in the "Big War". Judging by my own old man, and many of his contemporaries I met along the way, they were truly a great generation. And don't forget, they survived The Great Depression, and they really did save civilization as we knew it.

While the Vietnam War was going on, however, it was that same "Greatest Generation" that was running the country. Being the political leaders. And being the generals, as well. I had little good to say to my Dad about his peers when I got home in 1968. *(Don't waste your time scolding me on political correctness.)* Rather than venerating the Greatest Generation, I came home from Vietnam with a high regard for young people. If you were older than I, you were suspect. And that hasn't changed a whole lot.

I was apparently not alone. A diminutive young lady of Asian ancestry, when called upon to design a monument about the Vietnam War, created a huge memorial to the young people. Three-hundred-eighty young troopers of 5/7 Cav reside there. And, now 17 more of our men have died in the mideast. But, regardless of whether you are etched on The Wall, or are sitting on top of a tree at Ft. Stewart, all these troopers are Forever Soldiers now.

Many of my colleagues go to The Wall to see our men on the 11th of November — Veterans Day. Each visit brings additional new stories from the other guys, to go along with the same little things I always remember. Little things like:

"Garryowen, Sir. This is some great chow, sir. You better get you some."

"GARRYOWEN to you too, Hector."

What else is there to say?

"GARRYOWEN to you too, Joey."

And GARRYOWEN to all the men who ever served in combat with the Gray Horse Troop.

Memorial Service
December 27th, 2005

(Leaving Fort Stewart for Iraq)

Army Spc. Joseph Lucas
September 26, 1982 – December 15, 2005

Joe Lucas

QUE SON VALLEY – HUE – KHE SAHN – A SHAU VALLEY
October 1967 — June 1968

THOMAS C AUBERT ~ JAMES B MOORE ~ CRAIG D PINCHOT ~ JOHN E DAVIS
ROLLEEN C SORIM ~ EDWARD L BIEBER ~ WILLIAM FORD ~ ROBERT G TSCHUMPER
JOSEPH P PINK ~ LEROY HOPKINS JR ~ CHARLES E MULLIS ~ GEORGE M VINEYARD
NICK KOKALIS ~ ALLEN B GLINES (DSC) ~ LEE R DANIELSON ~ DOUGLAS M MCCRARY
LAWRENCE M JENNINGS ~ MICHAEL J DUNN ~ DAVID R BURSON ~ ROBERT J SIME
ROBERT F SHAW ~ WARREN D CAMPBELL ~ GEORGE H COLBERT ~ DEAN H MESSERSMITH
DANNIEL B HERRELL ~ ANTHONY J ESTRELLA ~ KENNETH D CHAPPELL ~ JAMES E GISH
JAMES A CORE ~ STEPHEN F JUMPER ~ BRUCE C LEISING ~ DAVID I HARNER
WILLIAM G NUEBEL ~ JAMES A WATSON ~ JAMES A BAILEY ~ RAUL G GUTIERREZ
MAX R SPANGLER ~ JAMES CASTALDI ~ RANDALL B ANDERSON ~ WILLIAM D PORT (MH)
JOSEPH L BOGOTKA ~ HERLIHY T LONG ~ ARCHIE BURNETTE JR ~ DANIEL MEADE
MICHAEL R ELWELL ~ WILFRED L SOLOMON SR ~ BERNARD P BREITENBACH
LEO P DUNSMORE (DSC) ~ LESLIE J FROLICH ~ ARNOLD E MELISH ~ MICHAEL M ALLEY
THOMAS D POOLE (DSC) ~ JOSEPH L OSTIFIN ~ GARY R CATES ~ LARRY L HACKLEMAN
NORMAN T D'AGOSTINO ~ WINFIELD W BECK ~ EDWARD L FRAZIER ~ WALTER ROBINSON
ZIGMUT P JABLONSKI JR ~ JOHN R LAWRENCE ~ LEE G TOLLEY ~ JERRY D EVANS (DSC)
JIMMIE D WHITLOCK ~ RICHARD J WILT ~ VERNON J WALKER ~ OTIS NICK
MICHAEL E MARTIN ~ RICHARD J GROAT ~ WILLIAM R WATT ~ CHARLIE J STRICKLAND
RICHARD P BRUCE ~ CLIFFORD L SELL ~ MICHAEL G LIPSIUS ~ CURTIS R RILEY
CHARLES S COX ~ ANDREW L MC DANIEL ~ DANIEL M KELLEY ~ DAVID L SCOTT
HUBIA J GUILLORY ~ BILLY K FORD ~ HENRY WUNDERLICH ~ DAVID L BARBER
JESSE CARMONA JR ~ BILLY W BRIDGEMAN ~ EDWARD L BROCK ~ VIRGIL J FOWLER
JESSIE F CROW ~ RICHARD P MARTINEZ ~ JOSE E BENITEZ-RIVERA ~ TERRY N BARTLING
CHARLES A GORDON ~ RONAL A EWING ~ JAMES G ROWE JR ~ ROBERT L DUTRA
HECTOR SANTIAGO-COLON (MH)

IRAQ & AFGHANISTAN
2005 - 2013

DAKOTAH L GOODING ~ RENE KNOX JR ~ CHAD W LAKE ~ CHRISTOPHER J TAYLOR
ARTHUR A MORA JR ~ RUSSELL H NAHVI ~ JOSE E ROSARIO ~ JOSEPH A LUCAS
WILLIAM R HOWDESHELL ~ CHARLES E BILBREY JR ~ JAIME RODRIGUEZ JR
NICHOLAS E RIEHL ~ EDDIE D TAMEZ ~ DAVID A KIRKPATRICK ~ CHRISTOPHER M WARD
DELFIN M SANTOS ~ WILBEL A ROBLES SANTA

William D. Port
12 January 1968

The Medal of Honor for conspicuous gallantry and intrepdiity in action at the risk of his life above and beyond the call of duty is awarded to Sgt. William D. Port. Sgt. Port distinguished himself while serving as a rifleman with Company C, which was conducting combat operations against an enemy force in the Que Son Valley. As Sgt. Port's platoon was moving to cut off a reported movement of enemy soldiers, the platoon came under heavy fire from an entrenched enemy force. The platoon was forced to withdraw due to the intensity and ferocity of the fire. Although wounded in the hand as the withdrawal began, Sgt. Port, with complete disregard for his safety, ran through the heavy fire to assist a wounded comrade back to the safety of the platoon perimeter. As the enemy forces assaulted in the perimeter, Sgt. Port and 3 comrades were in position behind an embankment when an enemy grenade landed in their midst. Sgt. Port, realizing the danger to his fellow soldiers, shouted the warning, "Grenade," and unhesitatingly hurled himself towards the grenade to shield his comrades from the explosion. Through his exemplary courage and devotion he saved the lives of his fellow soldiers and gave the members of his platoon the inspiration needed to hold their position. Sgt. Port's selfless concern for his comrades, at the risk of his life above and beyond the call of duty are in keeping with the highest tradition of the military service and reflect great credit on himself, his unit, and the U.S. Army.

James M. Sprayberry
25 April 1968

The Medal of Honor for conspicuous gallantry and intrepdiity in action at the risk of his life above and beyond the call of duty is awarded to Captain *(then First Lieutenant)* James M. Sprayberry, Armor, U.S. Army, who distinguished himself by exceptional bravery on 25 April 1968, while serving as Executive Officer of Company D, 5th Battalion, 7th Cavalry, 1st Cavalry Division *(Airmobile)*. On this date his company commander and a great number of men were wounded and separated from the main body of the company. A daylight attempt to rescue them was driven back by the well entrenched enemy's heavy fire. Capt. Sprayberry ...a volunteer night patrol to eliminate the intervening enemy bunkers and to relieve the surrounded element. The patrol soon began receiving enemy machine-gun fire. Capt. Sprayberry quickly moved the men to protective cover and without regard for his own safety, crawled within close range of the bunker from which the fire was coming. He silenced the machinegun with a hand grenade. Identifying several l-man enemy positions nearby, Capt. Sprayberry immediately attacked them with the rest of his grenades. He crawled back for more grenades and when 2 grenades were thrown at his men from a position to the front, Capt. Sprayberry, without hesitation, again exposed himself and charged the enemy-held bunker killing its occupants with a grenade. Placing 2 men to cover his advance, he crawled forward and neutralized 3 more bunkers with grenades. Immediately thereafter, Capt. Sprayberry was surprised by an enemy soldier who charged from a concealed position. He killed the soldier with his pistol and with continuing disregard for the danger neutralized another enemy emplacement. Capt. Sprayberry then established radio contact with the isolated men, directing them toward his position. When the 2 elements made contact he organized his men into litter parties to evacuate the wounded. As the evacuation was nearing completion, he observed an enemy machinegun... a grenade. Capt. Sprayberry returned to the rescue party, established security, and moved to friendly lines with the wounded. This rescue operation, which lasted approximately 7 1/2 hours, saved the lives of many of his fellow soldiers. Capt. Sprayberry personally killed 12 enemy soldiers, eliminated 2 machineguns, and destroyed numerous enemy bunkers. Capt. Sprayberry's indomitable spirit and gallant action at great personal risk to his life are in keeping with the highest traditions of the military service and reflect great credit upon himself, his unit, and the U.S. Army.

Hector Santiago-Colon
28 June 1968

The Medal of Honor for conspicuous gallantry and intrepidity in action above and beyond the call of duty is awarded to Specialist Fourth Class Hector Santiago-Colon, who distinguished himself at the cost of his life on 28 June 1968, while serving as a gunner in the mortar platoon with Company B, 5th Battalion, 7th Cavalry, 1st Cavalry Division (Airmobile). While serving as a perimeter sentry he detected movement in the heavily wooded area to his front and flanks. Immediately he alerted his fellow sentries in the area to move to their foxholes and remain alert for any enemy probing forces. From the wooded area around his position heavy enemy automatic weapons and small-arms fire suddenly broke out, but extreme darkness rendered difficult the precise location and identification of the enemy. Soon the muzzle flashes from enemy weapons indicated their position. Sp4c. Santiago-Colon and the other members of his position immediately began to repel the attackers, utilizing hand grenades, antipersonnel mines and small-arms fire. Due to the heavy volume of enemy fire and exploding grenades around them, a North Vietnamese soldier was able to crawl, undetected, to their position. Suddenly, the enemy soldier lobbed a hand grenade into Sp4c. Santiago-Colon's foxhole. Realizing that there was no time to throw the grenade out of his position, Sp4c. Santiago-Colon retrieved the grenade, tucked it in to his stomach and, turning away from his comrades, absorbed the full impact of the blast. His heroic self-sacrifice saved the lives of those who occupied the foxhole with him, and provided them with the inspiration to continue fighting until they had forced the enemy to retreat from the perimeter. By his gallantry at the cost of his life and in the highest traditions of the military service, Sp4c. Santiago-Colon has reflected great credit upon himself, his unit, and the U.S. Army.

Allen B. Glines
3 January 1968

The President of the United States of America, authorized by Act of Congress, July 9, 1918 *(amended by act of July 25, 1963)*, takes pride in presenting the Distinguished Service Cross *(Posthumously)* to Private First Class Allen Bruce Glines *(ASN: US-56648514)*, United States Army, for extraordinary heroism in connection with military operations involving conflict with an armed hostile force in the Republic of Vietnam, while serving with Company A, 5th Battalion (Airmobile), 7th Cavalry, 3d Brigade, 1st Cavalry Division. Private First Class Glines distinguished himself by exceptionally valorous actions on 3 January 1968 as a rifleman during a search and destroy mission in Hoi An Province. Private Glines was the point position for his unit, moving ahead of his platoon as it advanced across a series of open rice paddies. Suddenly a large, well armed enemy force placed heavy fire on the Platoon from concealed positions in a woodline. Private Glines immediately charged the enemy despite the fusillade. He moved forward in the open, intent only on destroying the enemy and aiding those elements of his platoon which were pinned down in the rice paddy. His accurate automatic rifle fire permitted his trapped comrades to reach cover. Assaulting the nearest bunker, he destroyed it, killing its three defenders. He then placed flanking fire on the enemy positions in his vicinity, drawing the insurgents' fire to himself as he assaulted a second bunker. He was mortally wounded before he reached it. Private First Class Glines' extraordinary heroism and devotion to duty, at the cost of his life, were in keeping with the highest traditions of the military service and reflect great credit upon himself, his unit and the United States Army.

Thomas D. Poole
12 February 1968

The President of the United States of America, authorized by Act of Congress, July 9, 1918 *(amended by act of July 25, 1963)*, takes pride in presenting the Distinguished Service Cross *(Posthumously)* to Private First Class Thomas Dewitt Poole *(ASN: US-67109268)*, United States Army, for extraordinary heroism in connection with military operations involving conflict with an armed hostile force in the Republic of Vietnam, while serving with Company A, 5th Battalion *(Airmobile)*, 7th Cavalry, 1st Cavalry Division *(Airmobile)*. Private First Class Poole distinguished himself by exceptionally valorous actions on 12 February 1968 as a rifleman during a search and destroy operation in Quan Huong Tra Province. His company was moving toward a treeline on the far side of a rice paddy when it was subjected to heavy mortar, recoilless rifle and small arms fire from a North Vietnamese Army force occupying entrenched and fortified positions in the woods. Private Poole's platoon was temporarily pinned down behind some mounds of earth, but soon began an assault on the enemy. Braving a hail of bullets and shrapnel. Private Poole charged across one hundred meters of open rice paddy and engaged the North Vietnamese at close range. Moving directly into the treeline, he personally assaulted an enemy bunker in his path, killing its three occupants with rifle fire. The savage fusillade delivered by other hostile bunker increased in intensity, and his platoon was ordered to withdraw and regroup. As Private Poole drew back across the rice paddy, he noticed a wounded platoon member lying exposed to the enemy weapons. Completely disregarding his safety, he moved to assist the fallen soldier. He was mortally wounded while attempting to rescue his comrade. Private First Class Poole's extraordinary heroism and devotion to duty, at the cost of his life, were in keeping with the highest traditions of the military service and reflect great credit upon himself, his unit, and the United States Army.

Leo P. Dunsmore
12 February 1968

The President of the United States of America, authorized by Act of Congress, July 9, 1918 *(amended by act of July 25, 1963)*, takes pride in presenting the Distinguished Service Cross *(Posthumously)* to Private First Class Leo Paul Dunsmore *(ASN: RA-11903314)*, United States Army, for extraordinary heroism in connection with military operations involving conflict with an armed hostile force in the Republic of Vietnam, while serving with Company A, 5th Battalion (Airmobile), 7th Cavalry, 1st Cavalry Division. Private First Class Dunsmore distinguished himself by exceptionally valorous actions on 12 February 1968 as a medic accompanying an infantry company during a search and destroy operation in Quan Huong Tra Province. The unit was moving toward a treeline on the far side of a rice paddy when it was subjected to heavy mortar, recoilless rifle and small arms fire from a North Vietnamese Army force occupying entrenched and fortified positions in the woods. Private Dunsmore's platoon, the lead element, was temporarily pinned down behind earthen grave mounds, but soon began to assault the enemy across the one hundred meters of open rice paddy. The platoon engaged the North Vietnamese at close range, but was forced to withdraw from the increasingly intense enemy fusillade. Seeing many casualties lying fully exposed to the enemy weapons, Private Dunsmore unhesitant moved back into the open terrain to aid his comrades. He repeatedly crossed the bullet-swept rice paddy to skillfully treat the casualties and carry them to safety. While administering aid to one fallen soldier, Private Dunsmore was mortally wounded by the relentless enemy fire. Private First Class Dunsmore extraordinary heroism and devotion to duty, at the cost of his life, were in keeping with the highest traditions of the military service and reflect great credit upon himself, his unit, and the United States Army.

William Phifer
23 February 1968

The President of the United States of America, authorized by Act of Congress, July 9, 1918 *(amended by act of July 25, 1963)*, takes pleasure in presenting the Distinguished Service Cross to Specialist Fourth Class William Phifer *(ASN: US-52757329)*, United States Army, for extraordinary heroism in connection with military operations involving conflict with an armed hostile force in the Republic of Vietnam, while serving with Company A, 5th Battalion, 7th Cavalry, 3d Brigade, 1st Cavalry Division *(Airmobile)*. Specialist Four Phifer distinguished himself by exceptionally valorous actions on 23 February 1968 during an attack against North Vietnamese regulars who were blocking his unit's entry into the city of Hue. His element came under heavy small arms and automatic weapons fire from the well entrenched enemy. When supporting aerial rocket artillery and gunships failed to silence the communist positions, Specialist Phifer began a one-man assault on the nearest bunker. Arming himself with several hand grenades, he crawled seventy-five meters through intense hostile fire to the base of the fortification. Exposing himself to the adjacent North Vietnamese positions, he twice crawled on top of the bunker to drop grenades inside, but the emplacement was not silenced. Specialist Phifer then climbed on the bunker a third time, and remained on top of it to shoot his pistol into the entrance after tossing another grenade inside. At the same time the occupants attempted to throw a grenade at him, but they were unable to release their grenade or dispose of his because of his pistol fire. Both grenades exploded within the bunker, killing the four North Vietnamese soldiers inside and wounding Specialist Phifer in the arm. Specialist Four Phifer's extraordinary heroism and devotion to duty were in keeping with the highest traditions of the military service and reflect great credit upon himself, his unit, and the United States Army.

Jerry D. Evans
23 February 1968

The President of the United States of America, authorized by Act of Congress, July 9, 1918 *(amended by act of July 25, 1963)*, takes pride in presenting the Distinguished Service Cross *(Posthumously)* to Specialist Fourth Class Jerry Dewain Evans *(ASN: US-52966929)*, United States Army, for extraordinary heroism in connection with military operations involving conflict with an armed hostile force in the Republic of Vietnam, while serving with Company A, 5th Battalion *(Airmobile)*, 7th Cavalry, 3d Brigade, 1st Cavalry Division. Specialist Four Evans distinguished himself by exceptionally valorous actions on 23 February 1968 as a rifleman of the an airmobile infantry company conducting an assault on a series of well fortified enemy bunker positions near Hue. Specialist Evans' company was immobilized by heavy enemy sniper fire from one of the bunker complexes. Realizing his unit would suffer heavy casualties unless it moved, he maneuvered across the bullet-swept terrain, attacking the bunker from which the company was receiving the most intense fire. Without regard for his personal safety, he mounted the fortification's roof and fired inside the emplacement, eliminating four enemy troops. Moving from the bunker, Specialist Four Evans was mortally wounded by sniper fire from another fortified position. Specialist Four Evans' extraordinary heroism and devotion to duty, at the cost of his life, were in keeping with the highest traditions of the military service and reflect great credit upon himself, his unit, and the United States Army.

October 1967 — June 1968

FRANCIS ROTHWEKK ~ MATT KOLENDICH ~ MICHAEL MILLIGAN ~ HUGH RATCLIFFE
HOWARD PRINCE ~ RONALD BUSTOS ~ MICHAEL FOX ~ THOMAS COLE ~ CLYDE REYES
WILLIAM WOOLEYHAM ~ GREGARIO TRUJILLO ~ BERNARD PAGANO ~ LANCE DAVIS
ROBERT TRIMBLE ~ CHARLIE NORWOOD ~ FRED IPPOLITO ~ HARLAN FEDDERSON
HENRY REESE ~ DAVID HARNER ~ MICHAEL MARTIN ~ JOHN HIATT ~ ROGER SPERAW
JOE REVELS ~ RICHARD PSCHIRRER ~ ANTHONY SIMS ~ LAREN EVANS THOMAS POOLE
RICHARD SHANNON ~ JAMES GILREATH ~ HERLIHY LONG ~ ANTHONY WILLIAMS
CHARLES GATES ~ ASHBY BOX ~ ELVIS CARTER ~ JOHN BAKEHOUSE ~ JOHN ROSENBURG
MICHAEL SPRAYBERRY ~ JOSEPH DROBNAK ~ GEORGE ROSS ~ WARREN FLENNIKEN
DONALD CASTEEL ~ PAUL DIGIACOMO ~ TERRY WEDEMORE ~ RICHARD WILT ~ JOHN ADAMS
ANRIAN CAVAZOS ~ EDWARD GILLIS ~ THOMAS GOLDEN ~ JAMES BORDEN ~ LARRY KIBBON
ROBERT PIERCE ~ CHARLES PRICE ~ ALLEN DILIE ~ ERNESTO ALVAREZ ~ DENNIS CARSWELL
MARVIN MAXWELL ~ JAMES THOMAS ~ LARRY COOK ~ ALONZO BEARD
BERNANRD BRIETENBACH ~ THOMAS POOLE ~ ROBERT LOWE ~ MICHAEL MOORE
JIM COLLINS ~ JOHN POORE ~ LAREN EVANS ~ CARL GREGGS ~ GEORGE BLANTON
STEPHEN LOVING ~ LAWRENCE CONCEPCION ~ DAVID ALEXANDER ~ HUBERT HUBIN
ANGEL MOLINA RODNEY RUSH ~ JOHN WEST ~ JOHN DITONNO ~ EDWARD GILLIS
JOHN LAPIOLI ~ JAMES VEASEY ROBERT HOEIZER ~ NICHOLAS FIORE ~ WILLIAM BELL
JOHN FINTON ~ MICHAEL BUSH ~ ORLEAN CLINTON ~ JACK MILLER ~ EDWARD LEWIS
EUGENE WILLIAMS ~ ANGEL ALBARBAN ~ EUGENE BASKINS ~ BENJAMIN HERNANDEZ
JOHN POORE ~ ROBERT WILLIS ~ ROBERT BUTLER ~ LARRY KIBBON ~ WILLIAM BLICKOS
CARLOS STERLING-WILLIAMS ~ ROBERT FONTAINE ~ CHRISTOPHER RICHARDSON
TERRY SANFORD ~ HECTOR SANTIAGO-COLON ~ JAMES LEONARD ~ FLOYD BOYD
WILLIAM HARPER ~ LARRY BINGHAM ~ WINFORD POPPHAN ~ ARTHUR HINSCH
DAVID ALEXANDER ~ DONALD BIRKBECK ~ JOHN GROCKI ~ FREDERICK BRIGGS
MICHAEL ROSENBERGER ~ EDWARD DOUCETTE ~ LEE RODRIGUEZ ~ DAVID CLINTON
JOHN WILLIAMS ~ HENRY WEBB ~ REMIE MARTENS ~ GEORGE KLEIN ~ JACK FISCHER
ROBERT KARDOS MICHAEL SHOEMAKER ~ THEODORE PAUZETTE ~ BRIAN GEESLER
RONALD BRITTON ~ THOMAS KYGER ~ MICHAEL SHAW ~ GEORGE FRY

JOSE QUINNONES-MERCADO ~ ANTHONY HARDY ~ ASHTEY OEX ~ MICHAEL MYCHALIK
JOHN THACKER ~ ROBERT TRIMBLE ~ PETER CASCIO ~ THOMAS MANN ~ MARIANO SALAS
ROBERT BURROWS ~ JOSEPH BERNARD ~ WILLIE GARMAN ~ EDWARD SANSONE
DAVID HEKKANEN ~ DONALD CARLSON ~ JOHN DEAN ~ THOMAS SHUTZ ~ GEORGE HOLBROOK
JAMES ROMBAKAS ~ ANTHONY ROGERS ~ SKIPPY MARCH ~ THOMAS LENT ~ GARY MCAFEE
ALFRED RAMIREZ ~ EDVIN BENTKS ~ EDWARD SHEAROCK ~ RONNIE CHILDERS
HAROLD GOTTESMAN ~ RONALD BUSTOS ~ JOSEPH SHULTZ ~ LLOYD BUTLER ~ JACK ANDERS
BRUCE KOOB~ MICHAEL ROSENBERGER CHARLES EKBERG ~ DAVID SCOTT ~ EUGENE GREENE
DENNIS MCGURRE ~ ANDREW WESTIN ~ HOWARD PRINCE ~ NORMAN STEWART
ROBERT CLARK ~ WADE NEWMAN ~ FREDERICK KRUPA ~ JOHN DITONNO ~ ANGEL MOLINA
JAMES BORDEN ~ OTIS TUCKER ~ GEORGE CRUZ ~ WILBUR LANE ~ WALTER BOWERS
JAMES AUSTIN ~ JOSEPH KUSCHMAN ~ WILLIAM OSBORNE ~ RICHARD WILT
CARLOS STERLING-WILLIAMS ~ BILLY FORD ~ DAVID MORRIS ~ MARK SCOTT ~ GARY FISCHER
ROGER CASE ~ GARY RATCLIFFE ~ OTHELLO ALEXANDER ~ ANTHONY WILLIAMS
HERMAN SCHUTT ~ EGBERTO TORO ~ LAJOIE GRIMES ~ JAMES KEYSHAW ~ BOBBIE JAMIESON
JAMES MEADE ~ BILLY FORD ~ MICHAEL DAVISON ~ JOHN WILLIAMS ~ KEITH NELSON
JAMES KING ~ WILLIAM PHIFER JOHN KAWANA ~ RONALD LEE ~ JIMMY LASTER
MICHAEL NEUZIL ~ ALFRED CARDENAS ~ THOMAS QUINLAN ~ STEVEN MCHULLEN
DAVID BIELSKI ~ LOUIS SCHWENT ~ JAMES FRYE ~ LOUIS SANCHEZ ~ VIRGIL EVANS
DANIEL NASE ~ FRANK DEFINO ~ RICHARD GROAT ~ RONALD WILLIAMS ~ CURTIS LENTZ
LARRY WOOD ~ THOMAS GUENTHER ~ BILLY STEWART ~ JIMMY TURNER ~ DEE JAMISON
JOHN DUFFY EZEKIAL FALLIN ~ GARY DAMRON ~ JOSE RIVERA-LOPEZ ~ PATRICK WEIGART
DUANE NORTON ~ JESSE THOMAS ~ HENRY BENTON ~ JAMES BLACK ~ CLYDE BIDDLE
DANIEL OLGARD ~ MICHAEL RUSHOLIVER RAGDALE ~ ROBERT OLLIS ~ ROBERT WOODS
GARY SPRY ~ RICHARD COCKROFT ~ ROBERT FOWLER ~ CHARLIE STRICKLAND
JOSEPH BROWN ~ WILLIE MITCHELL ~ WESLEY SMITH ~ ANDREW BASSO ~ KENNETH BROADUS
BILLY EVANS ~ ARTHUR ATON ~ ALBERT PALDO ~ JOSE QUINNONES-MERCADO ~ JAY MURRAY
SHELBEY STRINGFELLOW ~ RICHARD WEIGERINK ~ RUDOLF FRAZIER ~ JOHN OROZ
RONALD BROWN ~ CHARLES MILES ~ RICHARD HOCKENBERRY ~ DONALD HARVEY
JOHN DUFFY ~ GREGORY HOLLOWAY ~ LEE RODRIGUEZ ~ PETER VALENTE ~ LAWRENCE LUSK
RICHARD LIGHTHALL ~ WILLIE ALLEN ~ CLEVELAND CARLTON ~ PATRICK FLOHR
DANNY FIELDS ~ RALPH TALTON ~ MICHAEL SHOEMAKER ~ JOE RUSSELL ~ WALTER SUSALIA
PERRY SIMS ~ THOMAS YOUNG ~ MICHAEL ROSENBERGER ~ CARL OLSEN ~ JOHNNY WAGNER
RICHARD WINGARD ~ ASHLEY POWELL ~ JAMES DUSENBURY ~ DUANE SCHUTTS
ROBERT WOODS ~ ANDREW MCDANIEL ~ JAMES COCHRAN ~ MICHAEL MOORE ~ JIM COLLINS
MARK TUTTLE ~ MICHAEL PELIETIER ~ EDGAR MCKINNEY ~ MICHAEL GASTWIRTH
JAMES FLEISCHACKER ~ FRANCIS BROWN ~ FRANKLIN LAMBERT ~ MYLES OLDSON
JACOB DEBOAERD ~ BOB EPPERSON ~ NORMAN MCBRIDE ~ RODNEY WILSON
ERNEST SCHINKEL ~ HAROLD STEM ~ JACKIE TEAKLE ~ LILLY THOMAS ~ GILBERT GARCIA
NEIL MEYER ~ JIMMY GOUDY ~ JAMES GILMER ~ ALFRED WARREN ~ CLAUDE BROWN
RICHARD KNOLL ~ MICHAEL O'NEAL ~ CHARLES VANSICKLE ~ DAVID CASTENEDA
JOE GUERRA ~ JOE ANDERSON ~ VINCENT ANDREWS ~ KENNETH WAGNER ~ PAUL BALLARD
JOHN WELLING ~ HERMAN BODIFORD ~ PATSY ARACE ~ JACK JOHNSON ~ JAMES BUTLER
HERMAN GREENWOOD ~ RICHARD WORTHY ~ FLOYD BOYD ~ REMIE MARTENS ~ RICHARD
FRAME ~ DARRELL RICHARDSON ~   STEVEN SHEAR ~ MIKE EARLY ~ ELISWORTH KURTZ
CHARLES SINGLETON ~ VINCENT LAURICH ~ WILLIAM MINTZ ~ TOMMIE BATEMAN
JOE RUSSELL

This list is based only on the General Orders I found at the National Archives. It is far from complete because General Orders were not found for many who I personally know were wounded in action, for example, Wickham and Prince on 10 October at LZ Colt, and many men wounded on 23 October 1967 at Huong My. Nevertheless, this effort is intended to illustrate the intensity of the conflict in Vietnam from October 1967 through June 1968, as well as give credit to most of the men who took hits fighting with 5/7th Cav. I left my name off this list, because I only missed work for eight hours. Repeat names on this list means what they say, wounded more than once. There are about 325 names here, but I have no doubt the true number is well north of 350. Combined with the 100 men killed, 5/7th Cav sustained at least 450 casualties in this nine month period. We averaged about 450 men in the field in our four rifle companies during that period. It has been said that if you remained in the field in a rifle company in the 1st Cav for your entire twelve month tour, you would be dinged in one way or another. I know this to be true.

ACKNOWLEDGMENTS

Thanks first to Walter Tousey, West Point classmate, dear friend, and long time history professor at University of Illinois, who gave me the first real encouragement to finish this book. Lieutenant General (Ret) Jim Vaught, my combat leader, gave me critiques and input over the years, along with his friend, Richard Lovelace, from Conway, South Carolina, who found merit in this work and gave me structural ideas as well as encouragement. I also appreciate my primary buddies from the West Point Class of 1960, who so deftly concealed skepticism from hearing about this impending book for at least a decade — Sam Kouns, Dave Hogarth, Tyler Willson, Gene Brisach, Trent Crosby, Joe Naftzinger, Micky McManus, Mike Plummer, Ted Harcke, Hank Maloney and many others.

To the many 5/7th Cav veterans over the years who have shared stories and clarified events — particularly Juan Gonzalez, Jim Thomas, Bob Trimble, Doc McBride *(who read the early draft)*, Mike Sprayberry, Tom Solenberger, Frank Lambert, Vince Laurich, Howard Prince (who read the final draft) — and too many others to list. This book is for them and all the other veterans of 5/7th Cav in 1967-68.

A very big thanks also to Colonel Jody Petery, who invited me to ride with 5/7th Cav in Iraq in the spring of 2005. To Norman Lloyd, film-maker and long time CBS combat photographer, who helped me get to Iraq, and traveled with me. A special thanks to Captain Joel Jackson, A Troop Commander, who welcomed me into his unit and allowed me to ride on patrols with his 1st Platoon on numerous occasions. And to 1st Lieutenant Josh Rambo, and the men of the 1st Platoon *(Ace Red)* who made me feel almost like a member, in spite of being a way over the hill fossil — particularly PSG Reynolds, SSG Beau Saucier, SSG Godenschwager, SSG Ducksworth, Tony Pace, Michael Sankidota, and Nick Achison. Thanks, also to the C Troop commander, Captain Phil Poteet, who included me in his search operations and Iraqi Army training sessions.

Many thanks to my book designer Brian Gamel, who formatted this book into its final ready-to-print state and got me over the goal line.

And to my dear departed wife Nancy, who shared these experiences with me in the 60s, and persevered as an Army wife in spite of her own preferences. I also want to acknowledge my children, David, Chris, Kim and Jeff, who grew up in such stressful times, and did not roll their eyes in my presence when hearing about this long impending project. And lastly, thanks and big hugs to my wife Marty, who brought me back to life, put up with my constant dabbling with this book, shifted into being supportive, then very supportive, and lastly added her considerable editing and proofreading skills to its completion.

SELECTED BIBLIOGRAPHY

PUBLICATIONS

Bollinger, Gil. *Jim Gatchell, The Man and the Museum.* Buffalo, Wyoming: The Gatchell Museum Association, Inc., 1999.

Chloe, Bert. *Flashing Sabers: Memories of Vietnam 1967-1968.* Xlibris Corporation, 2005.

Coleman, J. D. *Memories of the First Team in Vietnam.* 1st Cavalry Division Information Office: Vietnam, 1969.

Fall, Bernard. *Street Without Joy.* Harrisburg, Pennsylvania: The Stackpole Company, 1961.

Halbertstam, David. *The Best and The Brightest.* New York: Random House, 1964.

Hammel, Eric. *Khe Sahn: Seige In the Clouds.* California: Pacifica Press, 1989.

Hammel, Eric. *Ambush Valley.* California: Pacifica Press, 1990.

Hammel, Eric. *Fire In the Streets: The Battle for Hue, Tet, 1968.* Chicago: Contemporary Books, 1991.

Herr, Michael. *Dispatches.* New York: Avon Books, 1978.

Karnow, Stanley. *Vietnam: A History.* New York: Viking, 1983.

Krohn, Charles A. *The Lost Battalion.* Westport, Connecticut: Praeger Publishing, 1993.

Nolan, Keith. *Battle for Hue: Tet 1968.* Novato, California: Presidio Press, 1978.

Nolan, Keith. *Search an Destroy: The Story of an Armored Cavalry Squadron in Viet Nam.* Zenith Press, 400 First Avenue North, Suite 300, Minneapolis, 2010.

Page, Tim and Pimlot, John. *NAM.* New York: Alfred A. Knopf, 1983.

Pisor, Robert. *The End of the Line: The Seige of Khe Sahn.* New York: Ballantine Books, 1982.

Stanton, Shelby. *The 1st Cav in Vietnam: Anatomy of a Division.* California: Presidio Press, 1987.

Smith, George W. *The Seige at Hue.* New York: Ballentine Books, 1999.

Tolson, Major General John J. *Airmobility: 1961-1971.* Washington, D.C.: Department of the Army, 1973.

Villard, Erik. *The 1968 Tet Offensive Battles of Quang Tri City and Hue.* US Army Center for Military History, 2000.

So totally comprehensive in capturing the sights, sounds and even smells of combat, those who were there will find this books engrossing. I found myself so engaged that I started to sweat and swear over the SNAFUs and casualties.

Charles A. Krohn
Writer

Charlie Baker has written an excellent book about the performance of America's soldiers in both Vietnam and Iraq based upon his personal experiences in both. He tells it like it was – citing the actual daily journals and the language of award recommendations that he himself wrote – and based upon actions he personally observed or listened to as they happened. This work is a must read for any student of that terrible thing called war!

Bob Totten
West Point, Class of 1960

This book is not just for military enthusiasts, but appeals to any audience. You will feel the intensity of war and the human costs that go with it. I cried, I laughed, and gained a heartfelt insight to what our soldiers must endure when duty calls from our Nation's leaders – whether they believed in the cause or not.

Kimberly Neil
Army Brat

21450013R00226

Made in the USA
Middletown, DE
30 June 2015